SHONEN JUMP MANGA EDITION

ASTRA
LOST IN SPACE

3

[SECRETS]

KENTA SHINOHARA

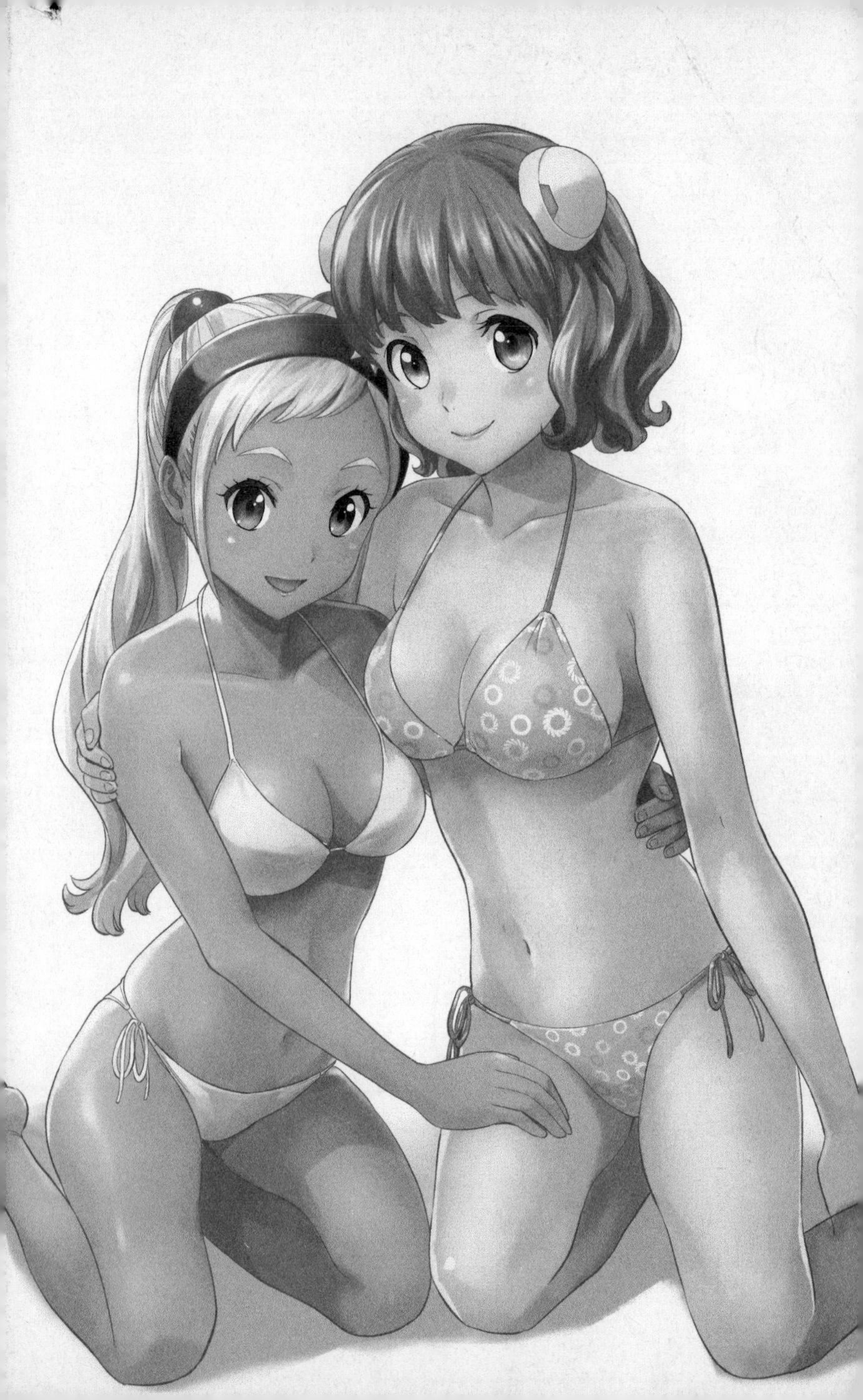

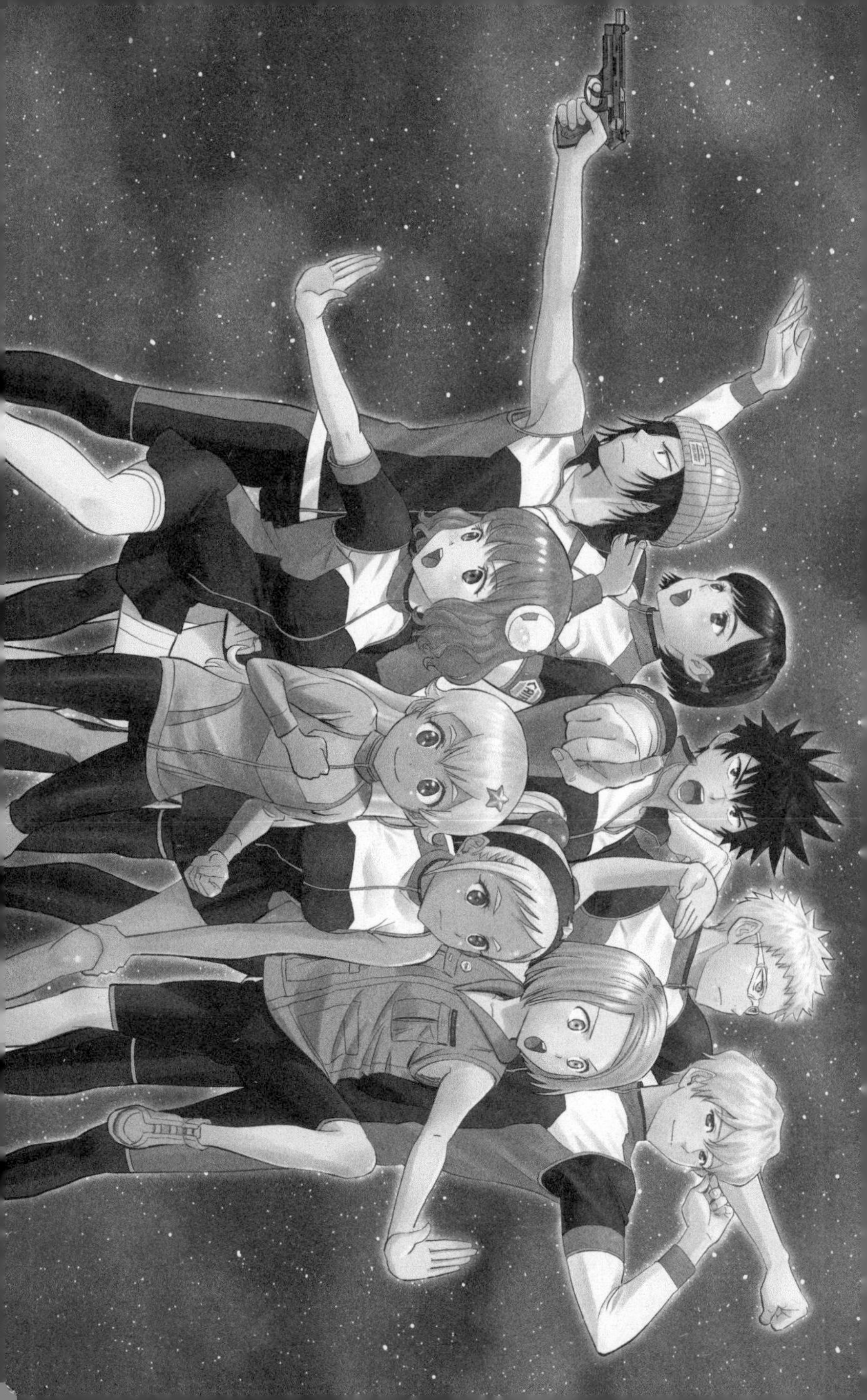

CHARACTERS&STORY

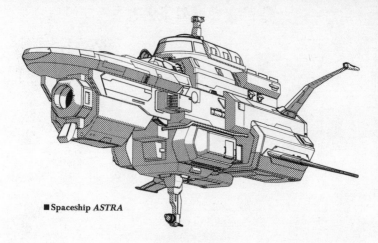

■ Spaceship *ASTRA*

STORY

It's the year 2063, and interstellar space travel has become the norm. A group of students from Caird High School is set to take off for a five-day camp on Planet McPa at the Mousanish Spaceport. However, shortly after arriving, the group encounters a mysterious glowing orb that swallows them up and spits them out into the depths of space. By a stroke of good luck, they find an abandoned spaceship where they can take shelter, but its long-range communications system is offline. Not only that, they quickly discover they weren't spat out above McPa as they initially thought, but were instead transported 5,000 light-years away! Critically short on both food and water, the group manages to piece together a string of five planets where they can forage for supplies while making their way home one planet at a time. But just as things barely get under way, they find out one of the crew may be a killer sent on a suicide mission to murder all of them!

The crew of the *Astra* arrives on the second planet, Shummoor, barely avoiding a disastrous crash landing. As everyone goes about foraging, Yun-hua falls into a depressive funk over how useless she feels. But when much of the crew falls ill from a poisonous spore cloud, Yun-hua sings to them, bringing them relief and comfort until a cure is found. With newfound confidence and deeper friendships, the crew of the *Astra* heads towards the third planet!

ASTRA
LOST IN SPACE

CHARACTERS

**Zack
Walker**

**Aries
Spring**

**Kanata
Hoshijima**

**Luca
Esposito**

**Funicia
Raffaeli**

**Quitterie
Raffaeli**

**Charce
Lacroix**

**Yun-hua
Lu**

**Ulgar
Zweig**

ASTRA
LOST IN SPACE
CONTENTS

3

[SECRETS]

ASTRA
LOST IN SPACE

#19

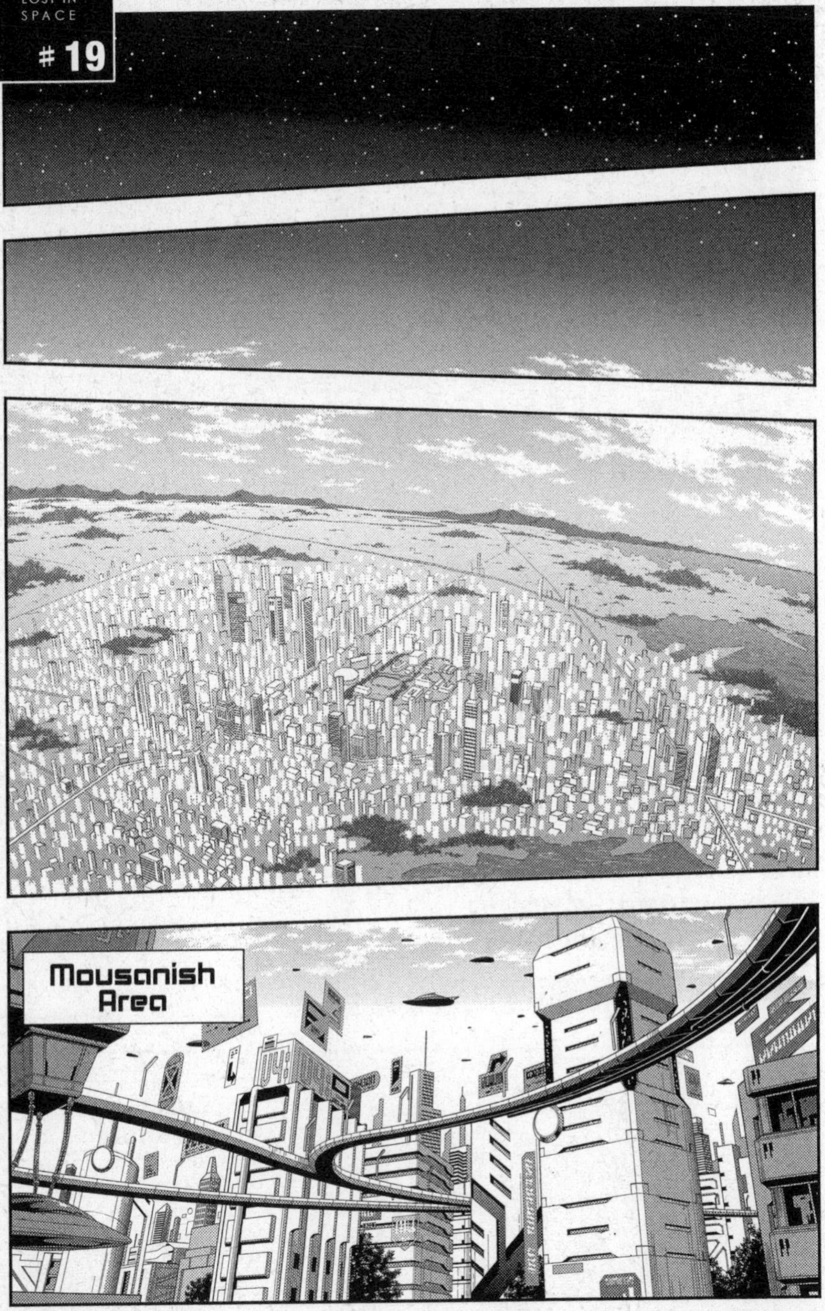
Mousanish Area

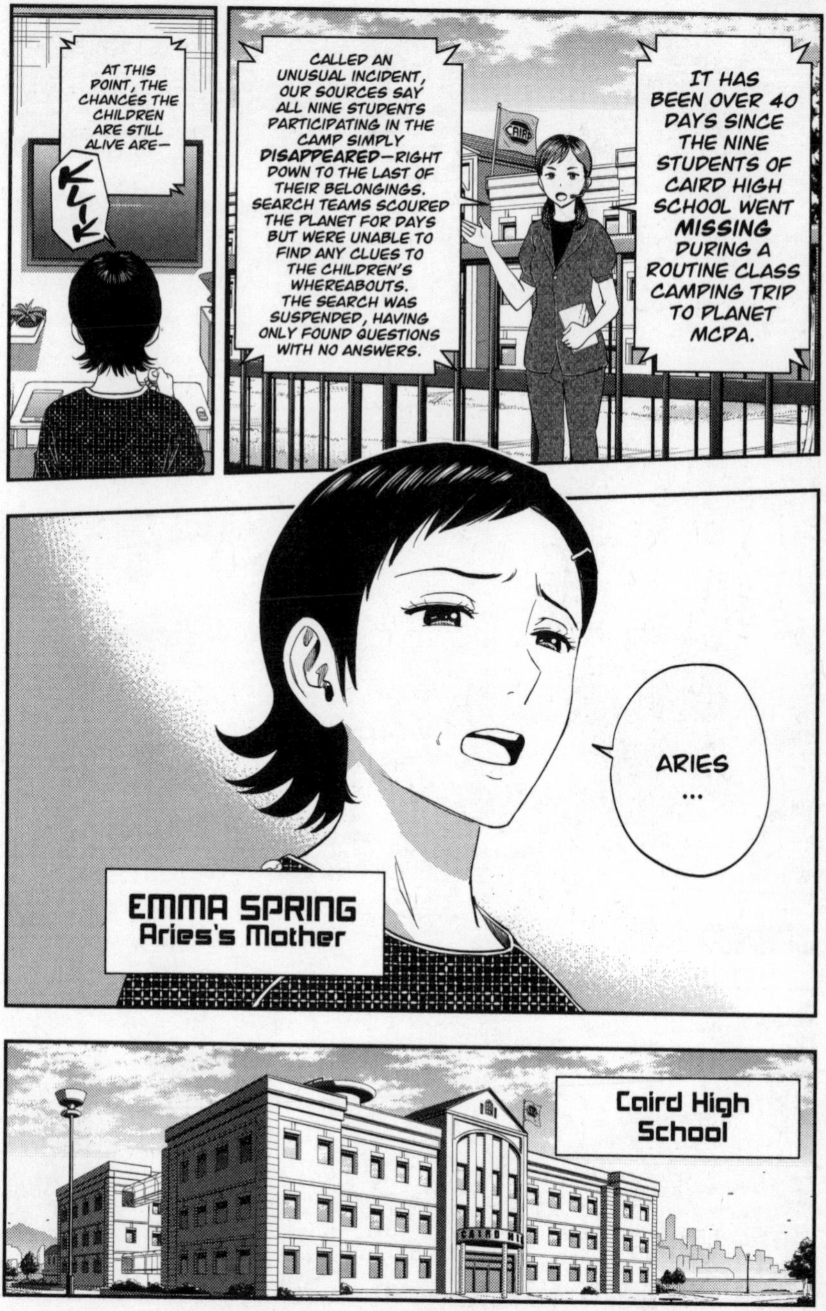
IT HAS BEEN OVER 40 DAYS SINCE THE NINE STUDENTS OF CAIRD HIGH SCHOOL WENT MISSING DURING A ROUTINE CLASS CAMPING TRIP TO PLANET MCPA.
CALLED AN UNUSUAL INCIDENT, OUR SOURCES SAY ALL NINE STUDENTS PARTICIPATING IN THE CAMP SIMPLY DISAPPEARED—RIGHT DOWN TO THE LAST OF THEIR BELONGINGS. SEARCH TEAMS SCOURED THE PLANET FOR DAYS BUT WERE UNABLE TO FIND ANY CLUES TO THE CHILDREN'S WHEREABOUTS. THE SEARCH WAS SUSPENDED, HAVING ONLY FOUND QUESTIONS WITH NO ANSWERS.
AT THIS POINT, THE CHANCES THE CHILDREN ARE STILL ALIVE ARE—
KLIK
ARIES ...
EMMA SPRING Aries's Mother
Caird High School

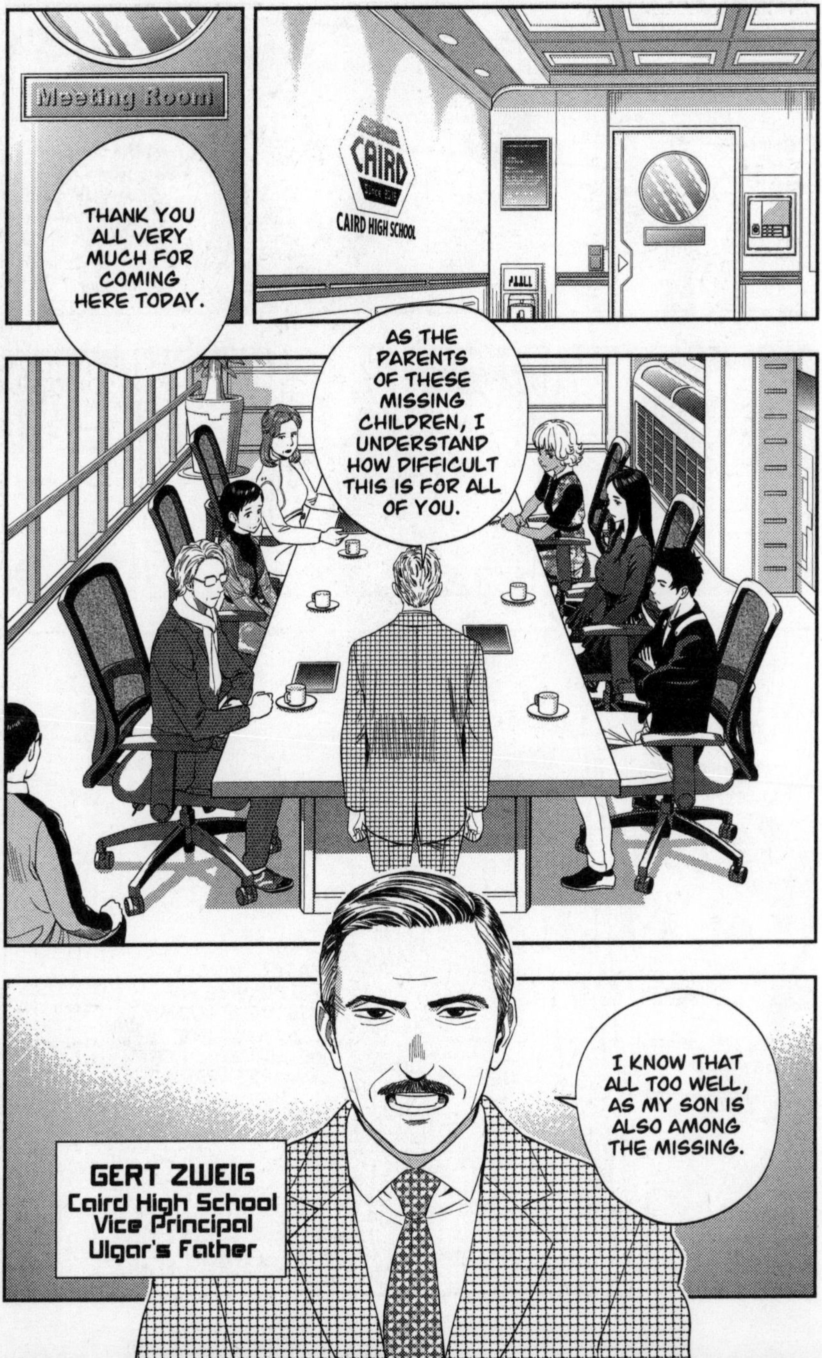
CAIRD
CAIRD HIGH SCHOOL
Meeting Room
THANK YOU ALL VERY MUCH FOR COMING HERE TODAY.
AS THE PARENTS OF THESE MISSING CHILDREN, I UNDERSTAND HOW DIFFICULT THIS IS FOR ALL OF YOU.
I KNOW THAT ALL TOO WELL, AS MY SON IS ALSO AMONG THE MISSING.
GERT ZWEIG
Caird High School Vice Principal Ulgar's Father

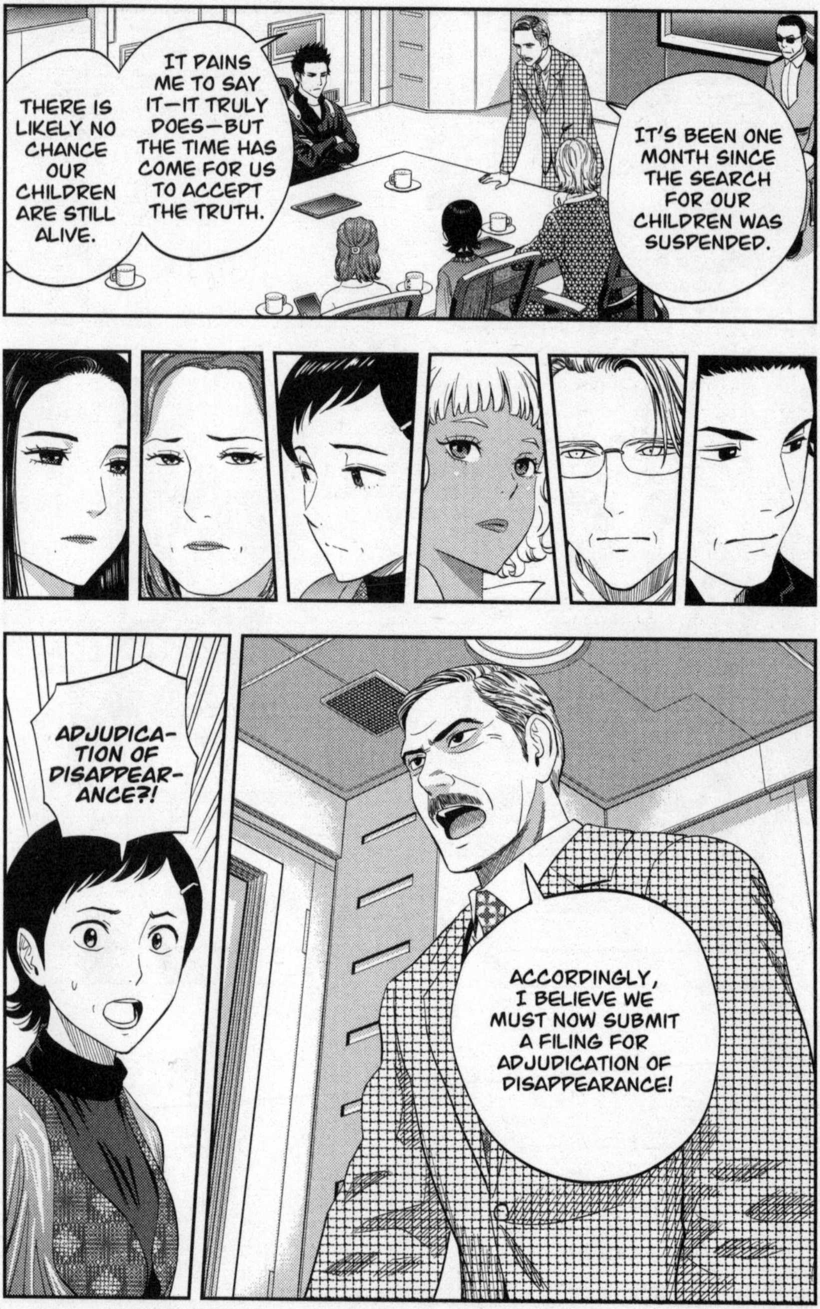
IT'S BEEN ONE MONTH SINCE THE SEARCH FOR OUR CHILDREN WAS SUSPENDED.
IT PAINS ME TO SAY IT—IT TRULY DOES—BUT THE TIME HAS COME FOR US TO ACCEPT THE TRUTH.
THERE IS LIKELY NO CHANCE OUR CHILDREN ARE STILL ALIVE.
ACCORDINGLY, I BELIEVE WE MUST NOW SUBMIT A FILING FOR ADJUDICATION OF DISAPPEARANCE!
ADJUDICA-TION OF DISAPPEAR-ANCE?!

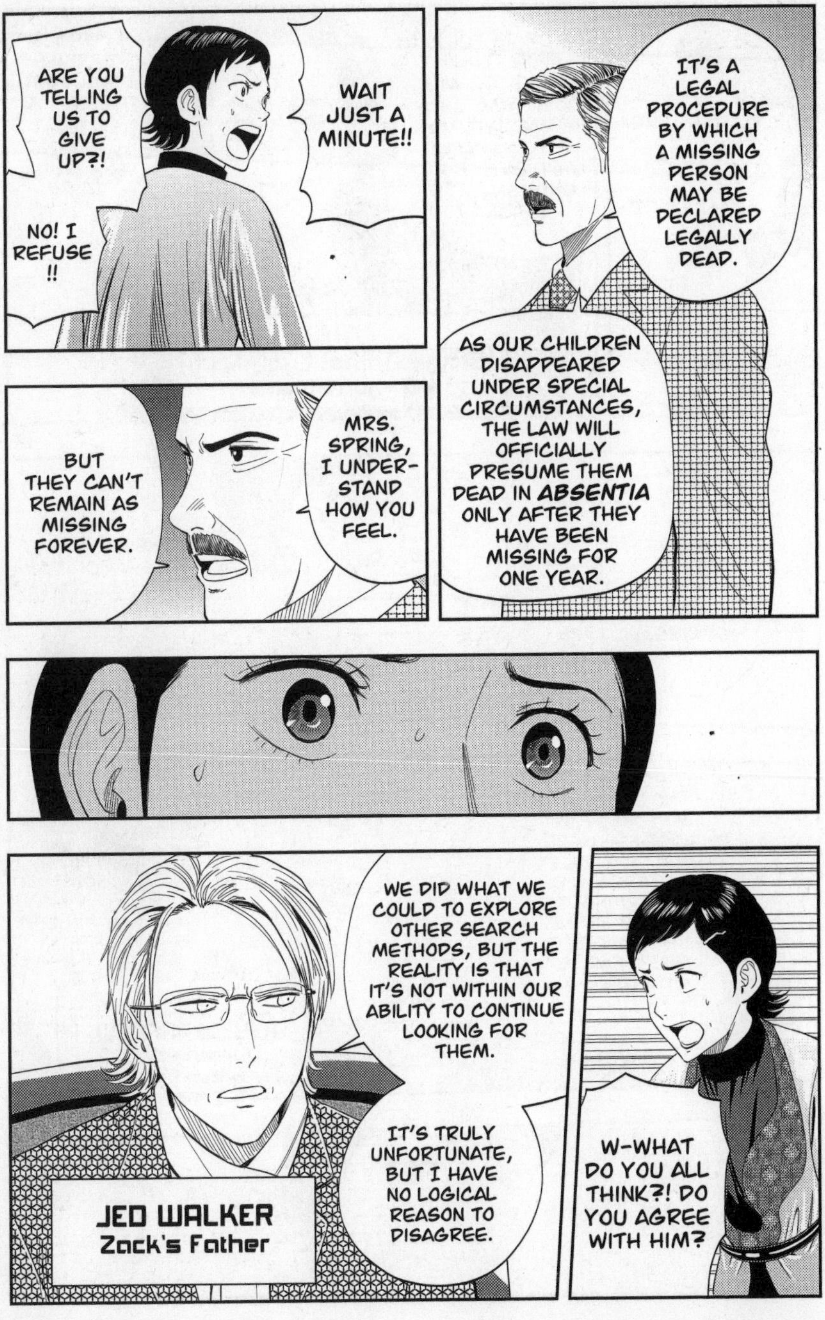
IT'S A LEGAL PROCEDURE BY WHICH A MISSING PERSON MAY BE DECLARED LEGALLY DEAD.
AS OUR CHILDREN DISAPPEARED UNDER SPECIAL CIRCUMSTANCES, THE LAW WILL OFFICIALLY PRESUME THEM DEAD IN ABSENTIA ONLY AFTER THEY HAVE BEEN MISSING FOR ONE YEAR.
WAIT JUST A MINUTE!!
ARE YOU TELLING US TO GIVE UP?!
NO! I REFUSE!!
MRS. SPRING, I UNDER-STAND HOW YOU FEEL.
BUT THEY CAN'T REMAIN AS MISSING FOREVER.
W-WHAT DO YOU ALL THINK?! DO YOU AGREE WITH HIM?
WE DID WHAT WE COULD TO EXPLORE OTHER SEARCH METHODS, BUT THE REALITY IS THAT IT'S NOT WITHIN OUR ABILITY TO CONTINUE LOOKING FOR THEM.
IT'S TRULY UNFORTUNATE, BUT I HAVE NO LOGICAL REASON TO DISAGREE.
JED WALKER
Zack's Father

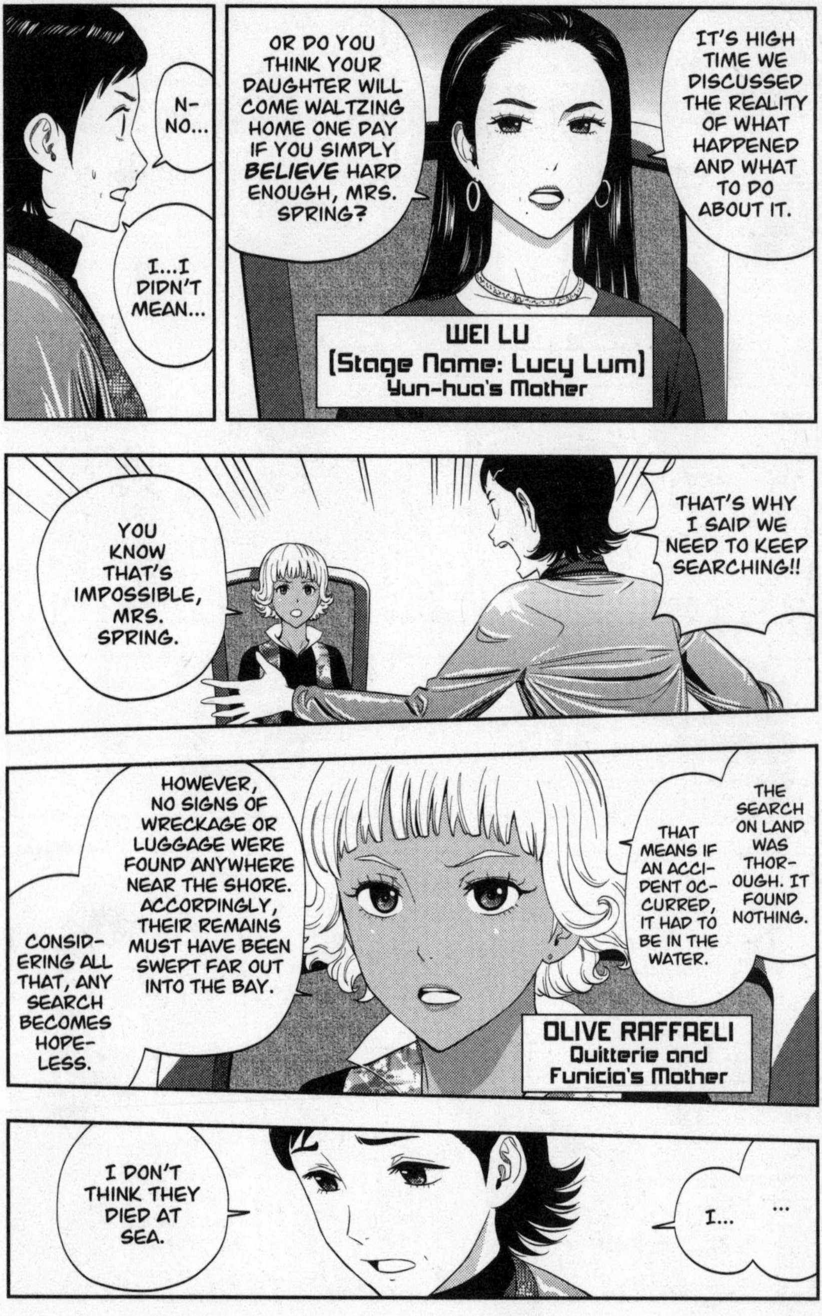
IT'S HIGH TIME WE DISCUSSED THE REALITY OF WHAT HAPPENED AND WHAT TO DO ABOUT IT.
OR DO YOU THINK YOUR DAUGHTER WILL COME WALTZING HOME ONE DAY IF YOU SIMPLY **BELIEVE** HARD ENOUGH, MRS. SPRING?
WEI LU
[Stage Name: Lucy Lum]
Yun-hua's Mother
N-NO...
I...I DIDN'T MEAN...
THAT'S WHY I SAID WE NEED TO KEEP SEARCHING!!
YOU KNOW THAT'S IMPOSSIBLE, MRS. SPRING.
THE SEARCH ON LAND WAS THOROUGH. IT FOUND NOTHING.
THAT MEANS IF AN ACCIDENT OCCURRED, IT HAD TO BE IN THE WATER.
HOWEVER, NO SIGNS OF WRECKAGE OR LUGGAGE WERE FOUND ANYWHERE NEAR THE SHORE. ACCORDINGLY, THEIR REMAINS MUST HAVE BEEN SWEPT FAR OUT INTO THE BAY.
CONSIDERING ALL THAT, ANY SEARCH BECOMES HOPELESS.
OLIVE RAFFAELI
Quitterie and Funicia's Mother
...
I...
I DON'T THINK THEY DIED AT SEA.

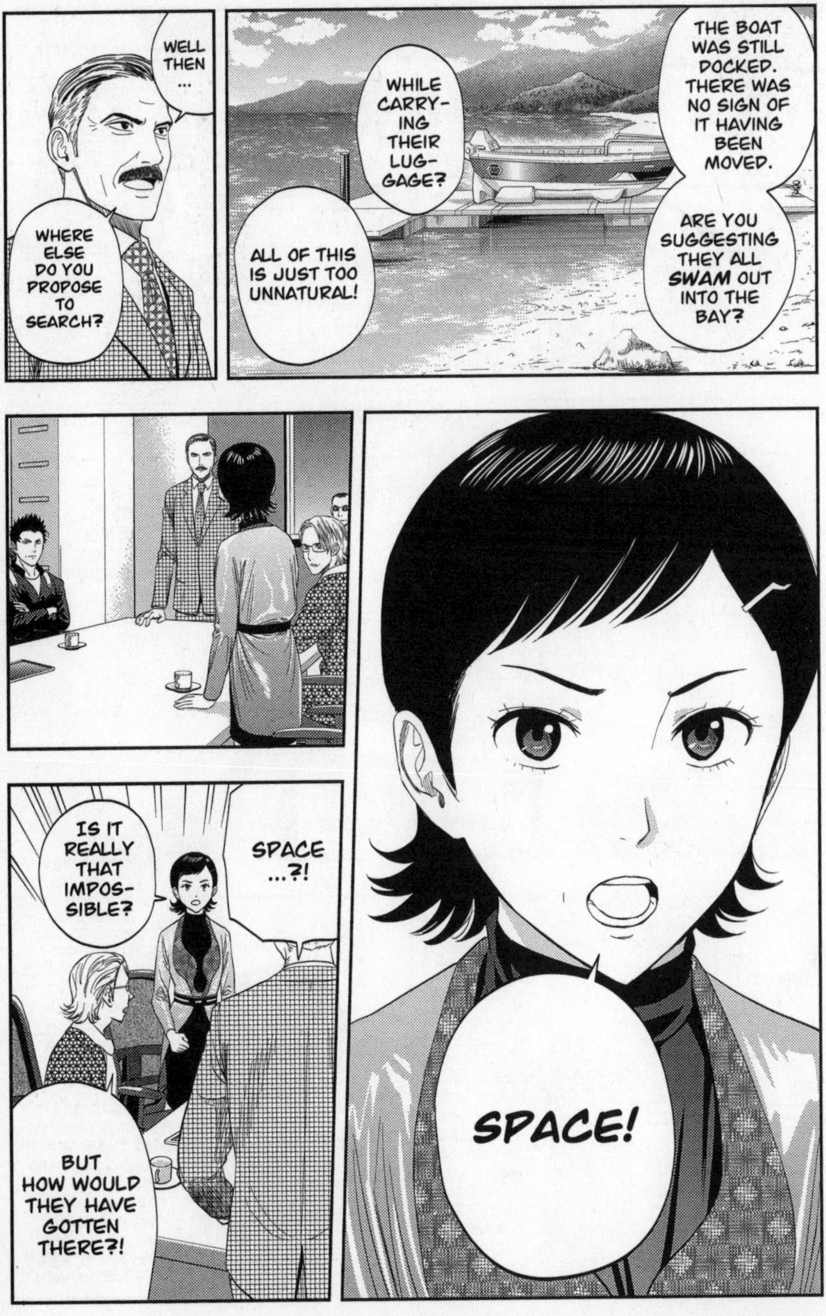
THE BOAT WAS STILL DOCKED. THERE WAS NO SIGN OF IT HAVING BEEN MOVED.
ARE YOU SUGGESTING THEY ALL SWAM OUT INTO THE BAY?
WHILE CARRYING THEIR LUGGAGE?
ALL OF THIS IS JUST TOO UNNATURAL!
WELL THEN ...
WHERE ELSE DO YOU PROPOSE TO SEARCH?
SPACE!
SPACE ...?!
IS IT REALLY THAT IMPOSSIBLE?
BUT HOW WOULD THEY HAVE GOTTEN THERE?!

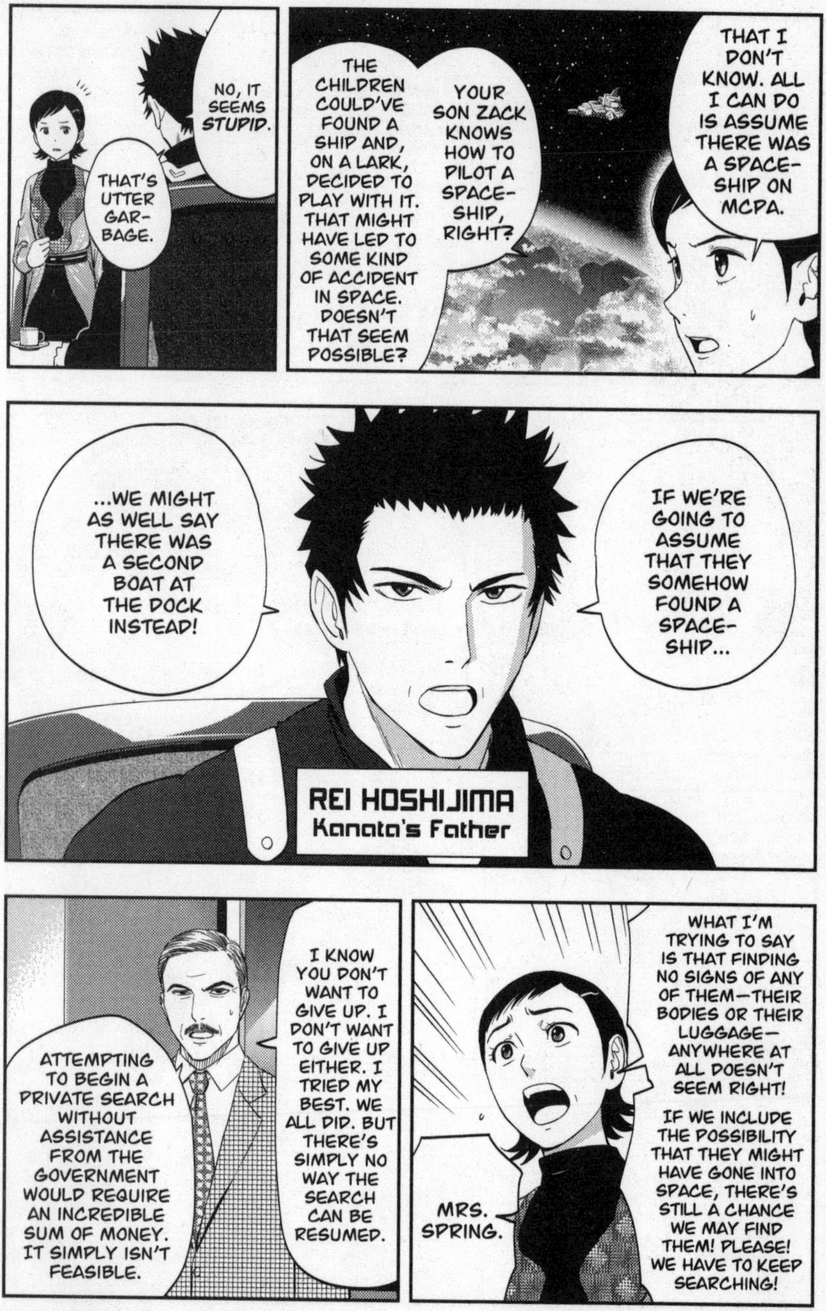
THAT I DON'T KNOW. ALL I CAN DO IS ASSUME THERE WAS A SPACE-SHIP ON MCPA.
YOUR SON ZACK KNOWS HOW TO PILOT A SPACE-SHIP, RIGHT?
THE CHILDREN COULD'VE FOUND A SHIP AND, ON A LARK, DECIDED TO PLAY WITH IT. THAT MIGHT HAVE LED TO SOME KIND OF ACCIDENT IN SPACE. DOESN'T THAT SEEM POSSIBLE?
NO, IT SEEMS STUPID.
THAT'S UTTER GAR-BAGE.
IF WE'RE GOING TO ASSUME THAT THEY SOMEHOW FOUND A SPACE-SHIP...
...WE MIGHT AS WELL SAY THERE WAS A SECOND BOAT AT THE DOCK INSTEAD!
REI HOSHIJIMA
Kanata's Father
WHAT I'M TRYING TO SAY IS THAT FINDING NO SIGNS OF ANY OF THEM—THEIR BODIES OR THEIR LUGGAGE—ANYWHERE AT ALL DOESN'T SEEM RIGHT!
IF WE INCLUDE THE POSSIBILITY THAT THEY MIGHT HAVE GONE INTO SPACE, THERE'S STILL A CHANCE WE MAY FIND THEM! PLEASE! WE HAVE TO KEEP SEARCHING!
MRS. SPRING.
I KNOW YOU DON'T WANT TO GIVE UP. I DON'T WANT TO GIVE UP EITHER. I TRIED MY BEST. WE ALL DID. BUT THERE'S SIMPLY NO WAY THE SEARCH CAN BE RESUMED.
ATTEMPTING TO BEGIN A PRIVATE SEARCH WITHOUT ASSISTANCE FROM THE GOVERNMENT WOULD REQUIRE AN INCREDIBLE SUM OF MONEY. IT SIMPLY ISN'T FEASIBLE.

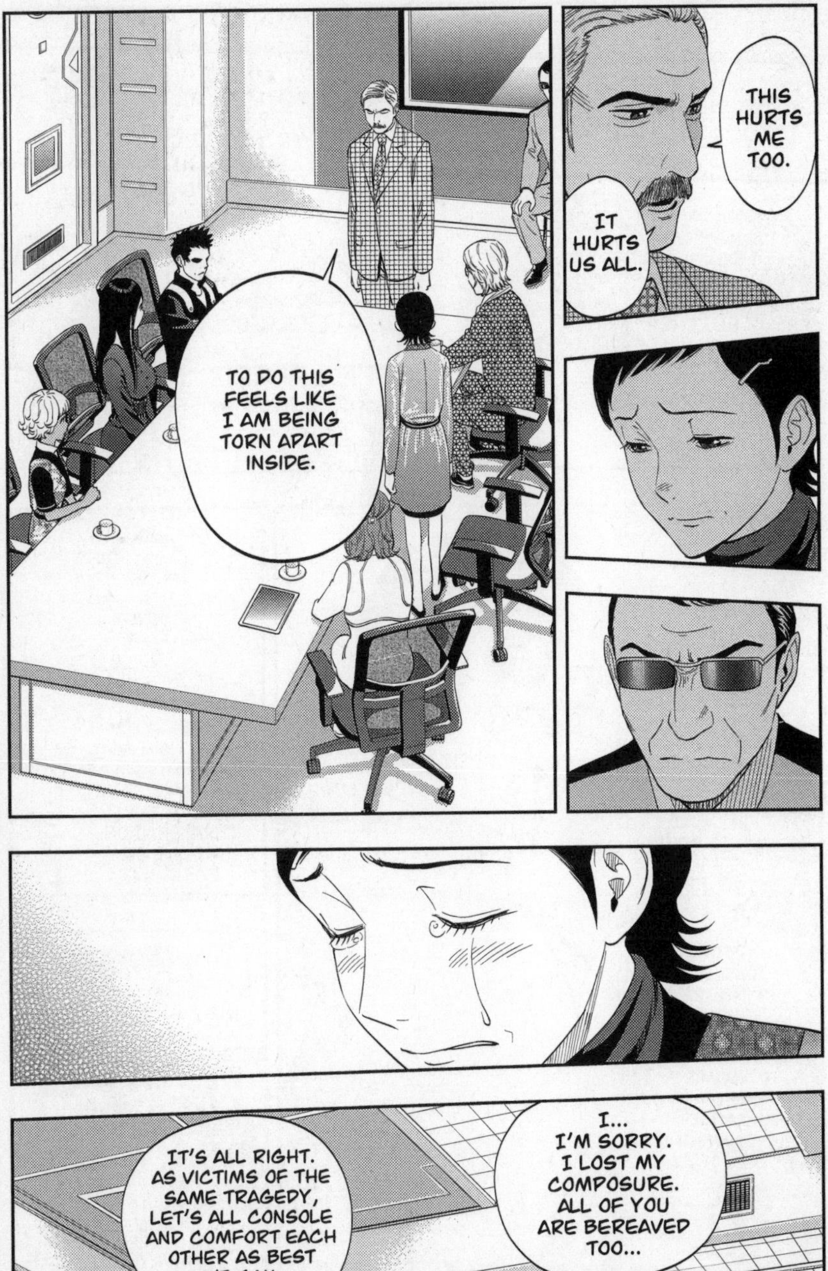
THIS HURTS ME TOO.
IT HURTS US ALL.
TO DO THIS FEELS LIKE I AM BEING TORN APART INSIDE.
I... I'M SORRY. I LOST MY COMPOSURE. ALL OF YOU ARE BEREAVED TOO...
IT'S ALL RIGHT. AS VICTIMS OF THE SAME TRAGEDY, LET'S ALL CONSOLE AND COMFORT EACH OTHER AS BEST WE CAN.

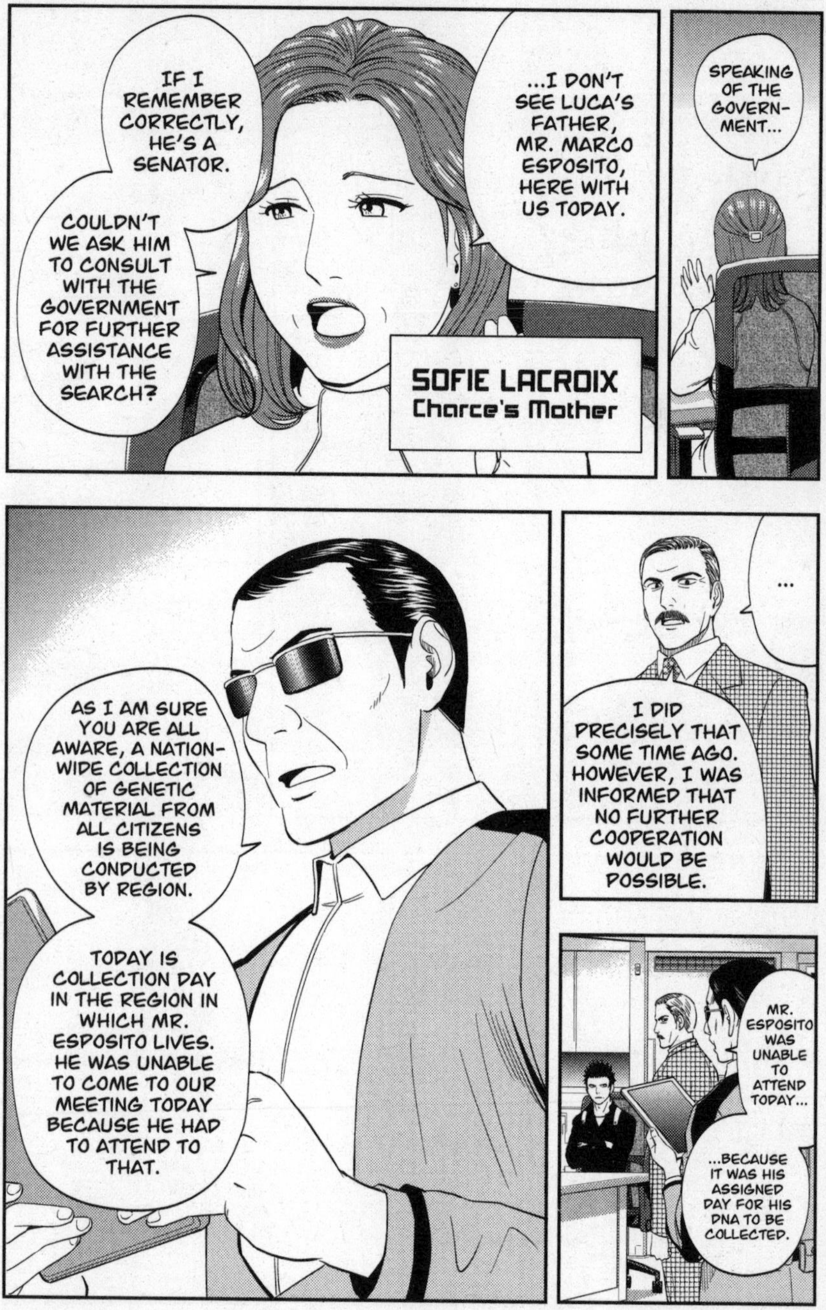
SPEAKING OF THE GOVERNMENT...
...I DON'T SEE LUCA'S FATHER, MR. MARCO ESPOSITO, HERE WITH US TODAY.
IF I REMEMBER CORRECTLY, HE'S A SENATOR.
COULDN'T WE ASK HIM TO CONSULT WITH THE GOVERNMENT FOR FURTHER ASSISTANCE WITH THE SEARCH?
SOFIE LACROIX Charce's Mother
...
I DID PRECISELY THAT SOME TIME AGO. HOWEVER, I WAS INFORMED THAT NO FURTHER COOPERATION WOULD BE POSSIBLE.
MR. ESPOSITO WAS UNABLE TO ATTEND TODAY...
...BECAUSE IT WAS HIS ASSIGNED DAY FOR HIS DNA TO BE COLLECTED.
AS I AM SURE YOU ARE ALL AWARE, A NATION-WIDE COLLECTION OF GENETIC MATERIAL FROM ALL CITIZENS IS BEING CONDUCTED BY REGION.
TODAY IS COLLECTION DAY IN THE REGION IN WHICH MR. ESPOSITO LIVES. HE WAS UNABLE TO COME TO OUR MEETING TODAY BECAUSE HE HAD TO ATTEND TO THAT.

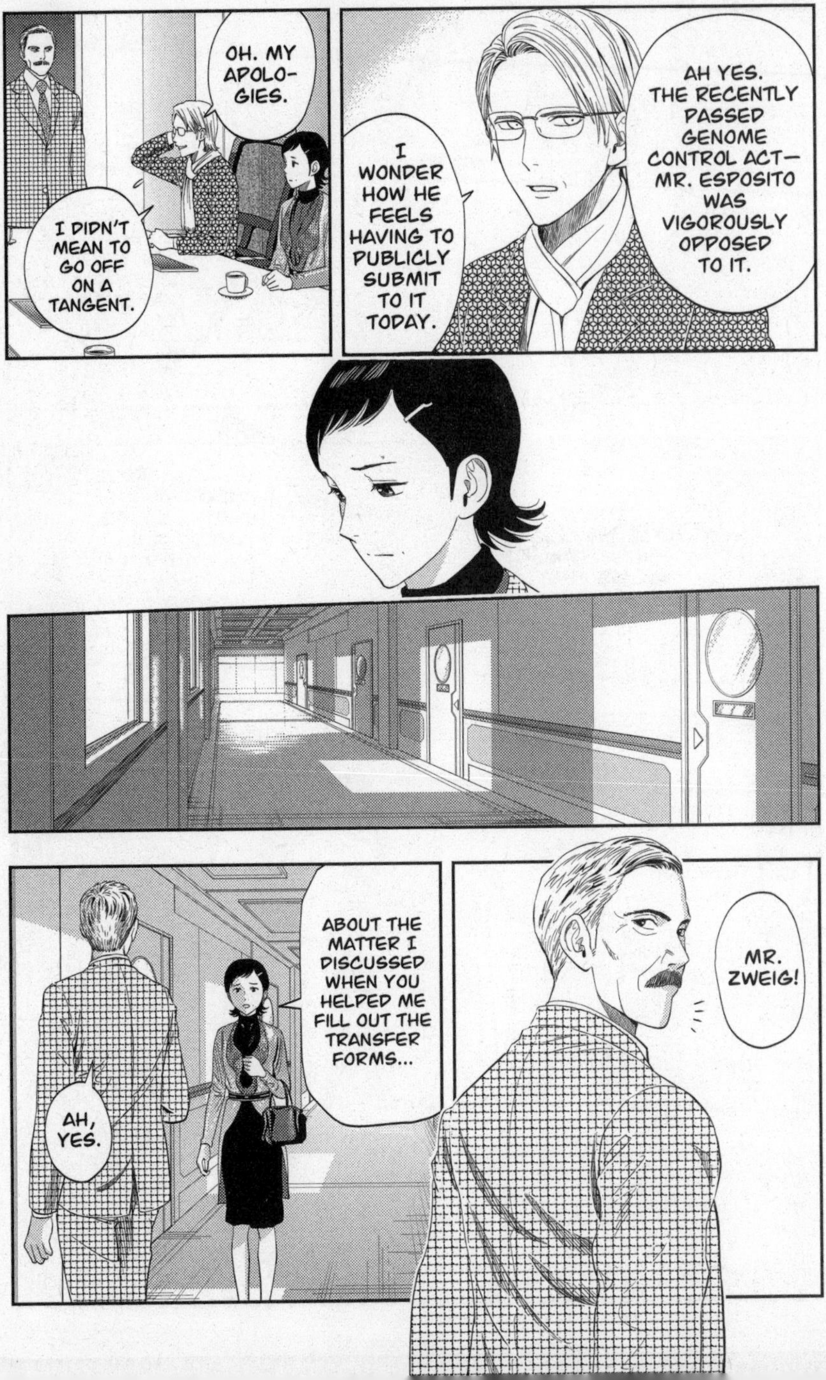
AH YES. THE RECENTLY PASSED GENOME CONTROL ACT—MR. ESPOSITO WAS VIGOROUSLY OPPOSED TO IT.
I WONDER HOW HE FEELS HAVING TO PUBLICLY SUBMIT TO IT TODAY.
OH. MY APOLO-GIES.
I DIDN'T MEAN TO GO OFF ON A TANGENT.
MR. ZWEIG!
ABOUT THE MATTER I DISCUSSED WHEN YOU HELPED ME FILL OUT THE TRANSFER FORMS...
AH, YES.

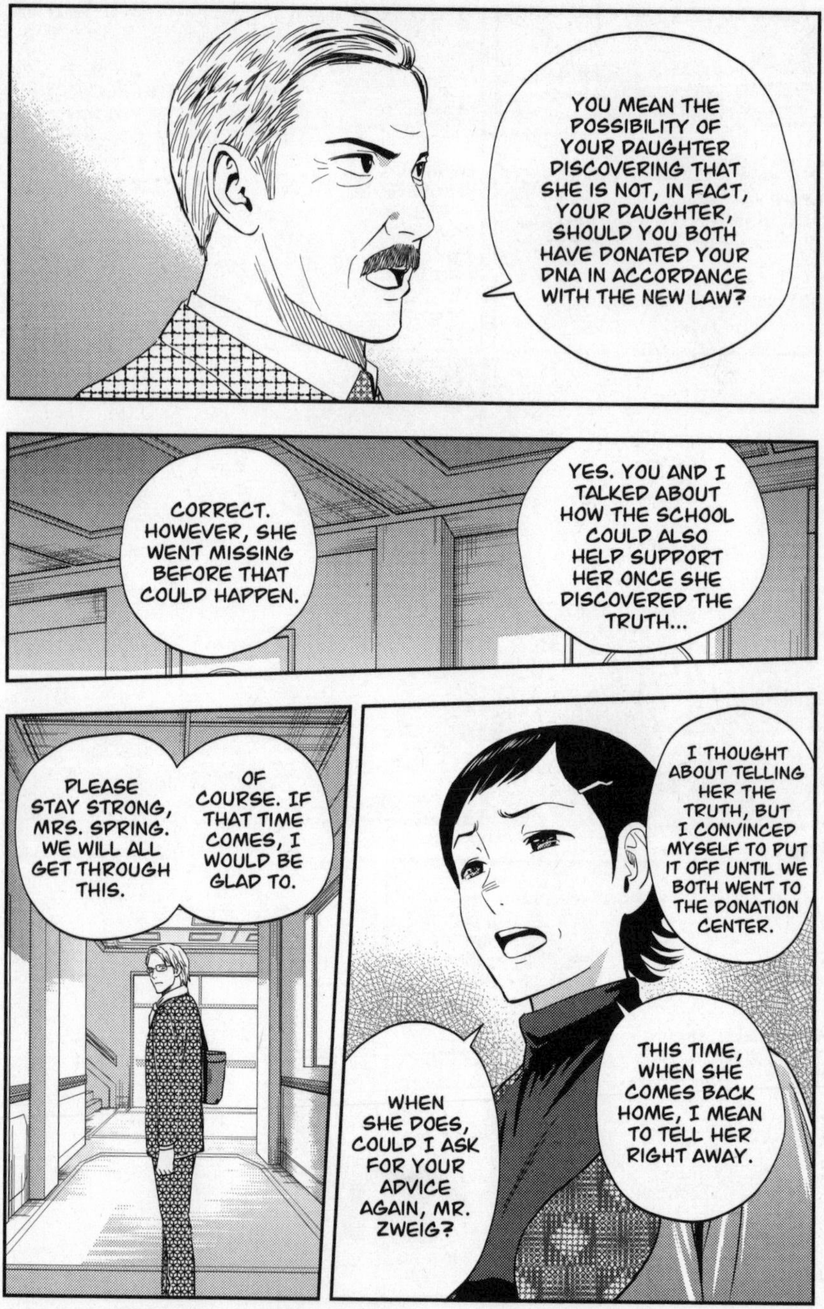
YOU MEAN THE POSSIBILITY OF YOUR DAUGHTER DISCOVERING THAT SHE IS NOT, IN FACT, YOUR DAUGHTER, SHOULD YOU BOTH HAVE DONATED YOUR DNA IN ACCORDANCE WITH THE NEW LAW?
YES. YOU AND I TALKED ABOUT HOW THE SCHOOL COULD ALSO HELP SUPPORT HER ONCE SHE DISCOVERED THE TRUTH...
CORRECT. HOWEVER, SHE WENT MISSING BEFORE THAT COULD HAPPEN.
I THOUGHT ABOUT TELLING HER THE TRUTH, BUT I CONVINCED MYSELF TO PUT IT OFF UNTIL WE BOTH WENT TO THE DONATION CENTER.
THIS TIME, WHEN SHE COMES BACK HOME, I MEAN TO TELL HER RIGHT AWAY.
WHEN SHE DOES, COULD I ASK FOR YOUR ADVICE AGAIN, MR. ZWEIG?
OF COURSE. IF THAT TIME COMES, I WOULD BE GLAD TO.
PLEASE STAY STRONG, MRS. SPRING. WE WILL ALL GET THROUGH THIS.

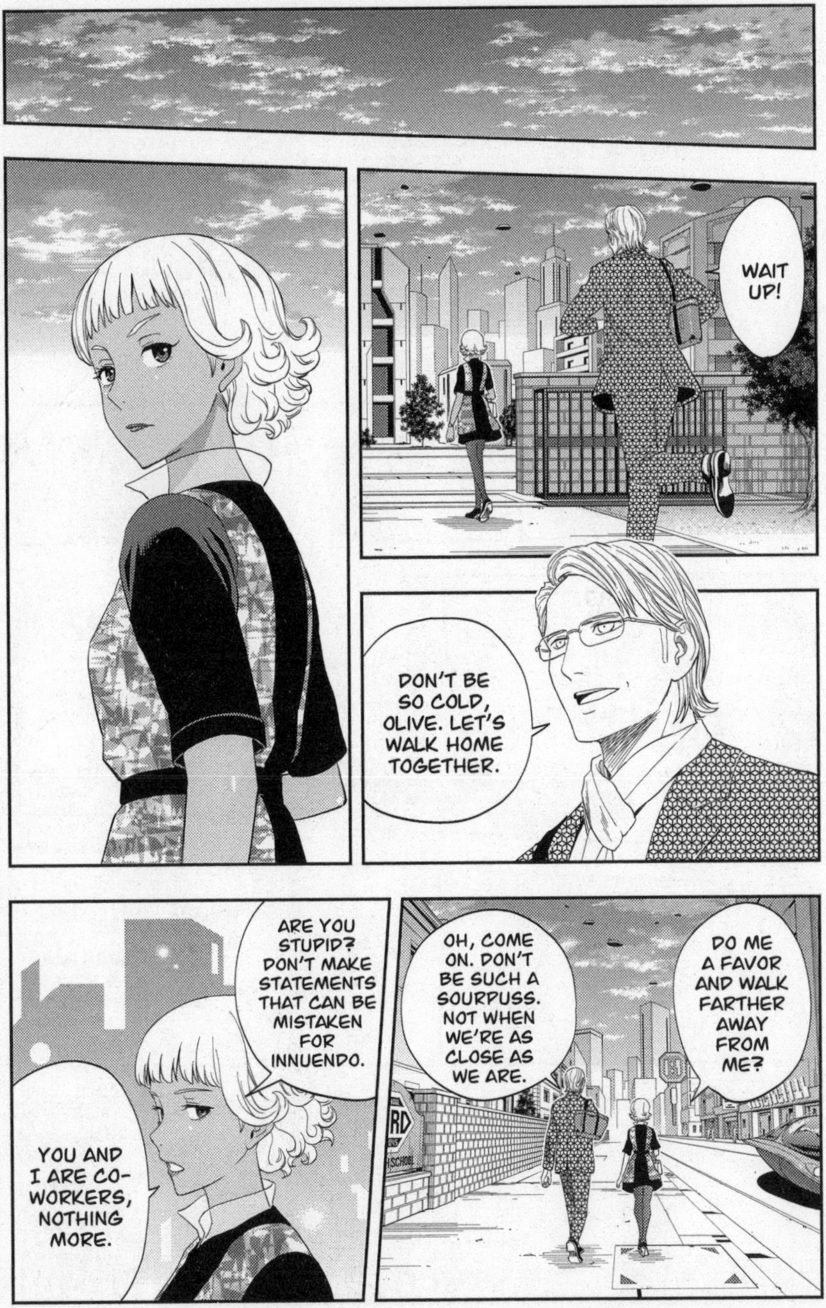
WAIT UP!
DON'T BE SO COLD, OLIVE. LET'S WALK HOME TOGETHER.
DO ME A FAVOR AND WALK FARTHER AWAY FROM ME?
OH, COME ON. DON'T BE SUCH A SOURPUSS. NOT WHEN WE'RE AS CLOSE AS WE ARE.
ARE YOU STUPID? DON'T MAKE STATEMENTS THAT CAN BE MISTAKEN FOR INNUENDO.
YOU AND I ARE CO-WORKERS, NOTHING MORE.

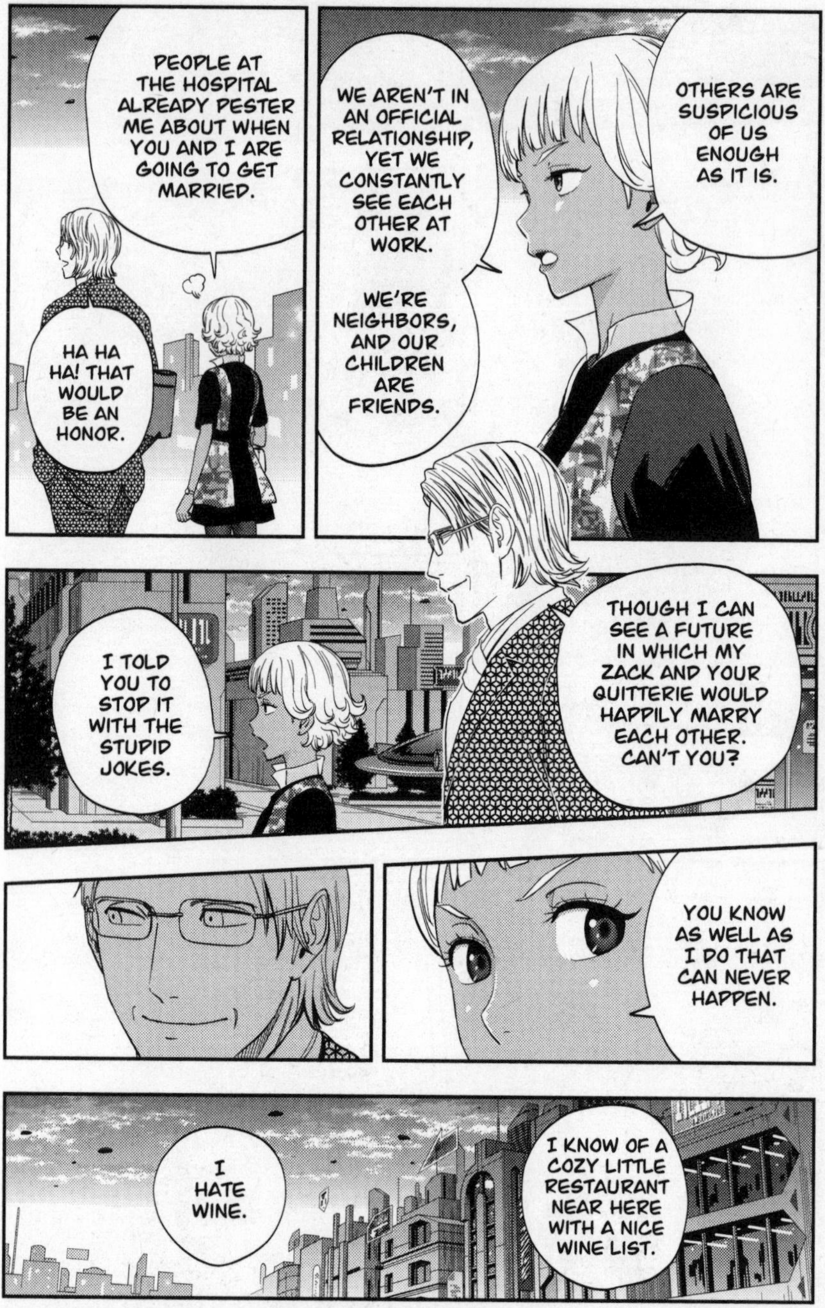
OTHERS ARE SUSPICIOUS OF US ENOUGH AS IT IS.
WE AREN'T IN AN OFFICIAL RELATIONSHIP, YET WE CONSTANTLY SEE EACH OTHER AT WORK.
WE'RE NEIGHBORS, AND OUR CHILDREN ARE FRIENDS.
PEOPLE AT THE HOSPITAL ALREADY PESTER ME ABOUT WHEN YOU AND I ARE GOING TO GET MARRIED.
HA HA HA! THAT WOULD BE AN HONOR.
THOUGH I CAN SEE A FUTURE IN WHICH MY ZACK AND YOUR QUITTERIE WOULD HAPPILY MARRY EACH OTHER. CAN'T YOU?
I TOLD YOU TO STOP IT WITH THE STUPID JOKES.
YOU KNOW AS WELL AS I DO THAT CAN NEVER HAPPEN.
I KNOW OF A COZY LITTLE RESTAURANT NEAR HERE WITH A NICE WINE LIST.
I HATE WINE.

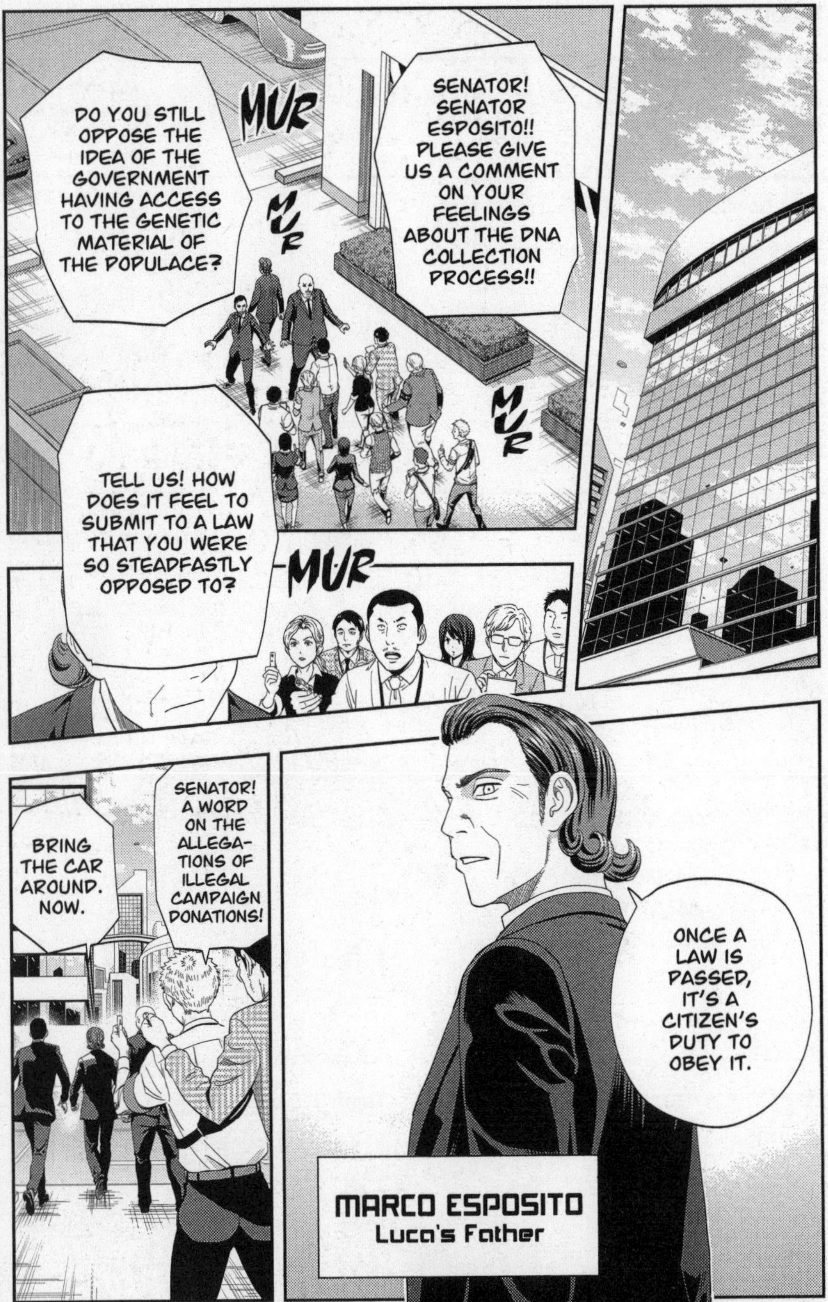
SENATOR! SENATOR ESPOSITO!! PLEASE GIVE US A COMMENT ON YOUR FEELINGS ABOUT THE DNA COLLECTION PROCESS!!
MUR
DO YOU STILL OPPOSE THE IDEA OF THE GOVERNMENT HAVING ACCESS TO THE GENETIC MATERIAL OF THE POPULACE?
MUR
MUR
MUR
TELL US! HOW DOES IT FEEL TO SUBMIT TO A LAW THAT YOU WERE SO STEADFASTLY OPPOSED TO?
ONCE A LAW IS PASSED, IT'S A CITIZEN'S DUTY TO OBEY IT.
MARCO ESPOSITO
Luca's Father
SENATOR! A WORD ON THE ALLEGATIONS OF ILLEGAL CAMPAIGN DONATIONS!
BRING THE CAR AROUND. NOW.

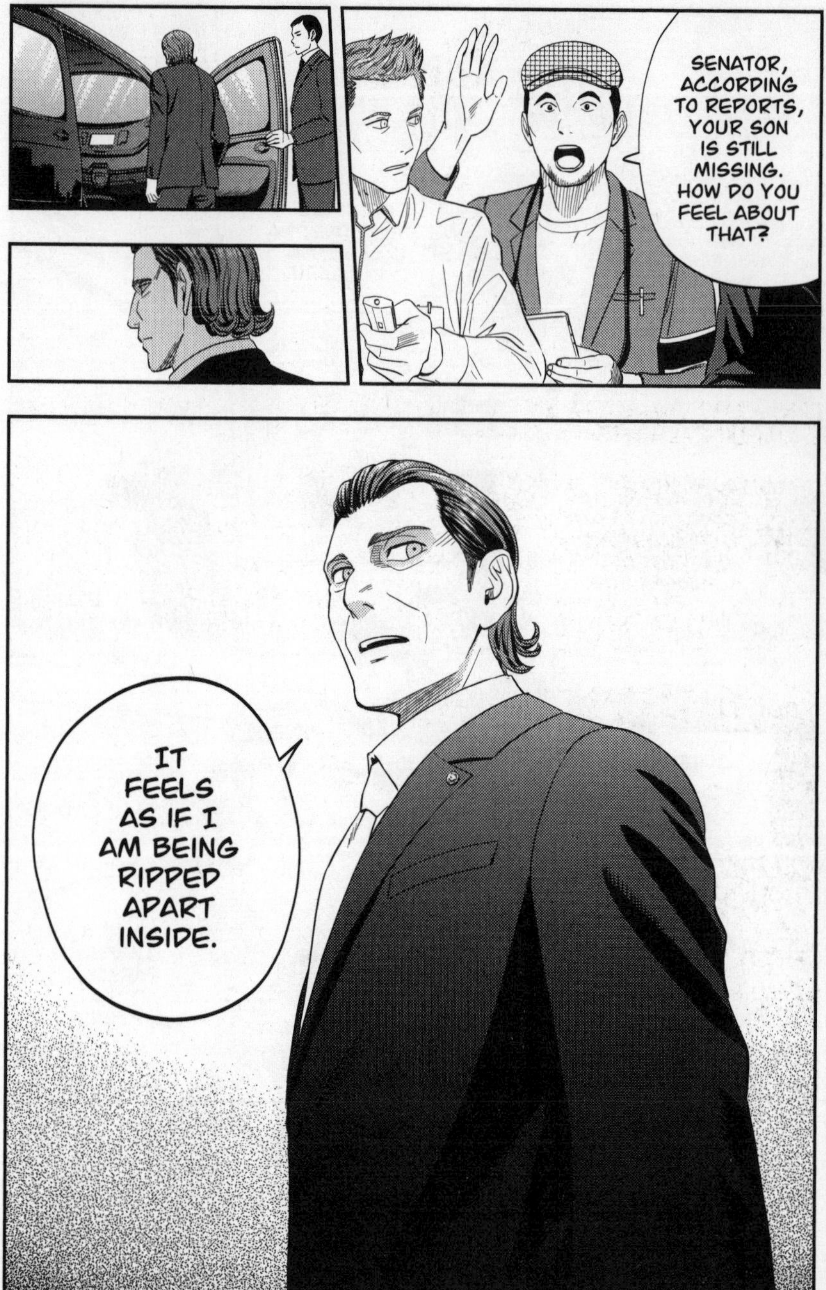
SENATOR, ACCORDING TO REPORTS, YOUR SON IS STILL MISSING. HOW DO YOU FEEL ABOUT THAT?
IT FEELS AS IF I AM BEING RIPPED APART INSIDE.

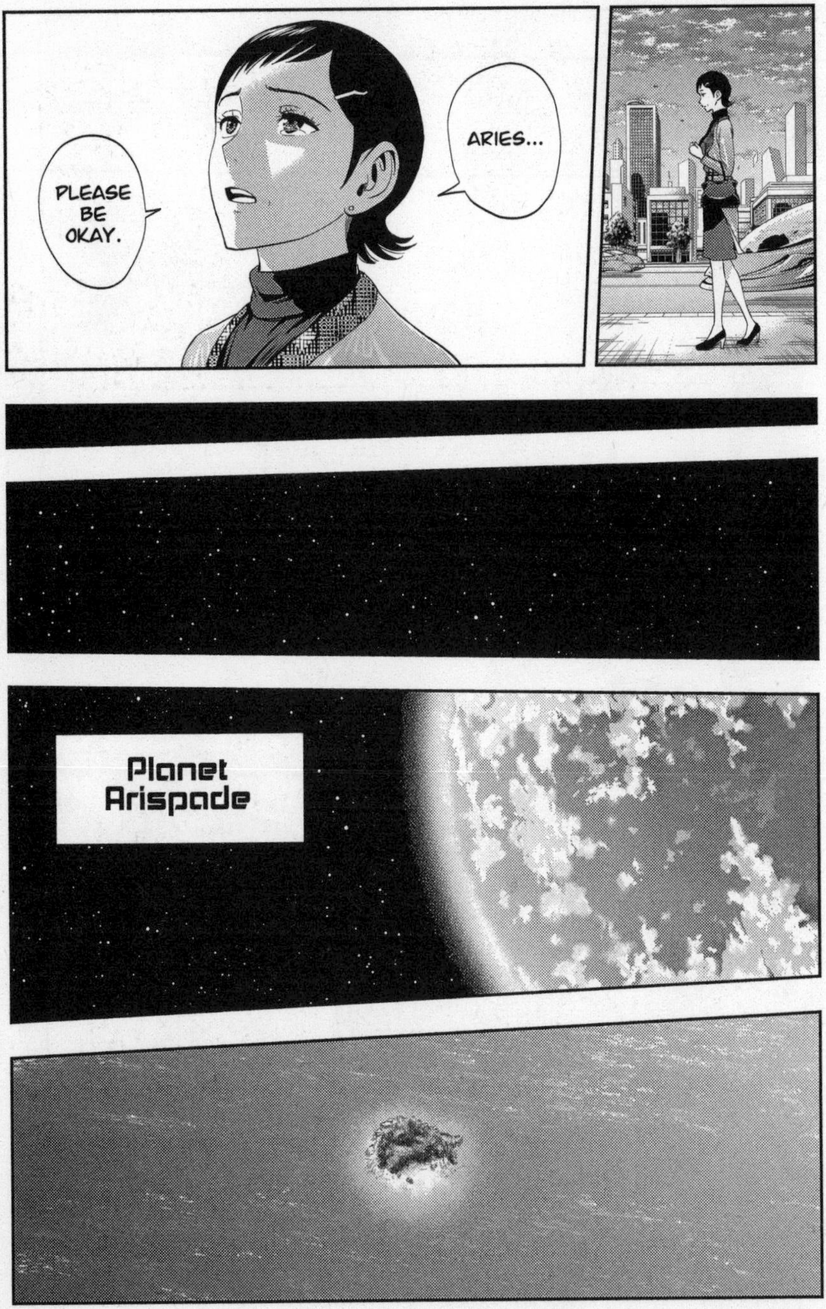
ARIES...
PLEASE BE OKAY.
Planet Arispade

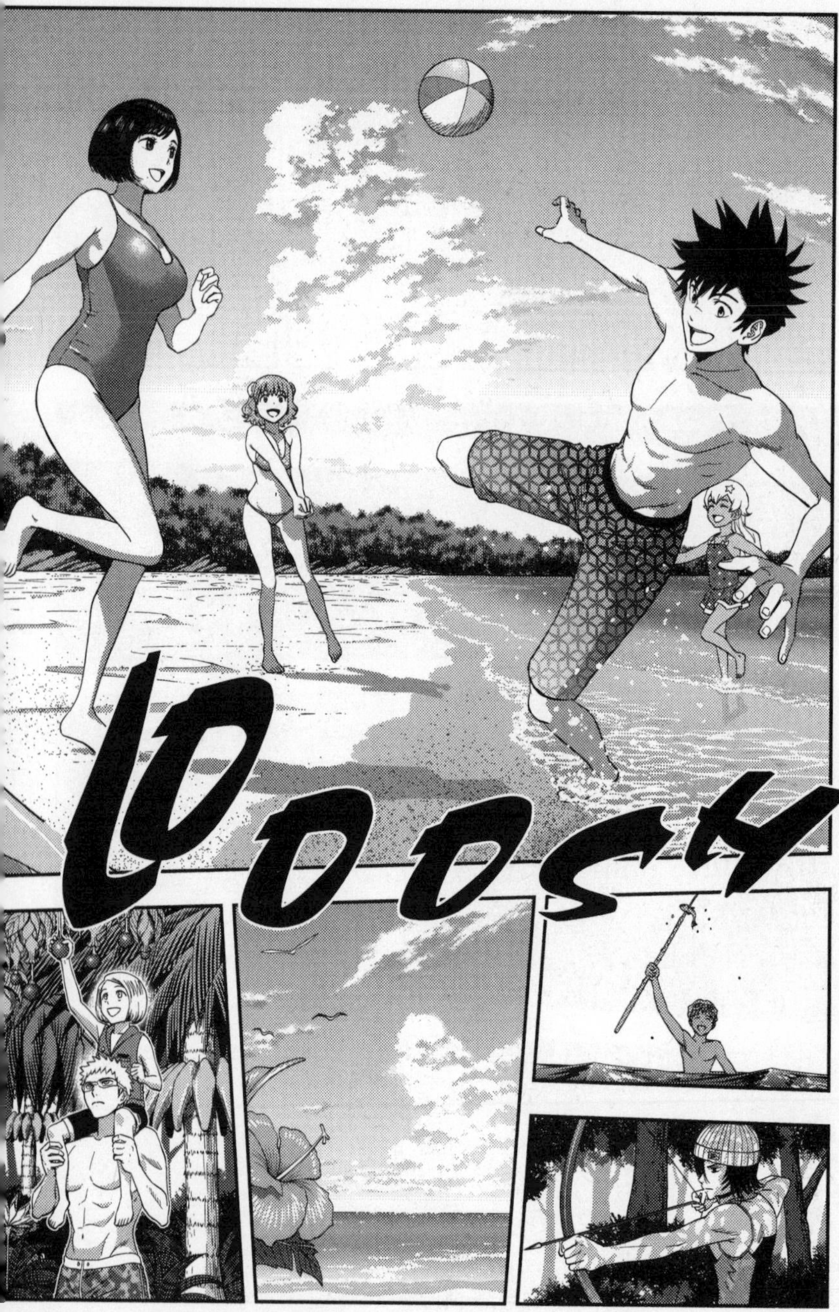
WOOSH

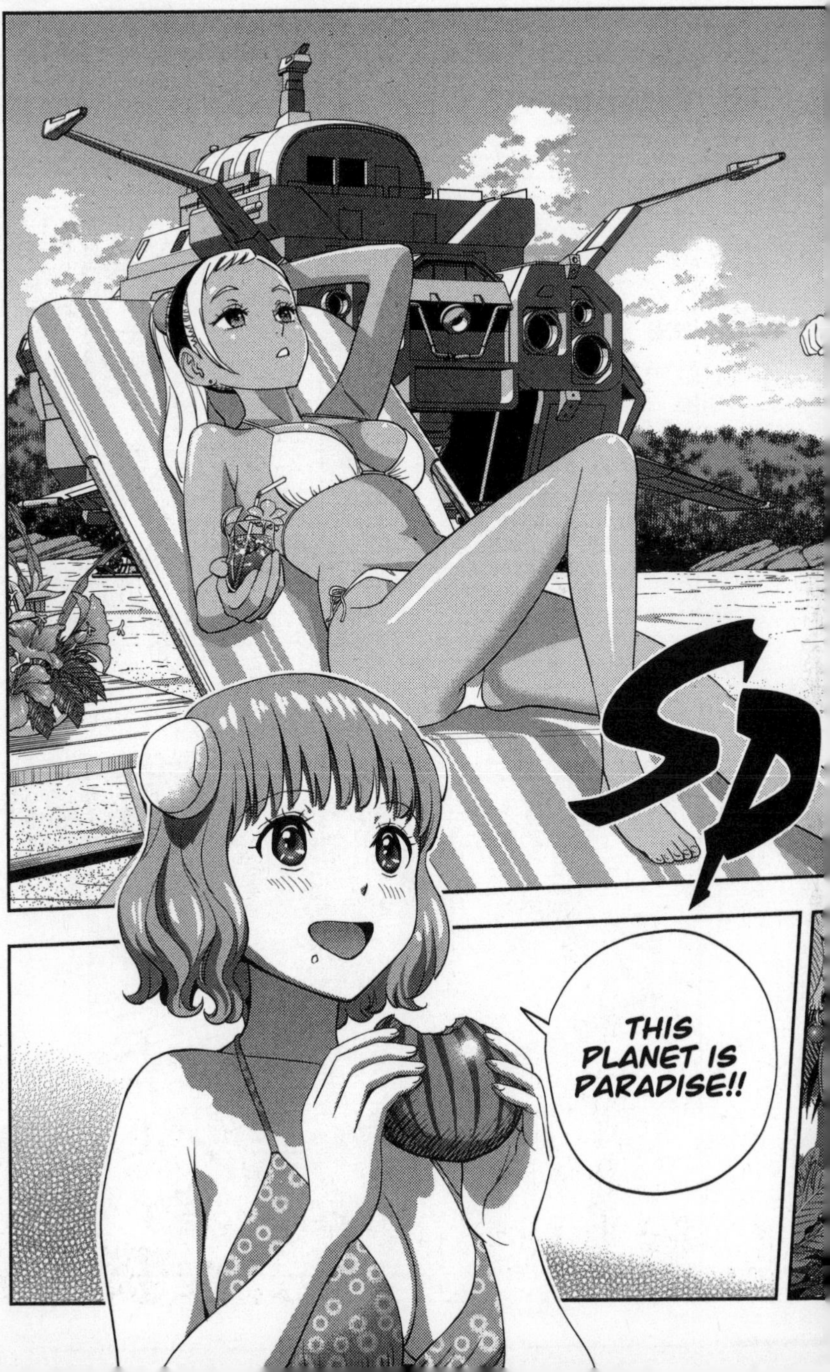
SP
THIS PLANET IS PARADISE!!

Material Collection

THE LOUNGE

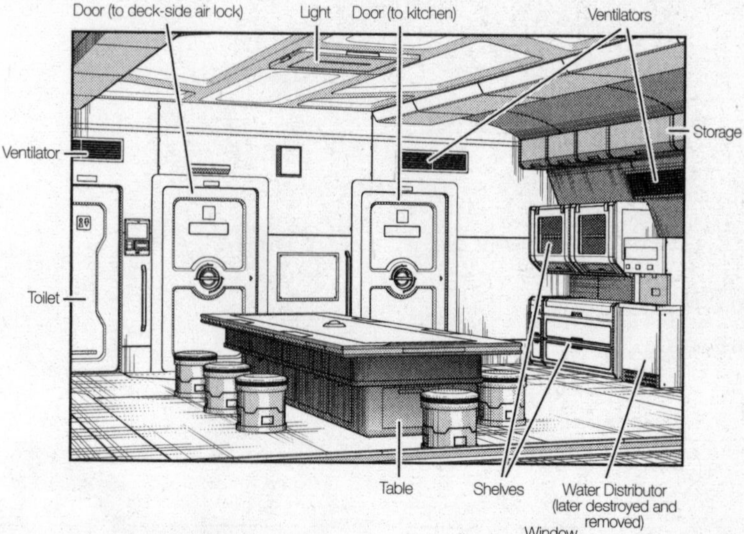
Door (to deck-side air lock)
Light
Door (to kitchen)
Ventilators
Storage
Ventilator
Toilet
Table
Shelves
Water Distributor (later destroyed and removed)

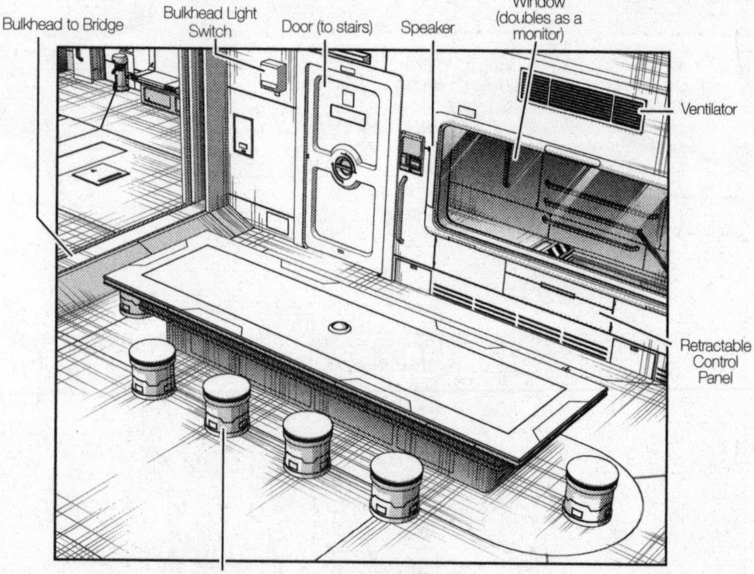
Bulkhead to Bridge
Bulkhead Light Switch
Door (to stairs)
Speaker
Window (doubles as a monitor)
Ventilator
Retractable Control Panel
Stool (emergency kit stored inside)

ASTRA
LOST IN SPACE
#20

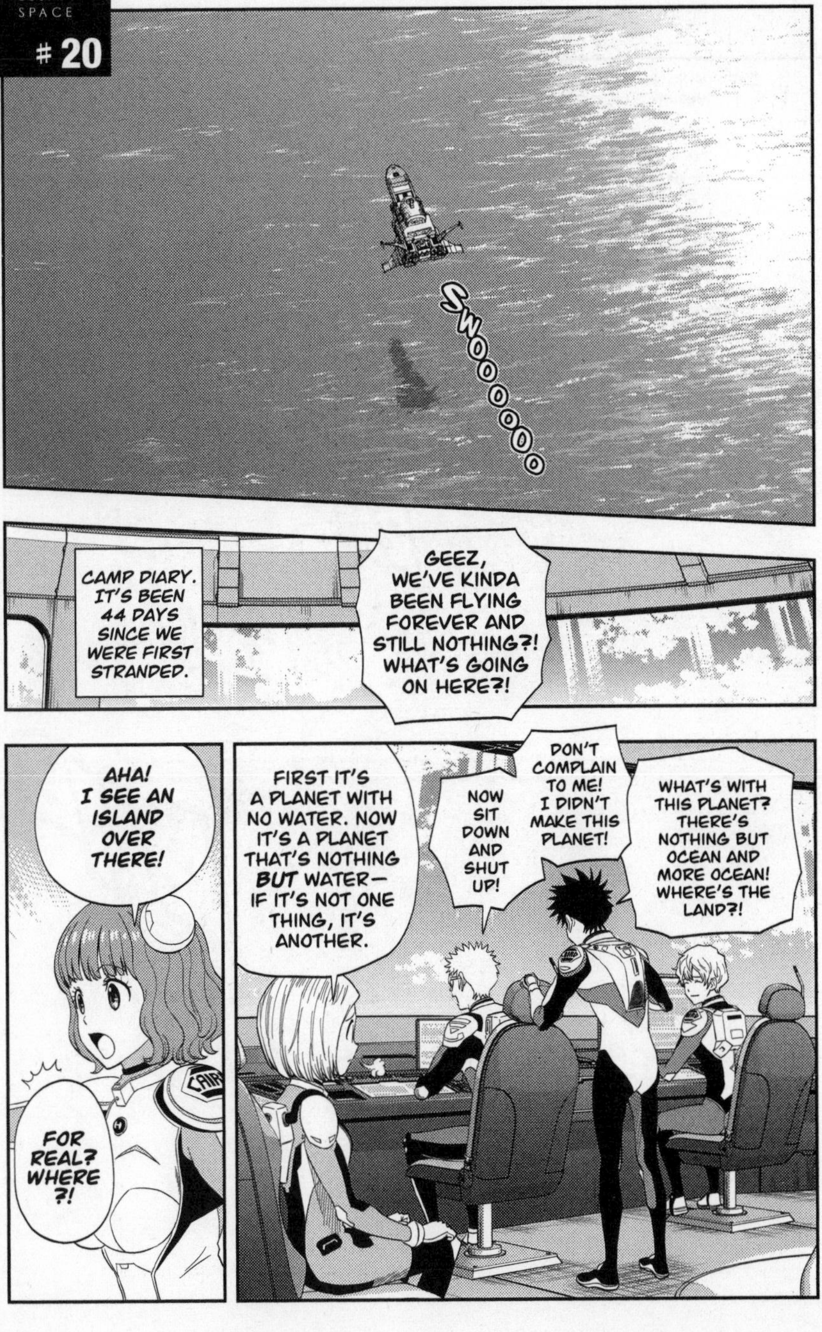
SWOOOOOO
GEEZ, WE'VE KINDA BEEN FLYING FOREVER AND STILL NOTHING?! WHAT'S GOING ON HERE?!
CAMP DIARY. IT'S BEEN 44 DAYS SINCE WE WERE FIRST STRANDED.
WHAT'S WITH THIS PLANET? THERE'S NOTHING BUT OCEAN AND MORE OCEAN! WHERE'S THE LAND?!
DON'T COMPLAIN TO ME! I DIDN'T MAKE THIS PLANET!
NOW SIT DOWN AND SHUT UP!
FIRST IT'S A PLANET WITH NO WATER. NOW IT'S A PLANET THAT'S NOTHING BUT WATER— IF IT'S NOT ONE THING, IT'S ANOTHER.
AHA! I SEE AN ISLAND OVER THERE!
FOR REAL? WHERE?!

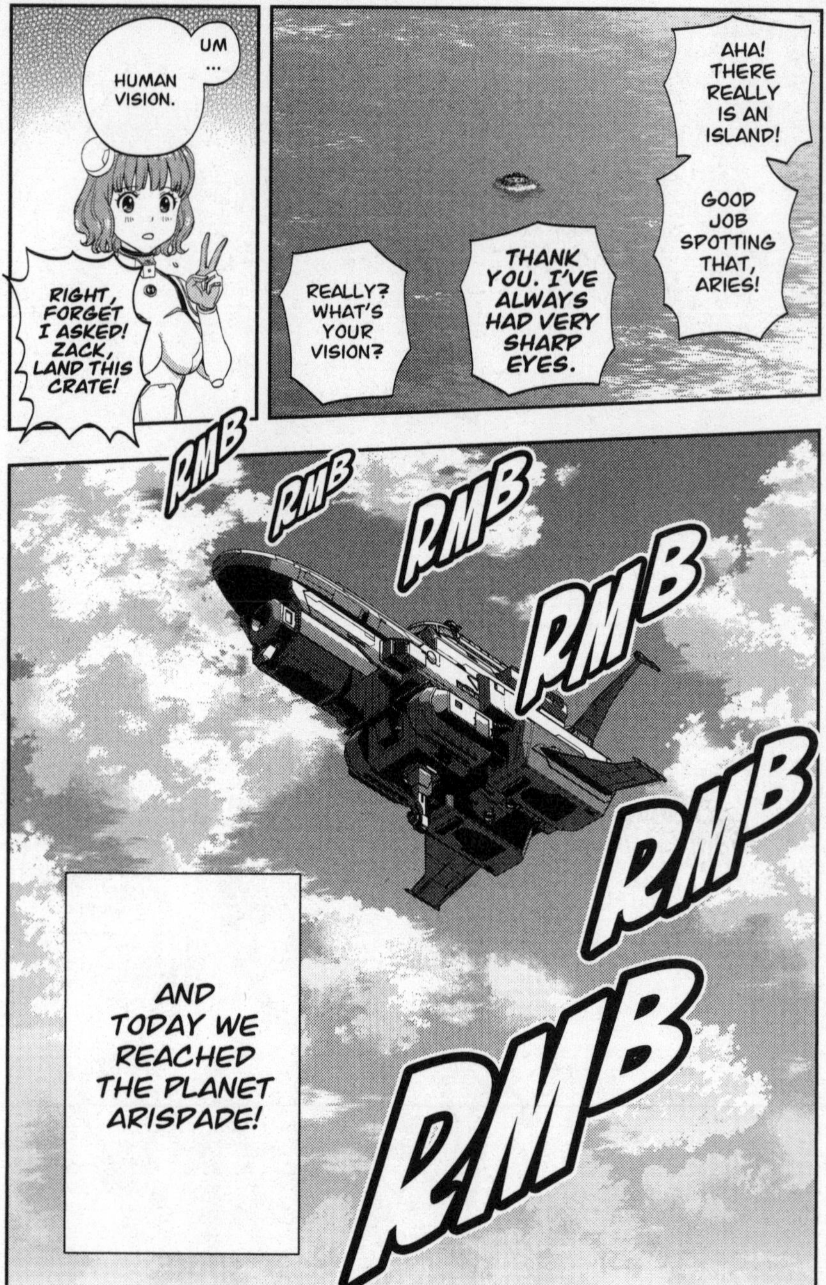
AHA! THERE REALLY IS AN ISLAND!
GOOD JOB SPOTTING THAT, ARIES!
THANK YOU. I'VE ALWAYS HAD VERY SHARP EYES.
REALLY? WHAT'S YOUR VISION?
UM ...
HUMAN VISION.
RIGHT, FORGET I ASKED! ZACK, LAND THIS CRATE!
RMB
RMB
RMB
RMB
RMB
RMB
AND TODAY WE REACHED THE PLANET ARISPADE!

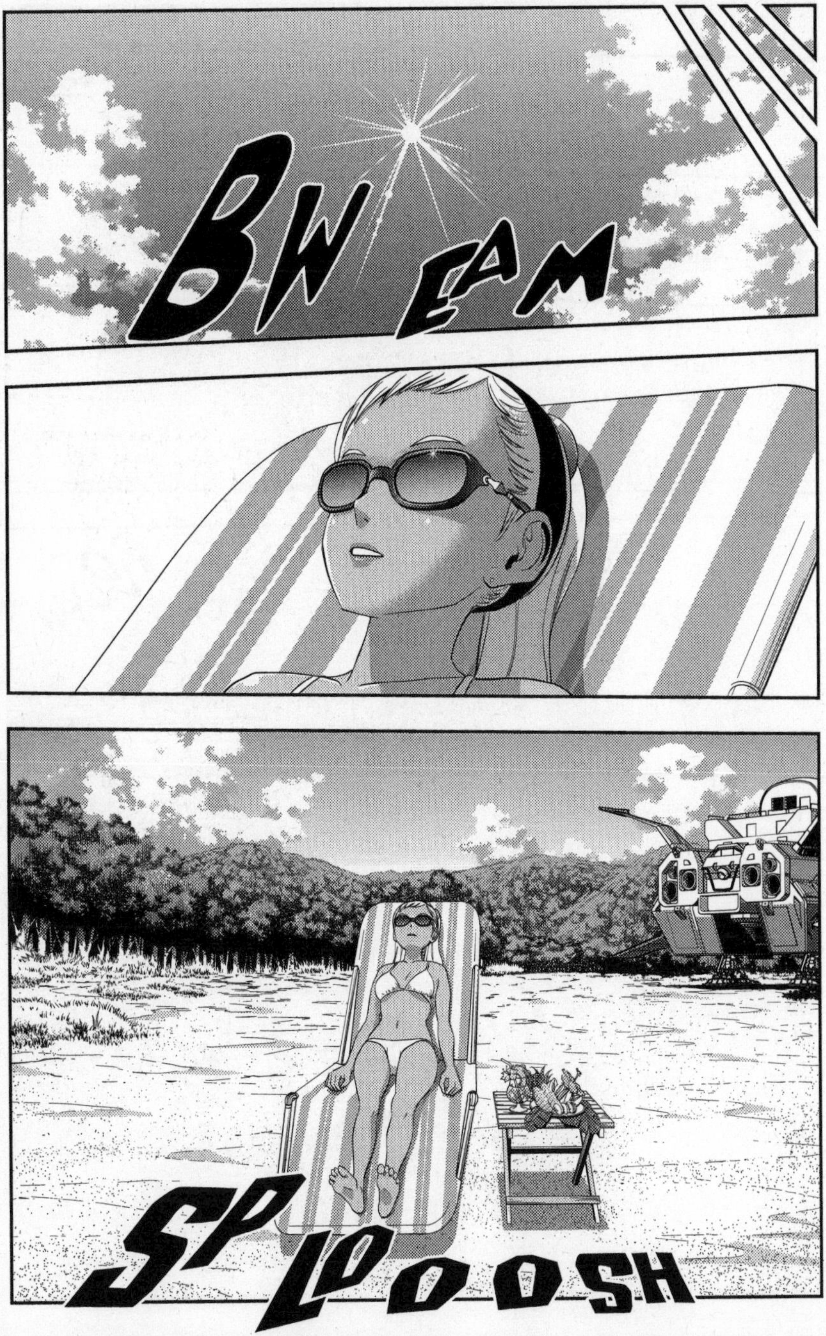
BWEAM
SPLOOOSH

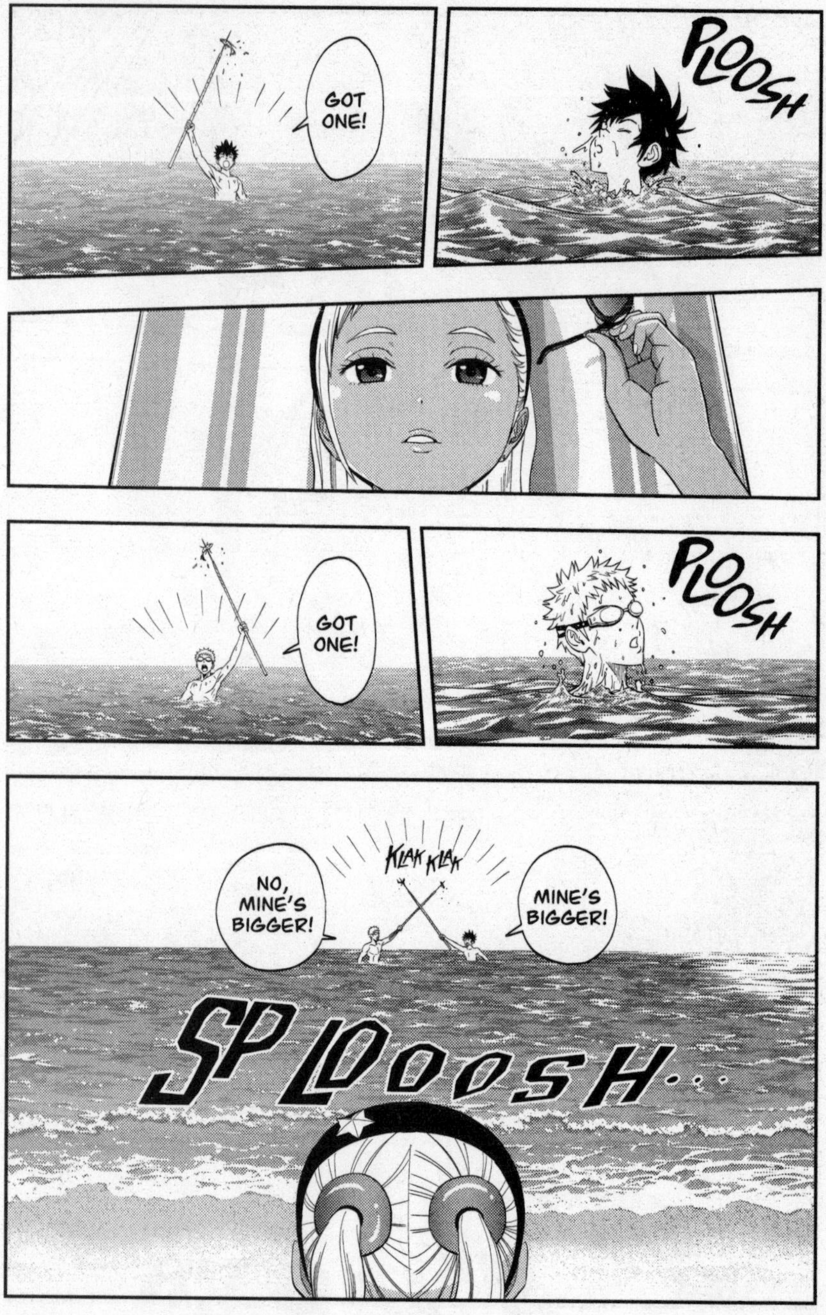
PLOOSH
GOT ONE!
PLOOSH
GOT ONE!
MINE'S BIGGER!
KLAK KLAK
NO, MINE'S BIGGER!
SPLOOOSH...

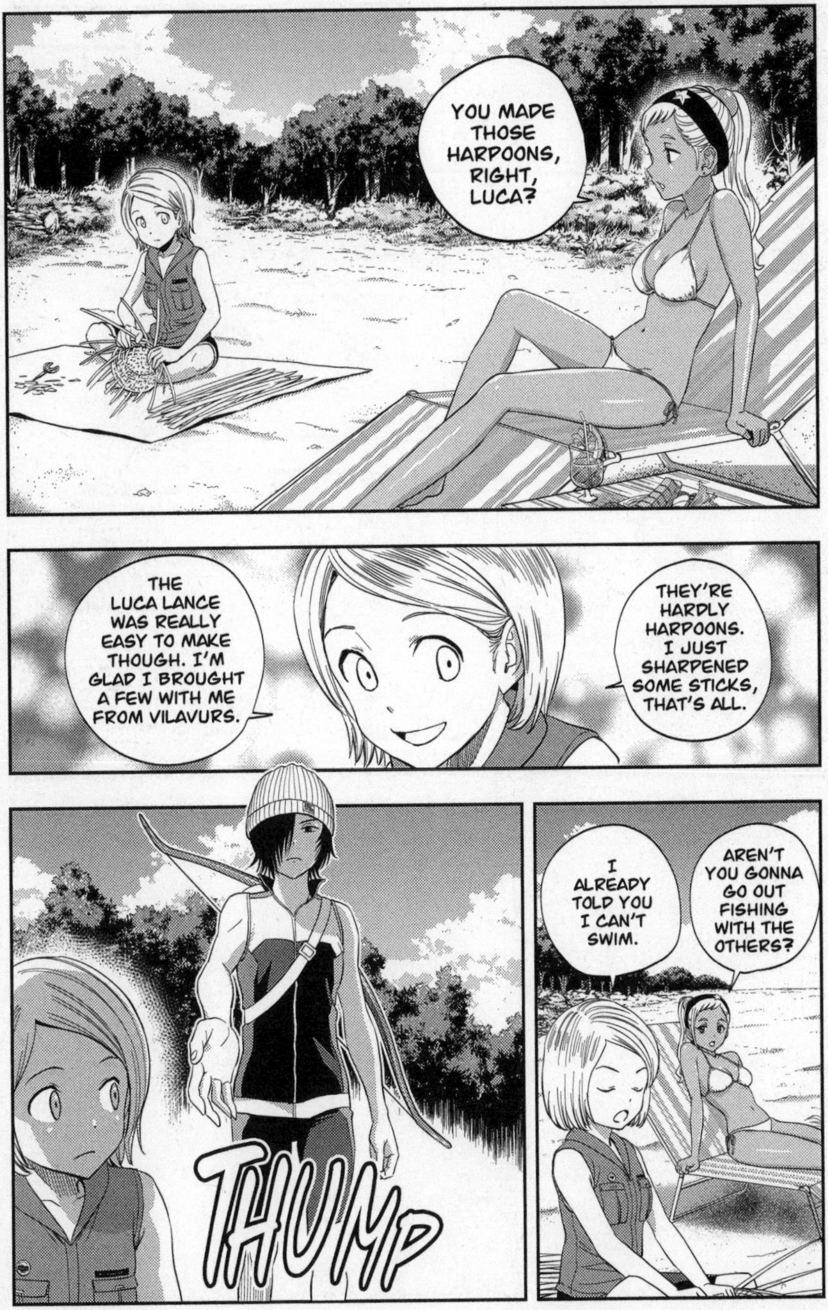
YOU MADE THOSE HARPOONS, RIGHT, LUCA?
THEY'RE HARDLY HARPOONS. I JUST SHARPENED SOME STICKS, THAT'S ALL.
THE LUCA LANCE WAS REALLY EASY TO MAKE THOUGH. I'M GLAD I BROUGHT A FEW WITH ME FROM VILAVURS.
AREN'T YOU GONNA GO OUT FISHING WITH THE OTHERS?
I ALREADY TOLD YOU I CAN'T SWIM.
THUMP

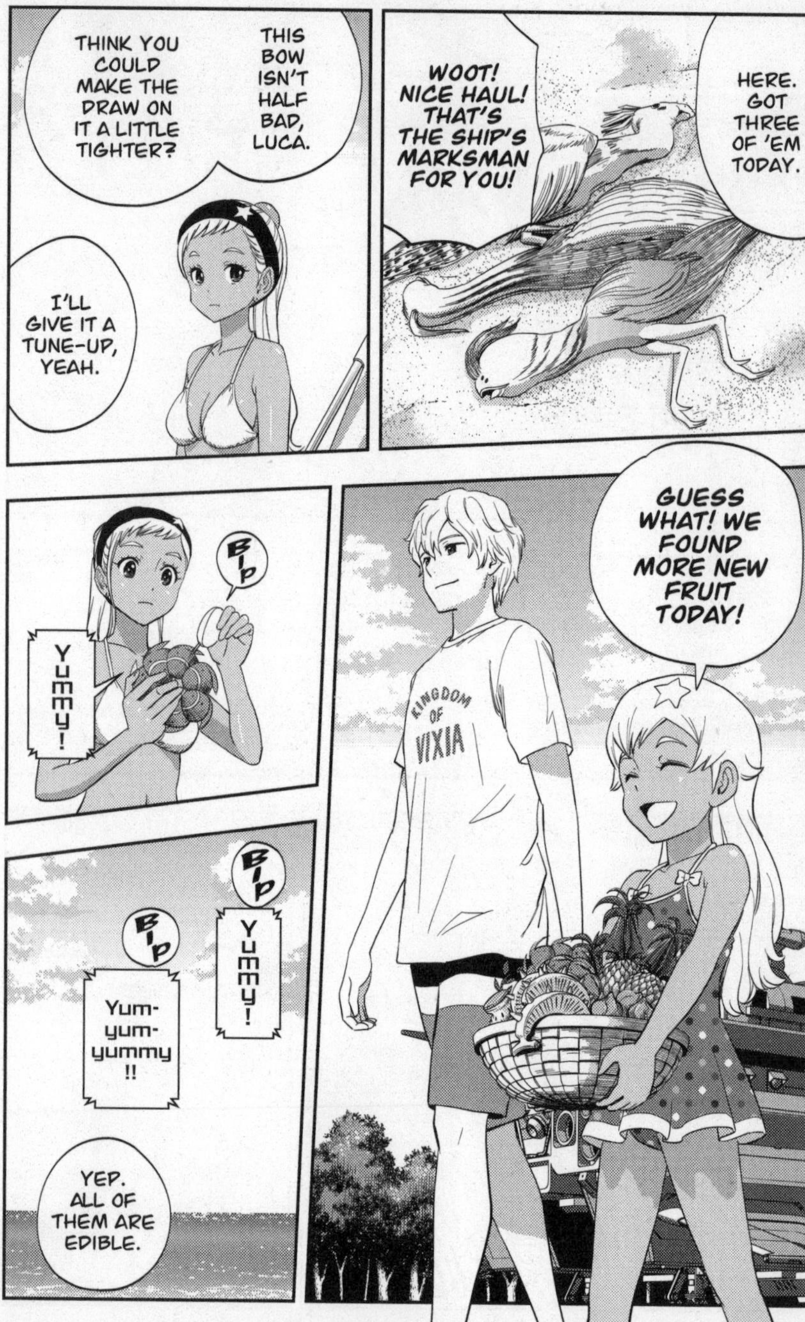
HERE. GOT THREE OF 'EM TODAY.
WOOT! NICE HAUL! THAT'S THE SHIP'S MARKSMAN FOR YOU!
THIS BOW ISN'T HALF BAD, LUCA.
THINK YOU COULD MAKE THE DRAW ON IT A LITTLE TIGHTER?
I'LL GIVE IT A TUNE-UP, YEAH.
GUESS WHAT! WE FOUND MORE NEW FRUIT TODAY!
KINGDOM OF VIXIA
BIP
Yummy!
BIP
Yummy!
BIP
Yum-yum-yummy!!
YEP. ALL OF THEM ARE EDIBLE.

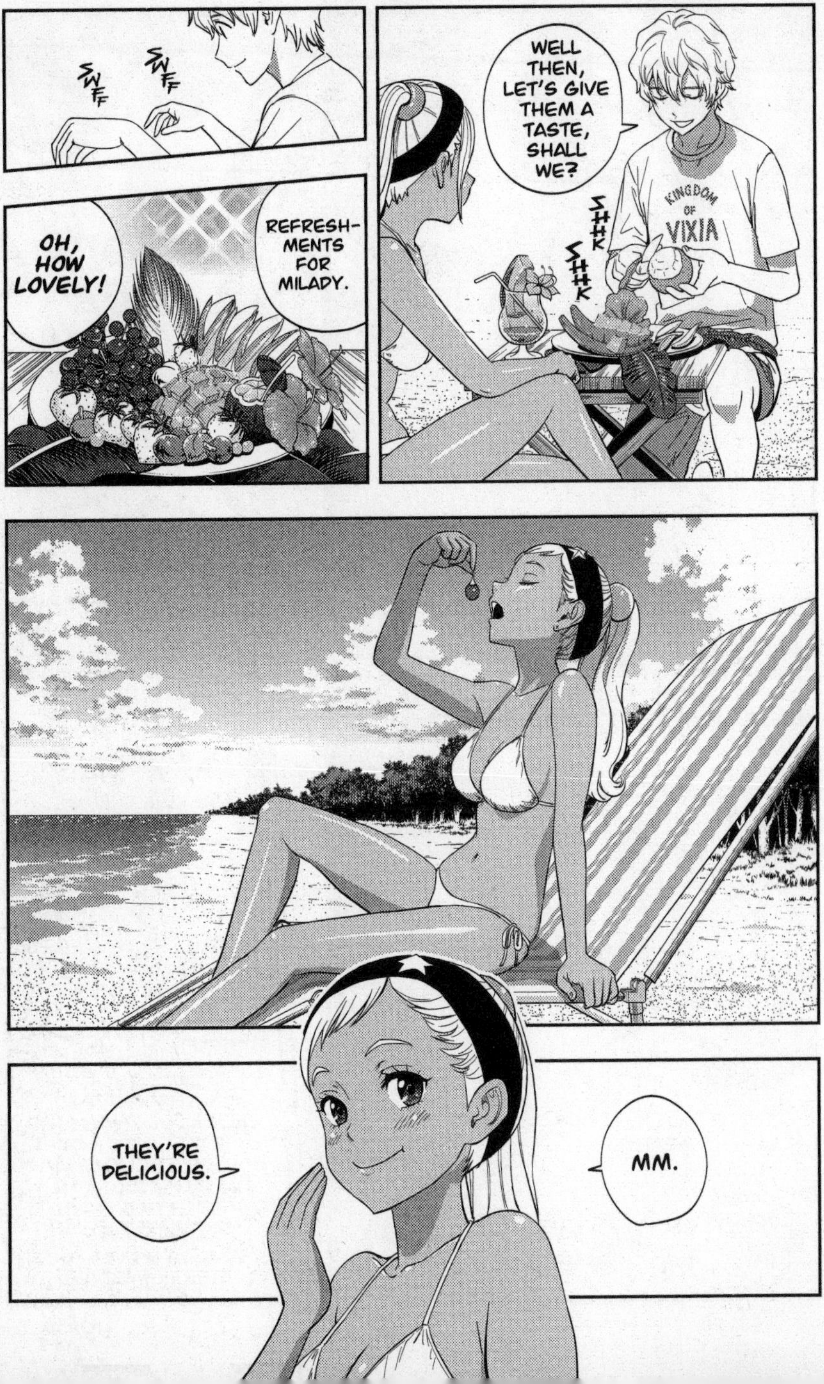
WELL THEN, LET'S GIVE THEM A TASTE, SHALL WE?
SHHK
SHHK
KINGDOM OF VIXIA
SWFF
SWFF
REFRESH-MENTS FOR MILADY.
OH, HOW LOVELY!
MM.
THEY'RE DELICIOUS.

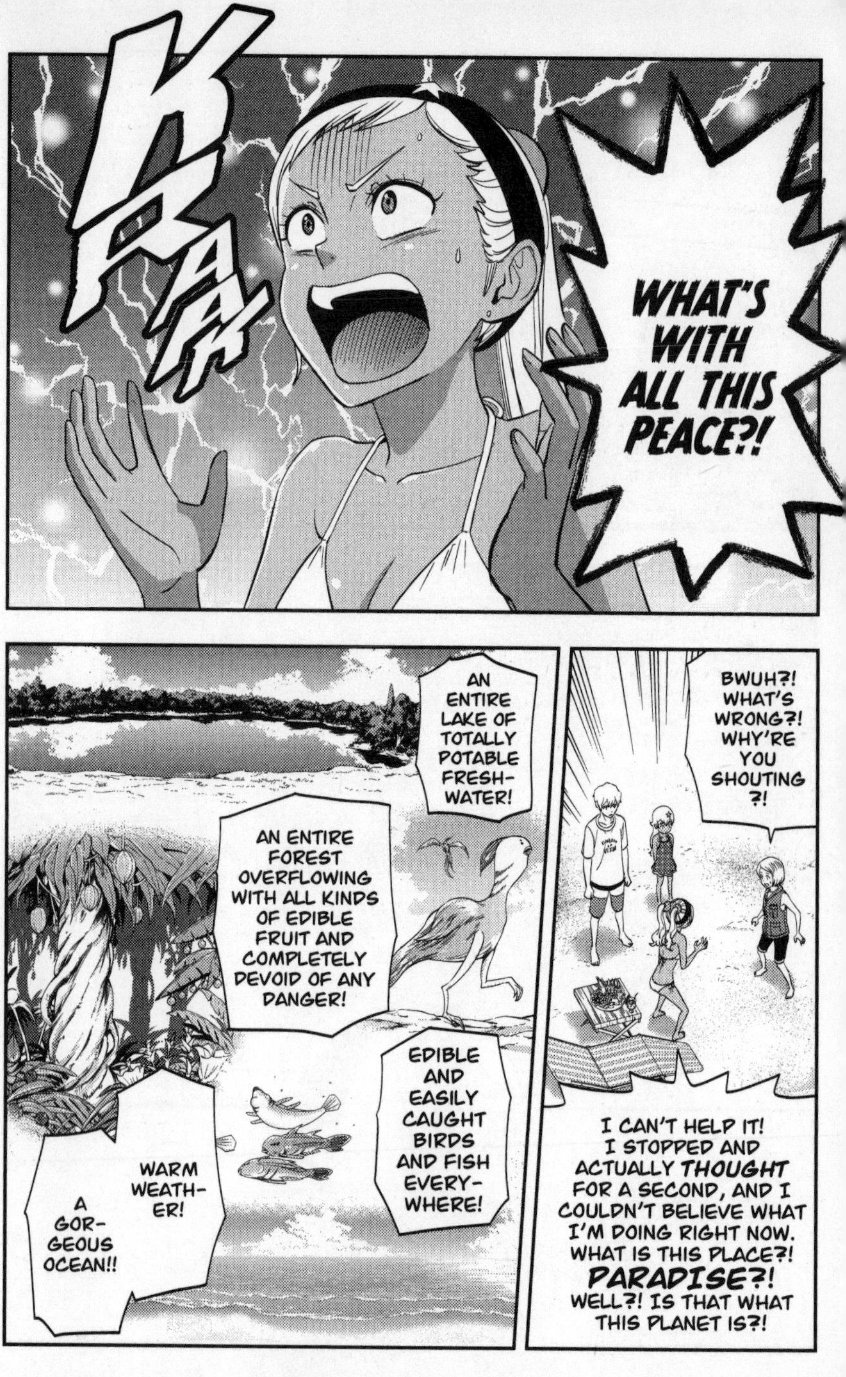
WHAT'S WITH ALL THIS PEACE?!
KRAK
BWUH?! WHAT'S WRONG?! WHY'RE YOU SHOUTING?!
I CAN'T HELP IT! I STOPPED AND ACTUALLY THOUGHT FOR A SECOND, AND I COULDN'T BELIEVE WHAT I'M DOING RIGHT NOW. WHAT IS THIS PLACE?! PARADISE?! WELL?! IS THAT WHAT THIS PLANET IS?!
AN ENTIRE LAKE OF TOTALLY POTABLE FRESH-WATER!
AN ENTIRE FOREST OVERFLOWING WITH ALL KINDS OF EDIBLE FRUIT AND COMPLETELY DEVOID OF ANY DANGER!
EDIBLE AND EASILY CAUGHT BIRDS AND FISH EVERY-WHERE!
WARM WEATH-ER!
A GOR-GEOUS OCEAN!!

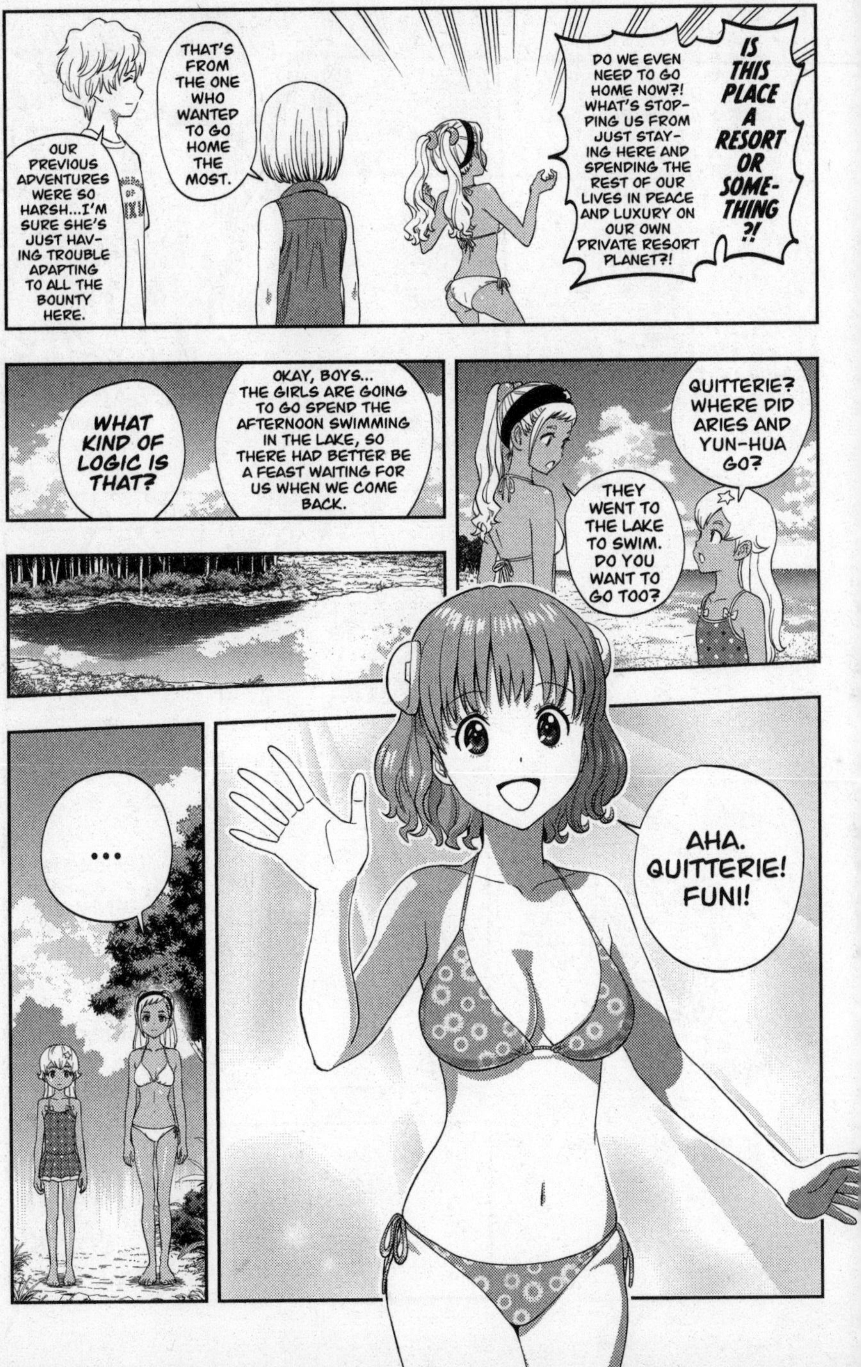
IS THIS PLACE A RESORT OR SOMETHING?!
DO WE EVEN NEED TO GO HOME NOW?! WHAT'S STOPPING US FROM JUST STAYING HERE AND SPENDING THE REST OF OUR LIVES IN PEACE AND LUXURY ON OUR OWN PRIVATE RESORT PLANET?!
THAT'S FROM THE ONE WHO WANTED TO GO HOME THE MOST.
OUR PREVIOUS ADVENTURES WERE SO HARSH...I'M SURE SHE'S JUST HAVING TROUBLE ADAPTING TO ALL THE BOUNTY HERE.
QUITTERIE? WHERE DID ARIES AND YUN-HUA GO?
THEY WENT TO THE LAKE TO SWIM. DO YOU WANT TO GO TOO?
OKAY, BOYS... THE GIRLS ARE GOING TO GO SPEND THE AFTERNOON SWIMMING IN THE LAKE, SO THERE HAD BETTER BE A FEAST WAITING FOR US WHEN WE COME BACK.
WHAT KIND OF LOGIC IS THAT?
AHA. QUITTERIE! FUNI!
...

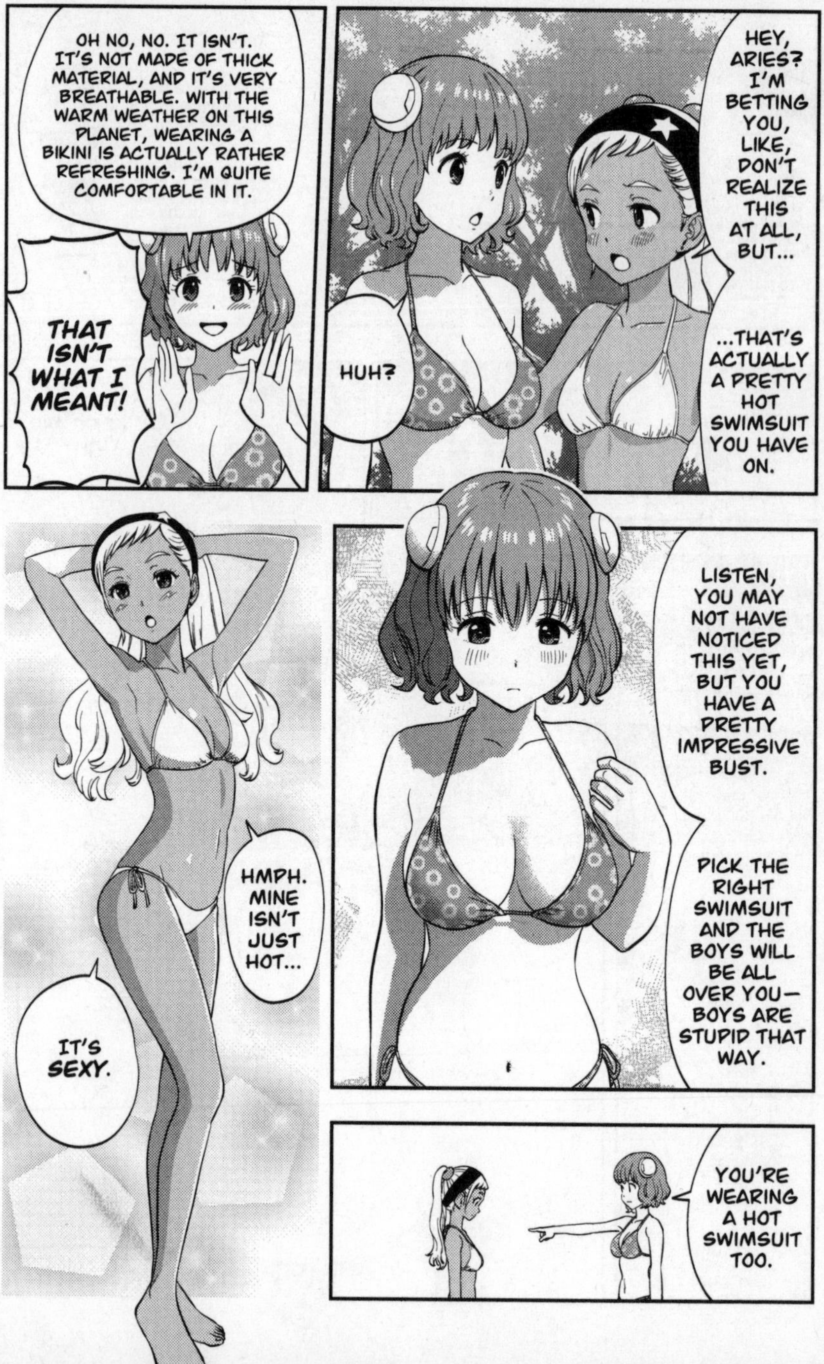
HEY, ARIES? I'M BETTING YOU, LIKE, DON'T REALIZE THIS AT ALL, BUT...
...THAT'S ACTUALLY A PRETTY HOT SWIMSUIT YOU HAVE ON.
HUH?
OH NO, NO. IT ISN'T. IT'S NOT MADE OF THICK MATERIAL, AND IT'S VERY BREATHABLE. WITH THE WARM WEATHER ON THIS PLANET, WEARING A BIKINI IS ACTUALLY RATHER REFRESHING. I'M QUITE COMFORTABLE IN IT.
THAT ISN'T WHAT I MEANT!
LISTEN, YOU MAY NOT HAVE NOTICED THIS YET, BUT YOU HAVE A PRETTY IMPRESSIVE BUST.
PICK THE RIGHT SWIMSUIT AND THE BOYS WILL BE ALL OVER YOU—BOYS ARE STUPID THAT WAY.
YOU'RE WEARING A HOT SWIMSUIT TOO.
HMPH. MINE ISN'T JUST HOT...
IT'S SEXY.

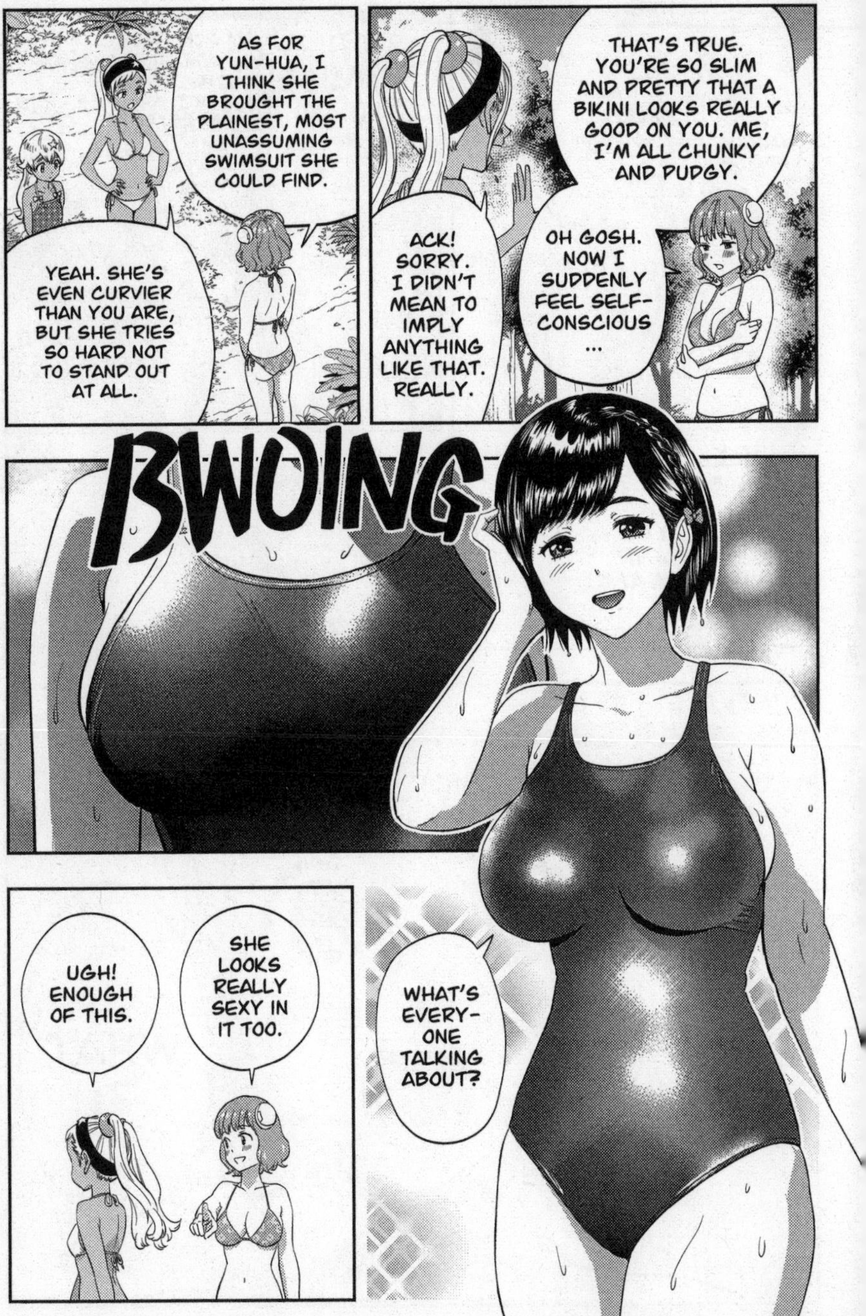

AS FOR YUN-HUA, I THINK SHE BROUGHT THE PLAINEST, MOST UNASSUMING SWIMSUIT SHE COULD FIND.
YEAH. SHE'S EVEN CURVIER THAN YOU ARE, BUT SHE TRIES SO HARD NOT TO STAND OUT AT ALL.
THAT'S TRUE. YOU'RE SO SLIM AND PRETTY THAT A BIKINI LOOKS REALLY GOOD ON YOU. ME, I'M ALL CHUNKY AND PUDGY.
OH GOSH. NOW I SUDDENLY FEEL SELF-CONSCIOUS...
ACK! SORRY. I DIDN'T MEAN TO IMPLY ANYTHING LIKE THAT. REALLY.
BWOING
UGH! ENOUGH OF THIS.
SHE LOOKS REALLY SEXY IN IT TOO.
WHAT'S EVERY-ONE TALKING ABOUT?

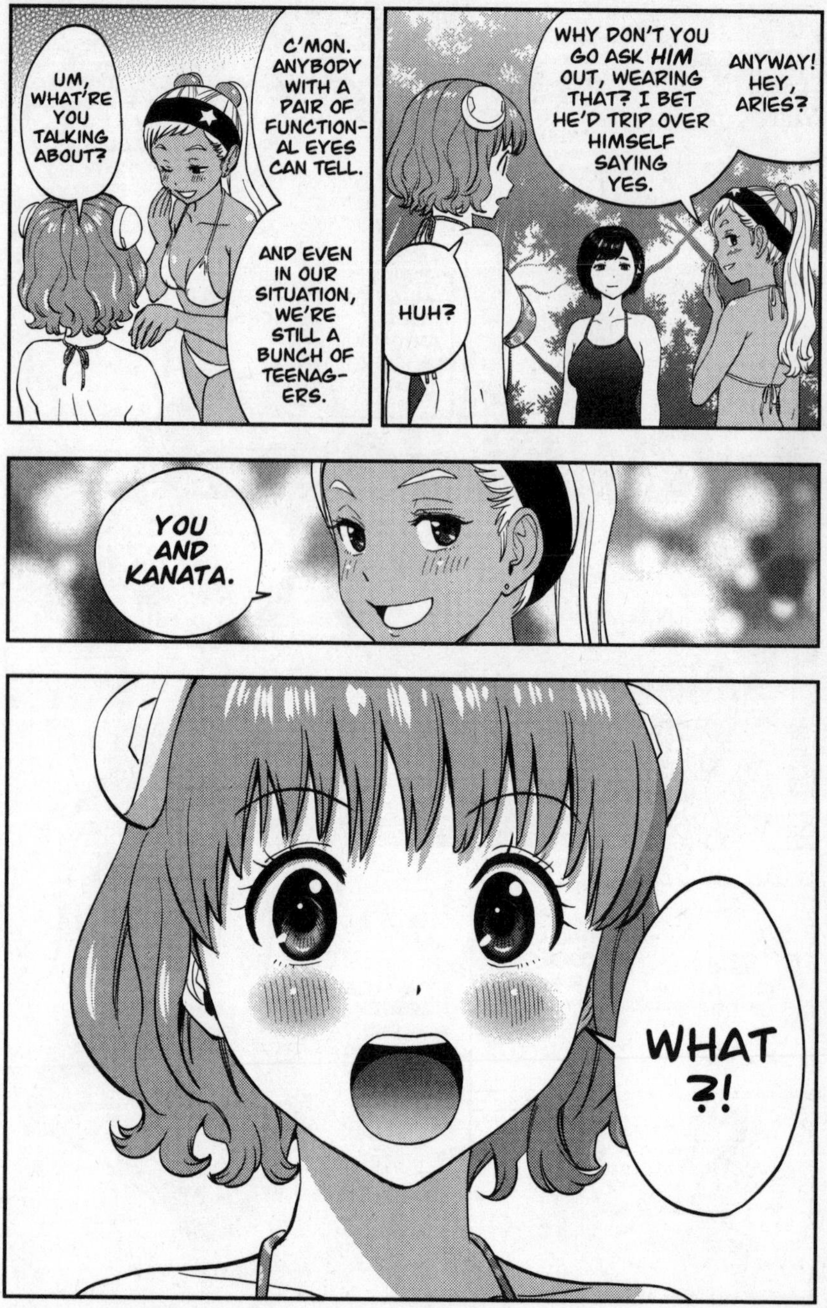
ANYWAY! HEY, ARIES?
WHY DON'T YOU GO ASK *HIM* OUT, WEARING THAT? I BET HE'D TRIP OVER HIMSELF SAYING YES.
HUH?
C'MON. ANYBODY WITH A PAIR OF FUNCTION-AL EYES CAN TELL.
AND EVEN IN OUR SITUATION, WE'RE STILL A BUNCH OF TEENAG-ERS.
UM, WHAT'RE YOU TALKING ABOUT?
YOU AND KANATA.
WHAT?!

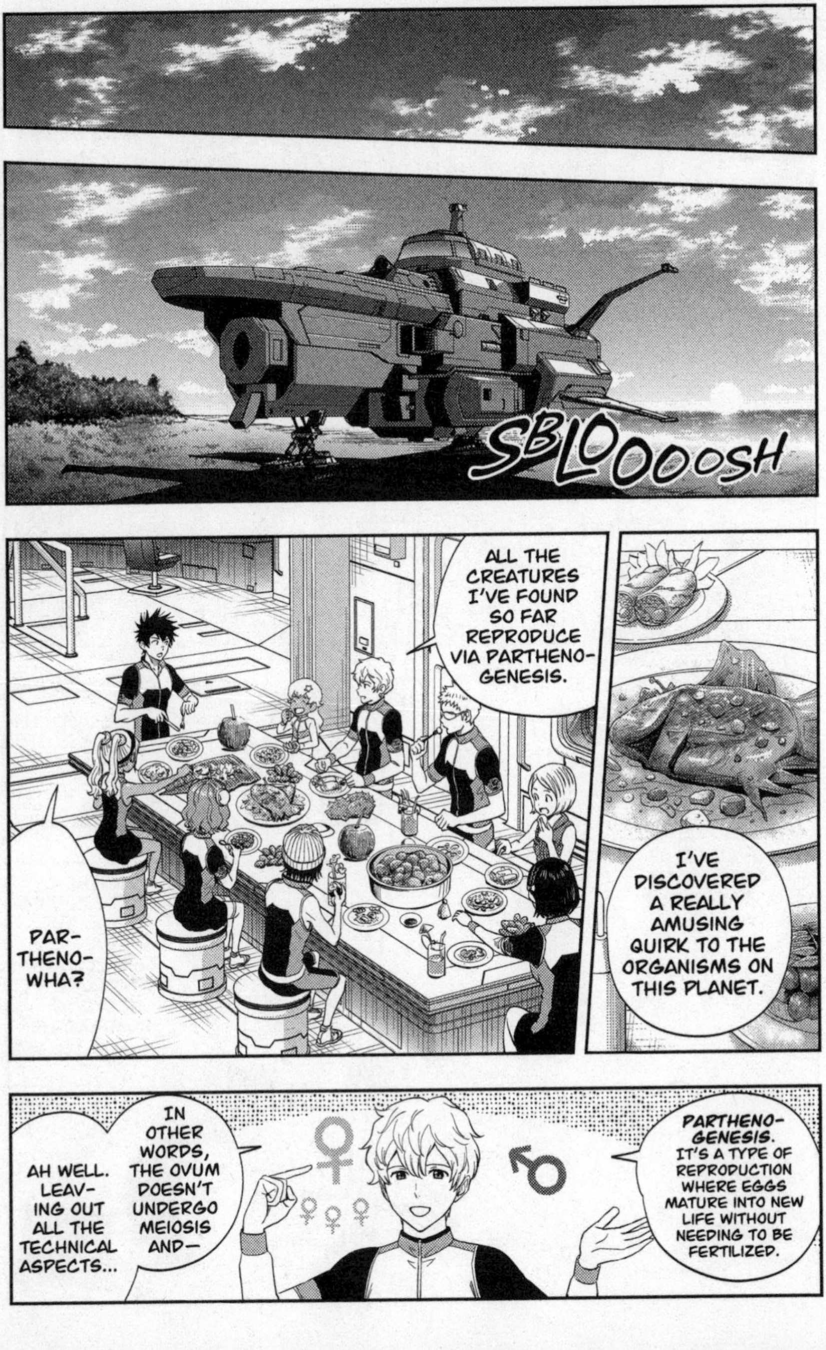
SBLOOOOOSH
I'VE DISCOVERED A REALLY AMUSING QUIRK TO THE ORGANISMS ON THIS PLANET.
ALL THE CREATURES I'VE FOUND SO FAR REPRODUCE VIA PARTHENO-GENESIS.
PAR-THENO-WHA?
PARTHENO-GENESIS. IT'S A TYPE OF REPRODUCTION WHERE EGGS MATURE INTO NEW LIFE WITHOUT NEEDING TO BE FERTILIZED.
IN OTHER WORDS, THE OVUM DOESN'T UNDERGO MEIOSIS AND—
AH WELL. LEAV-ING OUT ALL THE TECHNICAL ASPECTS...

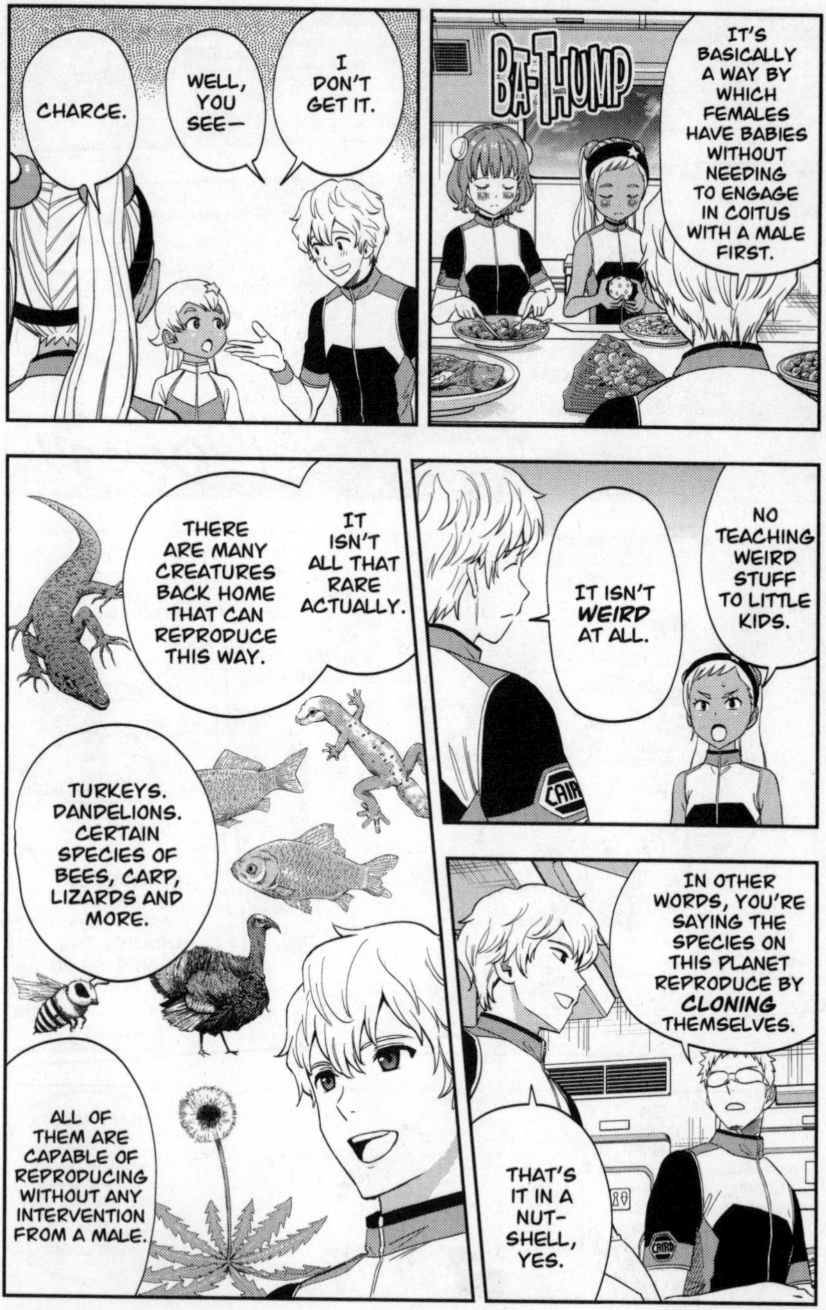
BA-THUMP
IT'S BASICALLY A WAY BY WHICH FEMALES HAVE BABIES WITHOUT NEEDING TO ENGAGE IN COITUS WITH A MALE FIRST.
I DON'T GET IT.
WELL, YOU SEE—
CHARCE.
NO TEACHING WEIRD STUFF TO LITTLE KIDS.
IT ISN'T **WEIRD** AT ALL.
IN OTHER WORDS, YOU'RE SAYING THE SPECIES ON THIS PLANET REPRODUCE BY **CLONING** THEMSELVES.
THAT'S IT IN A NUT-SHELL, YES.
IT ISN'T ALL THAT RARE ACTUALLY.
THERE ARE MANY CREATURES BACK HOME THAT CAN REPRODUCE THIS WAY.
TURKEYS. DANDELIONS. CERTAIN SPECIES OF BEES, CARP, LIZARDS AND MORE.
ALL OF THEM ARE CAPABLE OF REPRODUCING WITHOUT ANY INTERVENTION FROM A MALE.
CAIRD

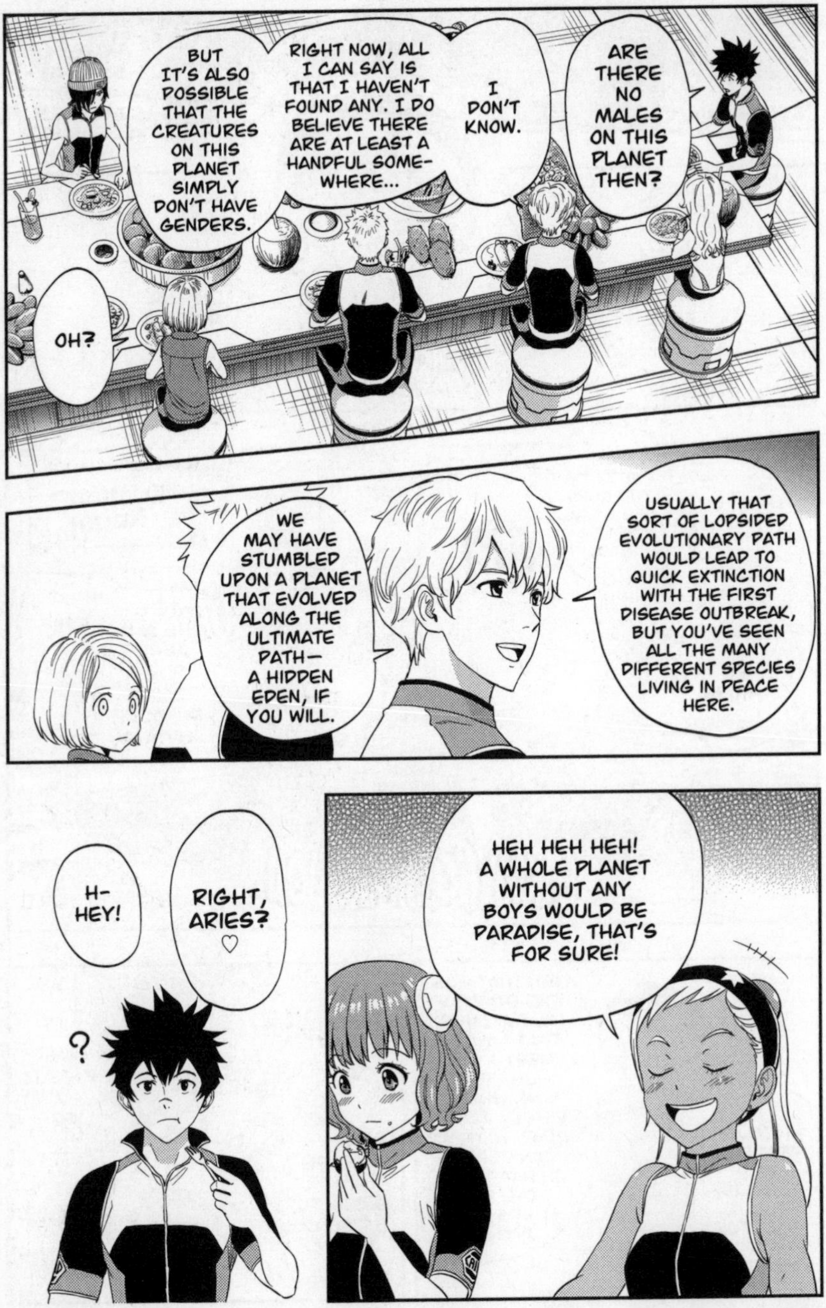
ARE THERE NO MALES ON THIS PLANET THEN?
I DON'T KNOW.
RIGHT NOW, ALL I CAN SAY IS THAT I HAVEN'T FOUND ANY. I DO BELIEVE THERE ARE AT LEAST A HANDFUL SOMEWHERE...
BUT IT'S ALSO POSSIBLE THAT THE CREATURES ON THIS PLANET SIMPLY DON'T HAVE GENDERS.
OH?
USUALLY THAT SORT OF LOPSIDED EVOLUTIONARY PATH WOULD LEAD TO QUICK EXTINCTION WITH THE FIRST DISEASE OUTBREAK, BUT YOU'VE SEEN ALL THE MANY DIFFERENT SPECIES LIVING IN PEACE HERE.
WE MAY HAVE STUMBLED UPON A PLANET THAT EVOLVED ALONG THE ULTIMATE PATH— A HIDDEN EDEN, IF YOU WILL.
HEH HEH HEH! A WHOLE PLANET WITHOUT ANY BOYS WOULD BE PARADISE, THAT'S FOR SURE!
RIGHT, ARIES? ♡
H-HEY!
?

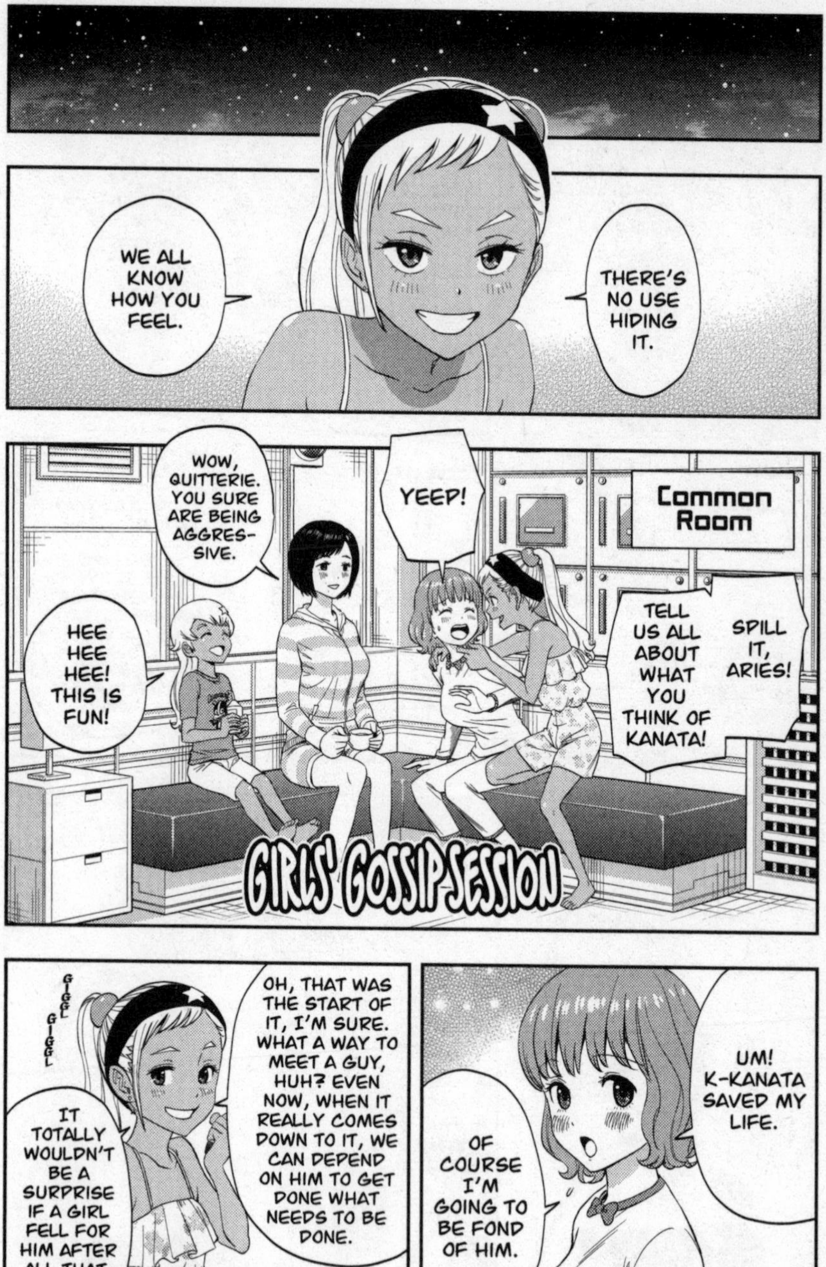
THERE'S NO USE HIDING IT.
WE ALL KNOW HOW YOU FEEL.
Common Room
SPILL IT, ARIES!
TELL US ALL ABOUT WHAT YOU THINK OF KANATA!
YEEP!
WOW, QUITTERIE. YOU SURE ARE BEING AGGRES-SIVE.
HEE HEE HEE! THIS IS FUN!
GIRLS' GOSSIP SESSION
UM! K-KANATA SAVED MY LIFE.
OF COURSE I'M GOING TO BE FOND OF HIM.
GIGGL GIGGL
OH, THAT WAS THE START OF IT, I'M SURE. WHAT A WAY TO MEET A GUY, HUH? EVEN NOW, WHEN IT REALLY COMES DOWN TO IT, WE CAN DEPEND ON HIM TO GET DONE WHAT NEEDS TO BE DONE.
IT TOTALLY WOULDN'T BE A SURPRISE IF A GIRL FELL FOR HIM AFTER ALL THAT.

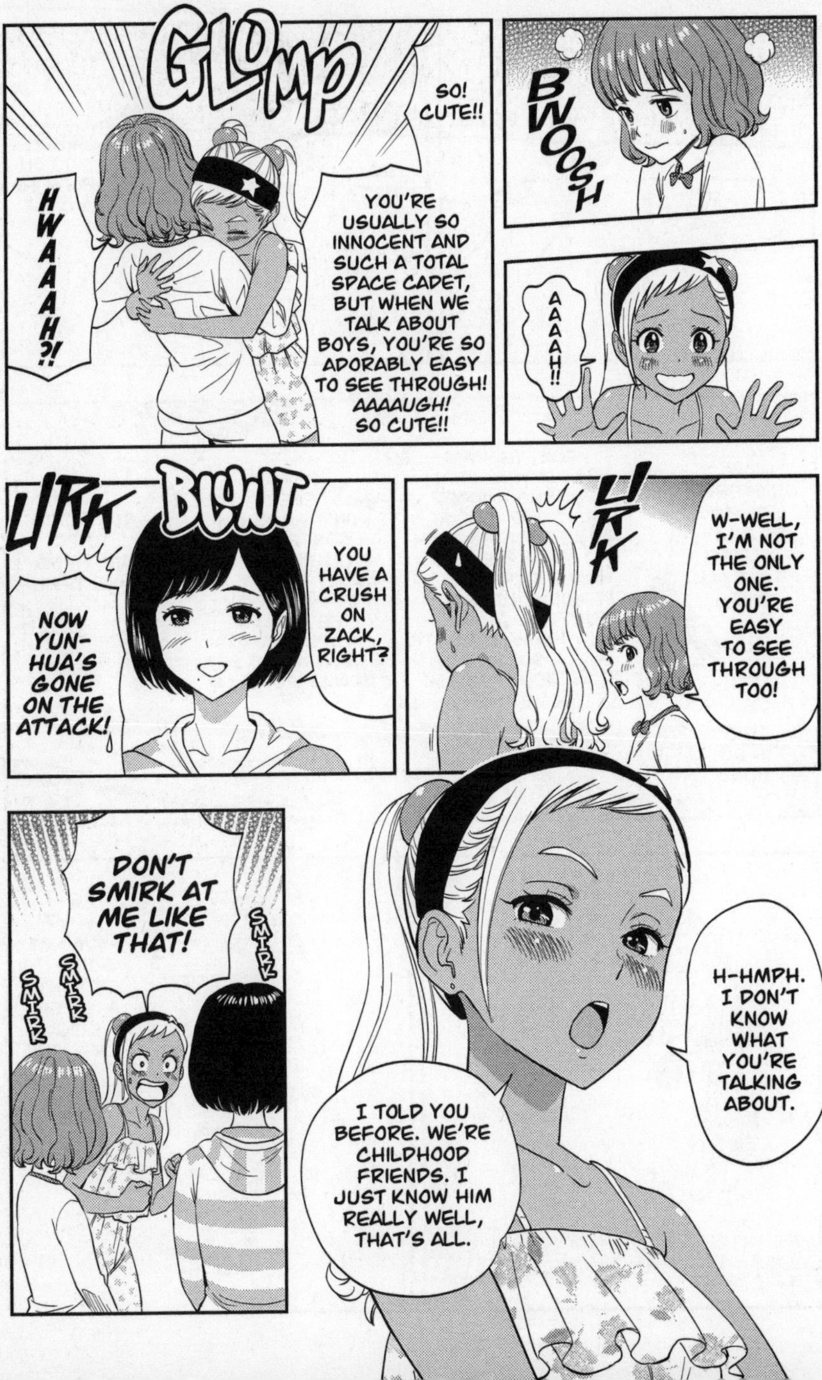
BWOOSH
AAAAH!!
GLOMP
SO! CUTE!!
YOU'RE USUALLY SO INNOCENT AND SUCH A TOTAL SPACE CADET, BUT WHEN WE TALK ABOUT BOYS, YOU'RE SO ADORABLY EASY TO SEE THROUGH! AAAAUGH! SO CUTE!!
HWAAAAH?!
URK
W-WELL, I'M NOT THE ONLY ONE. YOU'RE EASY TO SEE THROUGH TOO!
BLUNT
YOU HAVE A CRUSH ON ZACK, RIGHT?
URK
NOW YUN-HUA'S GONE ON THE ATTACK!
H-HMPH. I DON'T KNOW WHAT YOU'RE TALKING ABOUT.
I TOLD YOU BEFORE. WE'RE CHILDHOOD FRIENDS. I JUST KNOW HIM REALLY WELL, THAT'S ALL.
DON'T SMIRK AT ME LIKE THAT!
SMIRK
SMIRK
SMIRK

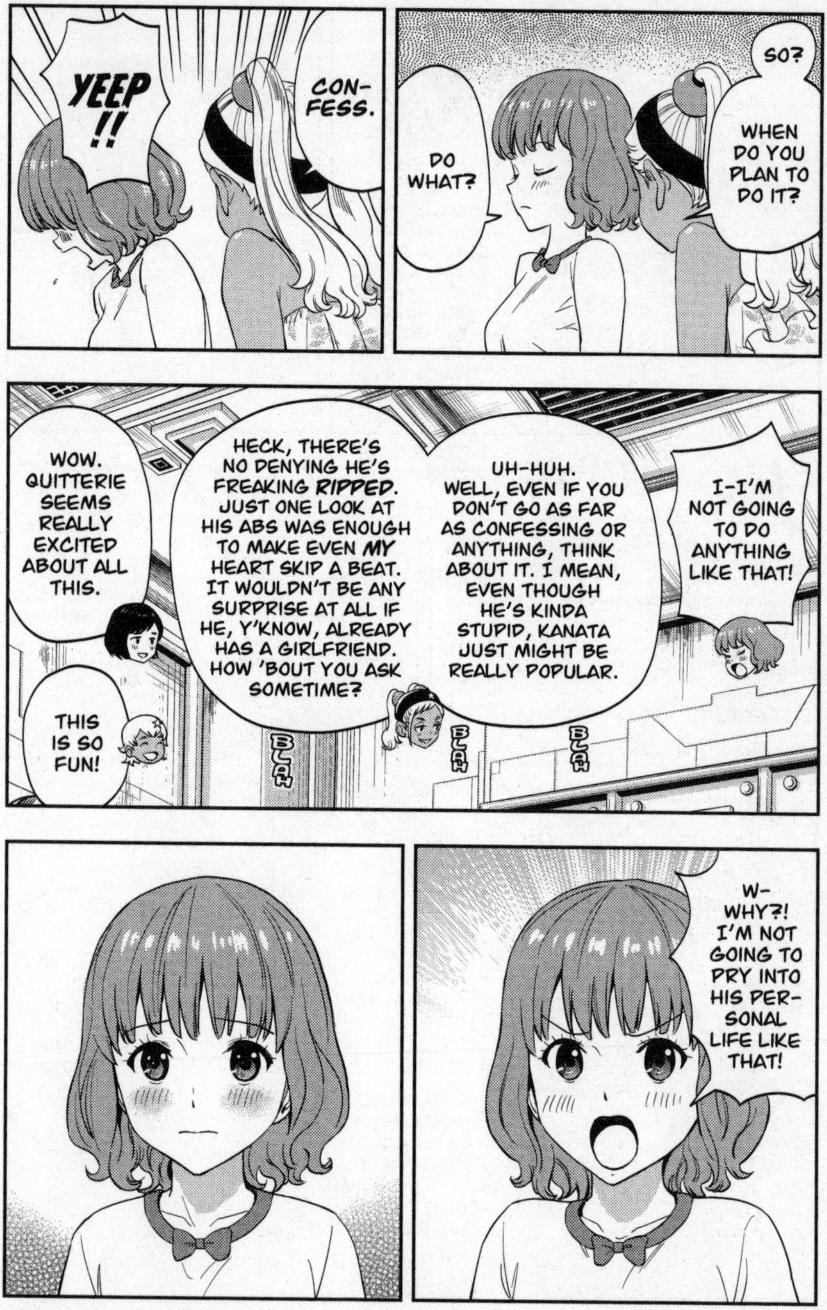
SO?
WHEN DO YOU PLAN TO DO IT?
DO WHAT?
CON-FESS.
YEEP !!
I-I'M NOT GOING TO DO ANYTHING LIKE THAT!
UH-HUH. WELL, EVEN IF YOU DON'T GO AS FAR AS CONFESSING OR ANYTHING, THINK ABOUT IT. I MEAN, EVEN THOUGH HE'S KINDA STUPID, KANATA JUST MIGHT BE REALLY POPULAR.
BLAH
BLAH
HECK, THERE'S NO DENYING HE'S FREAKING RIPPED. JUST ONE LOOK AT HIS ABS WAS ENOUGH TO MAKE EVEN MY HEART SKIP A BEAT. IT WOULDN'T BE ANY SURPRISE AT ALL IF HE, Y'KNOW, ALREADY HAS A GIRLFRIEND. HOW 'BOUT YOU ASK SOMETIME?
BLAH
WOW. QUITTERIE SEEMS REALLY EXCITED ABOUT ALL THIS.
THIS IS SO FUN!
W-WHY?! I'M NOT GOING TO PRY INTO HIS PER-SONAL LIFE LIKE THAT!

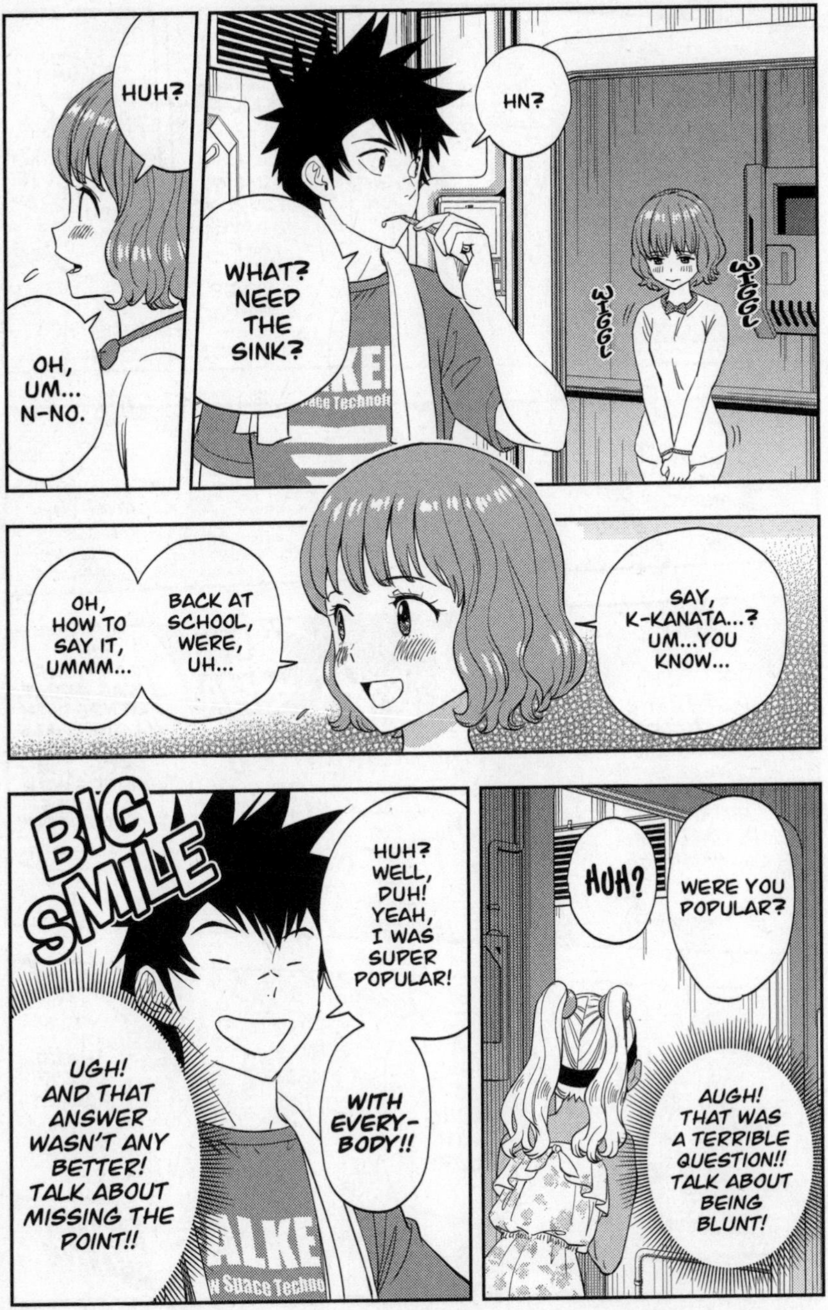
WIGGL
WIGGL
HN?
WHAT? NEED THE SINK?
HUH?
OH, UM... N-NO.
SAY, K-KANATA...? UM...YOU KNOW...
BACK AT SCHOOL, WERE, UH...
OH, HOW TO SAY IT, UMMM...
WERE YOU POPULAR?
HUH?
AUGH! THAT WAS A TERRIBLE QUESTION!! TALK ABOUT BEING BLUNT!
BIG SMILE
HUH? WELL, DUH! YEAH, I WAS SUPER POPULAR!
WITH EVERY-BODY!!
UGH! AND THAT ANSWER WASN'T ANY BETTER! TALK ABOUT MISSING THE POINT!!

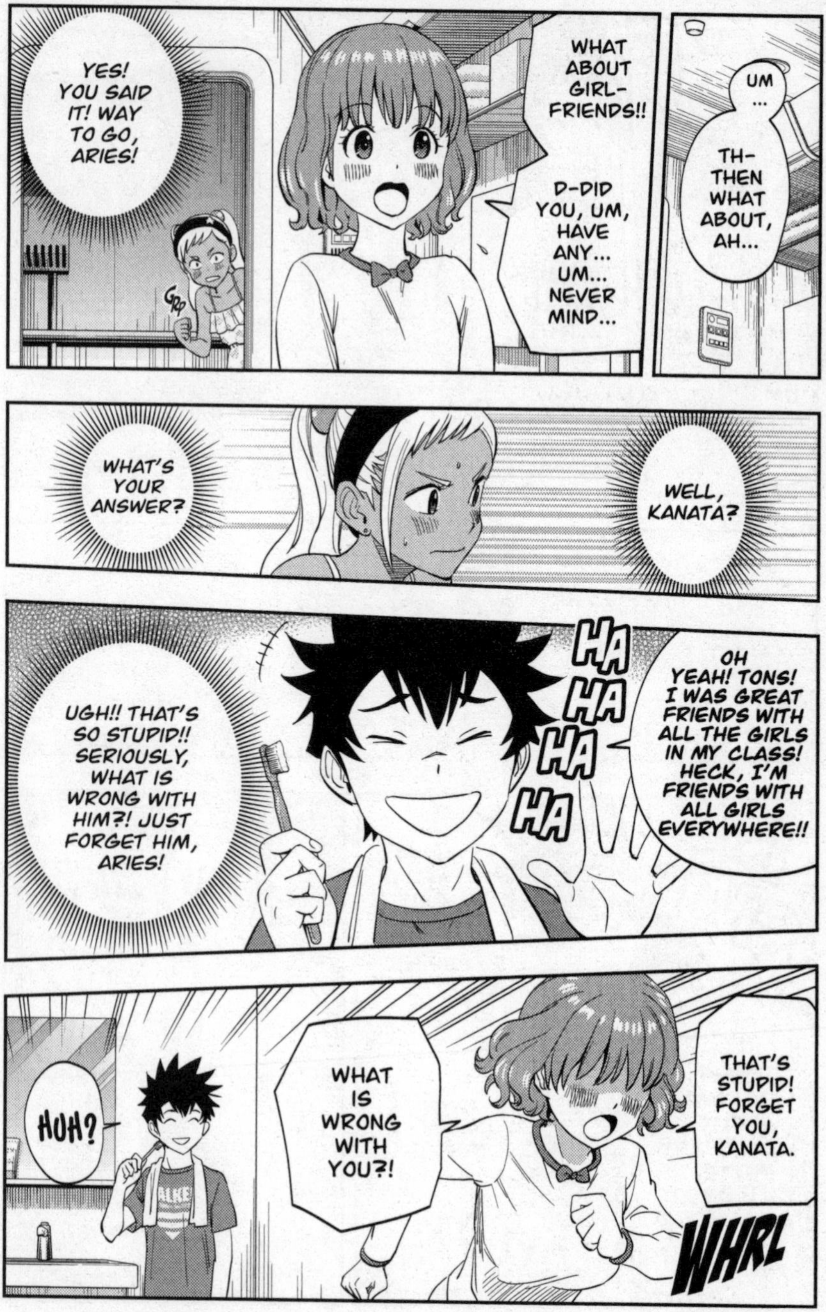
UM... TH-THEN WHAT ABOUT, AH...
WHAT ABOUT GIRL-FRIENDS!!
D-DID YOU, UM, HAVE ANY... UM... NEVER MIND...
YES! YOU SAID IT! WAY TO GO, ARIES!
GRP
WELL, KANATA?
WHAT'S YOUR ANSWER?
OH YEAH! TONS! I WAS GREAT FRIENDS WITH ALL THE GIRLS IN MY CLASS! HECK, I'M FRIENDS WITH ALL GIRLS EVERYWHERE!!
HA HA HA HA
UGH!! THAT'S SO STUPID!! SERIOUSLY, WHAT IS WRONG WITH HIM?! JUST FORGET HIM, ARIES!
THAT'S STUPID! FORGET YOU, KANATA.
WHRL
WHAT IS WRONG WITH YOU?!
HUH?

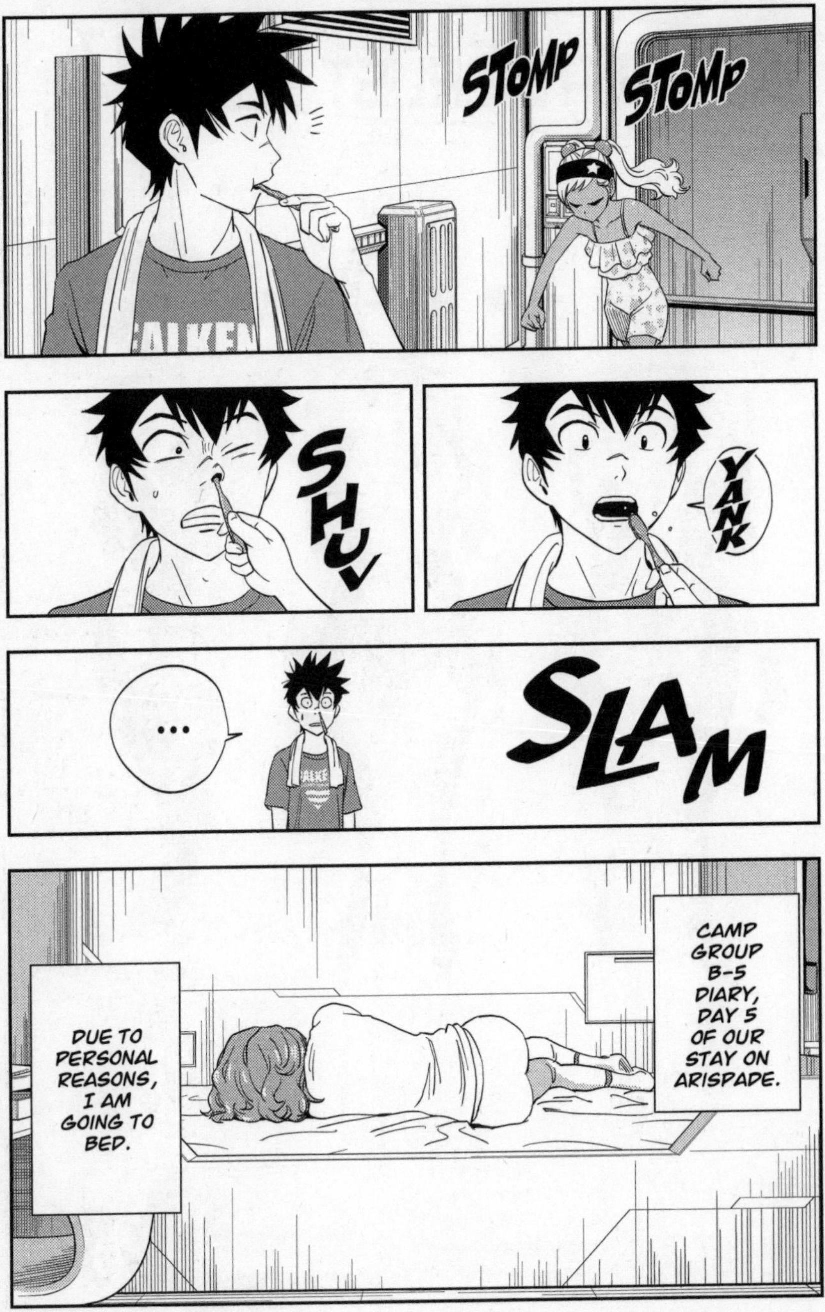
STOMP
STOMP
YANK
SHUV
SLAM
...
CAMP GROUP B-5 DIARY, DAY 5 OF OUR STAY ON ARISPADE.
DUE TO PERSONAL REASONS, I AM GOING TO BED.

Material Collection Costume Design

YUN-HUA'S CRUST SUIT

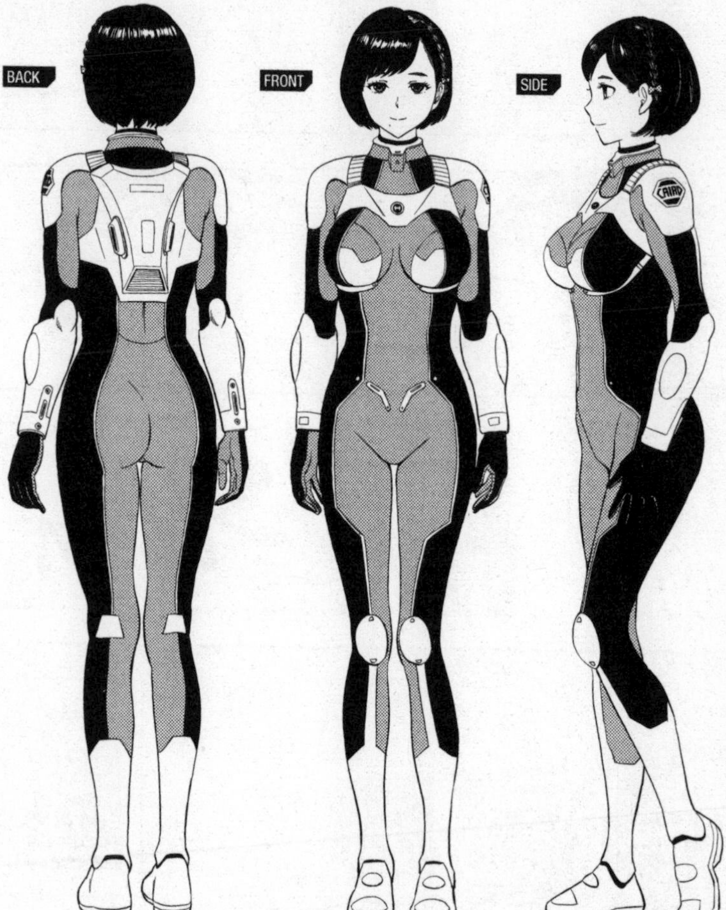
BACK
FRONT
SIDE
CAIRD

A Hyperion women's crust suit.

Purple.

Designed for curvier women.

Includes underwire support for the bust region.

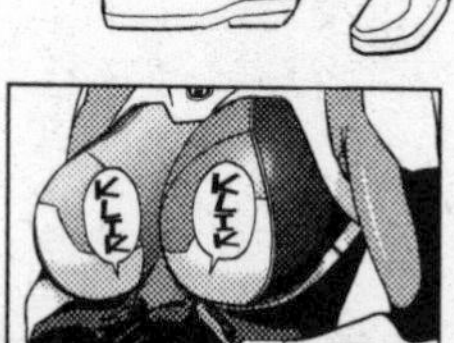
KLIK
KLIK

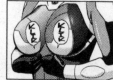

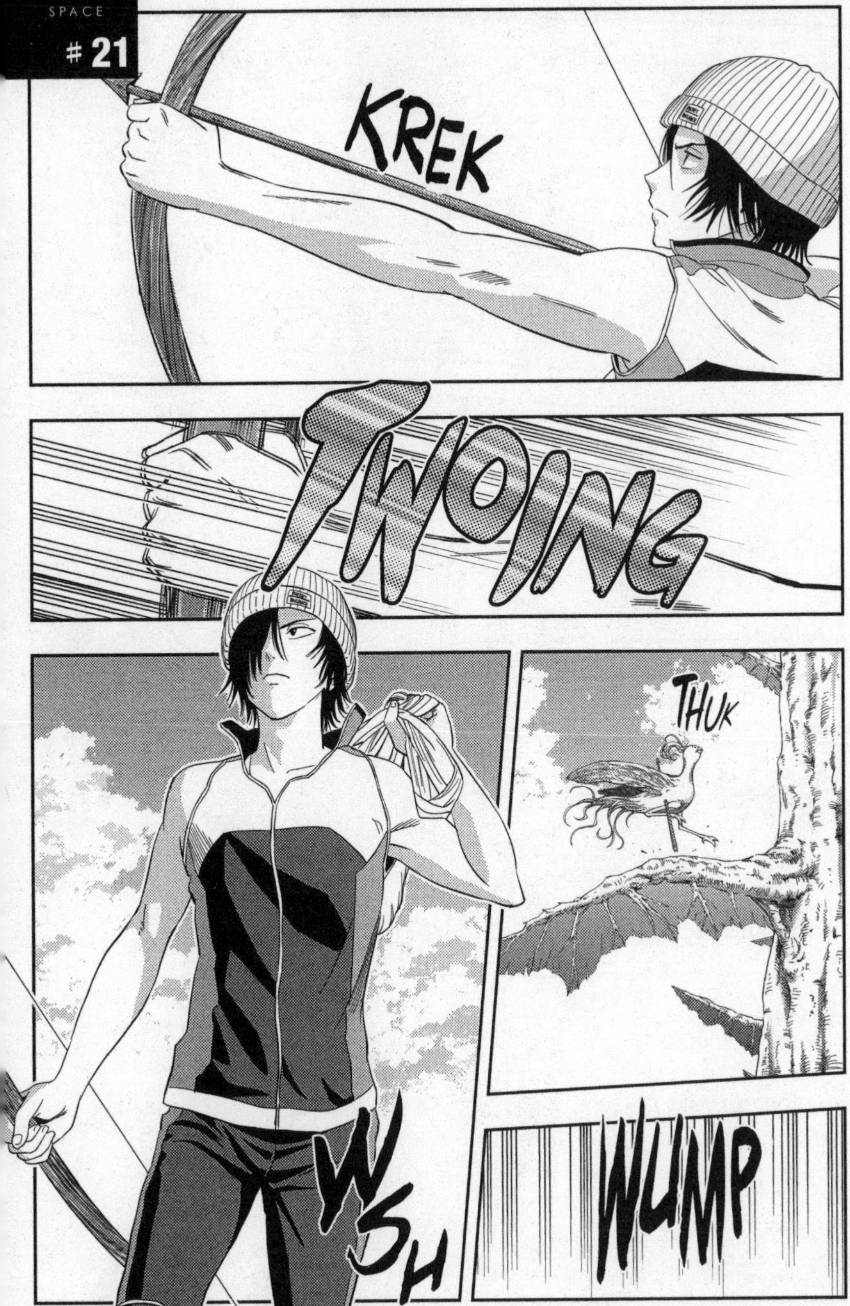
KREK
TWOING
THUK
WUMP
WSH

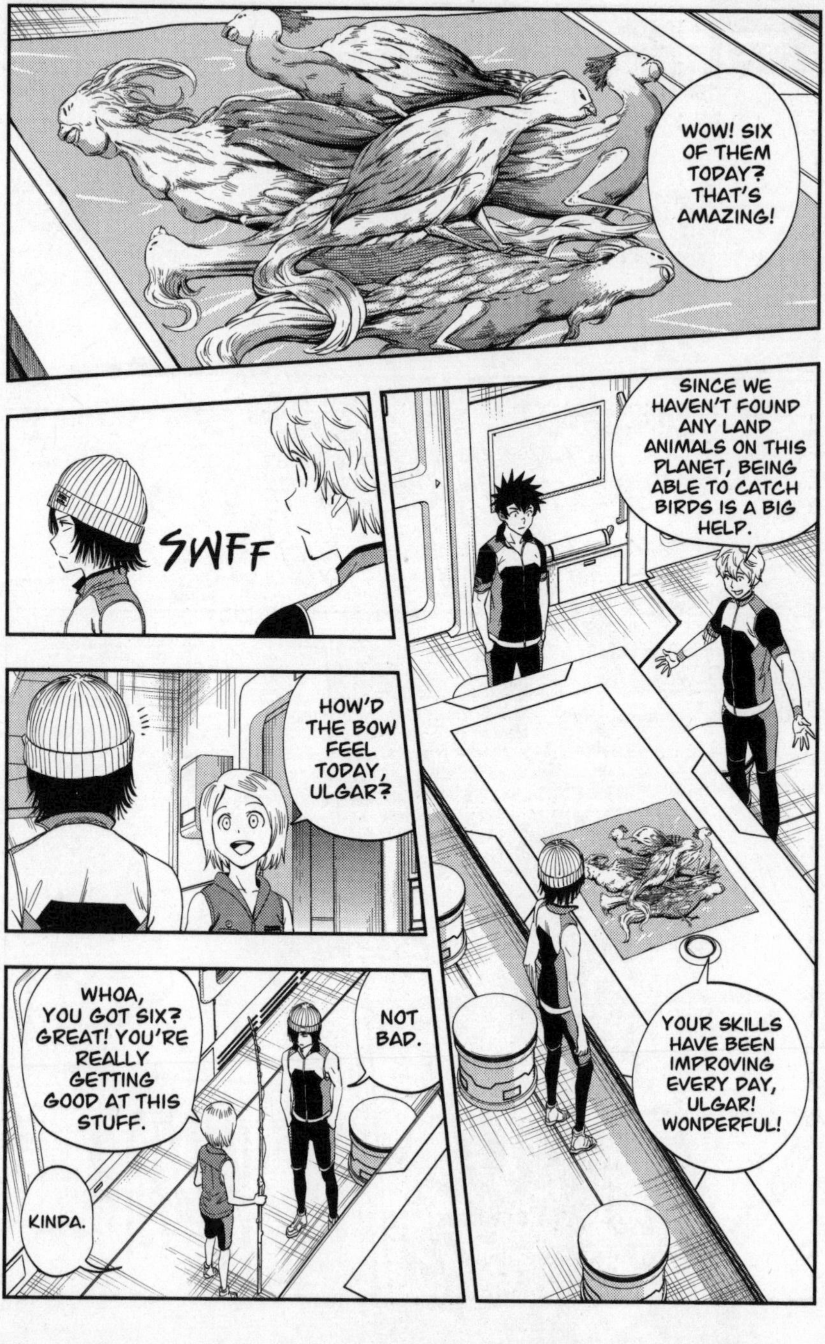
WOW! SIX OF THEM TODAY? THAT'S AMAZING!
SINCE WE HAVEN'T FOUND ANY LAND ANIMALS ON THIS PLANET, BEING ABLE TO CATCH BIRDS IS A BIG HELP.
YOUR SKILLS HAVE BEEN IMPROVING EVERY DAY, ULGAR! WONDERFUL!
SWFF
HOW'D THE BOW FEEL TODAY, ULGAR?
NOT BAD.
WHOA, YOU GOT SIX? GREAT! YOU'RE REALLY GETTING GOOD AT THIS STUFF.
KINDA.

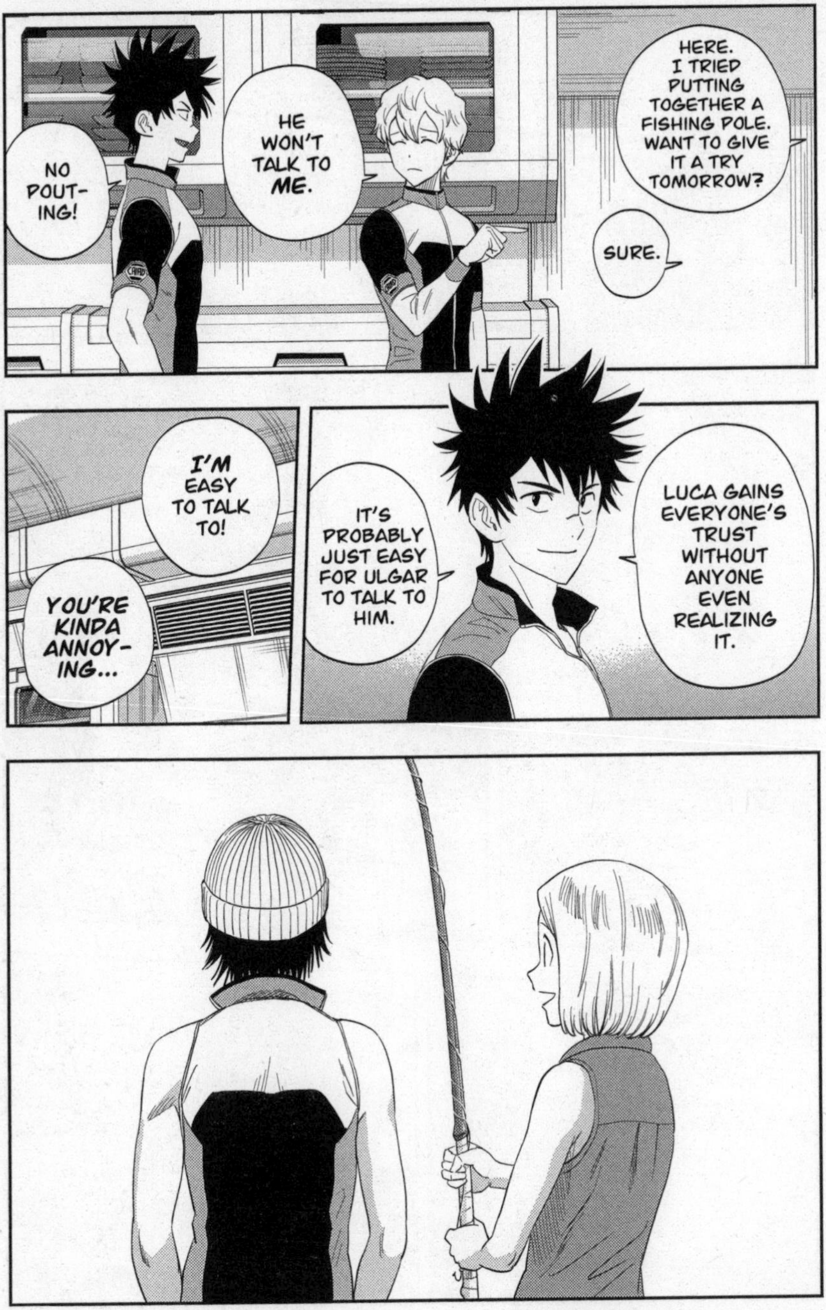
HERE. I TRIED PUTTING TOGETHER A FISHING POLE. WANT TO GIVE IT A TRY TOMORROW?
SURE.
HE WON'T TALK TO ME.
NO POUTING!
LUCA GAINS EVERYONE'S TRUST WITHOUT ANYONE EVEN REALIZING IT.
IT'S PROBABLY JUST EASY FOR ULGAR TO TALK TO HIM.
I'M EASY TO TALK TO!
YOU'RE KINDA ANNOYING...

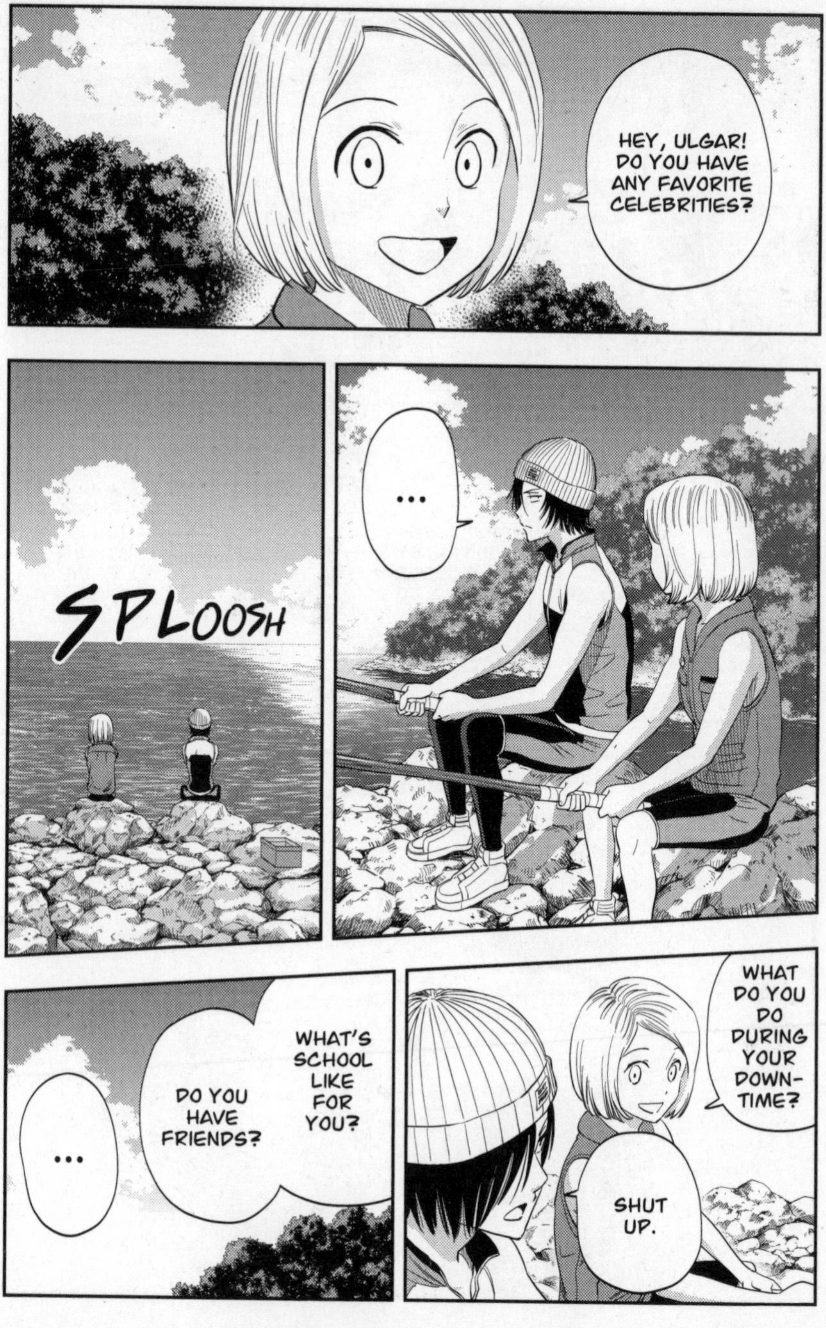
HEY, ULGAR! DO YOU HAVE ANY FAVORITE CELEBRITIES?
...
SPLOOSH
WHAT DO YOU DO DURING YOUR DOWN-TIME?
SHUT UP.
WHAT'S SCHOOL LIKE FOR YOU?
DO YOU HAVE FRIENDS?
...

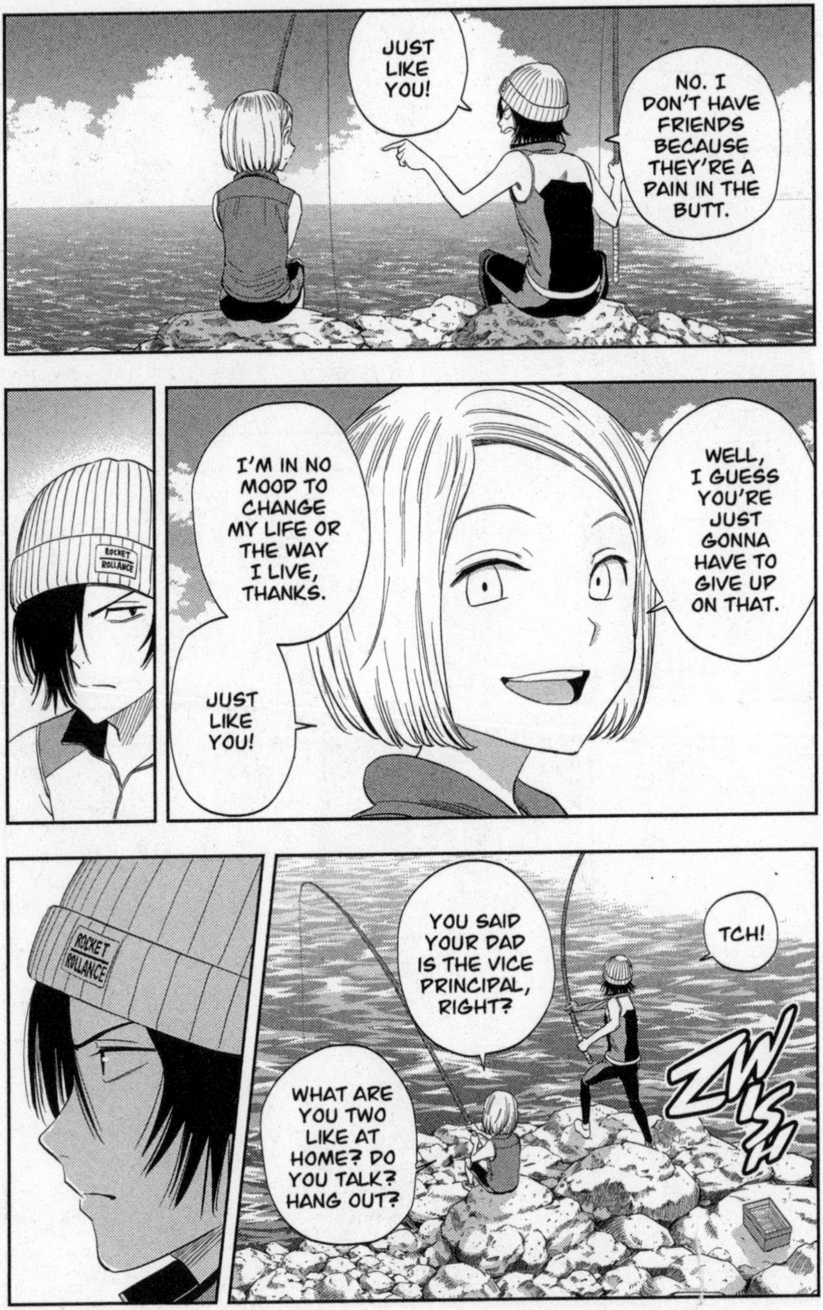
NO. I DON'T HAVE FRIENDS BECAUSE THEY'RE A PAIN IN THE BUTT.
JUST LIKE YOU!
WELL, I GUESS YOU'RE JUST GONNA HAVE TO GIVE UP ON THAT.
I'M IN NO MOOD TO CHANGE MY LIFE OR THE WAY I LIVE, THANKS.
JUST LIKE YOU!
ROCKET ROLLANCE
TCH!
YOU SAID YOUR DAD IS THE VICE PRINCIPAL, RIGHT?
ZWISH
WHAT ARE YOU TWO LIKE AT HOME? DO YOU TALK? HANG OUT?
ROCKET ROLLANCE

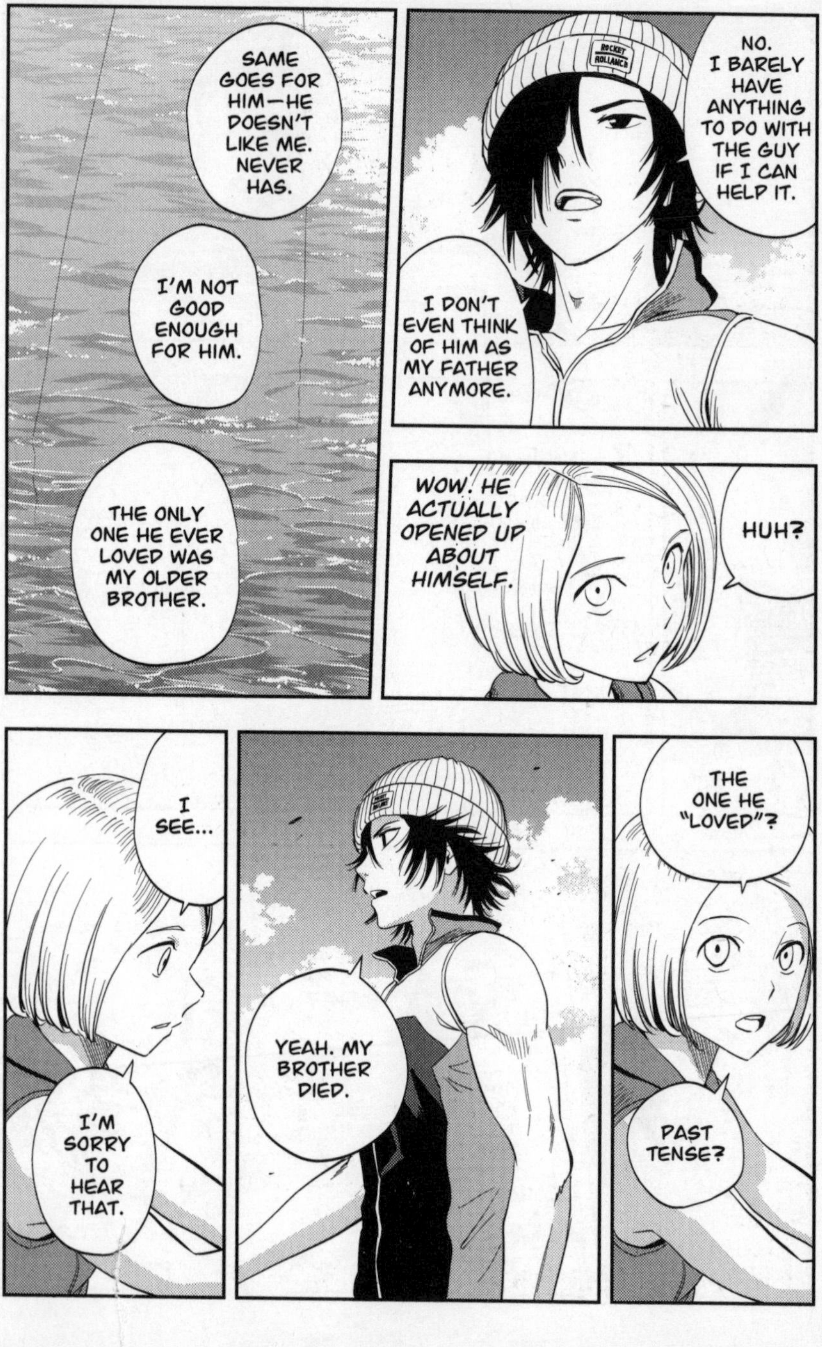
ROCKET ROLLANCE
NO. I BARELY HAVE ANYTHING TO DO WITH THE GUY IF I CAN HELP IT.
I DON'T EVEN THINK OF HIM AS MY FATHER ANYMORE.
HUH?
WOW. HE ACTUALLY OPENED UP ABOUT HIMSELF.
SAME GOES FOR HIM—HE DOESN'T LIKE ME. NEVER HAS.
I'M NOT GOOD ENOUGH FOR HIM.
THE ONLY ONE HE EVER LOVED WAS MY OLDER BROTHER.
THE ONE HE "LOVED"?
PAST TENSE?
YEAH. MY BROTHER DIED.
I SEE...
I'M SORRY TO HEAR THAT.

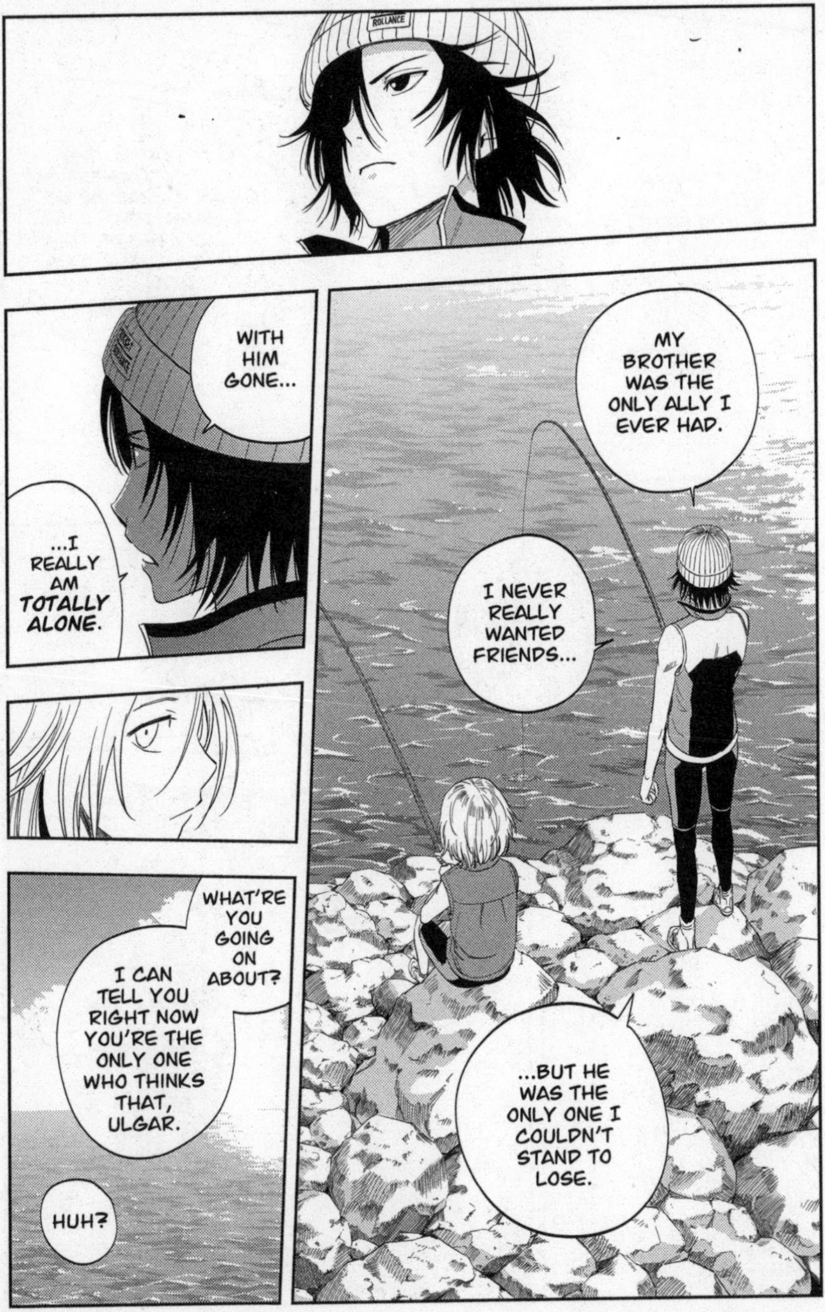
ROLLANCE
MY BROTHER WAS THE ONLY ALLY I EVER HAD.
I NEVER REALLY WANTED FRIENDS...
...BUT HE WAS THE ONLY ONE I COULDN'T STAND TO LOSE.
WITH HIM GONE...
...I REALLY AM TOTALLY ALONE.
WHAT'RE YOU GOING ON ABOUT?
I CAN TELL YOU RIGHT NOW YOU'RE THE ONLY ONE WHO THINKS THAT, ULGAR.
HUH?

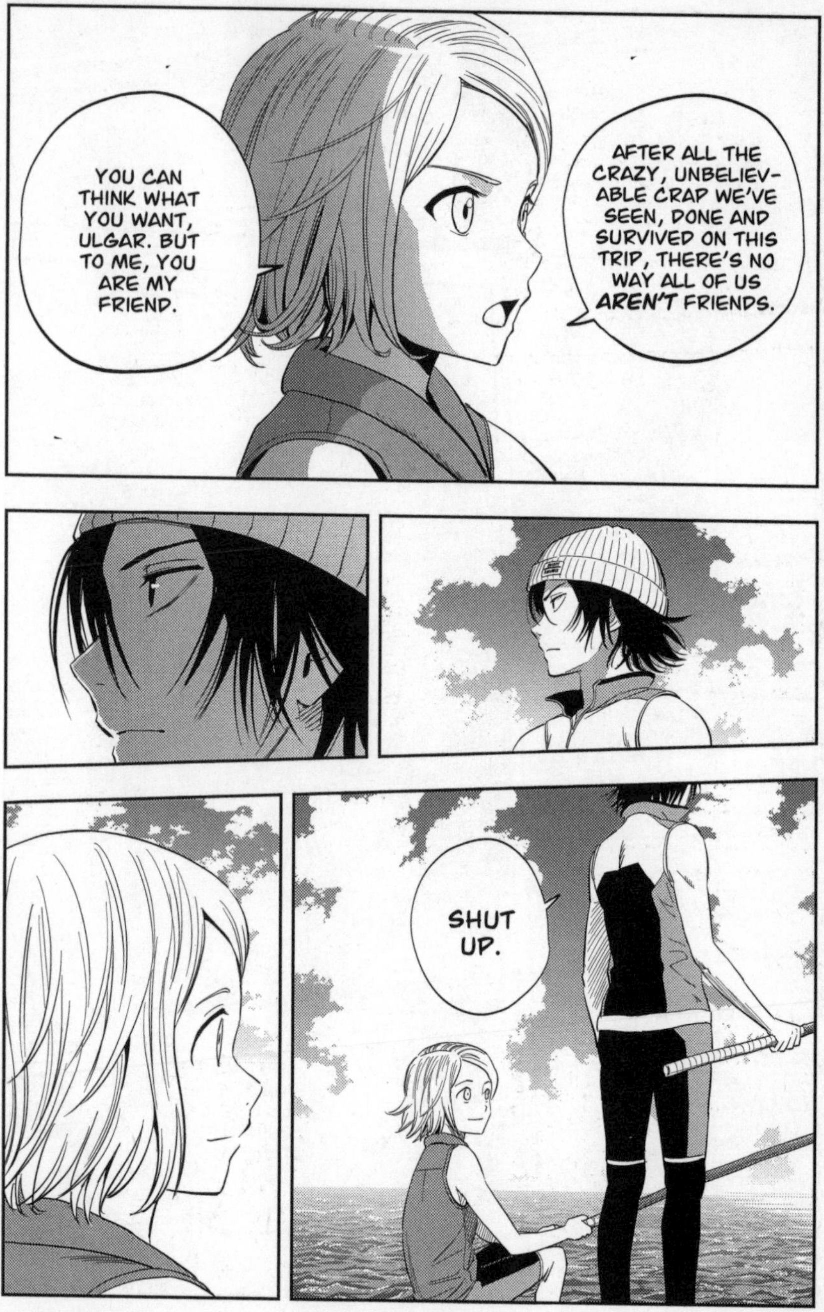
AFTER ALL THE CRAZY, UNBELIEVABLE CRAP WE'VE SEEN, DONE AND SURVIVED ON THIS TRIP, THERE'S NO WAY ALL OF US *AREN'T* FRIENDS.
YOU CAN THINK WHAT YOU WANT, ULGAR. BUT TO ME, YOU ARE MY FRIEND.
SHUT UP.

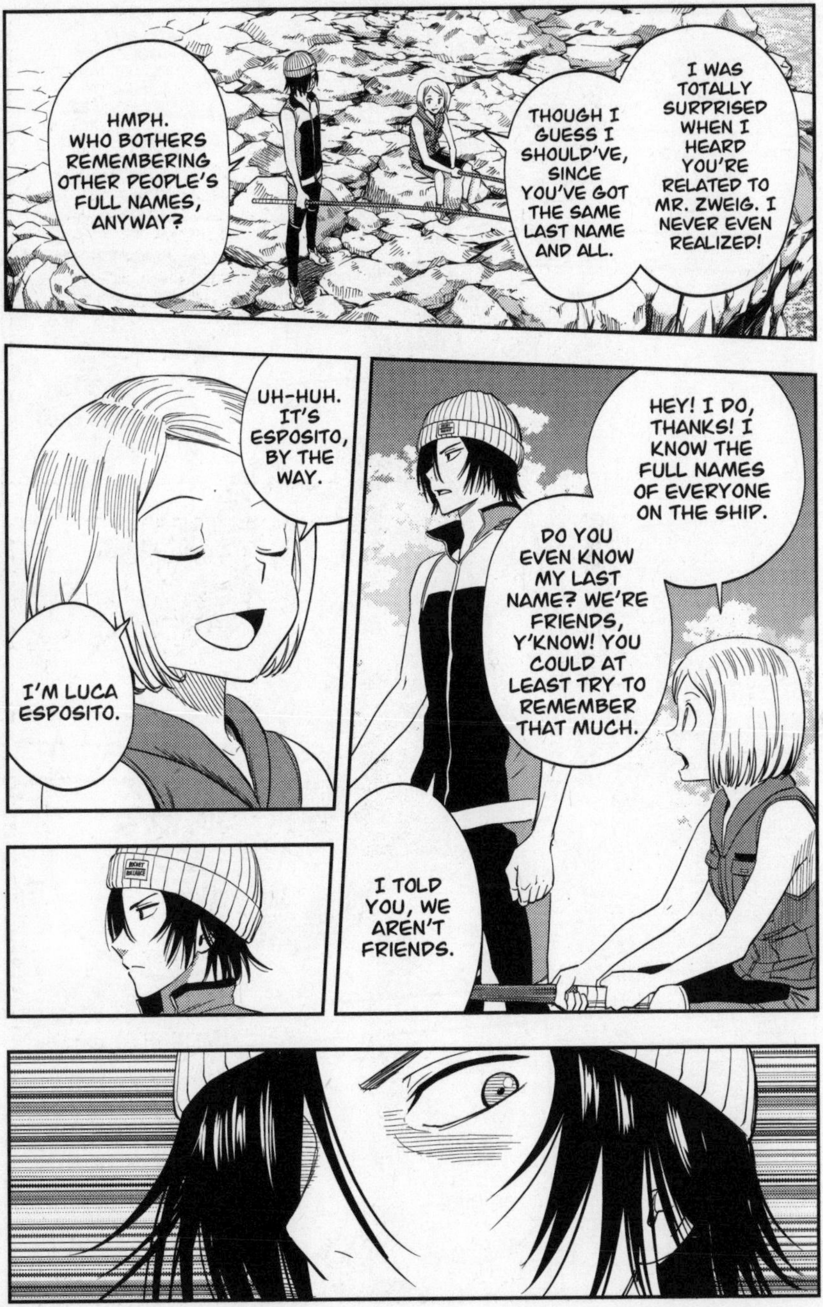
I WAS TOTALLY SURPRISED WHEN I HEARD YOU'RE RELATED TO MR. ZWEIG. I NEVER EVEN REALIZED!
THOUGH I GUESS I SHOULD'VE, SINCE YOU'VE GOT THE SAME LAST NAME AND ALL.
HMPH. WHO BOTHERS REMEMBERING OTHER PEOPLE'S FULL NAMES, ANYWAY?
HEY! I DO, THANKS! I KNOW THE FULL NAMES OF EVERYONE ON THE SHIP.
DO YOU EVEN KNOW MY LAST NAME? WE'RE FRIENDS, Y'KNOW! YOU COULD AT LEAST TRY TO REMEMBER THAT MUCH.
I TOLD YOU, WE AREN'T FRIENDS.
UH-HUH. IT'S ESPOSITO, BY THE WAY.
I'M LUCA ESPOSITO.

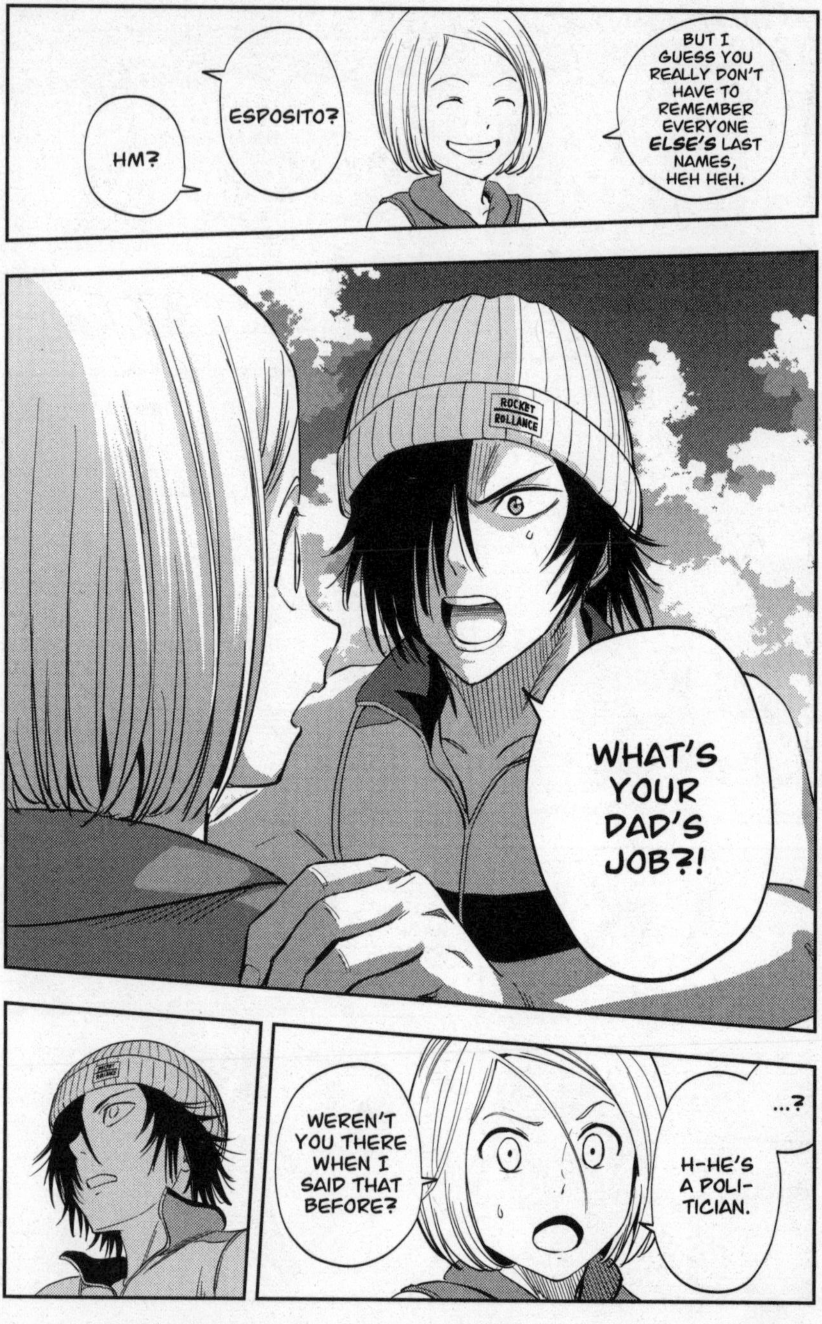
BUT I GUESS YOU REALLY DON'T HAVE TO REMEMBER EVERYONE **ELSE'S** LAST NAMES, HEH HEH.
ESPOSITO?
HM?
ROCKET ROLLANCE
WHAT'S YOUR DAD'S JOB?!
...?
H-HE'S A POLITICIAN.
WEREN'T YOU THERE WHEN I SAID THAT BEFORE?

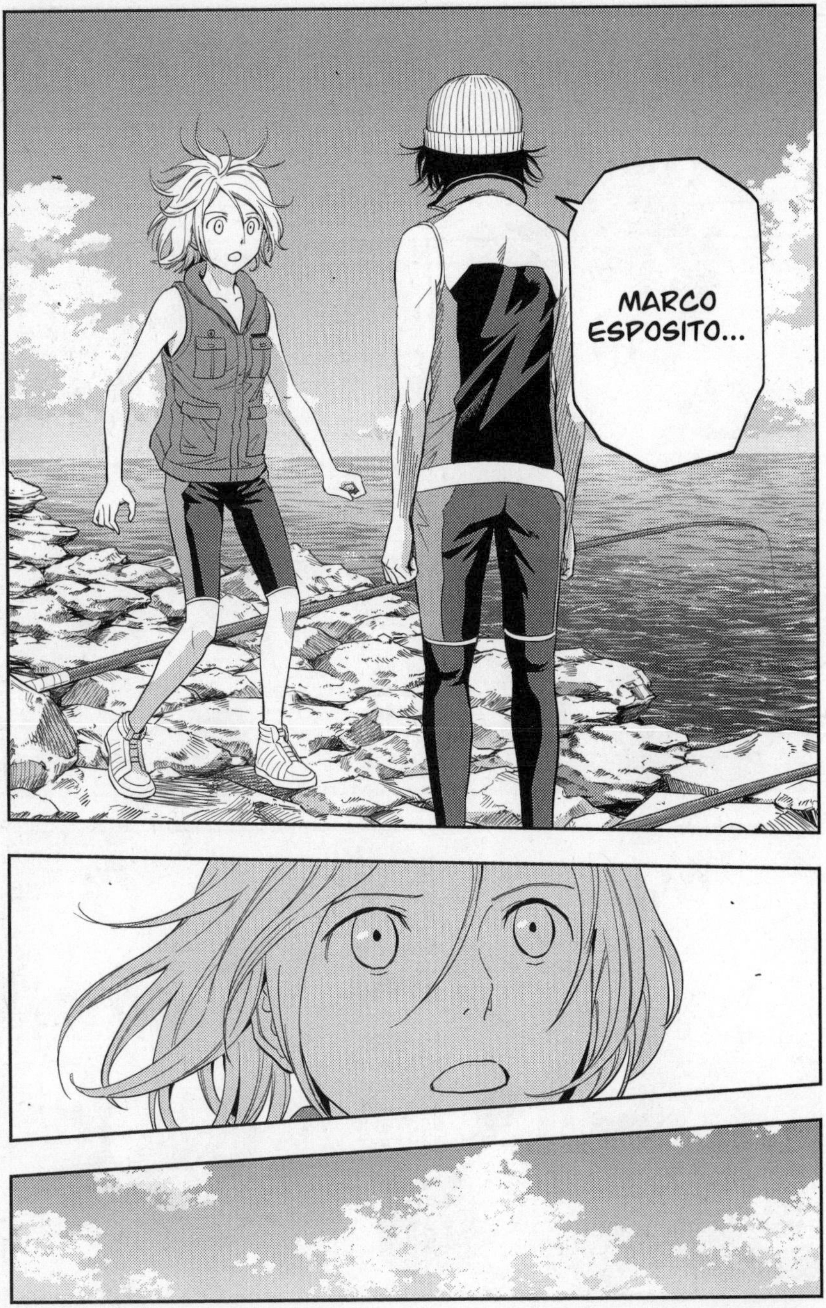
MARCO ESPOSITO...

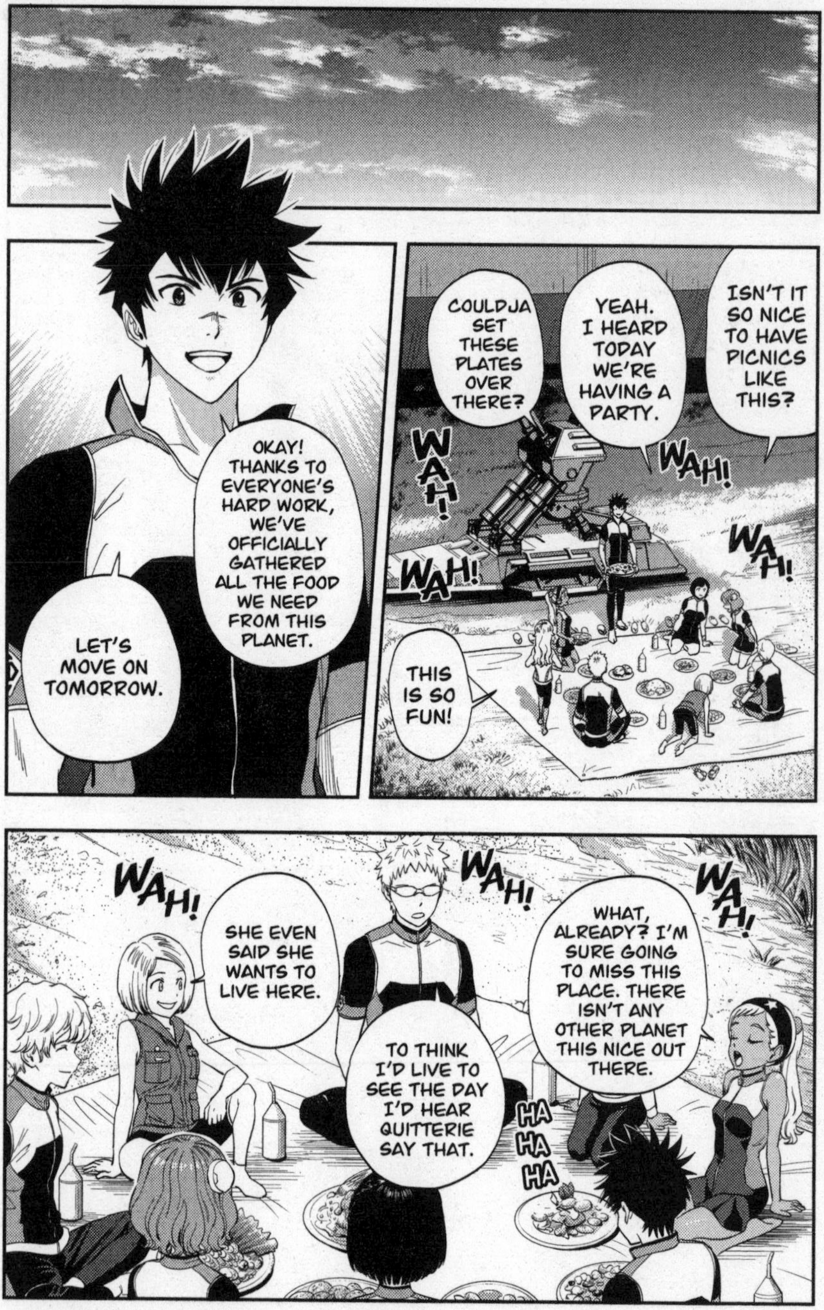
ISN'T IT SO NICE TO HAVE PICNICS LIKE THIS?
YEAH. I HEARD TODAY WE'RE HAVING A PARTY.
WAH!
COULDJA SET THESE PLATES OVER THERE?
WAH!
WAH!
WAH!
THIS IS SO FUN!
OKAY! THANKS TO EVERYONE'S HARD WORK, WE'VE OFFICIALLY GATHERED ALL THE FOOD WE NEED FROM THIS PLANET.
LET'S MOVE ON TOMORROW.
WAH!
WHAT, ALREADY? I'M SURE GOING TO MISS THIS PLACE. THERE ISN'T ANY OTHER PLANET THIS NICE OUT THERE.
WAH!
TO THINK I'D LIVE TO SEE THE DAY I'D HEAR QUITTERIE SAY THAT.
HA HA HA
SHE EVEN SAID SHE WANTS TO LIVE HERE.
WAH!

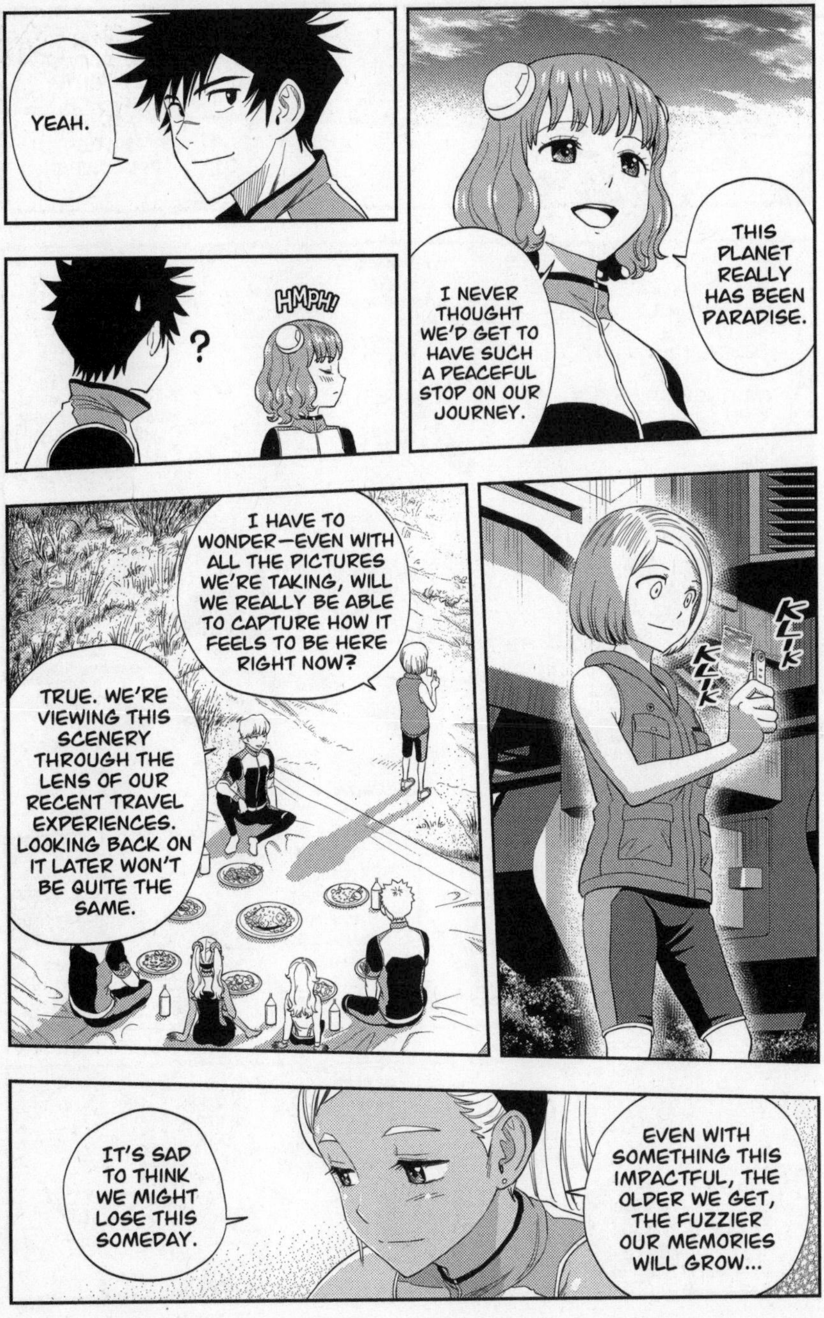
THIS PLANET REALLY HAS BEEN PARADISE.
I NEVER THOUGHT WE'D GET TO HAVE SUCH A PEACEFUL STOP ON OUR JOURNEY.
YEAH.
HMPH!
?
KLIK
KLIK
I HAVE TO WONDER—EVEN WITH ALL THE PICTURES WE'RE TAKING, WILL WE REALLY BE ABLE TO CAPTURE HOW IT FEELS TO BE HERE RIGHT NOW?
TRUE. WE'RE VIEWING THIS SCENERY THROUGH THE LENS OF OUR RECENT TRAVEL EXPERIENCES. LOOKING BACK ON IT LATER WON'T BE QUITE THE SAME.
EVEN WITH SOMETHING THIS IMPACTFUL, THE OLDER WE GET, THE FUZZIER OUR MEMORIES WILL GROW...
IT'S SAD TO THINK WE MIGHT LOSE THIS SOMEDAY.

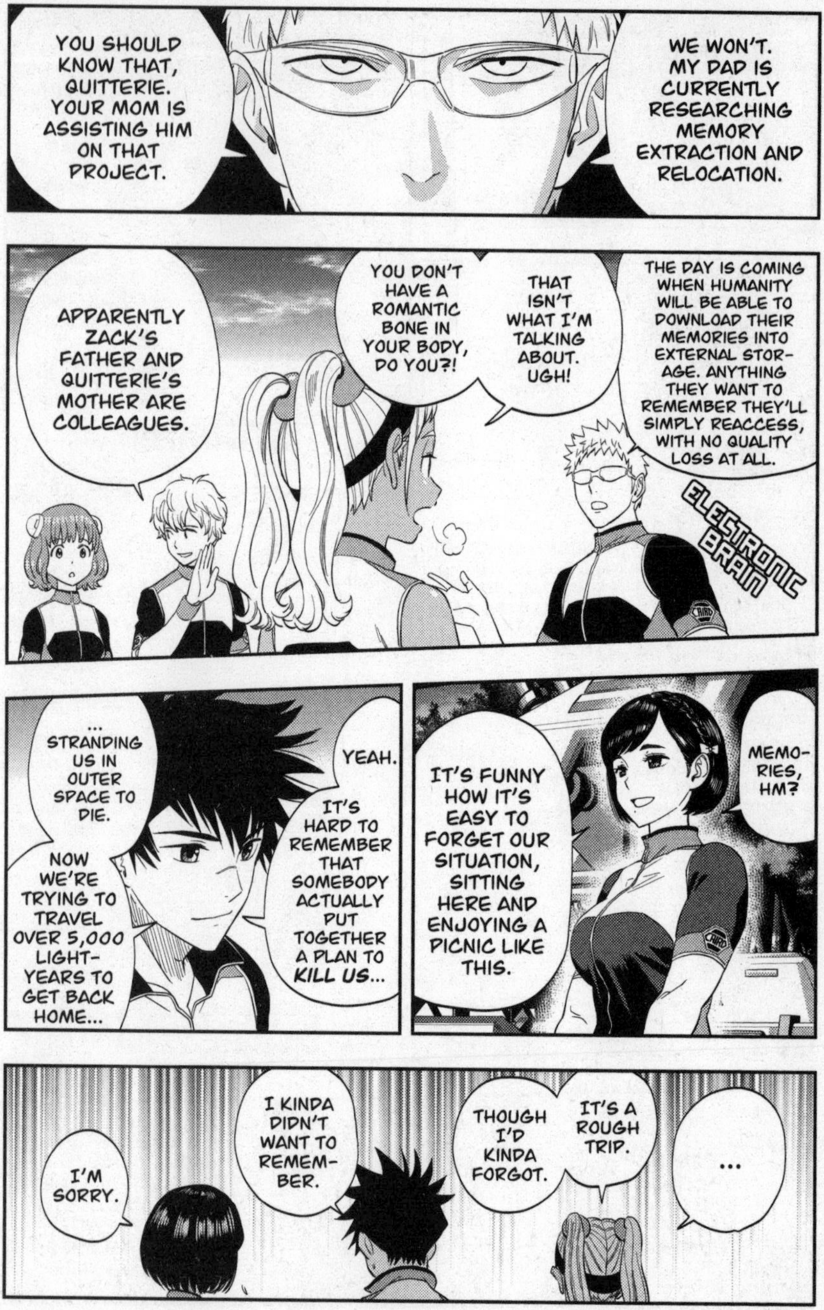
WE WON'T. MY DAD IS CURRENTLY RESEARCHING MEMORY EXTRACTION AND RELOCATION.
YOU SHOULD KNOW THAT, QUITTERIE. YOUR MOM IS ASSISTING HIM ON THAT PROJECT.
THE DAY IS COMING WHEN HUMANITY WILL BE ABLE TO DOWNLOAD THEIR MEMORIES INTO EXTERNAL STORAGE. ANYTHING THEY WANT TO REMEMBER THEY'LL SIMPLY REACCESS, WITH NO QUALITY LOSS AT ALL.
ELECTRONIC BRAIN
THAT ISN'T WHAT I'M TALKING ABOUT. UGH!
YOU DON'T HAVE A ROMANTIC BONE IN YOUR BODY, DO YOU?!
APPARENTLY ZACK'S FATHER AND QUITTERIE'S MOTHER ARE COLLEAGUES.
MEMORIES, HM?
IT'S FUNNY HOW IT'S EASY TO FORGET OUR SITUATION, SITTING HERE AND ENJOYING A PICNIC LIKE THIS.
YEAH.
IT'S HARD TO REMEMBER THAT SOMEBODY ACTUALLY PUT TOGETHER A PLAN TO KILL US...
...STRANDING US IN OUTER SPACE TO DIE.
NOW WE'RE TRYING TO TRAVEL OVER 5,000 LIGHT-YEARS TO GET BACK HOME...
...
IT'S A ROUGH TRIP.
THOUGH I'D KINDA FORGOT.
I KINDA DIDN'T WANT TO REMEMBER.
I'M SORRY.

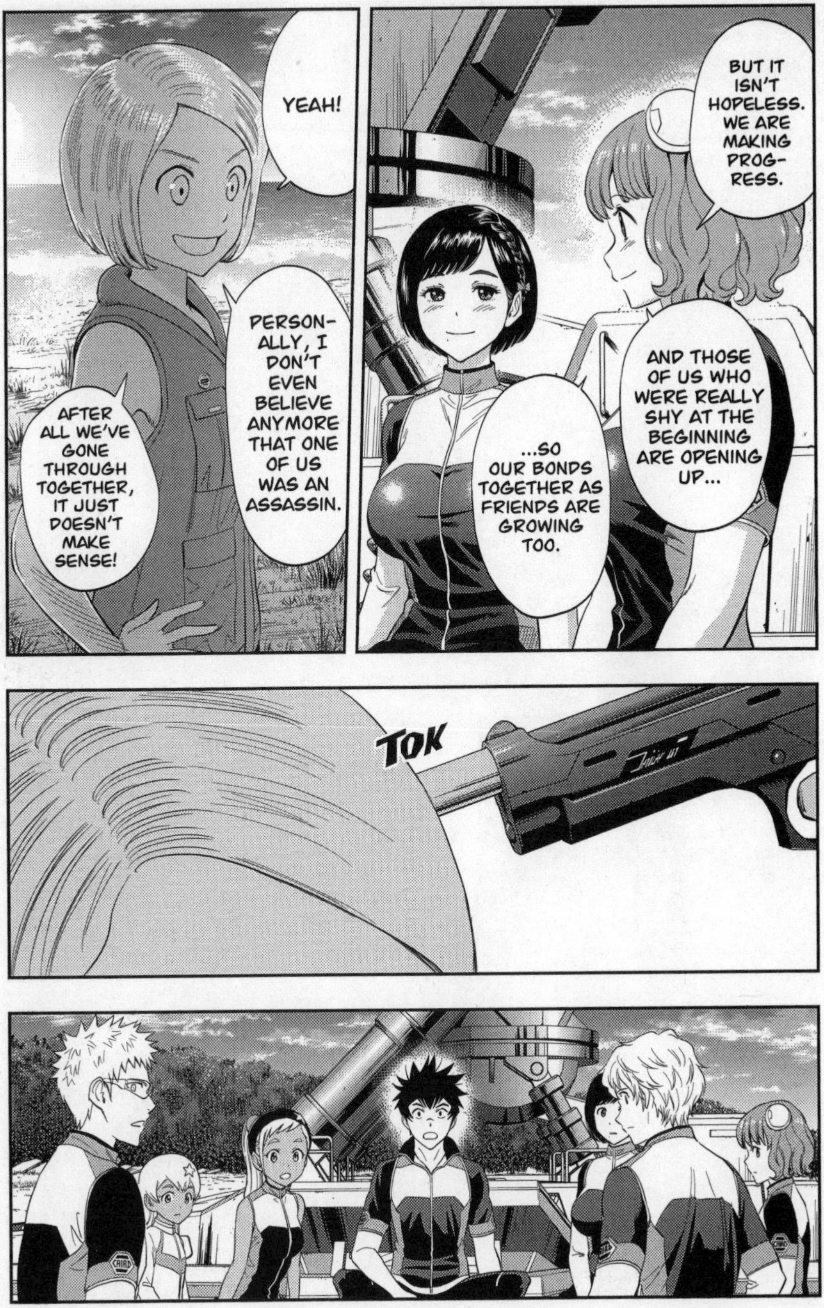
BUT IT ISN'T HOPELESS. WE ARE MAKING PROG-RESS.
AND THOSE OF US WHO WERE REALLY SHY AT THE BEGINNING ARE OPENING UP...
...SO OUR BONDS TOGETHER AS FRIENDS ARE GROWING TOO.
YEAH!
PERSON-ALLY, I DON'T EVEN BELIEVE ANYMORE THAT ONE OF US WAS AN ASSASSIN.
AFTER ALL WE'VE GONE THROUGH TOGETHER, IT JUST DOESN'T MAKE SENSE!
TOK

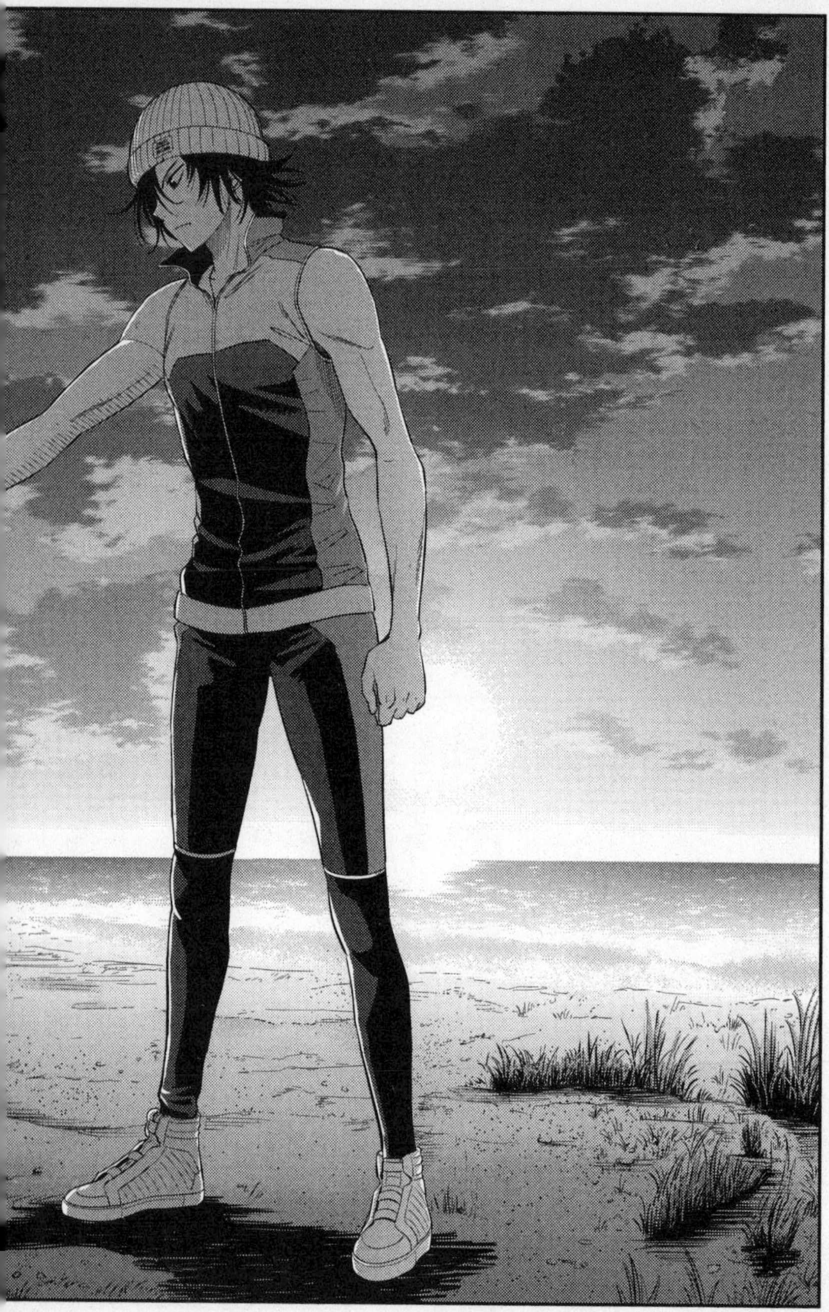

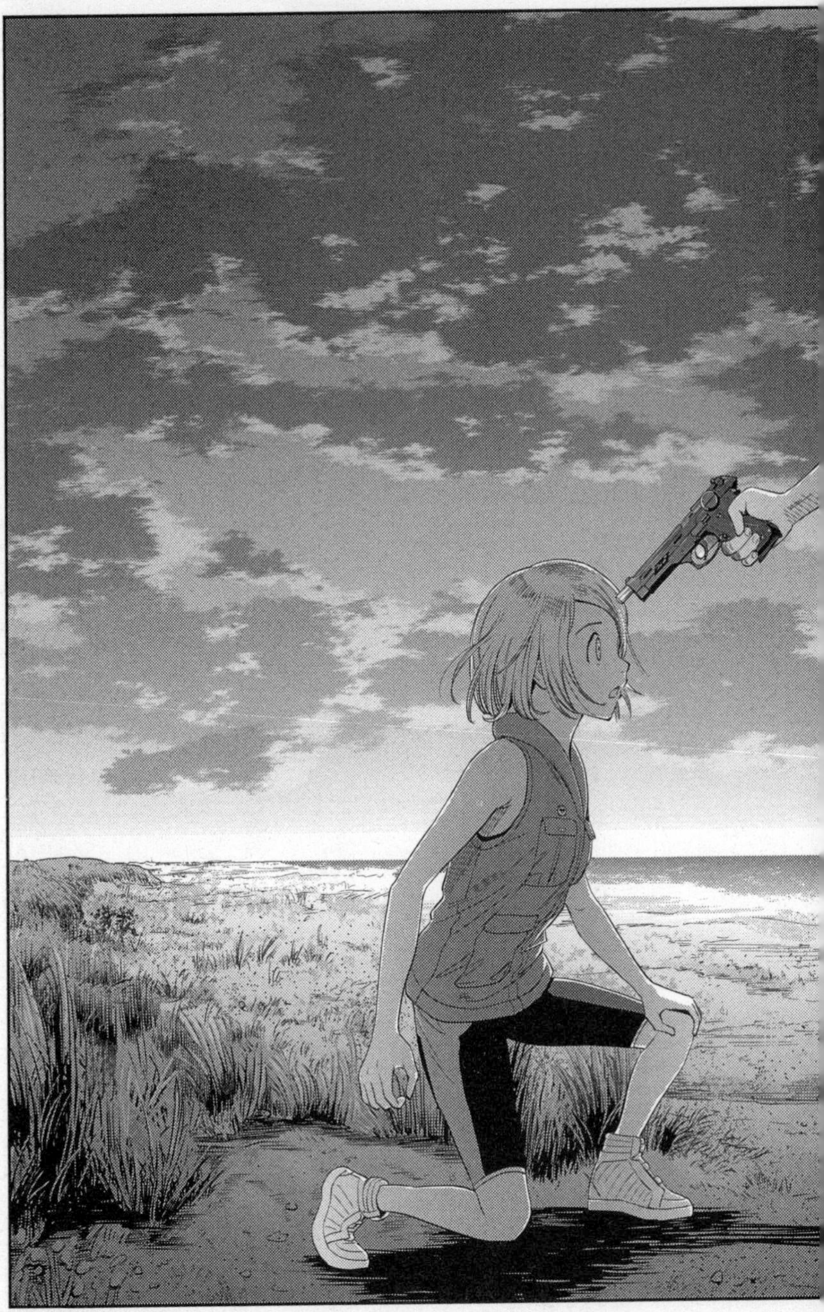

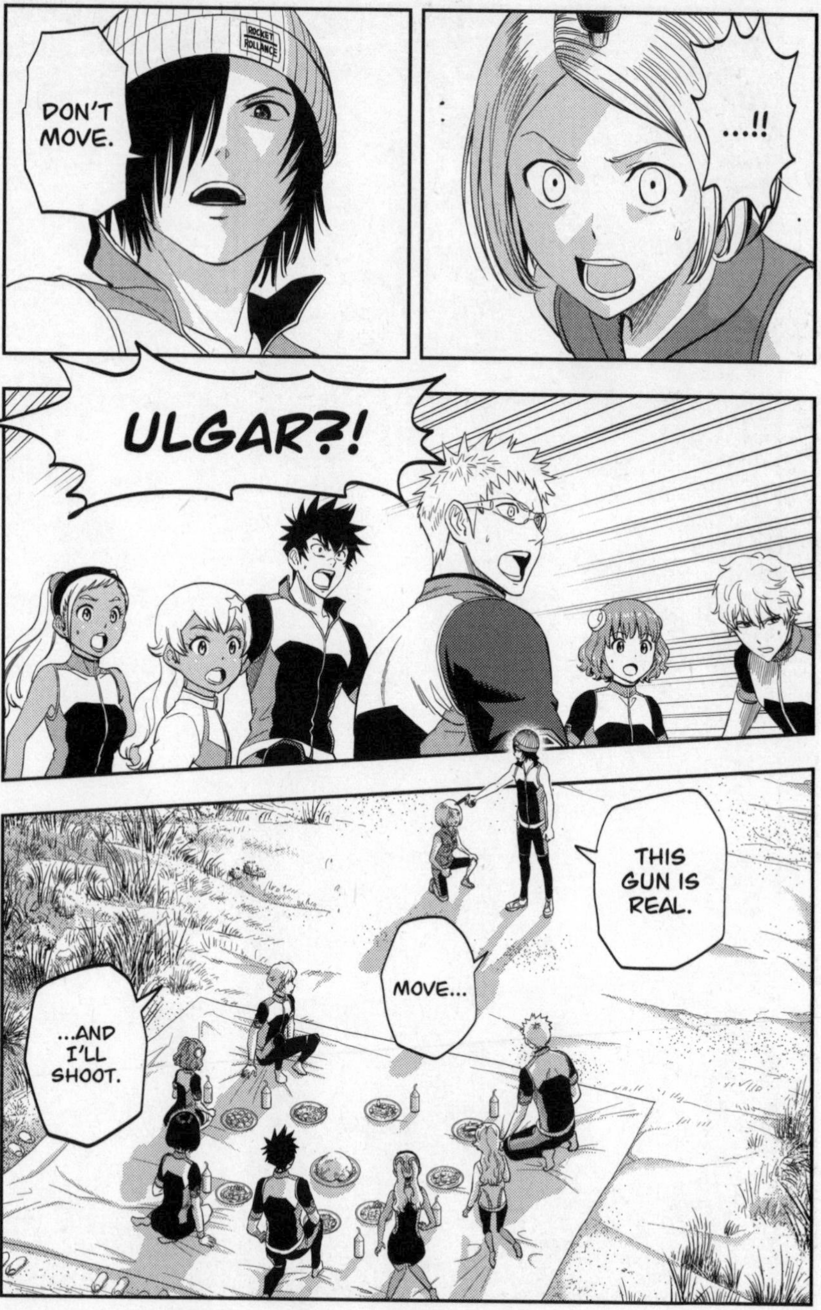
...!!
ROCKET ROLLANCE
DON'T MOVE.
ULGAR?!
THIS GUN IS REAL.
MOVE...
...AND I'LL SHOOT.

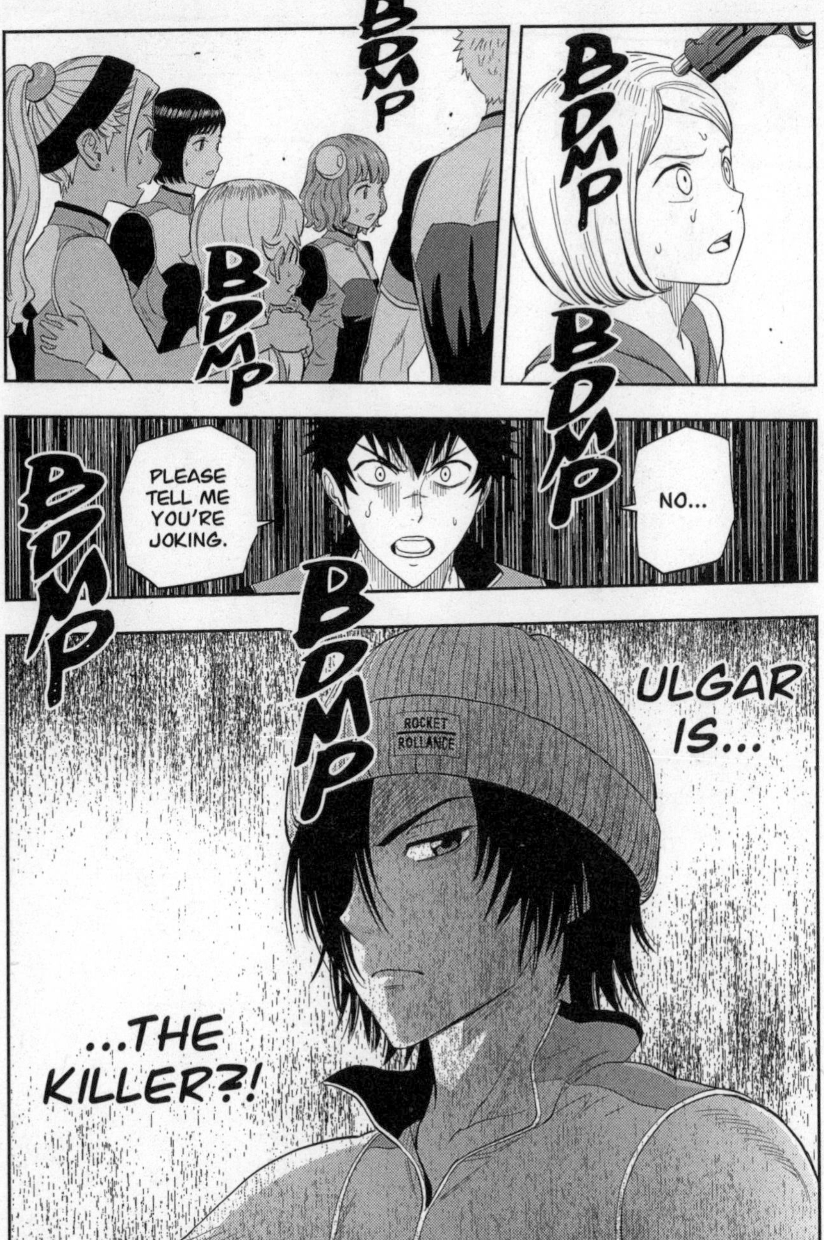
BDMP
BDMP
BDMP
BDMP
NO...
BDMP
PLEASE TELL ME YOU'RE JOKING.
BDMP
ULGAR IS...
BDMP
ROCKET ROLLANCE
...THE KILLER?!

Material Collection   Characters

YUN-HUA LU

D A T A

Name: **Yun-hua Lu**

Age: **17**

Birthday: **August 25**

Height: **5'10"**

Weight: **148 lbs.**

Blood Type: **B**

Eye Color: **Brown**

Hometown: **Mousanish District**

Daughter of worldwide singing sensation Lucy Lum. Due to her mother's parenting style, Yun-hua has a shy personality with a tendency to suppress any self-expression. She inherited her mother's love of singing and will sneak off to secluded locations to practice by herself.

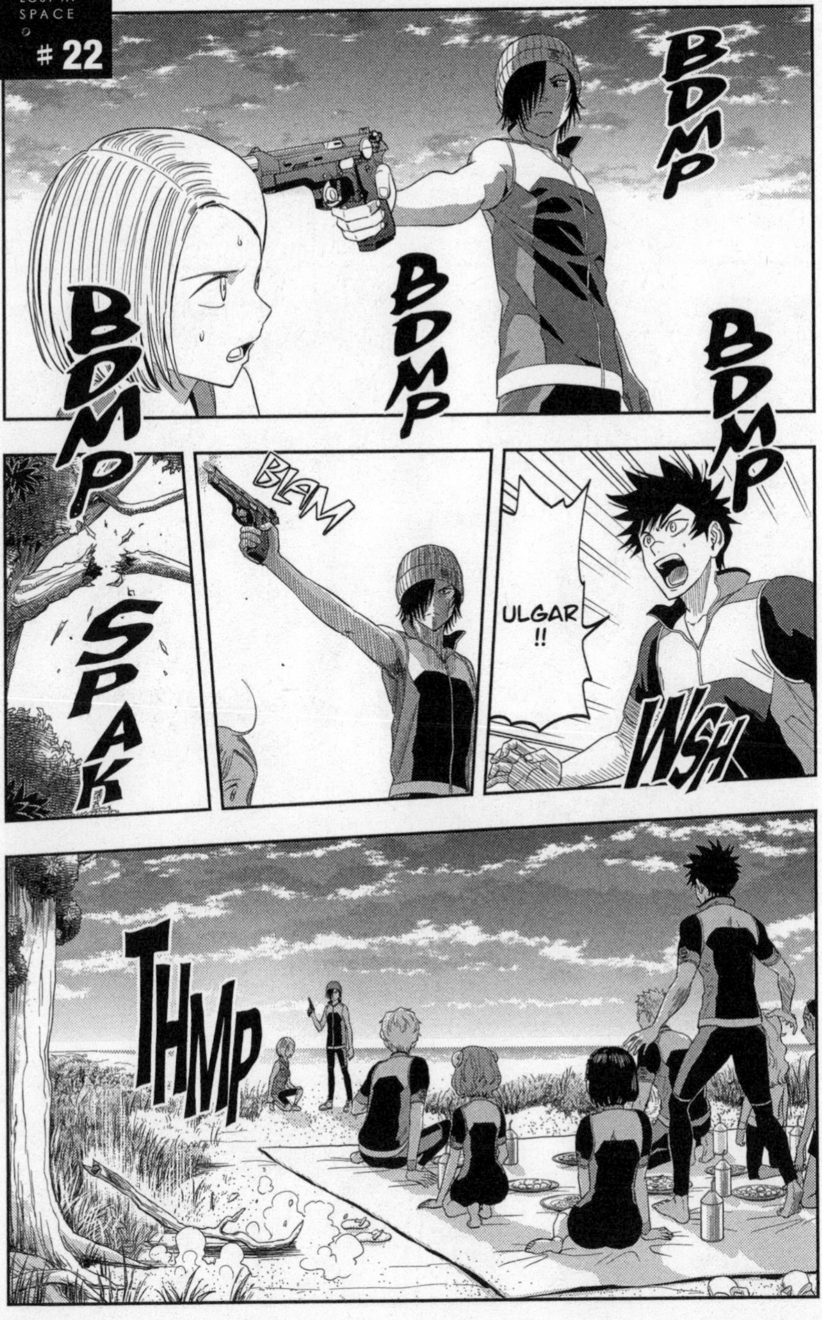
BDMP
BDMP
BDMP
BDMP
ULGAR !!
WSH
BLAM
SPAK
THMP

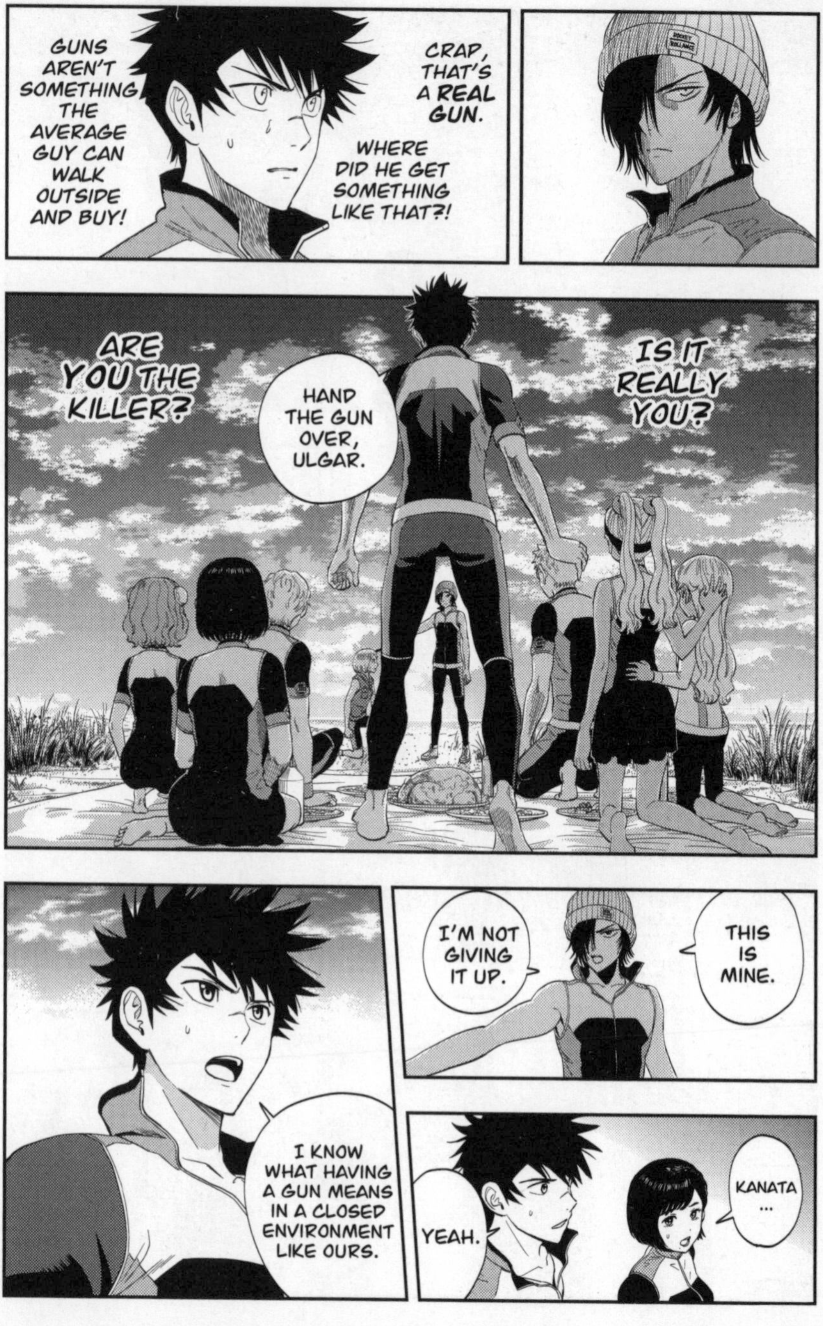
CRAP, THAT'S A REAL GUN.
WHERE DID HE GET SOMETHING LIKE THAT?!
GUNS AREN'T SOMETHING THE AVERAGE GUY CAN WALK OUTSIDE AND BUY!
IS IT REALLY YOU?
HAND THE GUN OVER, ULGAR.
ARE YOU THE KILLER?
THIS IS MINE.
I'M NOT GIVING IT UP.
KANATA ...
YEAH.
I KNOW WHAT HAVING A GUN MEANS IN A CLOSED ENVIRONMENT LIKE OURS.

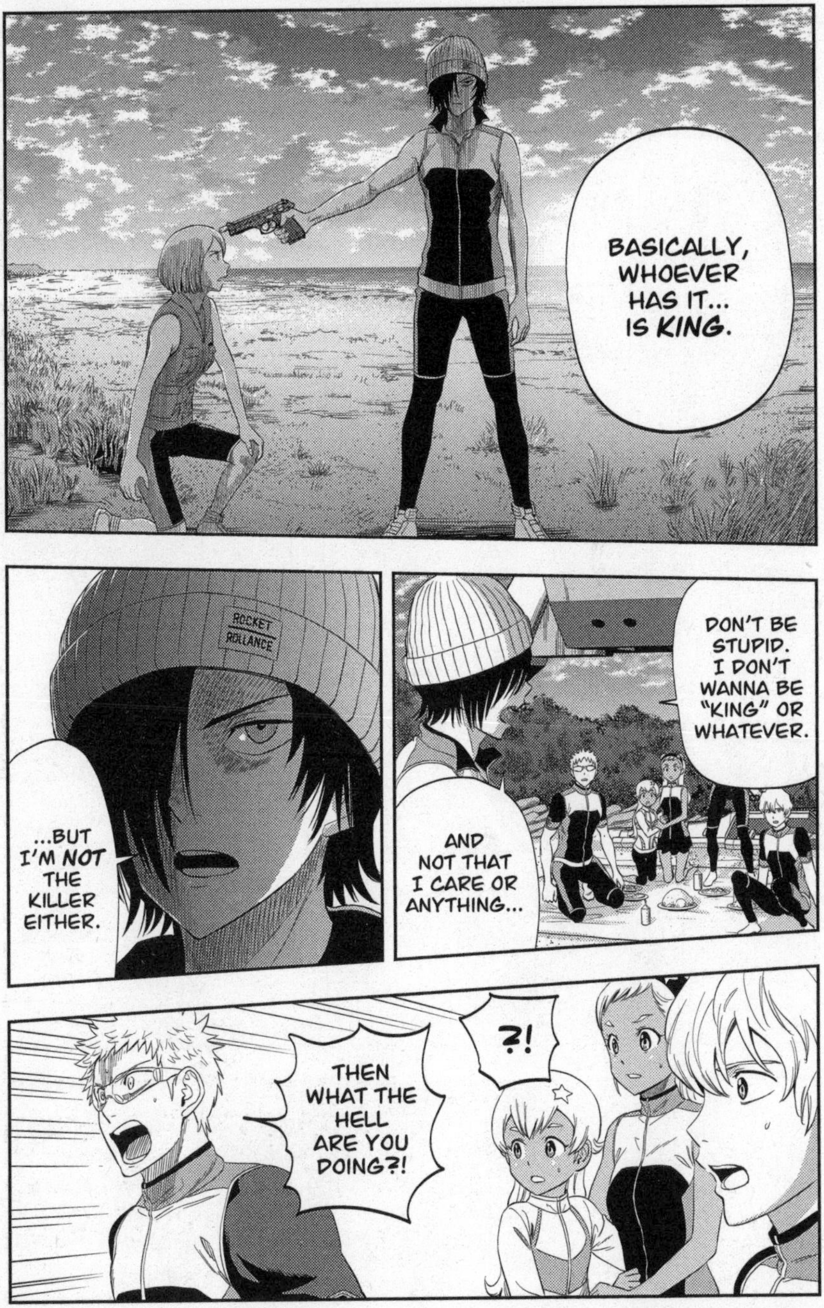
BASICALLY, WHOEVER HAS IT... IS KING.
DON'T BE STUPID. I DON'T WANNA BE "KING" OR WHATEVER.
AND NOT THAT I CARE OR ANYTHING...
ROCKET ROLLANCE
...BUT I'M NOT THE KILLER EITHER.
?!
THEN WHAT THE HELL ARE YOU DOING?!

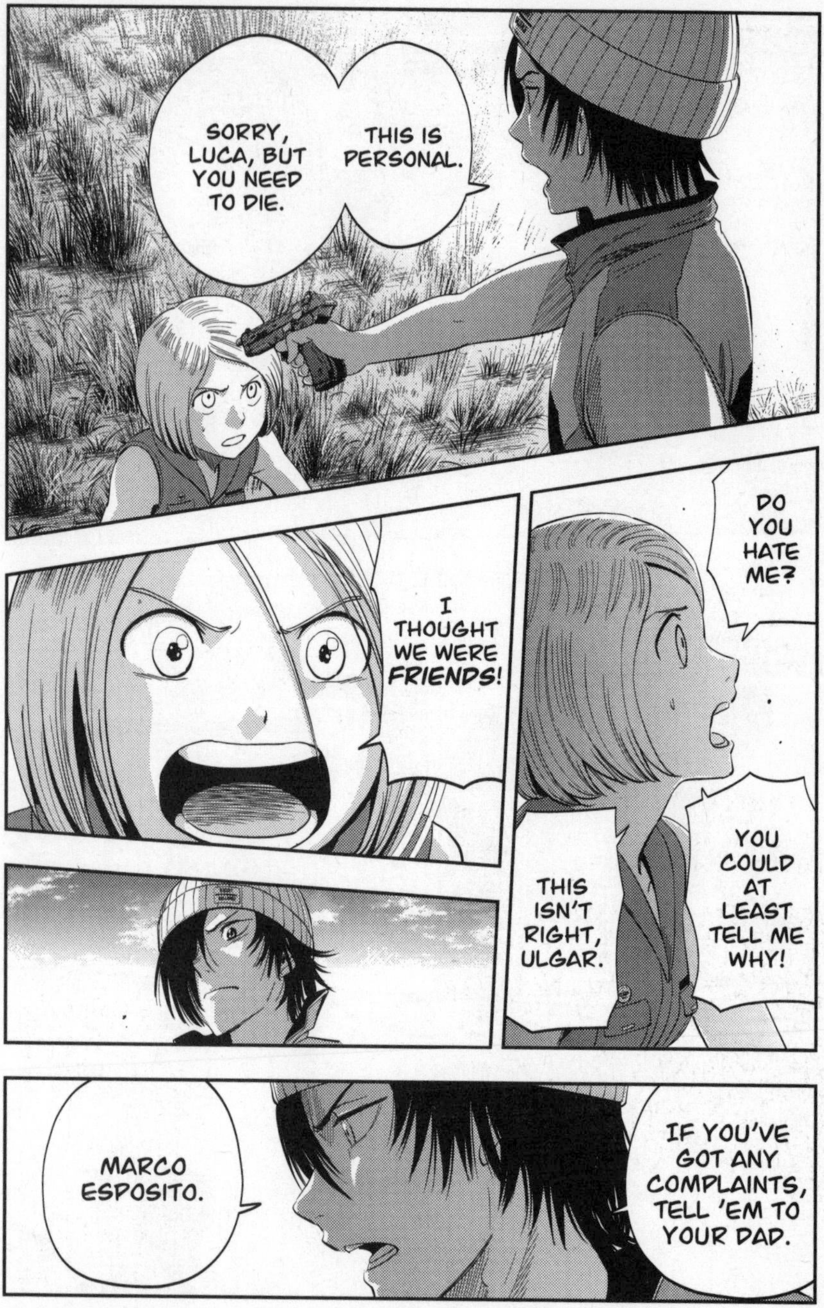
THIS IS PERSONAL.
SORRY, LUCA, BUT YOU NEED TO DIE.
DO YOU HATE ME?
YOU COULD AT LEAST TELL ME WHY!
THIS ISN'T RIGHT, ULGAR.
I THOUGHT WE WERE **FRIENDS**!
IF YOU'VE GOT ANY COMPLAINTS, TELL 'EM TO YOUR DAD.
MARCO ESPOSITO.

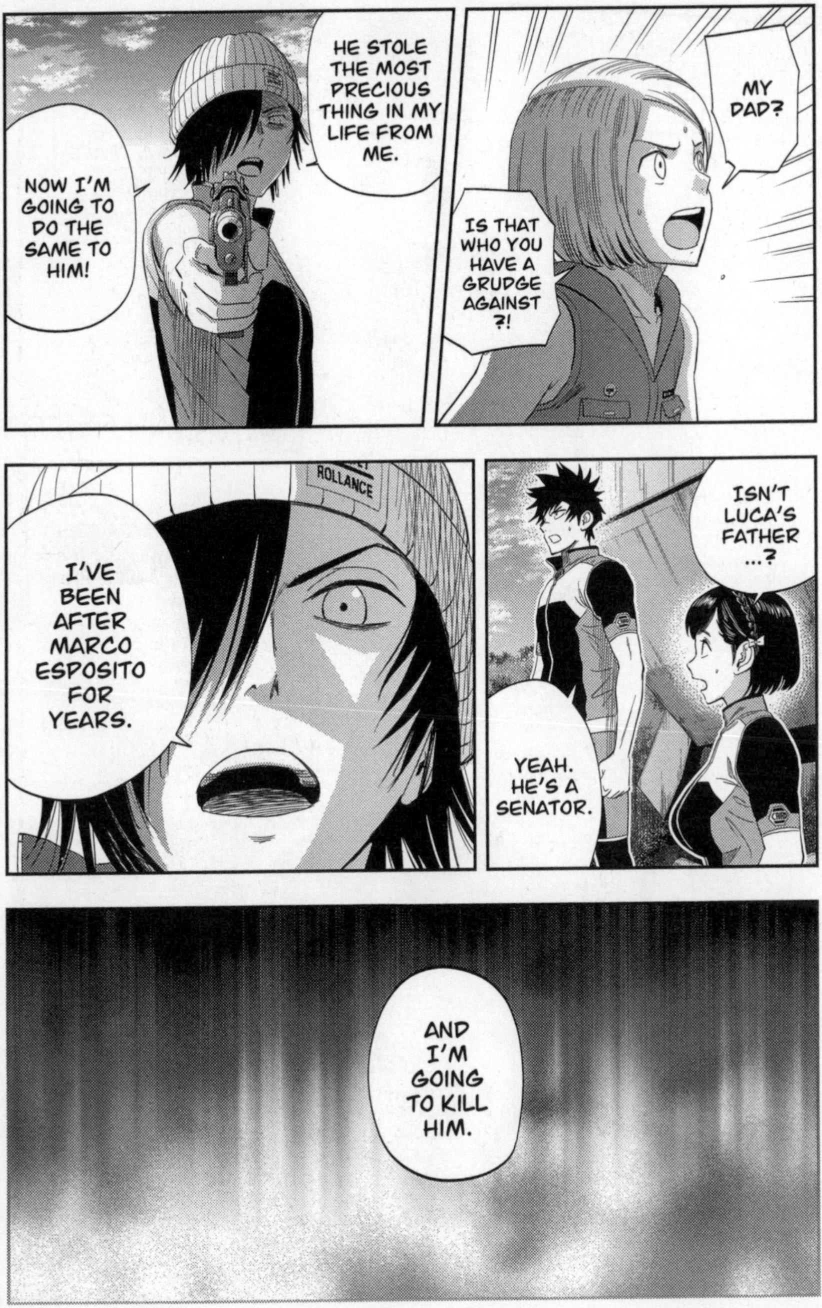
MY DAD?
IS THAT WHO YOU HAVE A GRUDGE AGAINST ?!
HE STOLE THE MOST PRECIOUS THING IN MY LIFE FROM ME.
NOW I'M GOING TO DO THE SAME TO HIM!
ISN'T LUCA'S FATHER ...?
YEAH. HE'S A SENATOR.
ROLLANCE
I'VE BEEN AFTER MARCO ESPOSITO FOR YEARS.
AND I'M GOING TO KILL HIM.

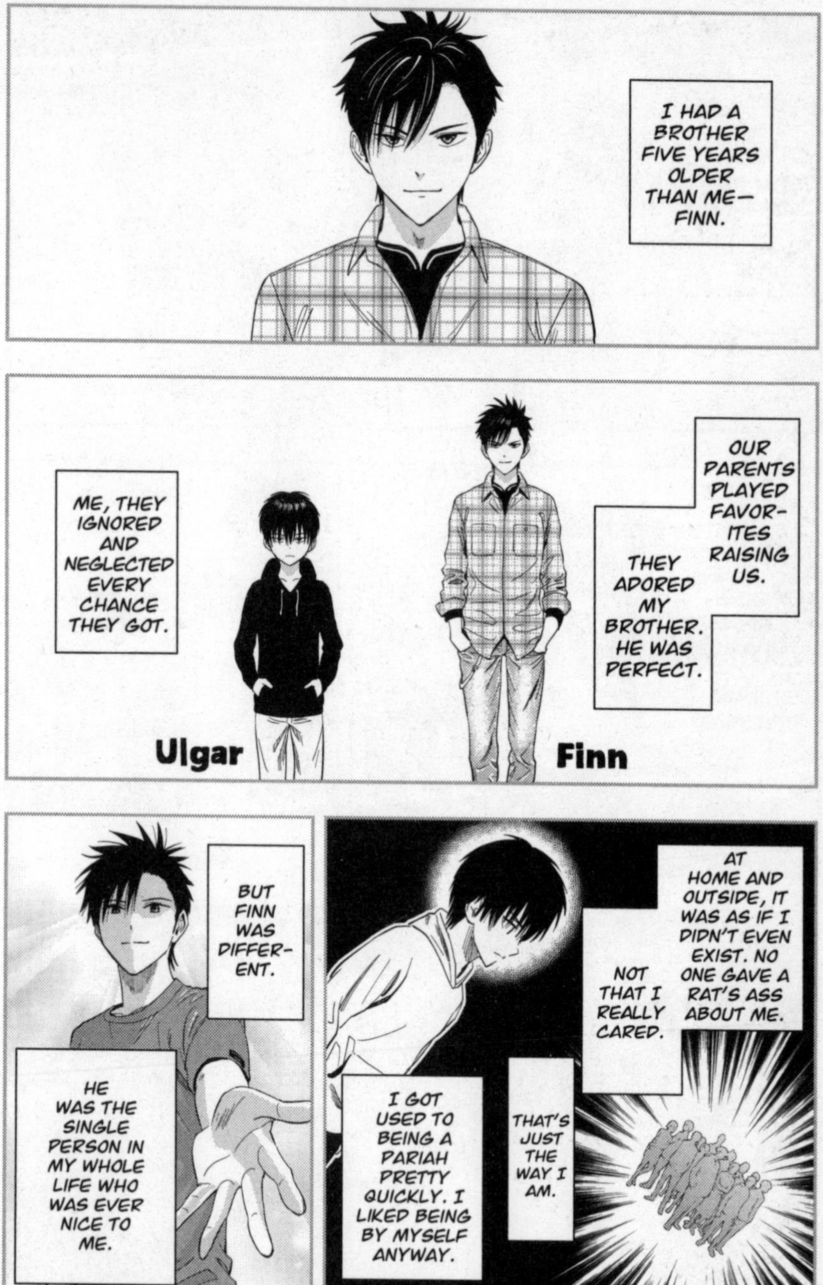
I HAD A BROTHER FIVE YEARS OLDER THAN ME—FINN.
OUR PARENTS PLAYED FAVOR-ITES RAISING US.
THEY ADORED MY BROTHER. HE WAS PERFECT.
ME, THEY IGNORED AND NEGLECTED EVERY CHANCE THEY GOT.
Finn
Ulgar
AT HOME AND OUTSIDE, IT WAS AS IF I DIDN'T EVEN EXIST. NO ONE GAVE A RAT'S ASS ABOUT ME.
NOT THAT I REALLY CARED.
THAT'S JUST THE WAY I AM.
I GOT USED TO BEING A PARIAH PRETTY QUICKLY. I LIKED BEING BY MYSELF ANYWAY.
BUT FINN WAS DIFFER-ENT.
HE WAS THE SINGLE PERSON IN MY WHOLE LIFE WHO WAS EVER NICE TO ME.

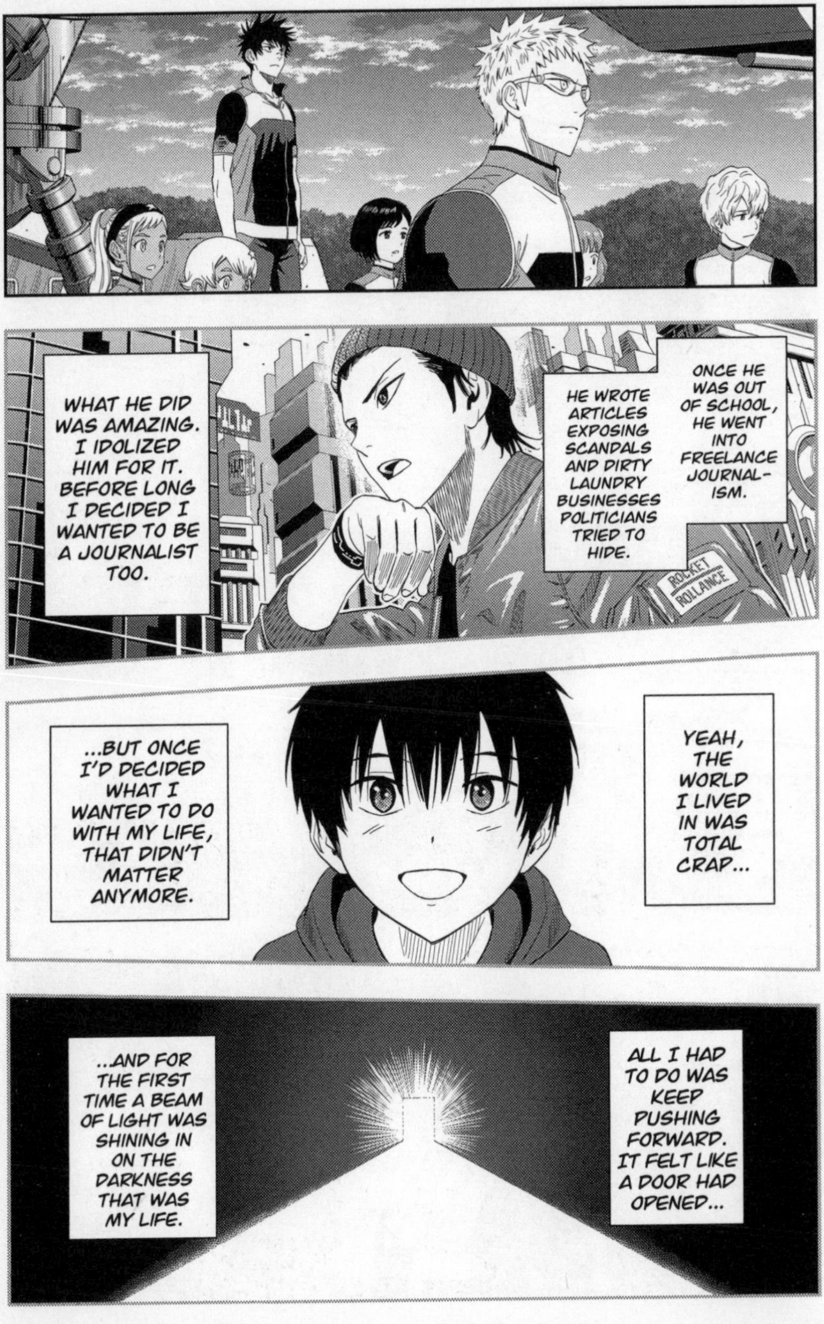

ONCE HE WAS OUT OF SCHOOL, HE WENT INTO FREELANCE JOURNAL-ISM.
HE WROTE ARTICLES EXPOSING SCANDALS AND DIRTY LAUNDRY BUSINESSES POLITICIANS TRIED TO HIDE.
ROCKET ROLLANCE
WHAT HE DID WAS AMAZING. I IDOLIZED HIM FOR IT. BEFORE LONG I DECIDED I WANTED TO BE A JOURNALIST TOO.
YEAH, THE WORLD I LIVED IN WAS TOTAL CRAP...
...BUT ONCE I'D DECIDED WHAT I WANTED TO DO WITH MY LIFE, THAT DIDN'T MATTER ANYMORE.
ALL I HAD TO DO WAS KEEP PUSHING FORWARD. IT FELT LIKE A DOOR HAD OPENED...
...AND FOR THE FIRST TIME A BEAM OF LIGHT WAS SHINING IN ON THE DARKNESS THAT WAS MY LIFE.

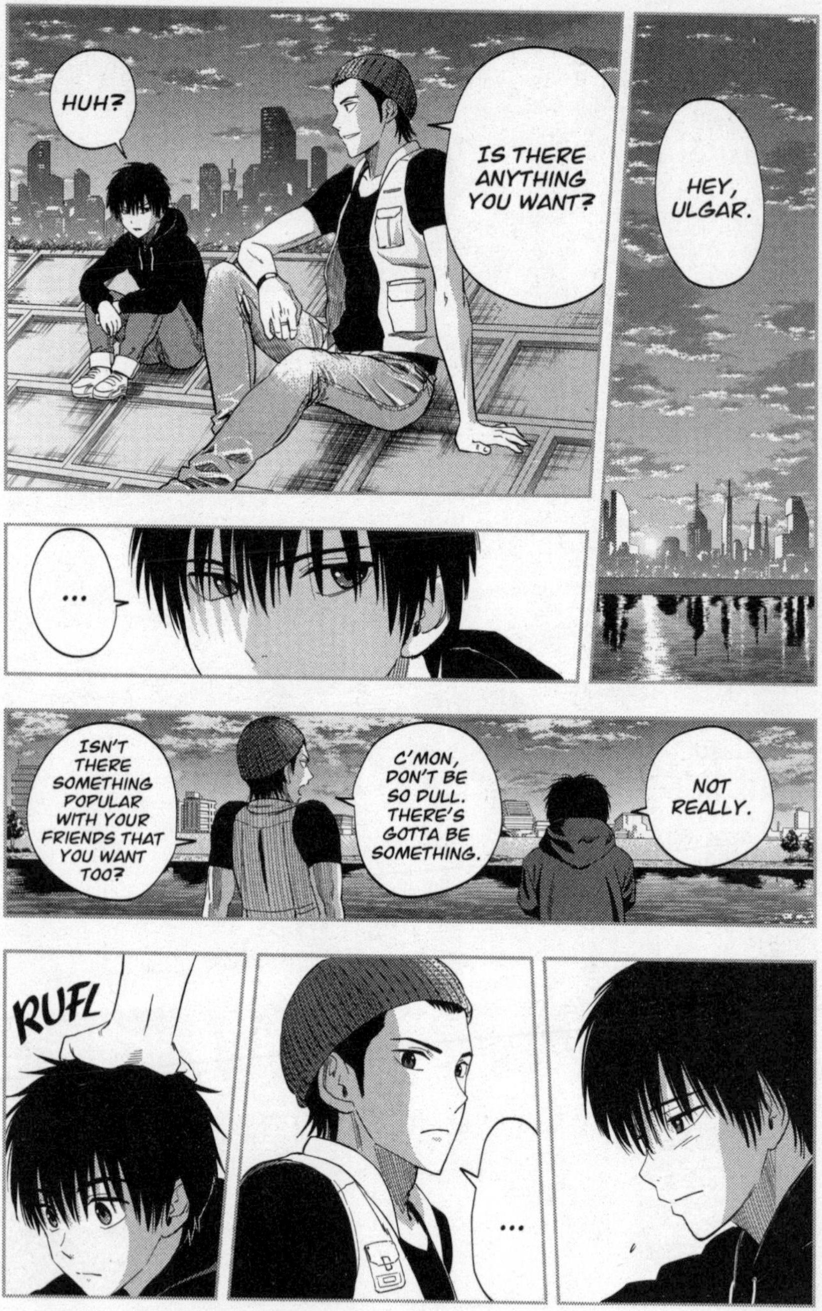
HEY, ULGAR.
IS THERE ANYTHING YOU WANT?
HUH?
...
NOT REALLY.
C'MON, DON'T BE SO DULL. THERE'S GOTTA BE SOMETHING.
ISN'T THERE SOMETHING POPULAR WITH YOUR FRIENDS THAT YOU WANT TOO?
...
RUFL

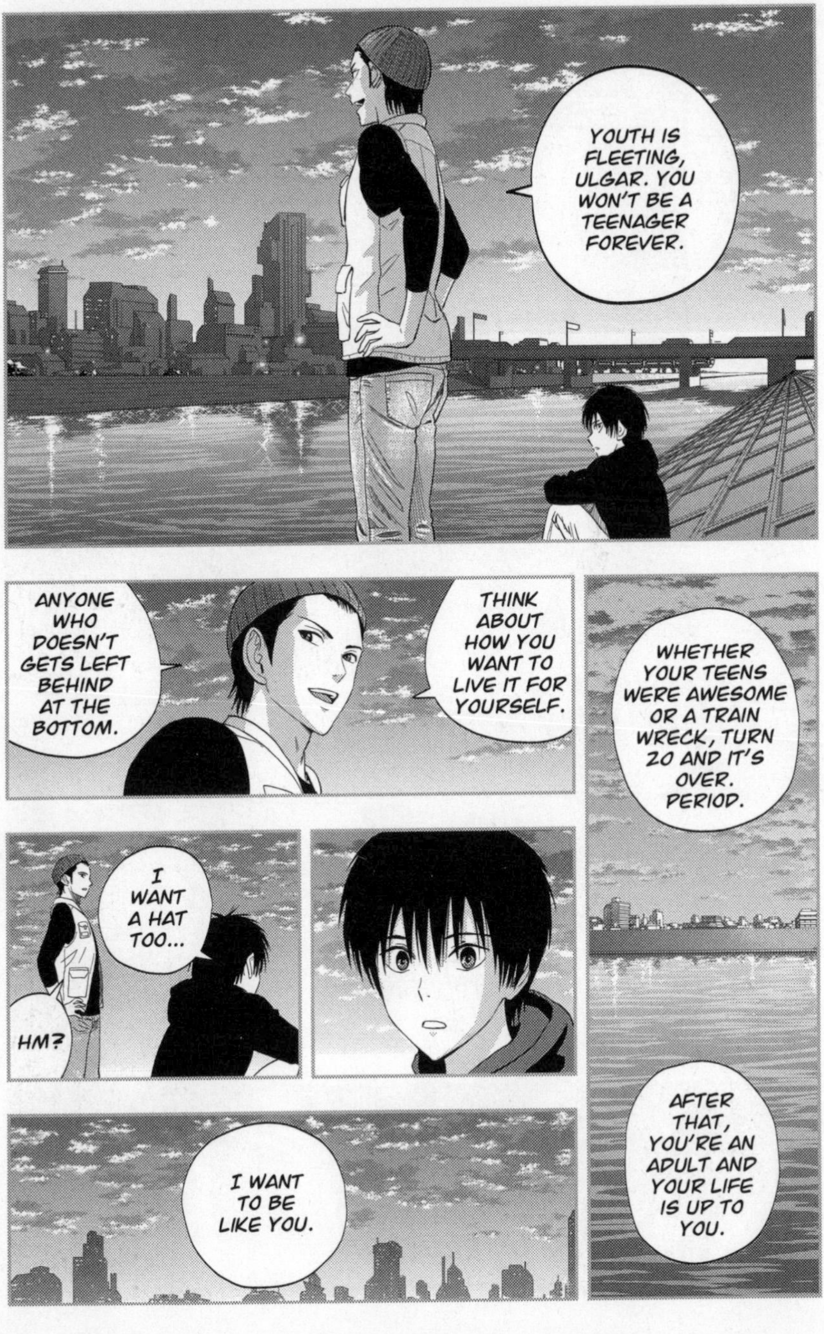
YOUTH IS FLEETING, ULGAR. YOU WON'T BE A TEENAGER FOREVER.
WHETHER YOUR TEENS WERE AWESOME OR A TRAIN WRECK, TURN 20 AND IT'S OVER. PERIOD.
AFTER THAT, YOU'RE AN ADULT AND YOUR LIFE IS UP TO YOU.
THINK ABOUT HOW YOU WANT TO LIVE IT FOR YOURSELF.
ANYONE WHO DOESN'T GETS LEFT BEHIND AT THE BOTTOM.
I WANT A HAT TOO...
HM?
I WANT TO BE LIKE YOU.

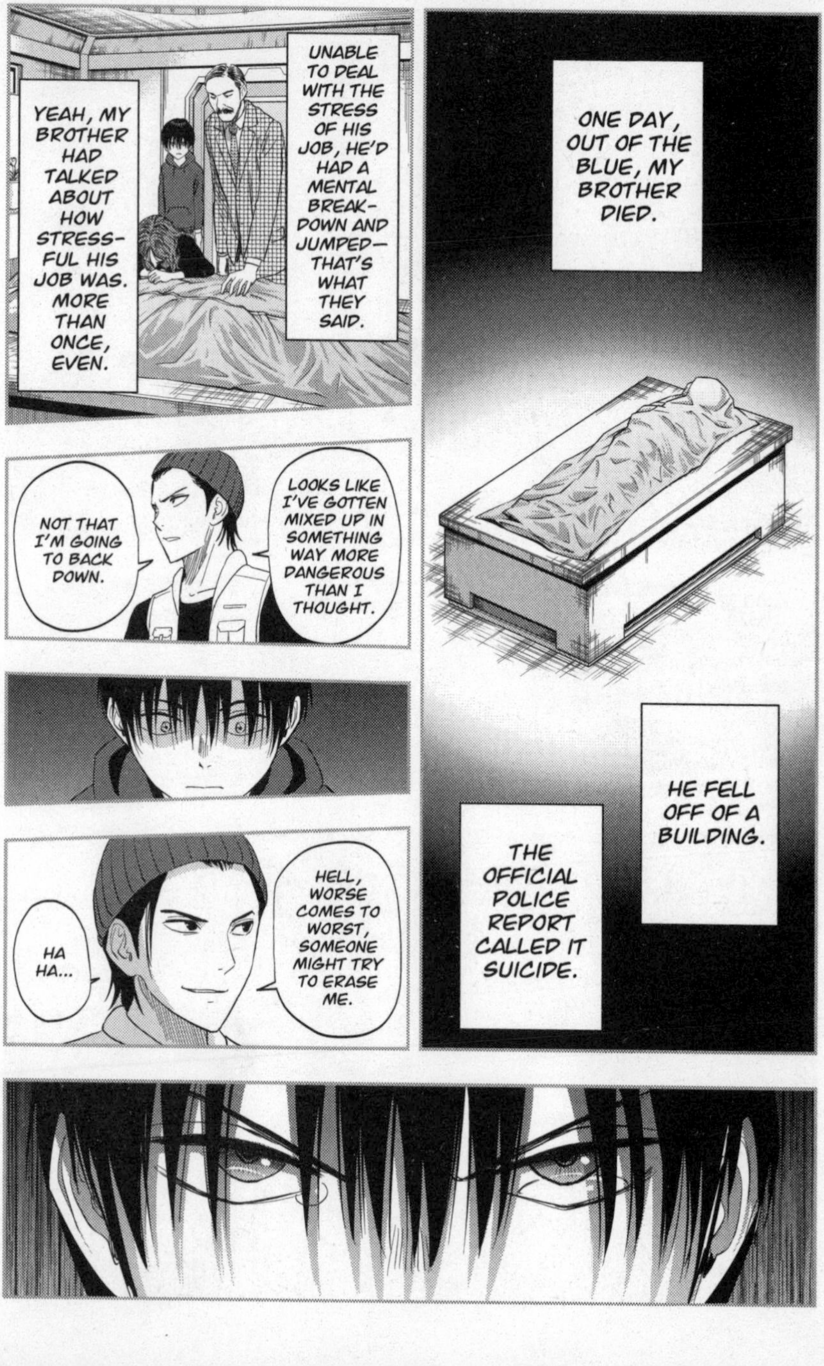
ONE DAY, OUT OF THE BLUE, MY BROTHER DIED.
HE FELL OFF OF A BUILDING.
THE OFFICIAL POLICE REPORT CALLED IT SUICIDE.
UNABLE TO DEAL WITH THE STRESS OF HIS JOB, HE'D HAD A MENTAL BREAK-DOWN AND JUMPED—THAT'S WHAT THEY SAID.
YEAH, MY BROTHER HAD TALKED ABOUT HOW STRESS-FUL HIS JOB WAS. MORE THAN ONCE, EVEN.
LOOKS LIKE I'VE GOTTEN MIXED UP IN SOMETHING WAY MORE DANGEROUS THAN I THOUGHT.
NOT THAT I'M GOING TO BACK DOWN.
HELL, WORSE COMES TO WORST, SOMEONE MIGHT TRY TO ERASE ME.
HA HA...

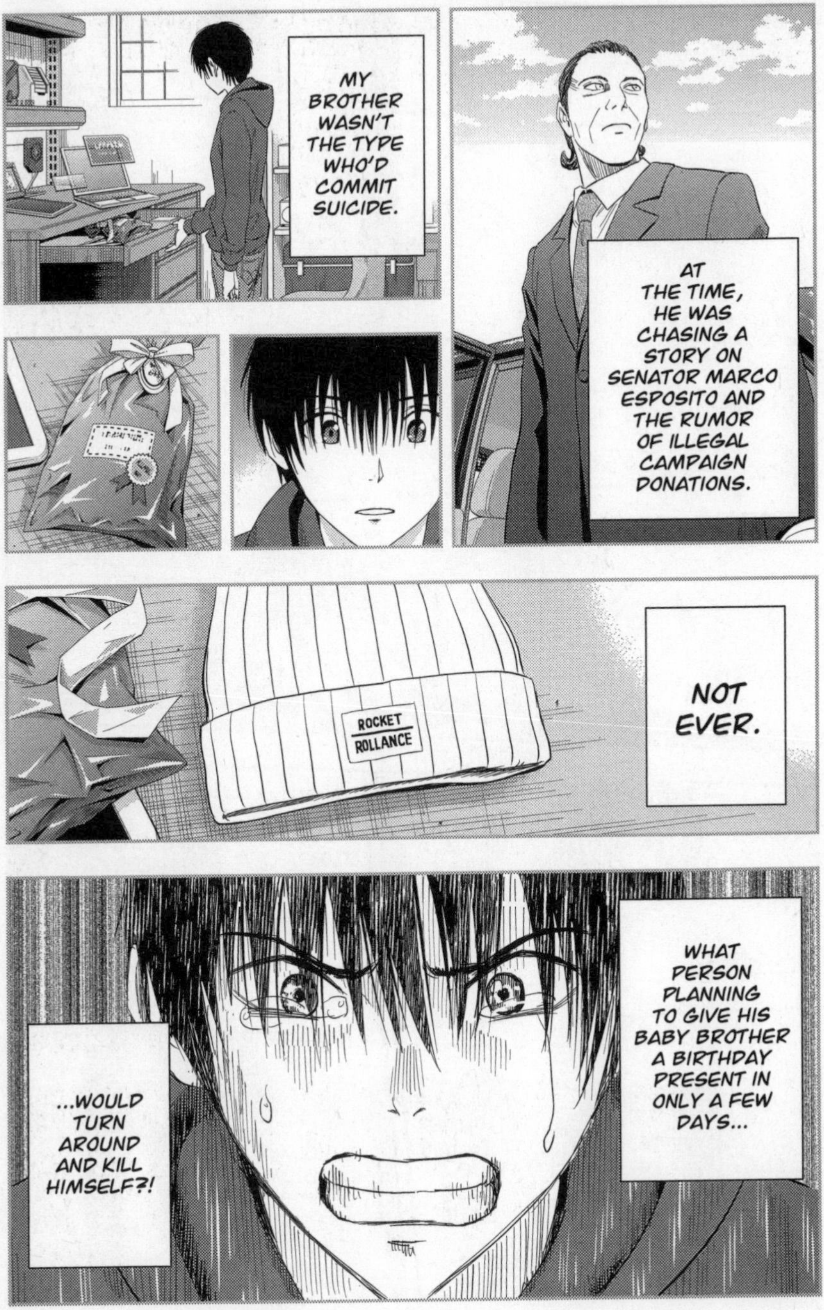
AT THE TIME, HE WAS CHASING A STORY ON SENATOR MARCO ESPOSITO AND THE RUMOR OF ILLEGAL CAMPAIGN DONATIONS.
MY BROTHER WASN'T THE TYPE WHO'D COMMIT SUICIDE.
NOT EVER.
ROCKET
ROLLANCE
WHAT PERSON PLANNING TO GIVE HIS BABY BROTHER A BIRTHDAY PRESENT IN ONLY A FEW DAYS...
...WOULD TURN AROUND AND KILL HIMSELF?!

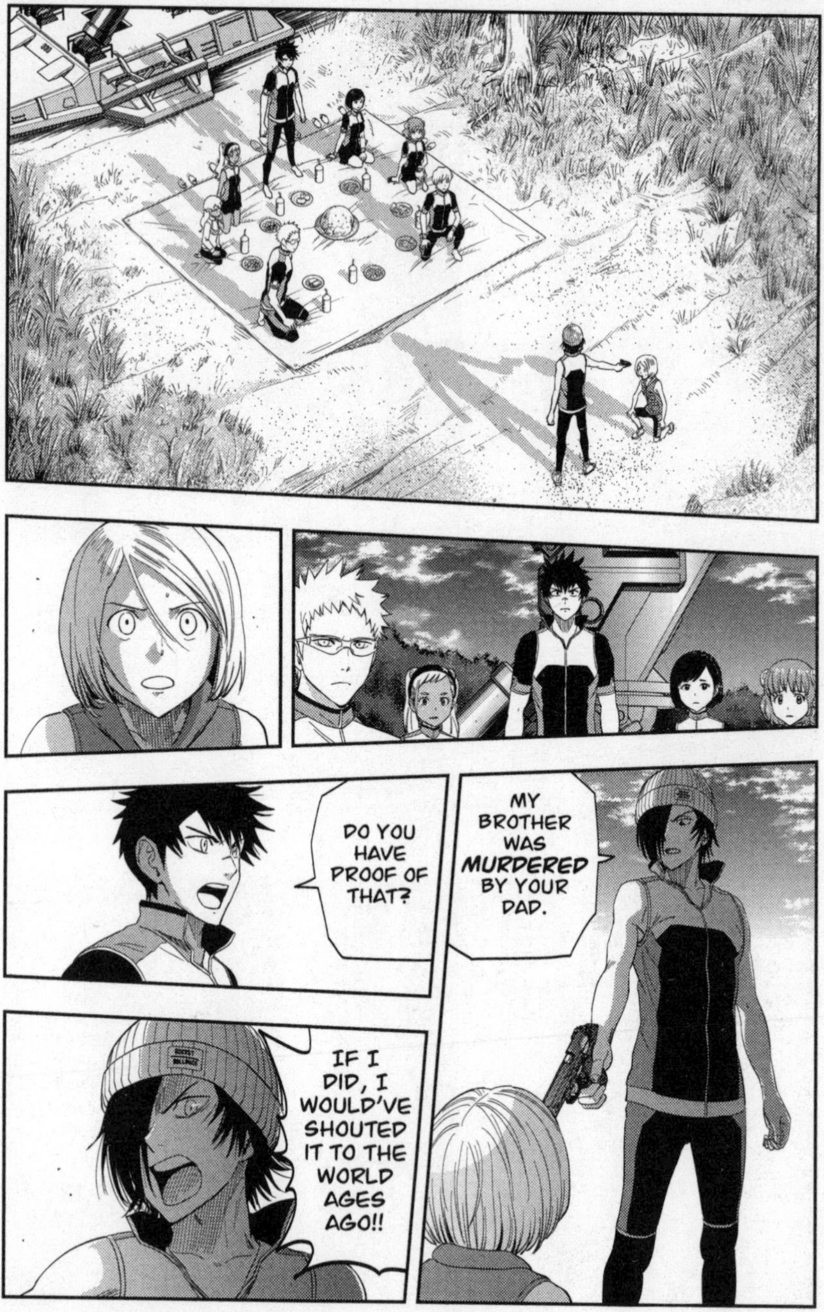
MY BROTHER WAS MURDERED BY YOUR DAD.
DO YOU HAVE PROOF OF THAT?
IF I DID, I WOULD'VE SHOUTED IT TO THE WORLD AGES AGO!!

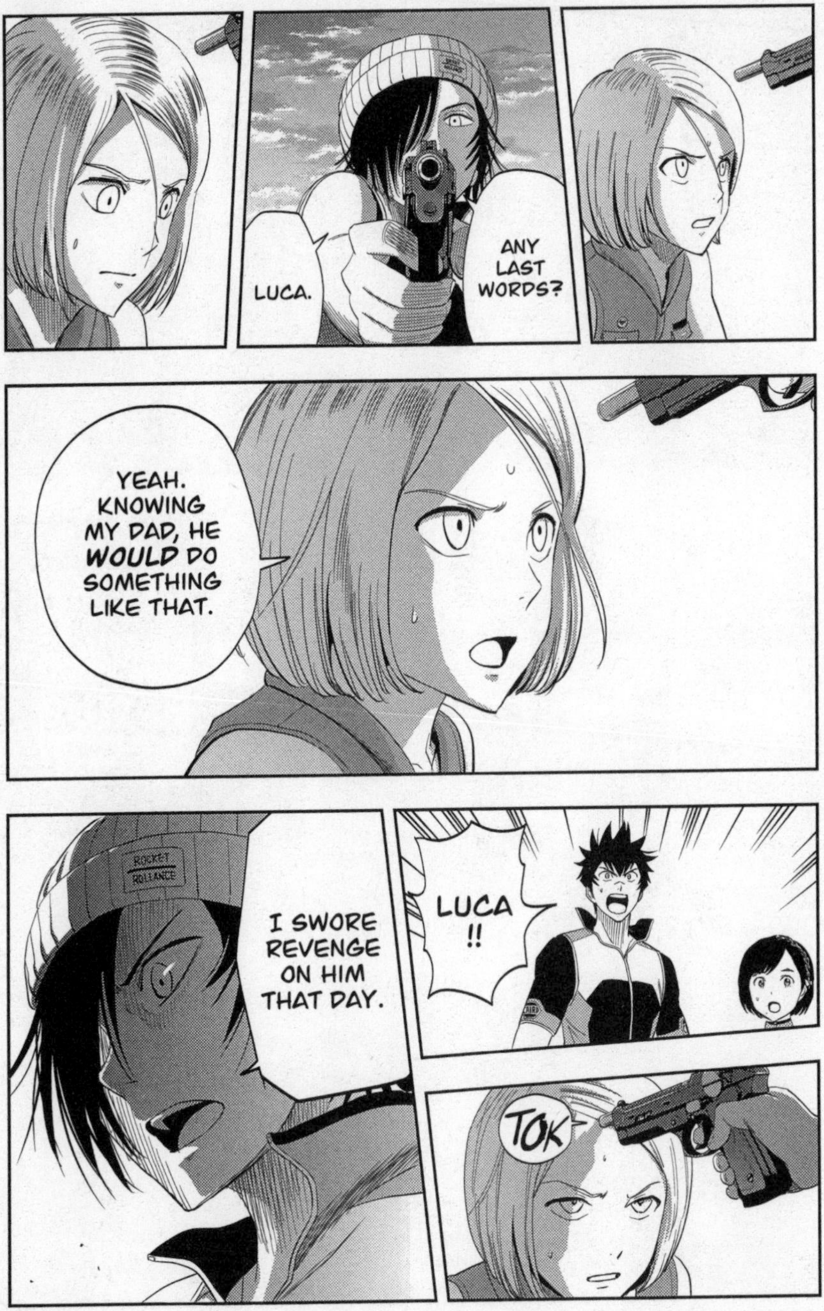
ANY LAST WORDS?
LUCA.
YEAH. KNOWING MY DAD, HE WOULD DO SOMETHING LIKE THAT.
LUCA!!
TOK
I SWORE REVENGE ON HIM THAT DAY.
ROCKET ROLLANCE

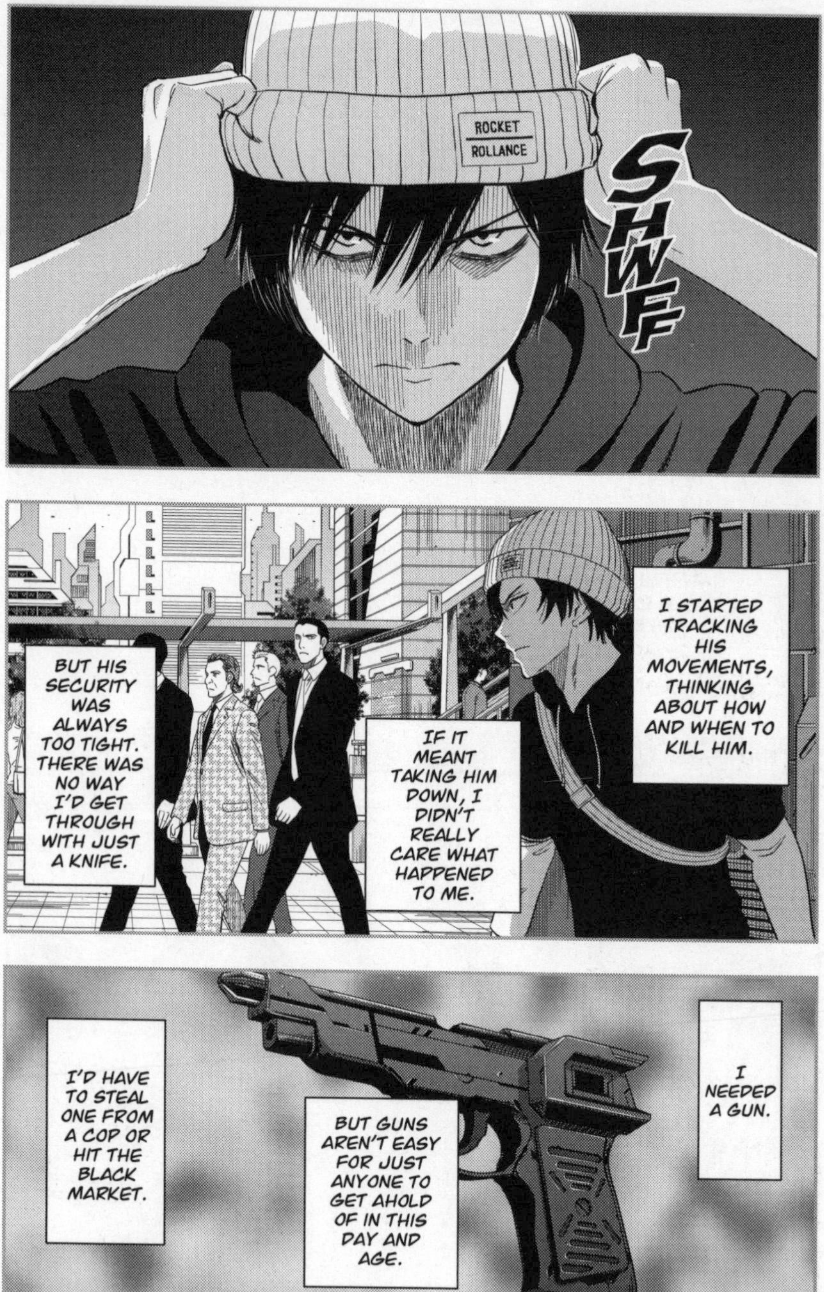
ROCKET ROLLANCE
SHWFF
I STARTED TRACKING HIS MOVEMENTS, THINKING ABOUT HOW AND WHEN TO KILL HIM.
IF IT MEANT TAKING HIM DOWN, I DIDN'T REALLY CARE WHAT HAPPENED TO ME.
BUT HIS SECURITY WAS ALWAYS TOO TIGHT. THERE WAS NO WAY I'D GET THROUGH WITH JUST A KNIFE.
I NEEDED A GUN.
BUT GUNS AREN'T EASY FOR JUST ANYONE TO GET AHOLD OF IN THIS DAY AND AGE.
I'D HAVE TO STEAL ONE FROM A COP OR HIT THE BLACK MARKET.

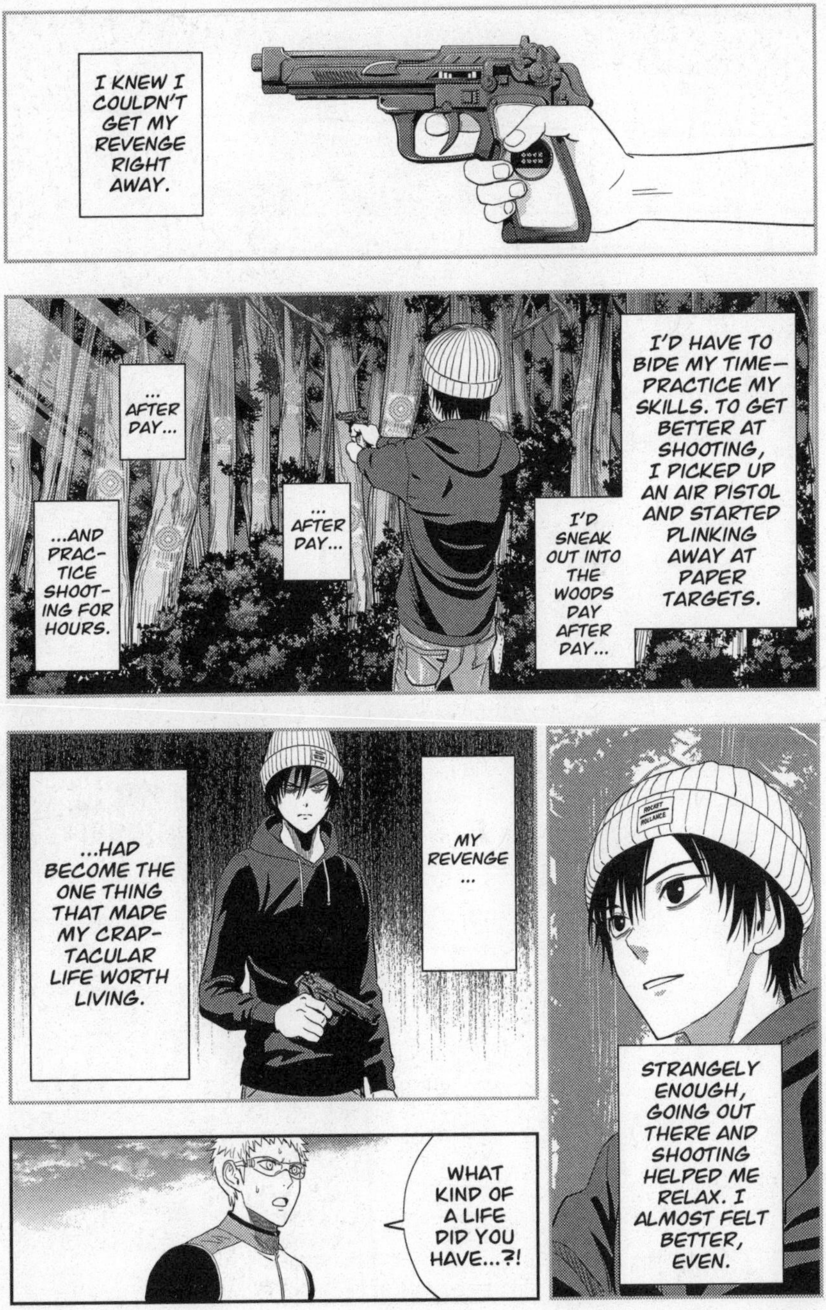

I KNEW I COULDN'T GET MY REVENGE RIGHT AWAY.
I'D HAVE TO BIDE MY TIME—PRACTICE MY SKILLS. TO GET BETTER AT SHOOTING, I PICKED UP AN AIR PISTOL AND STARTED PLINKING AWAY AT PAPER TARGETS.
I'D SNEAK OUT INTO THE WOODS DAY AFTER DAY...
...AFTER DAY...
...AFTER DAY...
...AND PRACTICE SHOOTING FOR HOURS.
STRANGELY ENOUGH, GOING OUT THERE AND SHOOTING HELPED ME RELAX. I ALMOST FELT BETTER, EVEN.
MY REVENGE...
...HAD BECOME THE ONE THING THAT MADE MY CRAPTACULAR LIFE WORTH LIVING.
WHAT KIND OF A LIFE DID YOU HAVE...?!

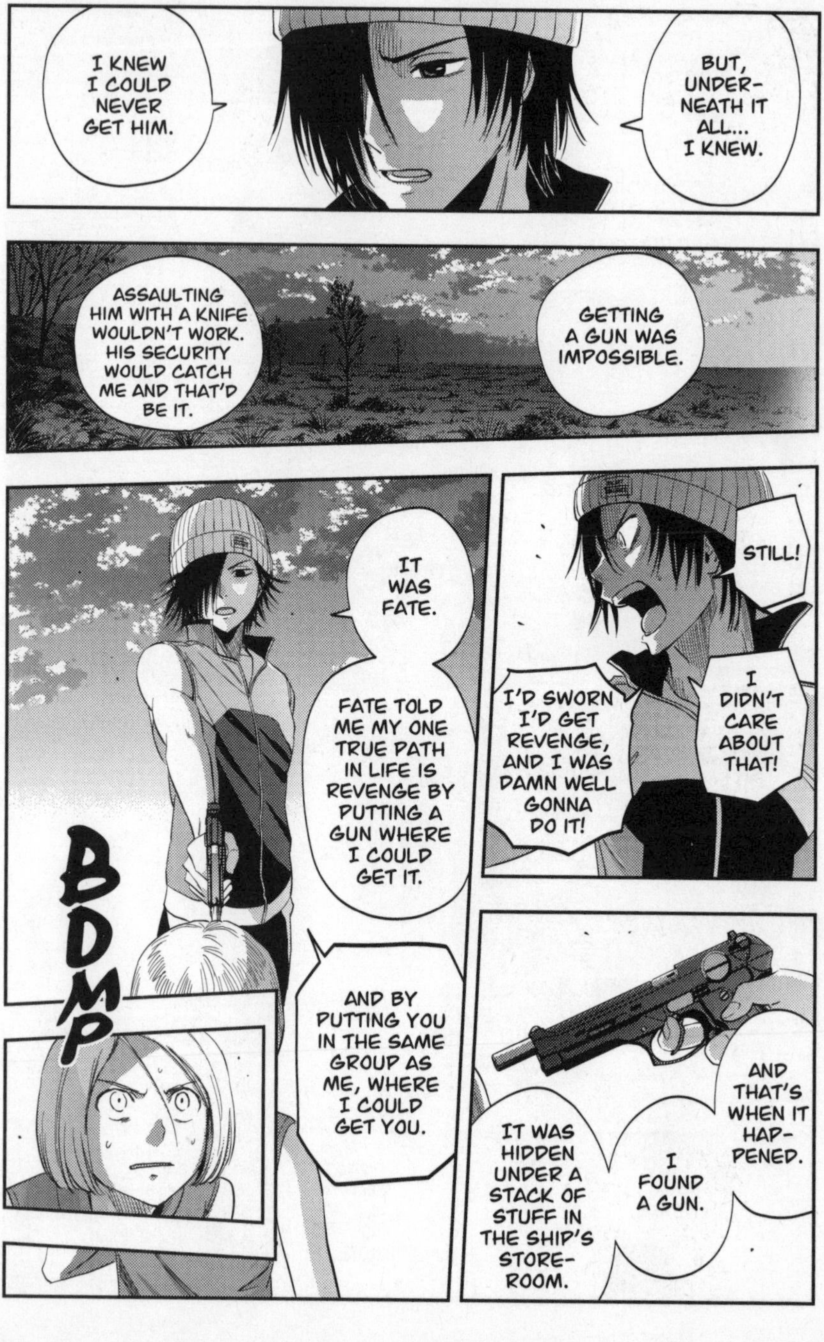
BUT, UNDER-NEATH IT ALL... I KNEW.
I KNEW I COULD NEVER GET HIM.
GETTING A GUN WAS IMPOSSIBLE.
ASSAULTING HIM WITH A KNIFE WOULDN'T WORK. HIS SECURITY WOULD CATCH ME AND THAT'D BE IT.
STILL!
I DIDN'T CARE ABOUT THAT!
I'D SWORN I'D GET REVENGE, AND I WAS DAMN WELL GONNA DO IT!
AND THAT'S WHEN IT HAP-PENED.
I FOUND A GUN.
IT WAS HIDDEN UNDER A STACK OF STUFF IN THE SHIP'S STORE-ROOM.
IT WAS FATE.
FATE TOLD ME MY ONE TRUE PATH IN LIFE IS REVENGE BY PUTTING A GUN WHERE I COULD GET IT.
AND BY PUTTING YOU IN THE SAME GROUP AS ME, WHERE I COULD GET YOU.
BDMP

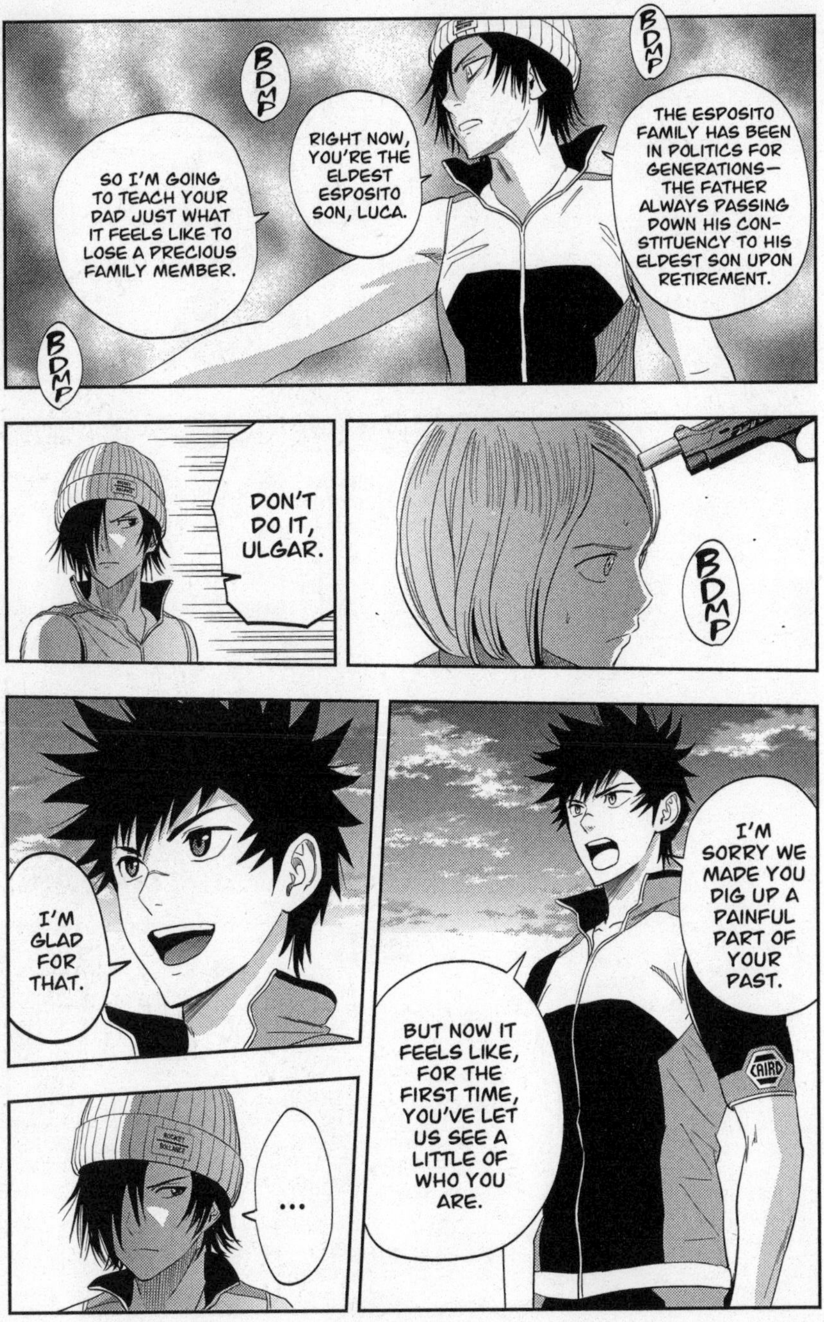
BDMP
THE ESPOSITO FAMILY HAS BEEN IN POLITICS FOR GENERATIONS—THE FATHER ALWAYS PASSING DOWN HIS CONSTITUENCY TO HIS ELDEST SON UPON RETIREMENT.
RIGHT NOW, YOU'RE THE ELDEST ESPOSITO SON, LUCA.
BDMP
SO I'M GOING TO TEACH YOUR DAD JUST WHAT IT FEELS LIKE TO LOSE A PRECIOUS FAMILY MEMBER.
BDMP
BDMP
DON'T DO IT, ULGAR.
I'M SORRY WE MADE YOU DIG UP A PAINFUL PART OF YOUR PAST.
BUT NOW IT FEELS LIKE, FOR THE FIRST TIME, YOU'VE LET US SEE A LITTLE OF WHO YOU ARE.
CAIRD
I'M GLAD FOR THAT.
...

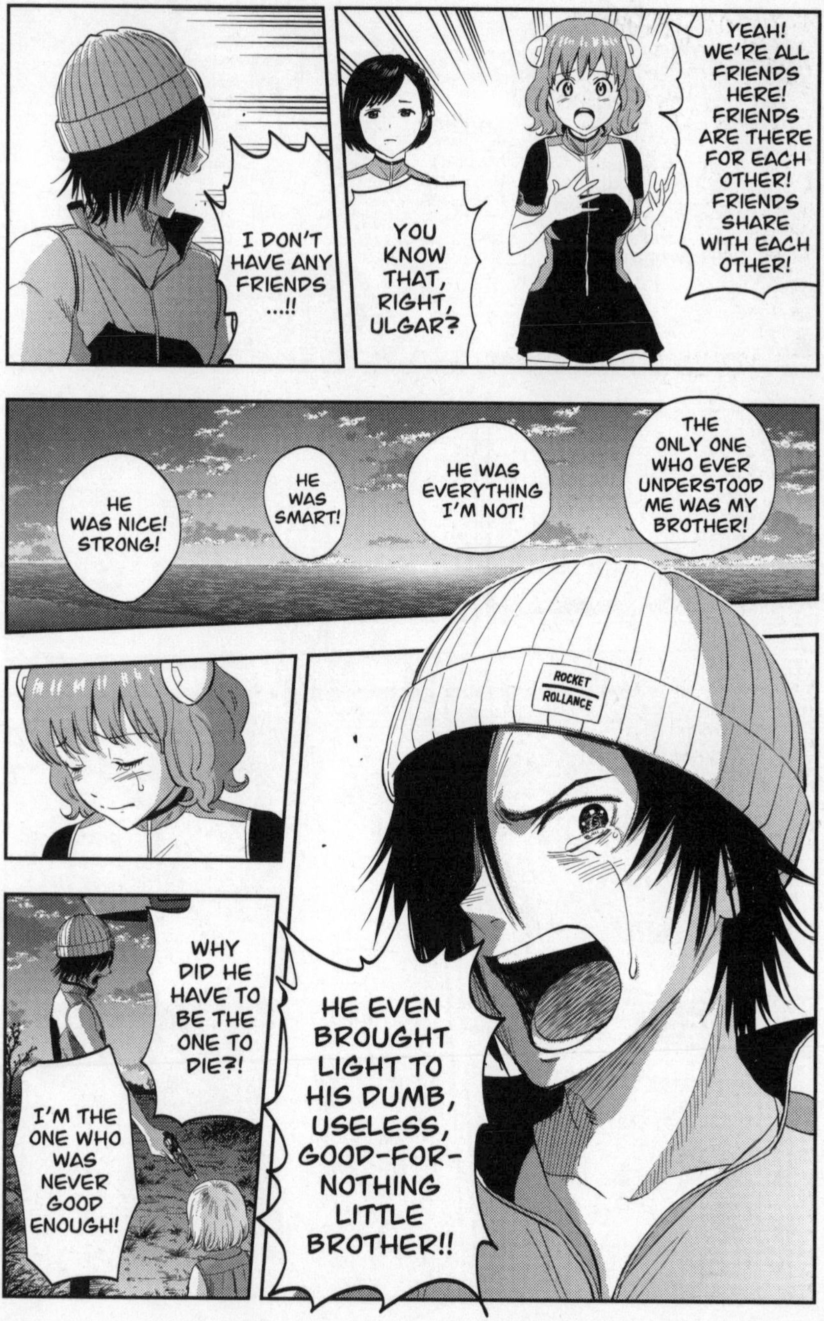
YEAH! WE'RE ALL FRIENDS HERE! FRIENDS ARE THERE FOR EACH OTHER! FRIENDS SHARE WITH EACH OTHER!
YOU KNOW THAT, RIGHT, ULGAR?
I DON'T HAVE ANY FRIENDS ...!!
THE ONLY ONE WHO EVER UNDERSTOOD ME WAS MY BROTHER!
HE WAS EVERYTHING I'M NOT!
HE WAS SMART!
HE WAS NICE! STRONG!
ROCKET ROLLANCE
HE EVEN BROUGHT LIGHT TO HIS DUMB, USELESS, GOOD-FOR-NOTHING LITTLE BROTHER!!
WHY DID HE HAVE TO BE THE ONE TO DIE?!
I'M THE ONE WHO WAS NEVER GOOD ENOUGH!

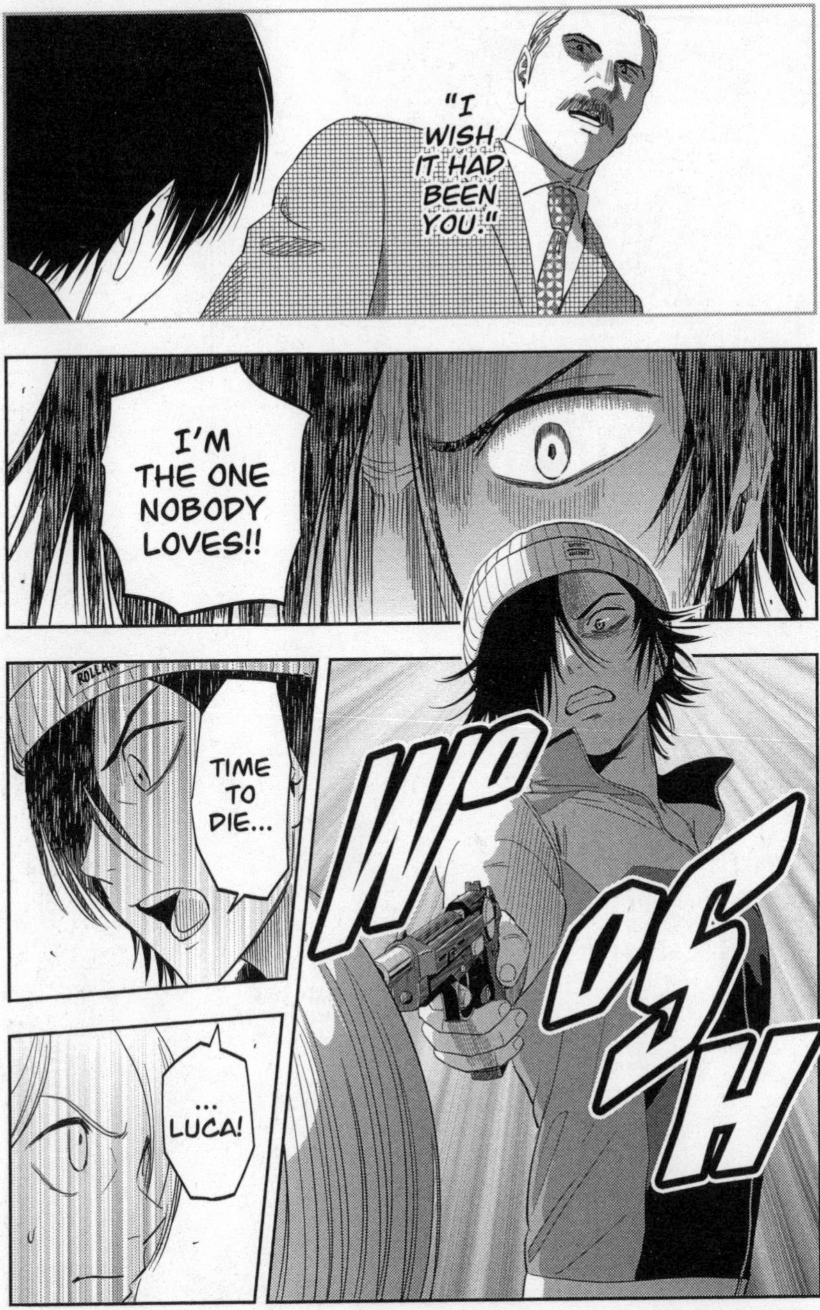
"I WISH IT HAD BEEN YOU."
I'M THE ONE NOBODY LOVES!!
WOOSH
TIME TO DIE...
...LUCA!

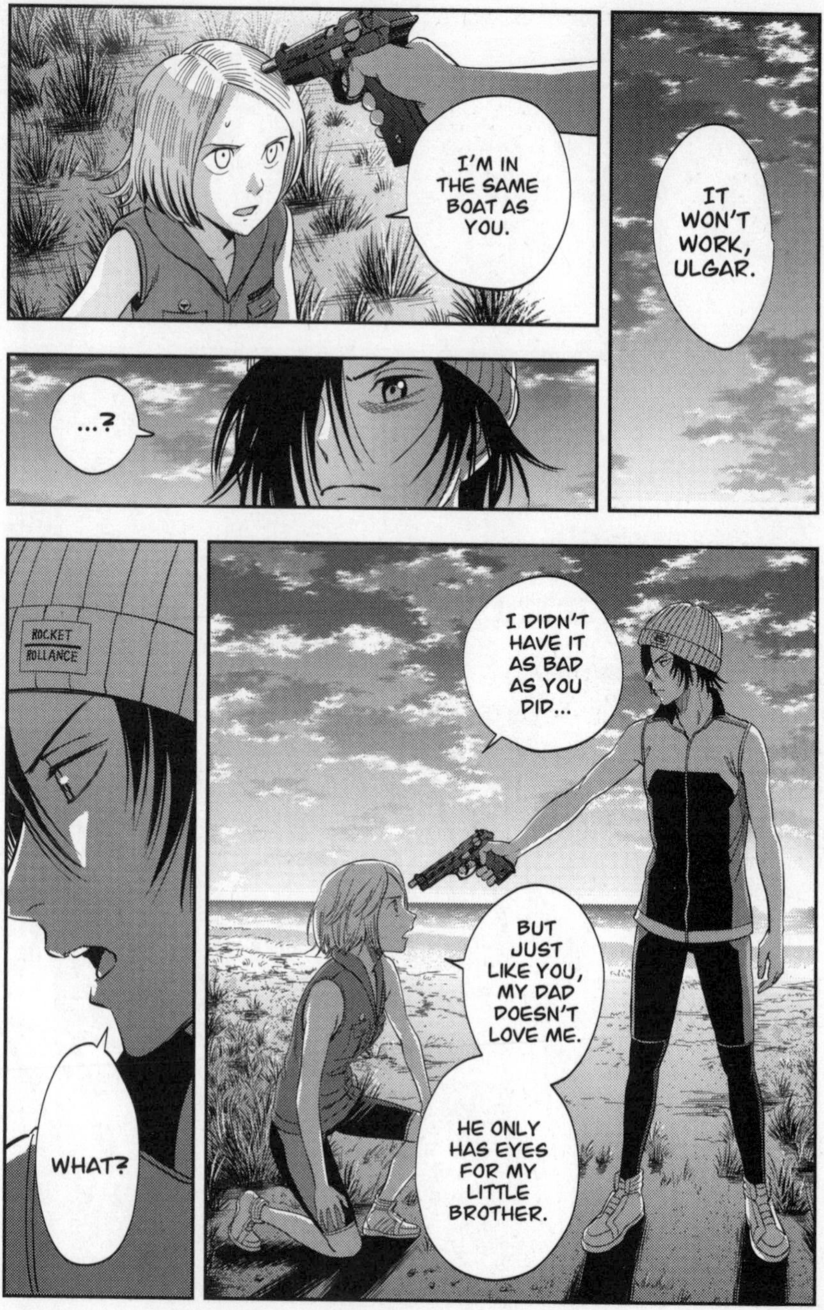
IT WON'T WORK, ULGAR.
I'M IN THE SAME BOAT AS YOU.
...?
I DIDN'T HAVE IT AS BAD AS YOU DID...
BUT JUST LIKE YOU, MY DAD DOESN'T LOVE ME.
HE ONLY HAS EYES FOR MY LITTLE BROTHER.
ROCKET ROLLANCE
WHAT?

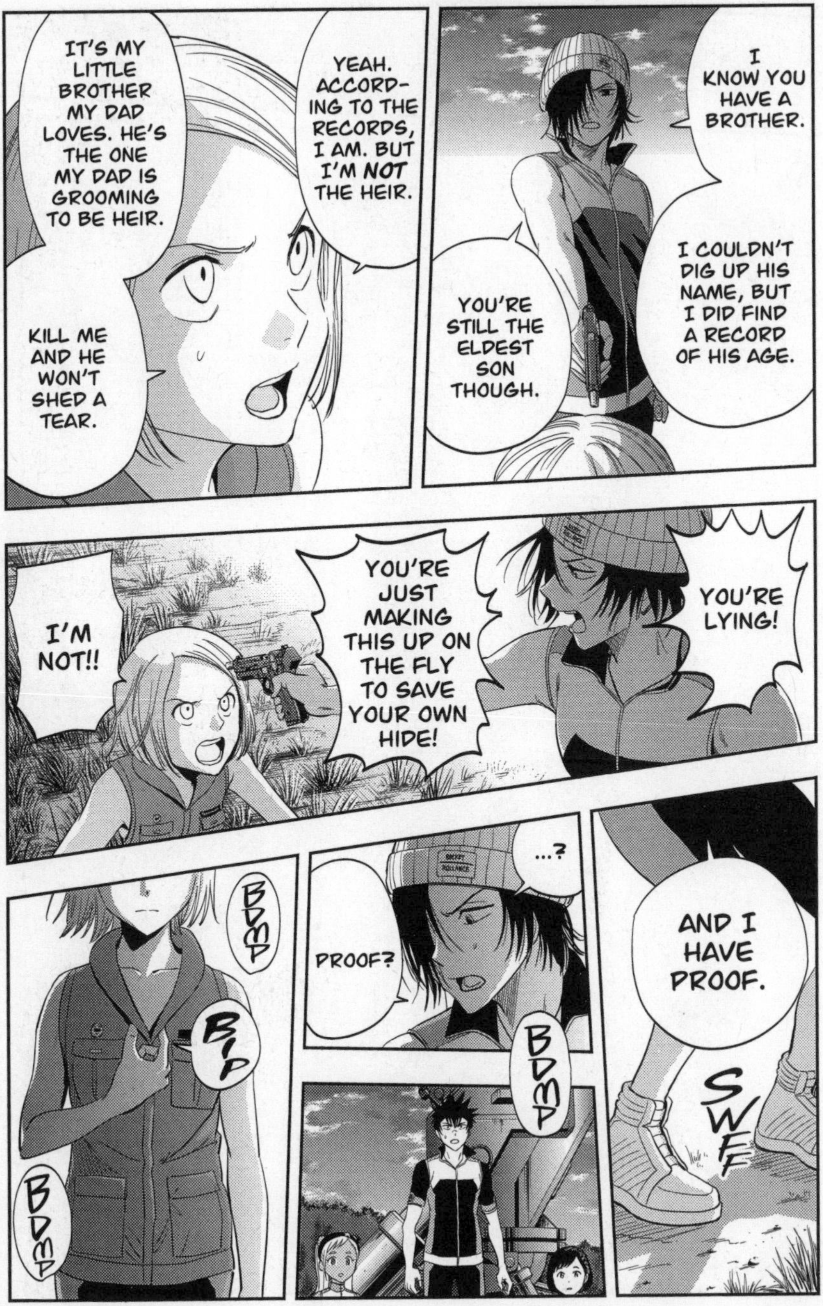
I KNOW YOU HAVE A BROTHER.
I COULDN'T DIG UP HIS NAME, BUT I DID FIND A RECORD OF HIS AGE.
YOU'RE STILL THE ELDEST SON THOUGH.
YEAH. ACCORDING TO THE RECORDS, I AM. BUT I'M **NOT** THE HEIR.
IT'S MY LITTLE BROTHER MY DAD LOVES. HE'S THE ONE MY DAD IS GROOMING TO BE HEIR.
KILL ME AND HE WON'T SHED A TEAR.
YOU'RE LYING!
YOU'RE JUST MAKING THIS UP ON THE FLY TO SAVE YOUR OWN HIDE!
I'M NOT!!
AND I HAVE PROOF.
SWFF
...?
PROOF?
BDMP
BDMP
RIP
BDMP

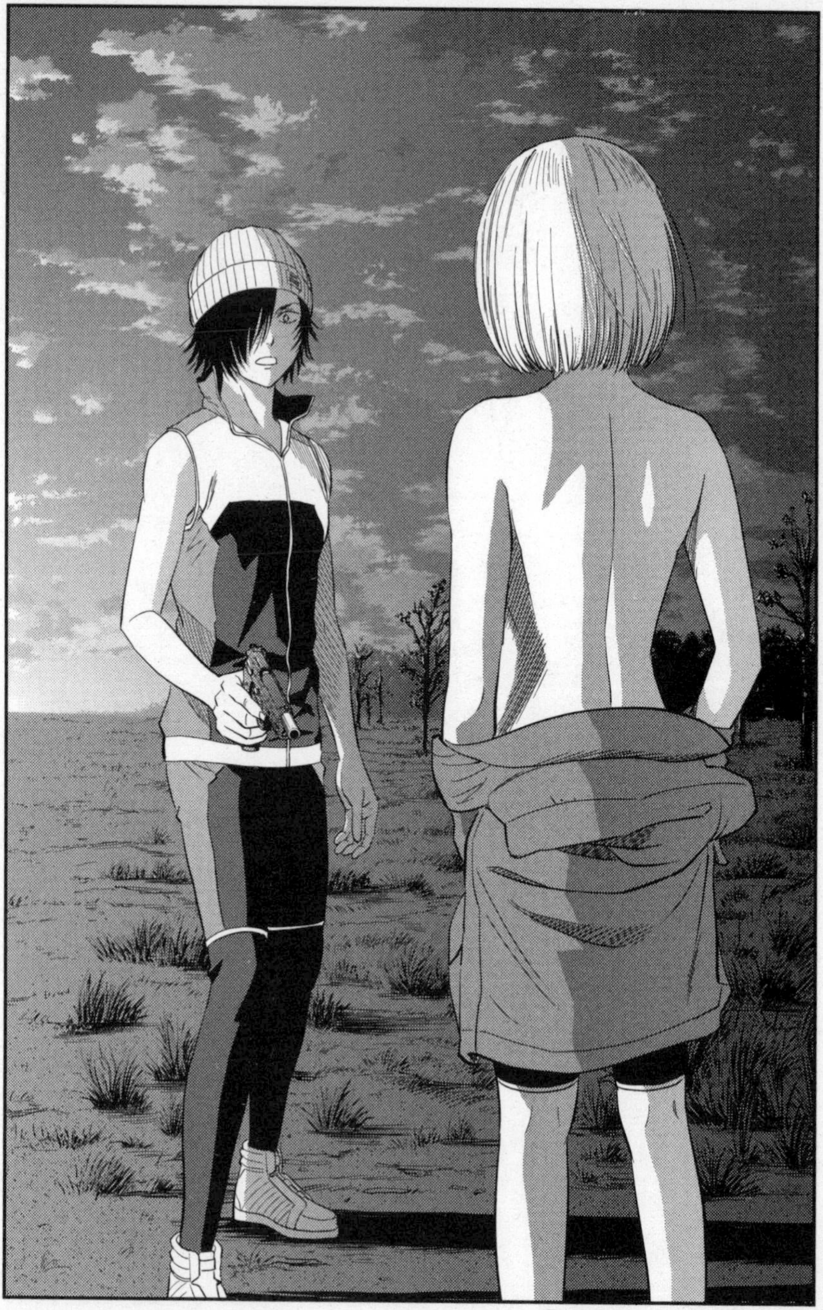

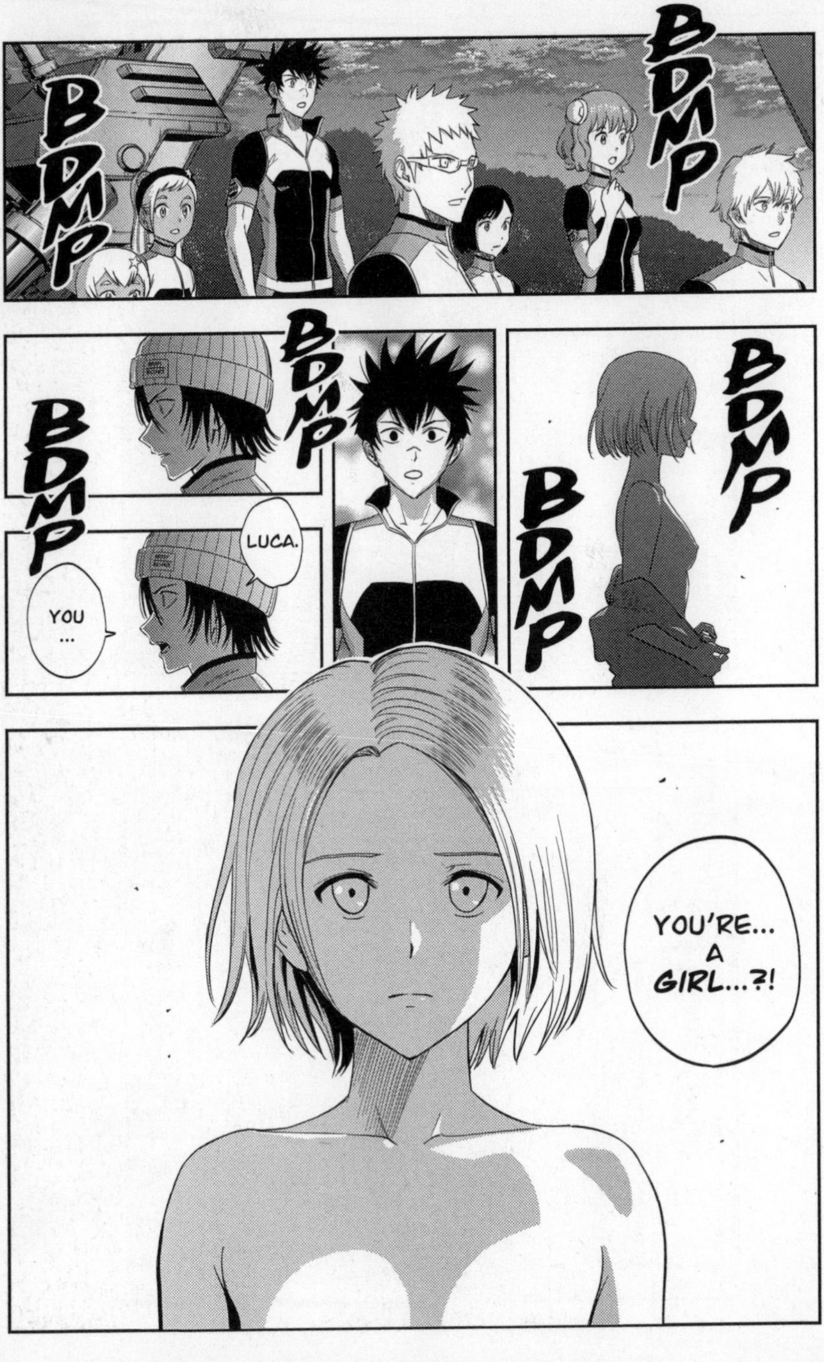
BDMP
BDMP
BDMP
BDMP
BDMP
BDMP
LUCA.
YOU ...
YOU'RE... A GIRL...?!

Material Collection

PRIVATE ROOMS

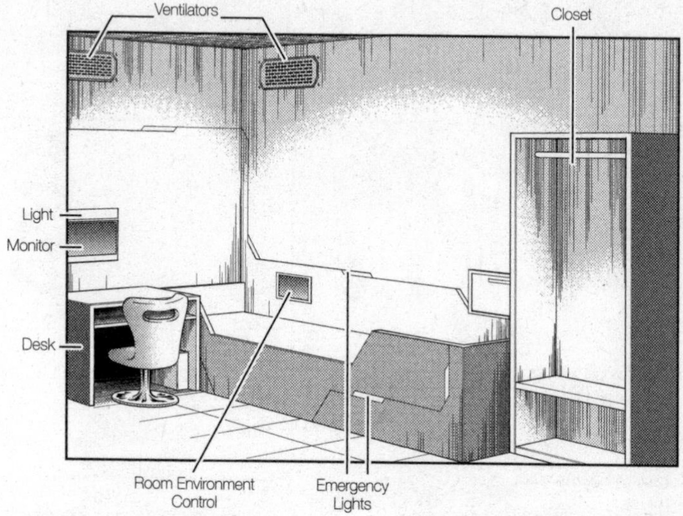
Ventilators
Closet
Light
Monitor
Desk
Room Environment Control
Emergency Lights

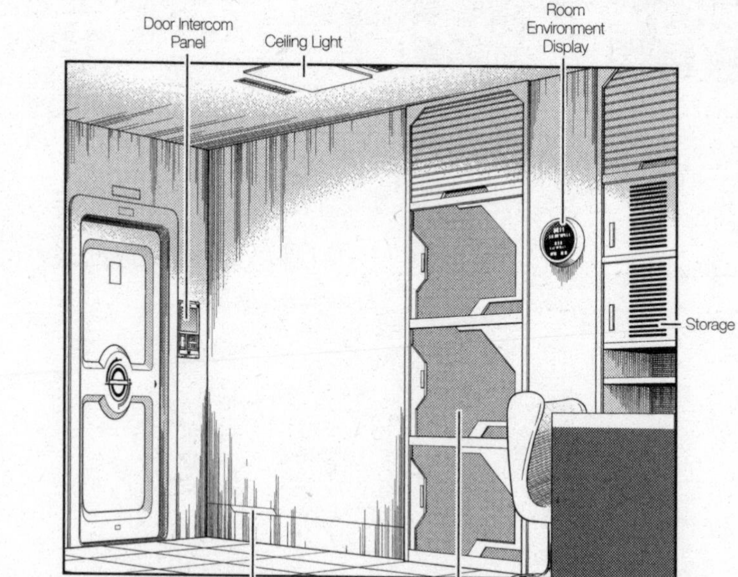
Door Intercom Panel
Ceiling Light
Room Environment Display
Storage
Emergency Light
Storage

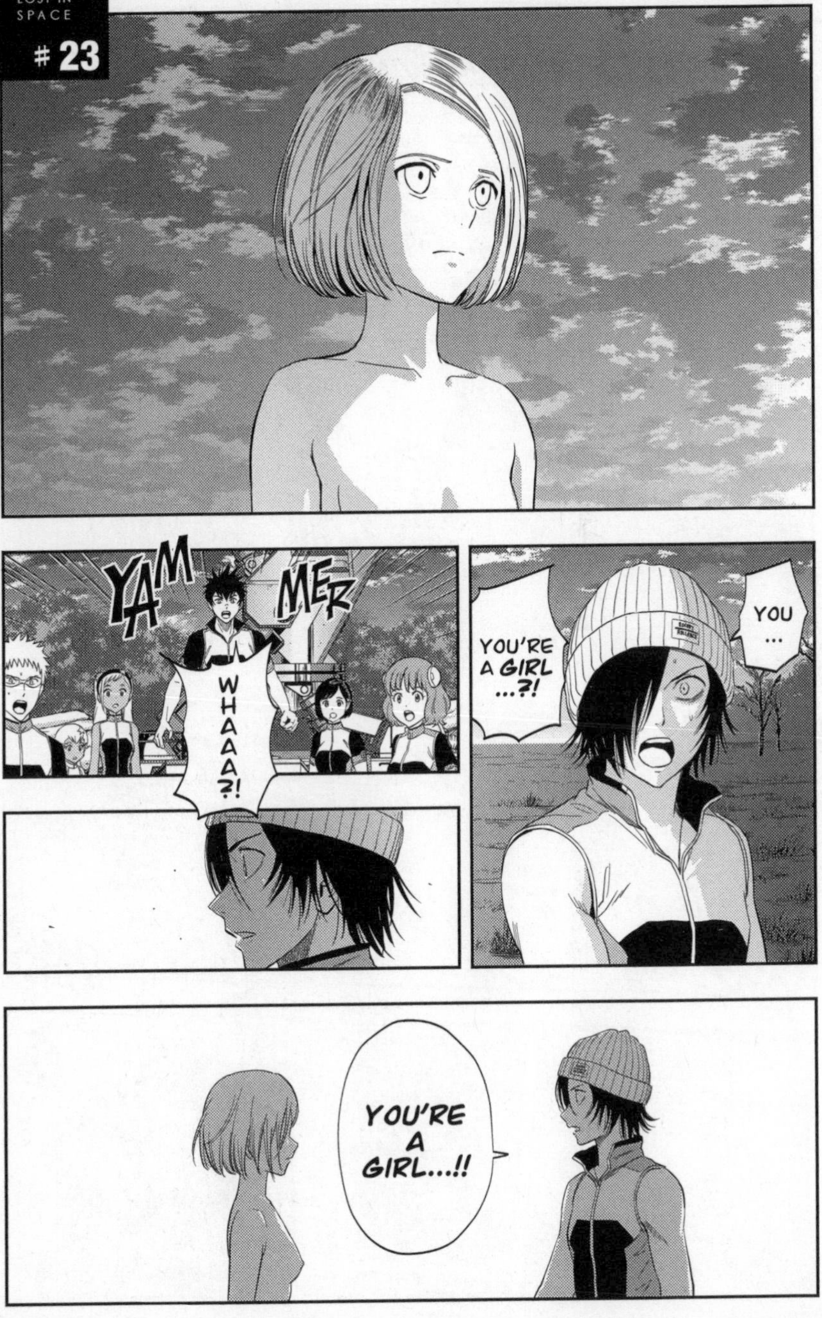
YOU ...
YOU'RE A GIRL ...?!
YAM MER
WHAAAA?!
YOU'RE A GIRL...!!

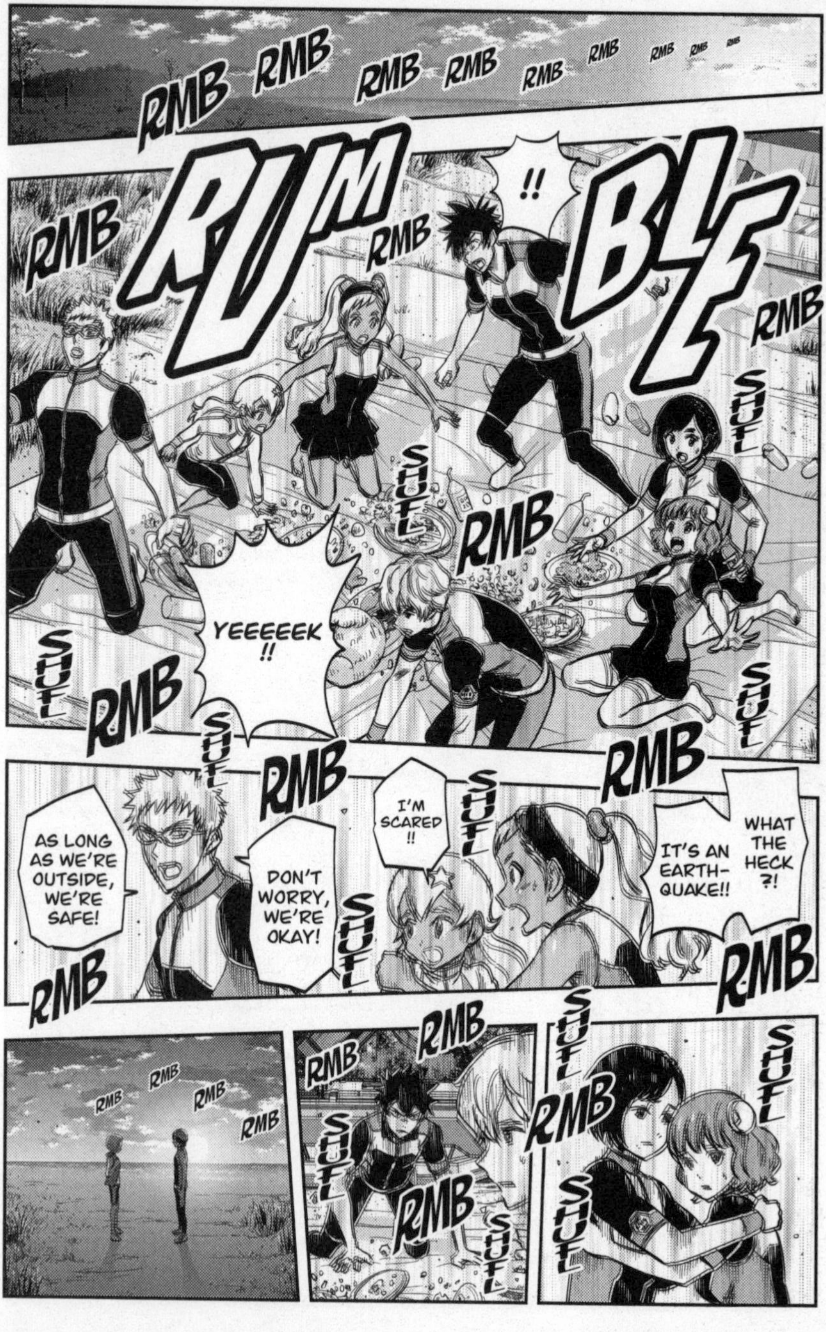
RMB RMB RMB RMB RMB RMB RMB RMB RMB
RUMBLE
!!
RMB
RMB
RMB
SHUFL
SHUFL
RMB
YEEEEEK!!
SHUFL
RMB
SHUFL
SHUFL
RMB
RMB
WHAT THE HECK?!
IT'S AN EARTHQUAKE!!
RMB
SHUFL
I'M SCARED!!
SHUFL
DON'T WORRY, WE'RE OKAY!
AS LONG AS WE'RE OUTSIDE, WE'RE SAFE!
RMB
SHUFL
SHUFL
RMB
SHUFL
RMB
RMB
RMB
SHUFL
SHUFL
RMB RMB RMB RMB

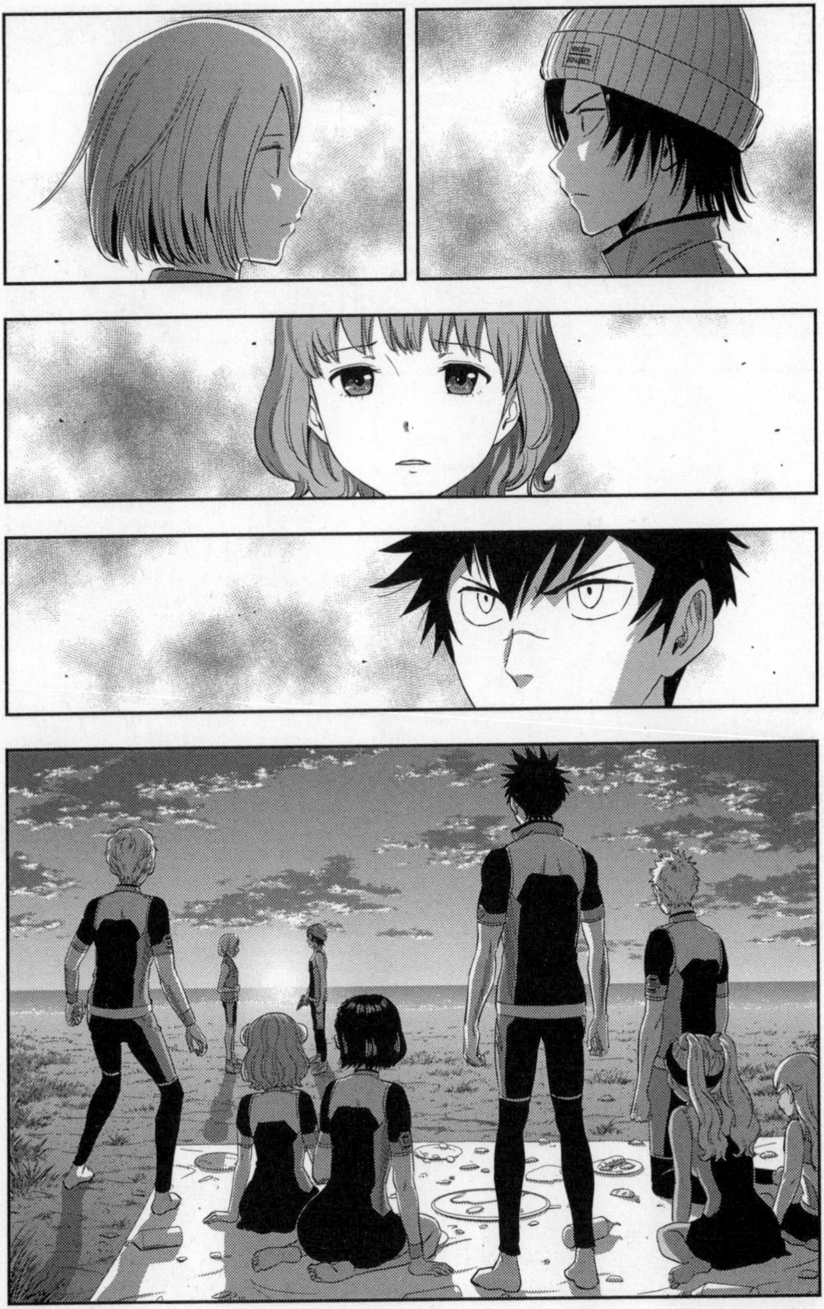

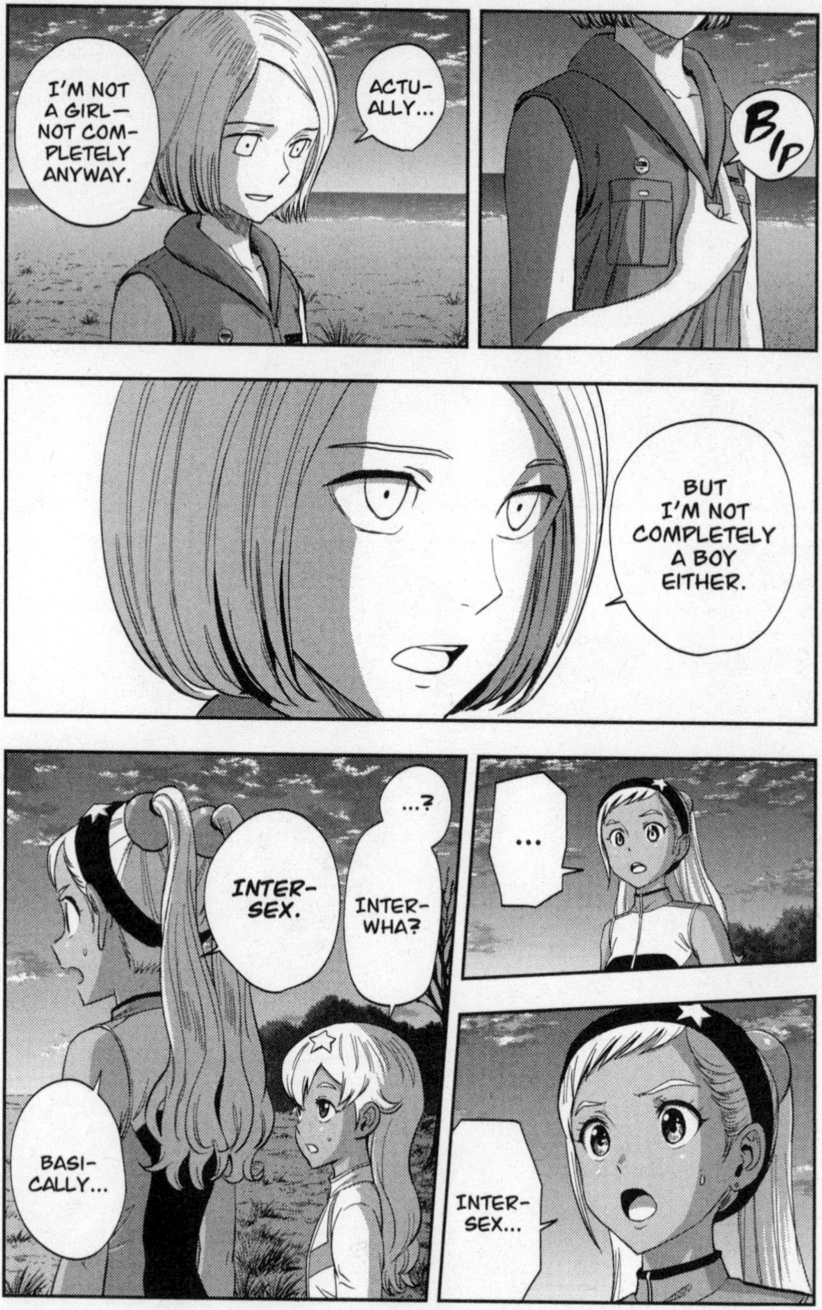
BIP
ACTU-ALLY...
I'M NOT A GIRL— NOT COM-PLETELY ANYWAY.
BUT I'M NOT COMPLETELY A BOY EITHER.
...
INTER-SEX...
...?
INTER-WHA?
INTER-SEX.
BASI-CALLY...

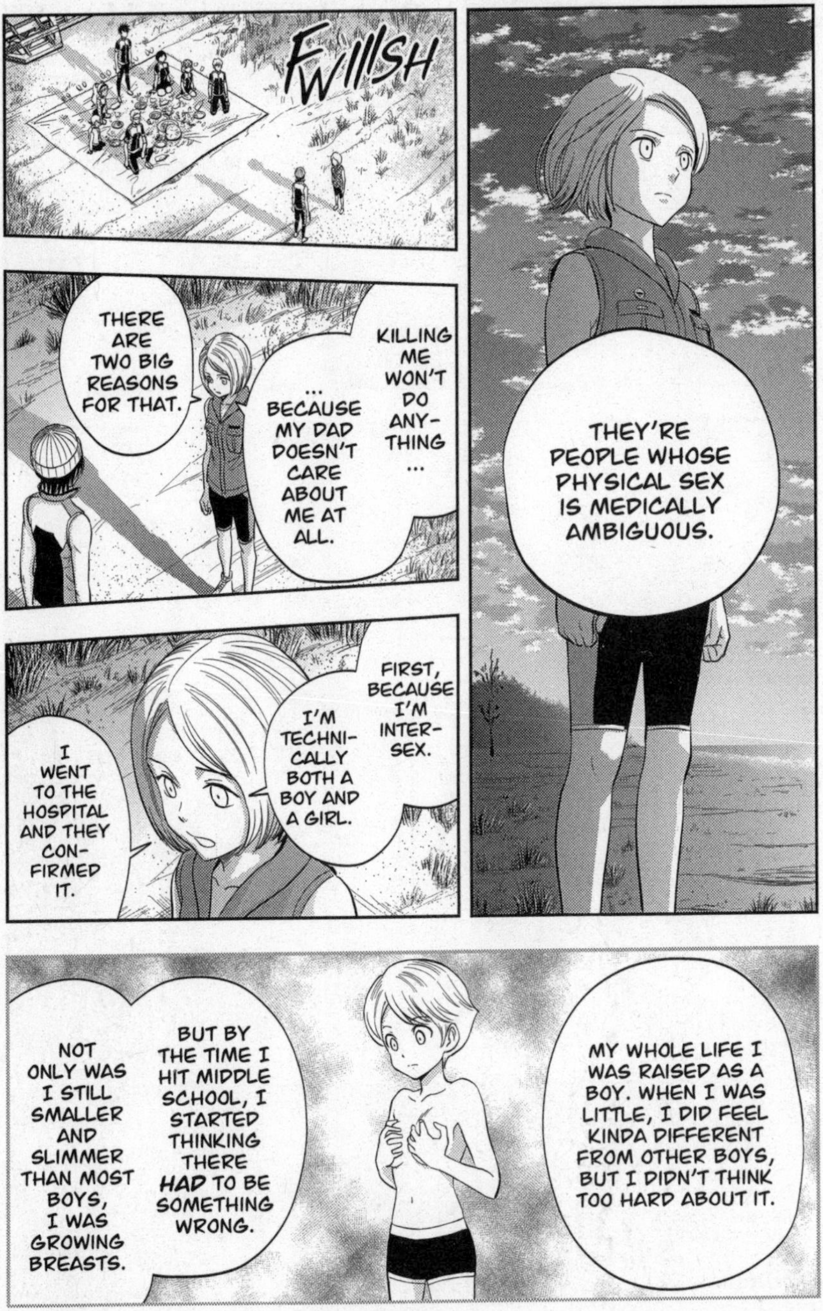
FWIIISH
KILLING ME WON'T DO ANYTHING...
...BECAUSE MY DAD DOESN'T CARE ABOUT ME AT ALL.
THERE ARE TWO BIG REASONS FOR THAT.
FIRST, BECAUSE I'M INTERSEX.
I'M TECHNICALLY BOTH A BOY AND A GIRL.
I WENT TO THE HOSPITAL AND THEY CONFIRMED IT.
THEY'RE PEOPLE WHOSE PHYSICAL SEX IS MEDICALLY AMBIGUOUS.
MY WHOLE LIFE I WAS RAISED AS A BOY. WHEN I WAS LITTLE, I DID FEEL KINDA DIFFERENT FROM OTHER BOYS, BUT I DIDN'T THINK TOO HARD ABOUT IT.
BUT BY THE TIME I HIT MIDDLE SCHOOL, I STARTED THINKING THERE HAD TO BE SOMETHING WRONG.
NOT ONLY WAS I STILL SMALLER AND SLIMMER THAN MOST BOYS, I WAS GROWING BREASTS.

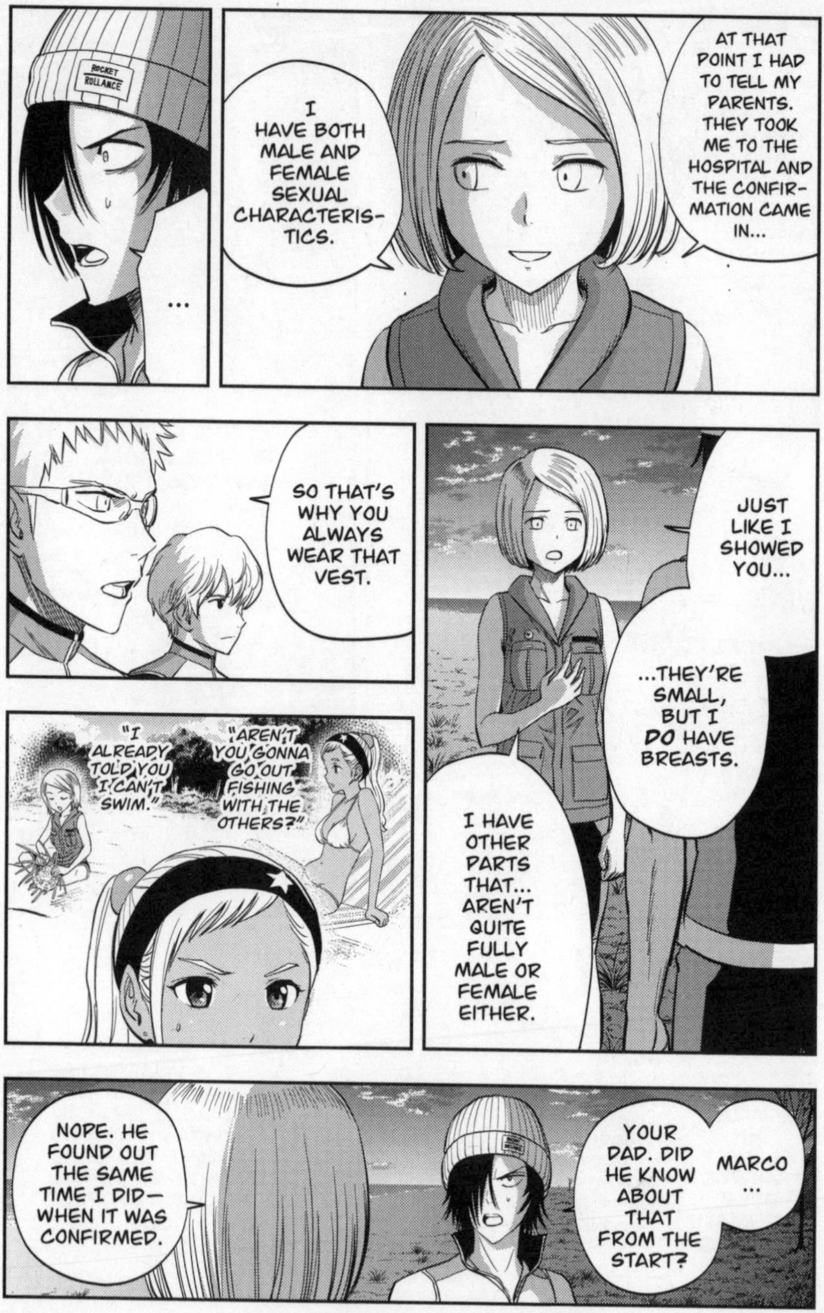
AT THAT POINT I HAD TO TELL MY PARENTS. THEY TOOK ME TO THE HOSPITAL AND THE CONFIRMATION CAME IN...
I HAVE BOTH MALE AND FEMALE SEXUAL CHARACTERISTICS.
ROCKET ROLLANCE
...
JUST LIKE I SHOWED YOU...
...THEY'RE SMALL, BUT I **DO** HAVE BREASTS.
I HAVE OTHER PARTS THAT... AREN'T QUITE FULLY MALE OR FEMALE EITHER.
SO THAT'S WHY YOU ALWAYS WEAR THAT VEST.
"AREN'T YOU GONNA GO OUT FISHING WITH THE OTHERS?"
"I ALREADY TOLD YOU I CAN'T SWIM."
MARCO...
YOUR DAD. DID HE KNOW ABOUT THAT FROM THE START?
NOPE. HE FOUND OUT THE SAME TIME I DID—WHEN IT WAS CONFIRMED.

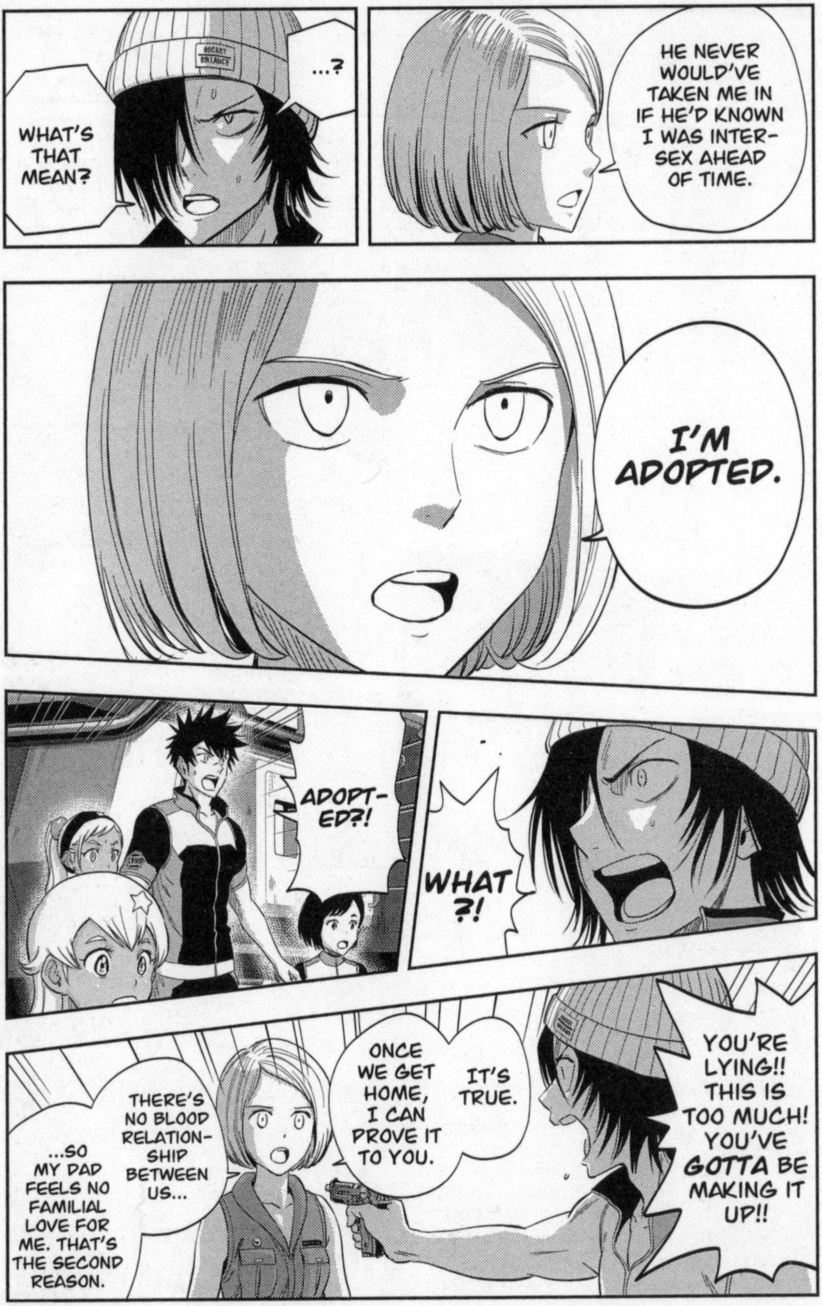
HE NEVER WOULD'VE TAKEN ME IN IF HE'D KNOWN I WAS INTERSEX AHEAD OF TIME.
...?
WHAT'S THAT MEAN?
I'M ADOPTED.
WHAT?!
ADOPTED?!
YOU'RE LYING!! THIS IS TOO MUCH! YOU'VE GOTTA BE MAKING IT UP!!
IT'S TRUE.
ONCE WE GET HOME, I CAN PROVE IT TO YOU.
THERE'S NO BLOOD RELATIONSHIP BETWEEN US...
...SO MY DAD FEELS NO FAMILIAL LOVE FOR ME. THAT'S THE SECOND REASON.

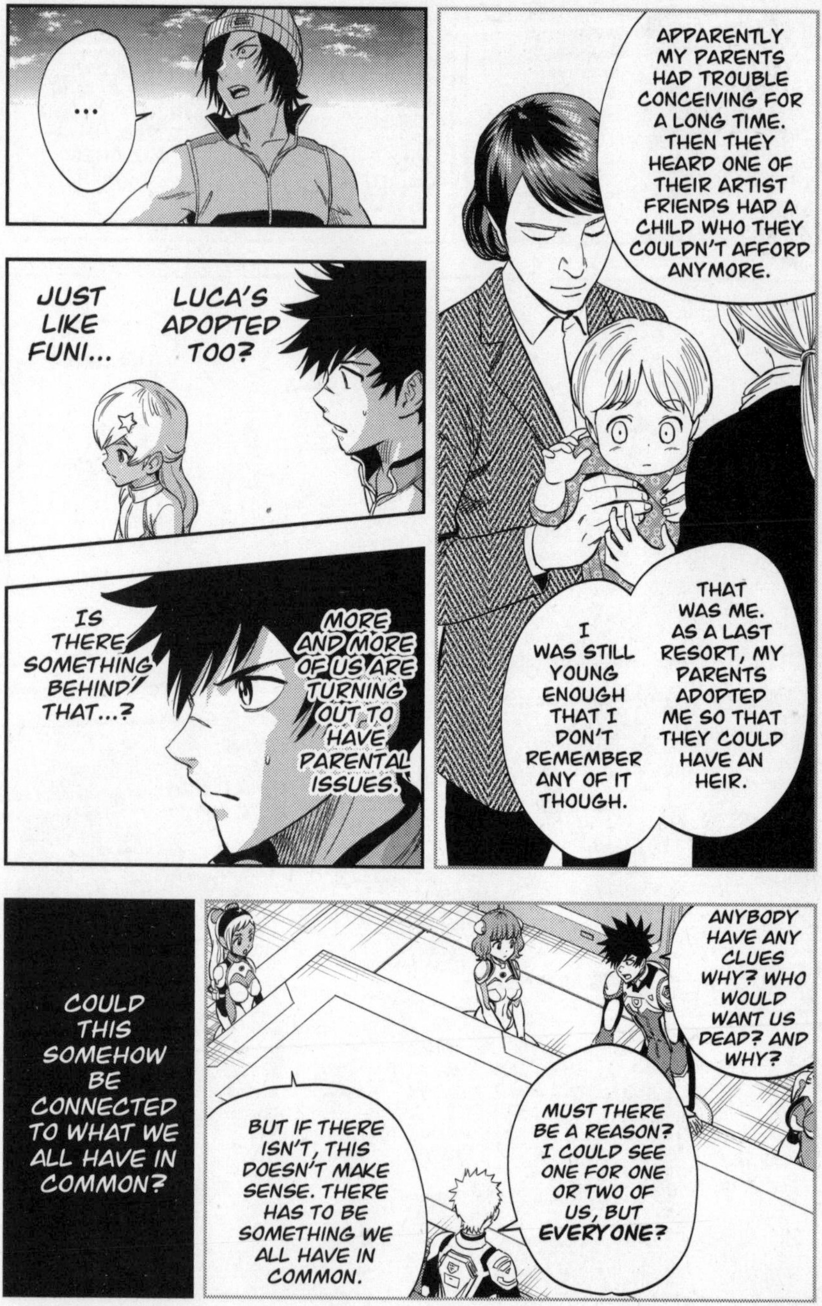
APPARENTLY MY PARENTS HAD TROUBLE CONCEIVING FOR A LONG TIME. THEN THEY HEARD ONE OF THEIR ARTIST FRIENDS HAD A CHILD WHO THEY COULDN'T AFFORD ANYMORE.
THAT WAS ME. AS A LAST RESORT, MY PARENTS ADOPTED ME SO THAT THEY COULD HAVE AN HEIR.
I WAS STILL YOUNG ENOUGH THAT I DON'T REMEMBER ANY OF IT THOUGH.
...
LUCA'S ADOPTED TOO?
JUST LIKE FUNI...
MORE AND MORE OF US ARE TURNING OUT TO HAVE PARENTAL ISSUES.
IS THERE SOMETHING BEHIND THAT...?
ANYBODY HAVE ANY CLUES WHY? WHO WOULD WANT US DEAD? AND WHY?
MUST THERE BE A REASON? I COULD SEE ONE FOR ONE OR TWO OF US, BUT **EVERYONE**?
BUT IF THERE ISN'T, THIS DOESN'T MAKE SENSE. THERE HAS TO BE SOMETHING WE ALL HAVE IN COMMON.
COULD THIS SOMEHOW BE CONNECTED TO WHAT WE ALL HAVE IN COMMON?

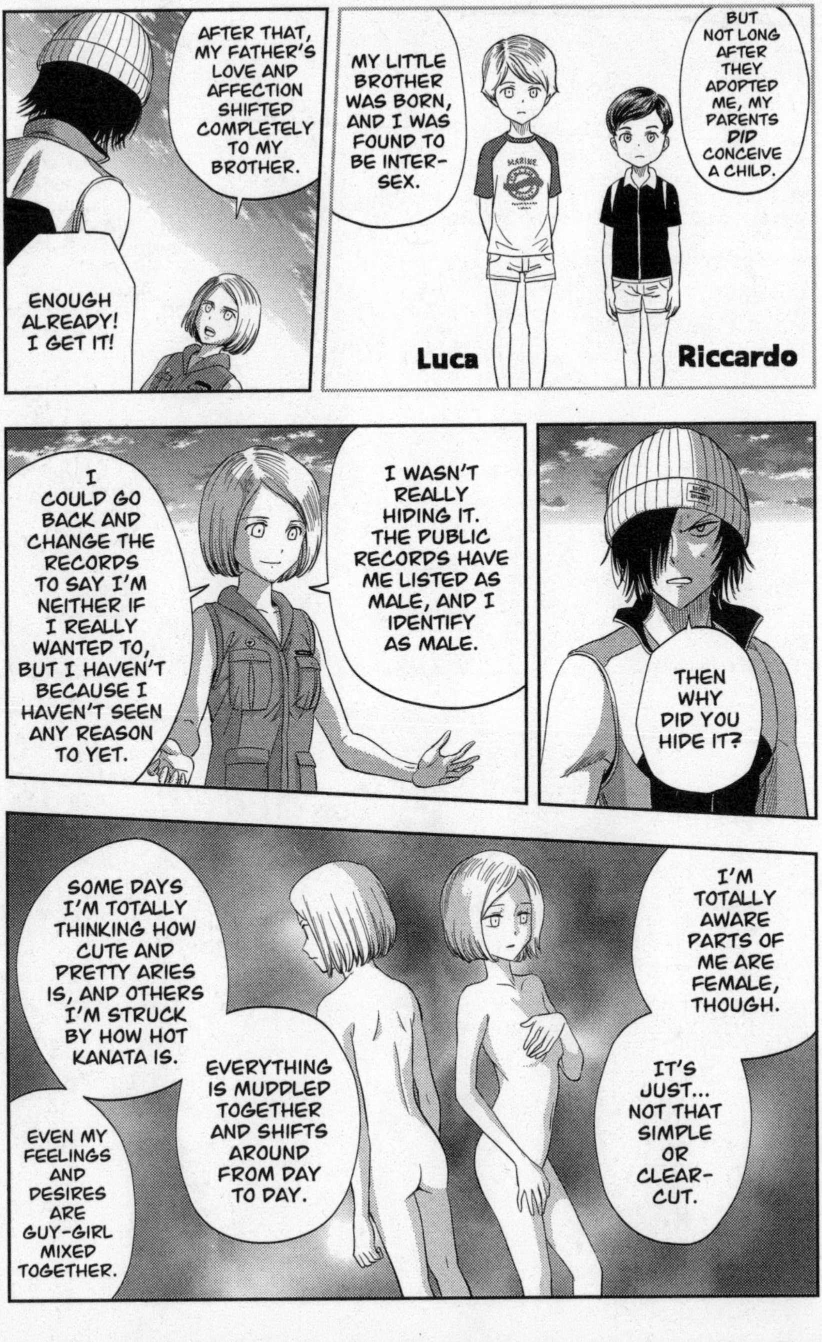
BUT NOT LONG AFTER THEY ADOPTED ME, MY PARENTS DID CONCEIVE A CHILD.
MY LITTLE BROTHER WAS BORN, AND I WAS FOUND TO BE INTER-SEX.
Riccardo
Luca
AFTER THAT, MY FATHER'S LOVE AND AFFECTION SHIFTED COMPLETELY TO MY BROTHER.
ENOUGH ALREADY! I GET IT!
THEN WHY DID YOU HIDE IT?
I WASN'T REALLY HIDING IT. THE PUBLIC RECORDS HAVE ME LISTED AS MALE, AND I IDENTIFY AS MALE.
I COULD GO BACK AND CHANGE THE RECORDS TO SAY I'M NEITHER IF I REALLY WANTED TO, BUT I HAVEN'T BECAUSE I HAVEN'T SEEN ANY REASON TO YET.
I'M TOTALLY AWARE PARTS OF ME ARE FEMALE, THOUGH.
SOME DAYS I'M TOTALLY THINKING HOW CUTE AND PRETTY ARIES IS, AND OTHERS I'M STRUCK BY HOW HOT KANATA IS.
IT'S JUST... NOT THAT SIMPLE OR CLEAR-CUT.
EVERYTHING IS MUDDLED TOGETHER AND SHIFTS AROUND FROM DAY TO DAY.
EVEN MY FEELINGS AND DESIRES ARE GUY-GIRL MIXED TOGETHER.

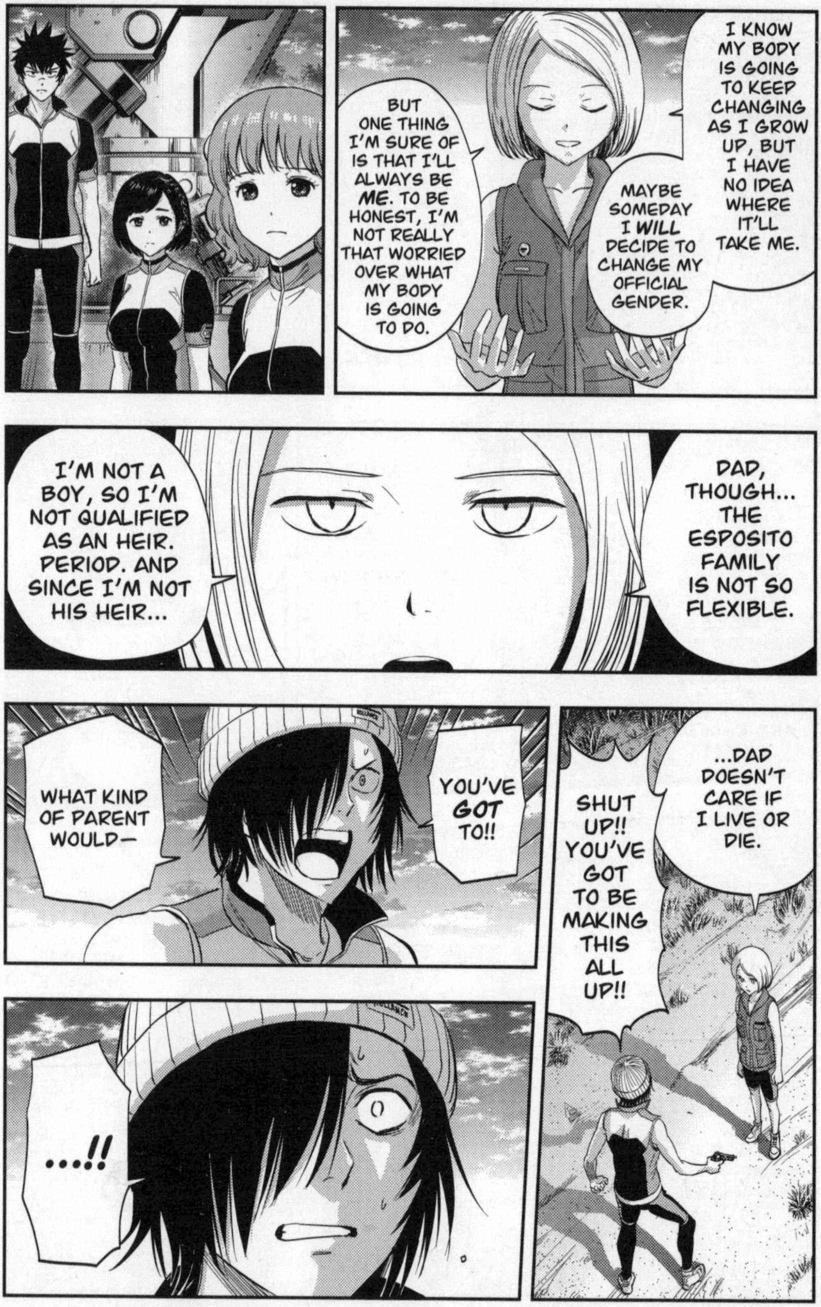

I KNOW MY BODY IS GOING TO KEEP CHANGING AS I GROW UP, BUT I HAVE NO IDEA WHERE IT'LL TAKE ME.
MAYBE SOMEDAY I WILL DECIDE TO CHANGE MY OFFICIAL GENDER.
BUT ONE THING I'M SURE OF IS THAT I'LL ALWAYS BE ME. TO BE HONEST, I'M NOT REALLY THAT WORRIED OVER WHAT MY BODY IS GOING TO DO.
DAD, THOUGH... THE ESPOSITO FAMILY IS NOT SO FLEXIBLE.
I'M NOT A BOY, SO I'M NOT QUALIFIED AS AN HEIR. PERIOD. AND SINCE I'M NOT HIS HEIR...
...DAD DOESN'T CARE IF I LIVE OR DIE.
SHUT UP!! YOU'VE GOT TO BE MAKING THIS ALL UP!!
YOU'VE GOT TO!!
WHAT KIND OF PARENT WOULD—
...!!

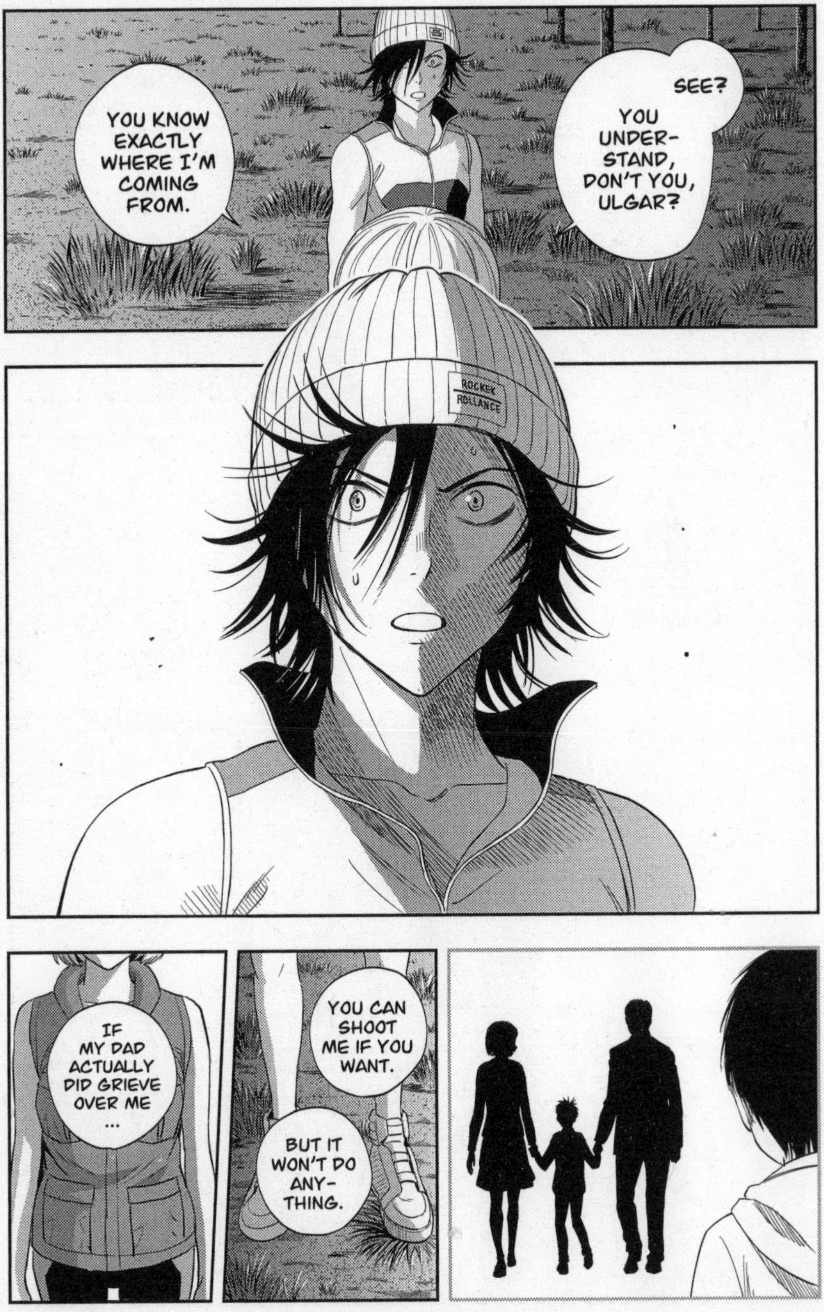
SEE?
YOU UNDER-STAND, DON'T YOU, ULGAR?
YOU KNOW EXACTLY WHERE I'M COMING FROM.
YOU CAN SHOOT ME IF YOU WANT.
BUT IT WON'T DO ANY-THING.
IF MY DAD ACTUALLY DID GRIEVE OVER ME ...

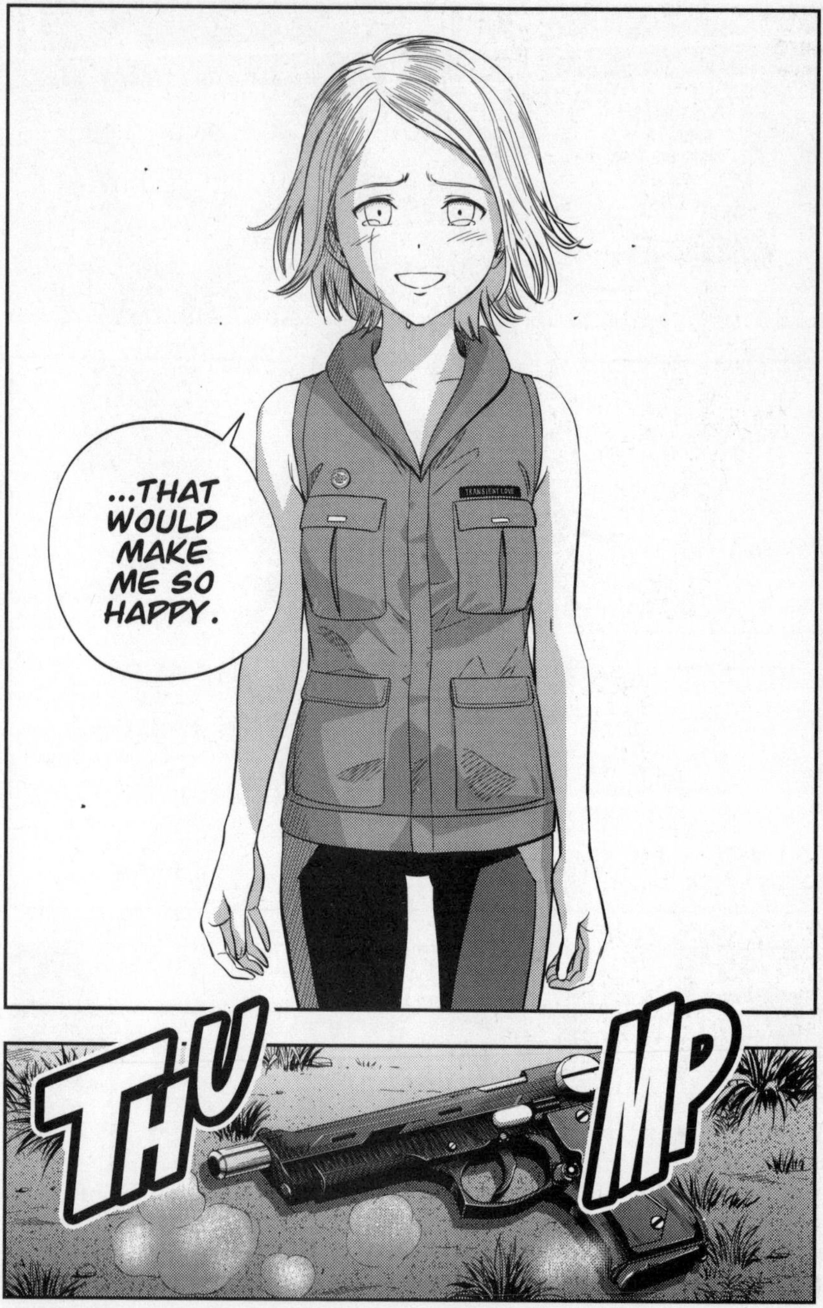
...THAT WOULD MAKE ME SO HAPPY.
THUMP

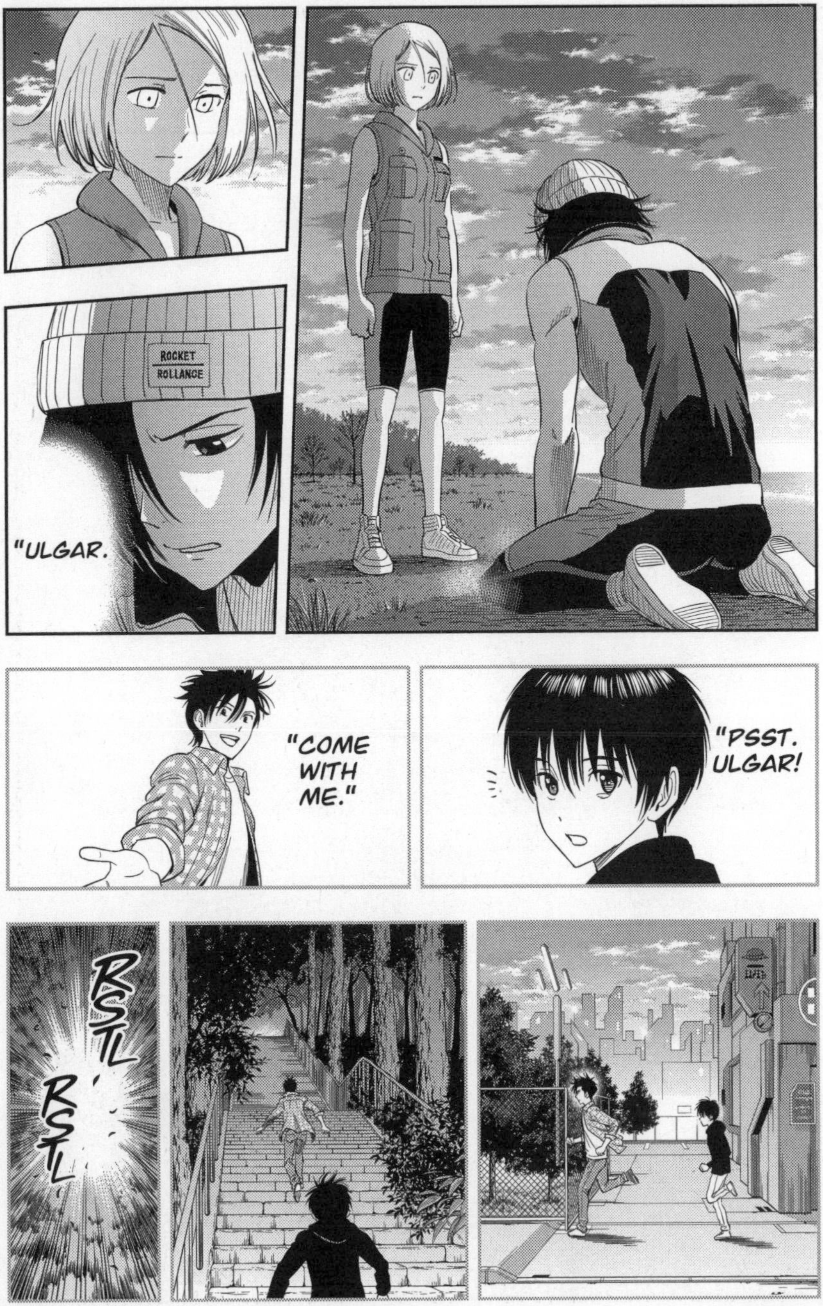
"ULGAR.
"PSST. ULGAR!
"COME WITH ME."
RSTL RSTL

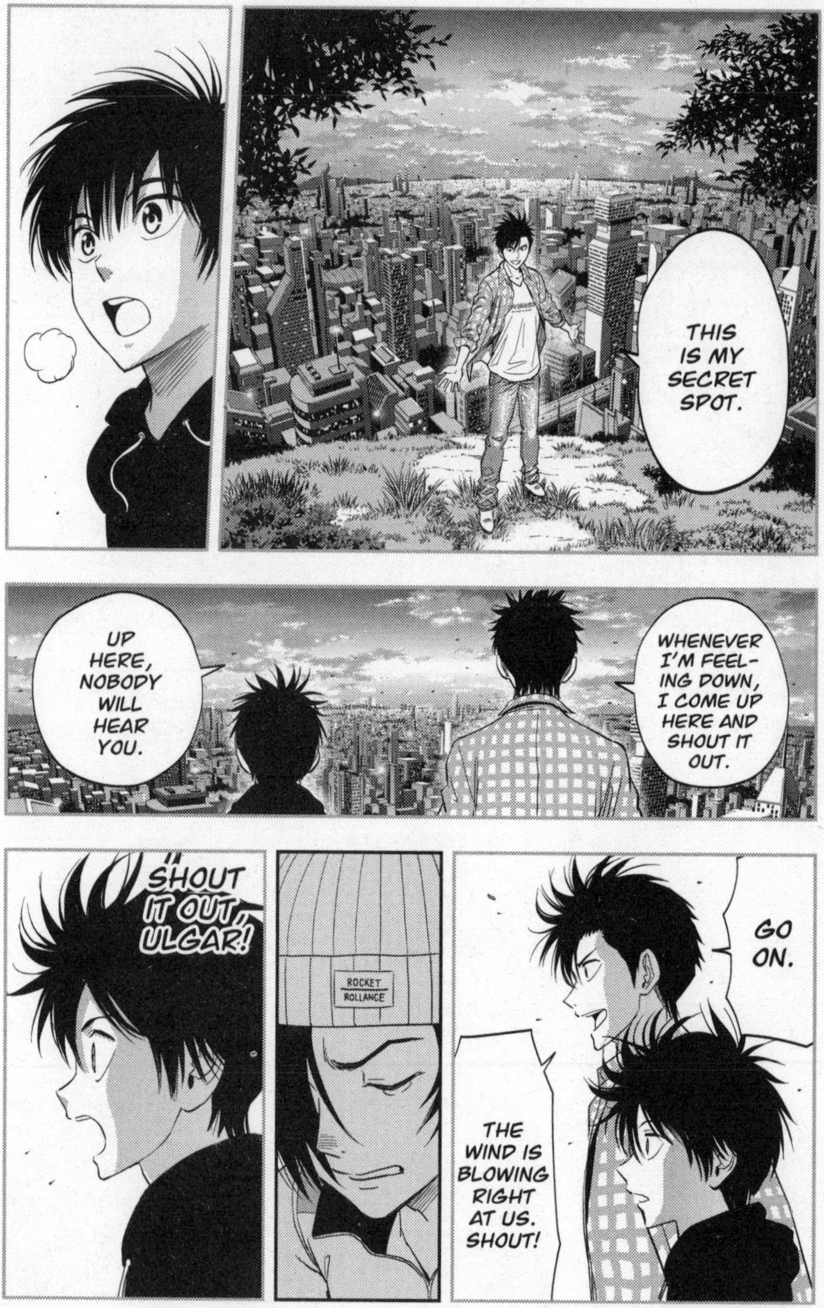
THIS IS MY SECRET SPOT.
WHENEVER I'M FEEL-ING DOWN, I COME UP HERE AND SHOUT IT OUT.
UP HERE, NOBODY WILL HEAR YOU.
GO ON.
THE WIND IS BLOWING RIGHT AT US. SHOUT!
ROCKET ROLLANCE
"SHOUT IT OUT, ULGAR!

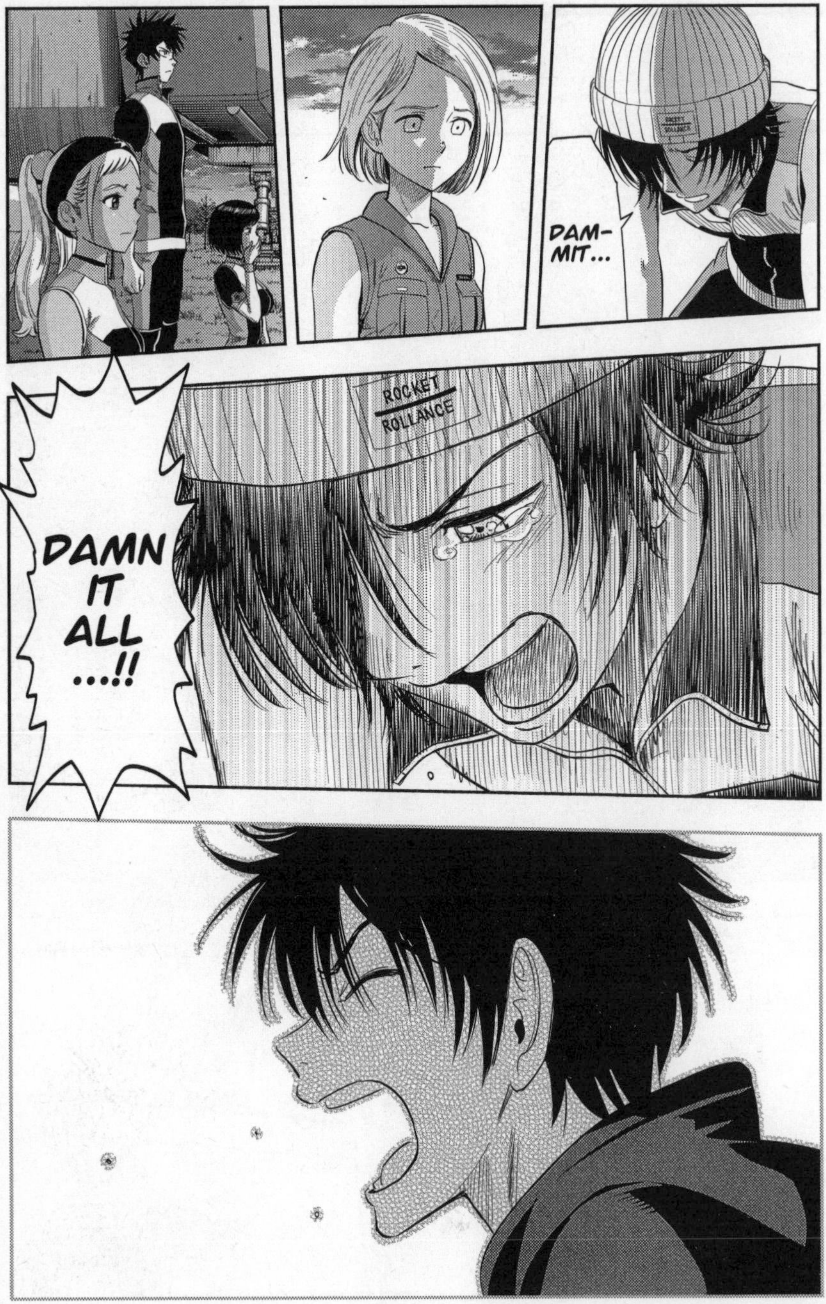
DAM-
MIT...
ROCKET
ROLLANCE
DAMN IT ALL ...!!

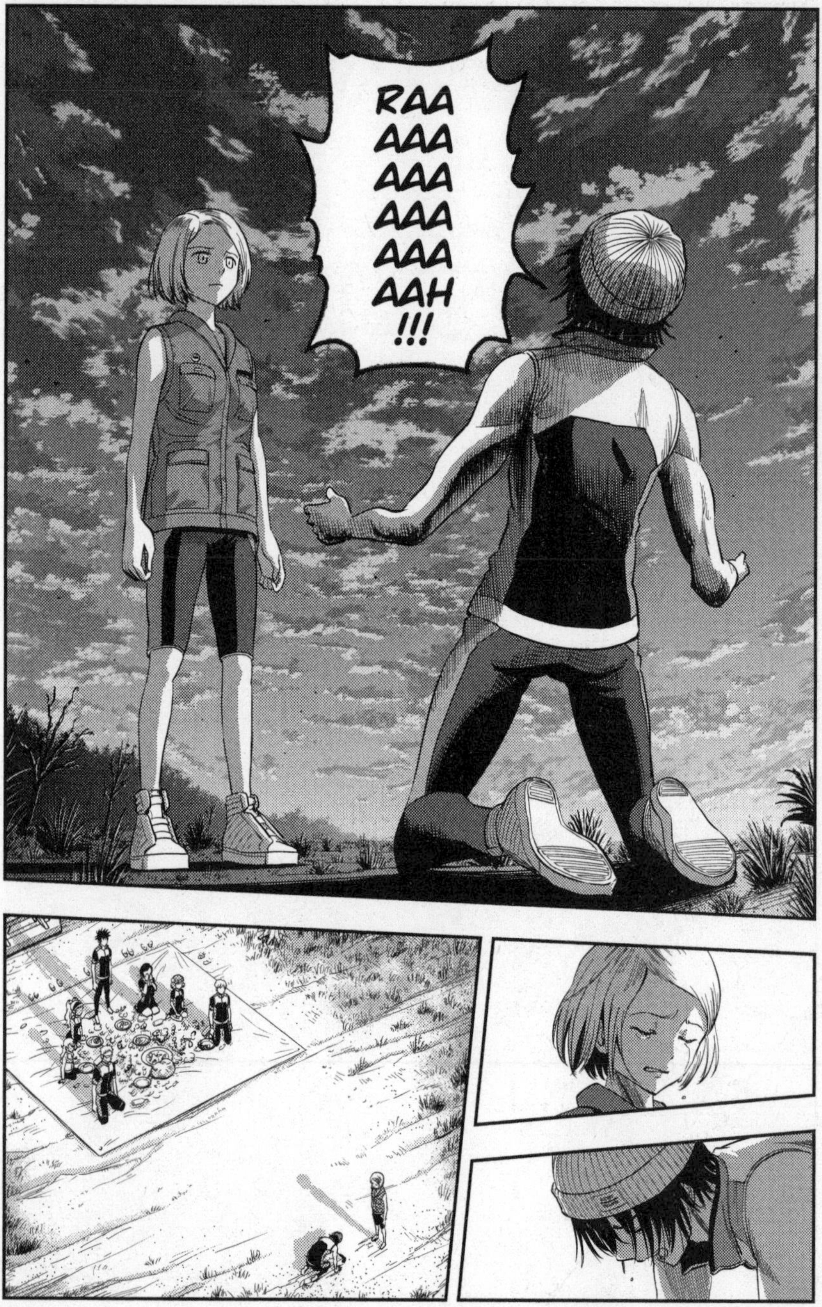
RAAAAAAAAAAAAAAAAAH!!!

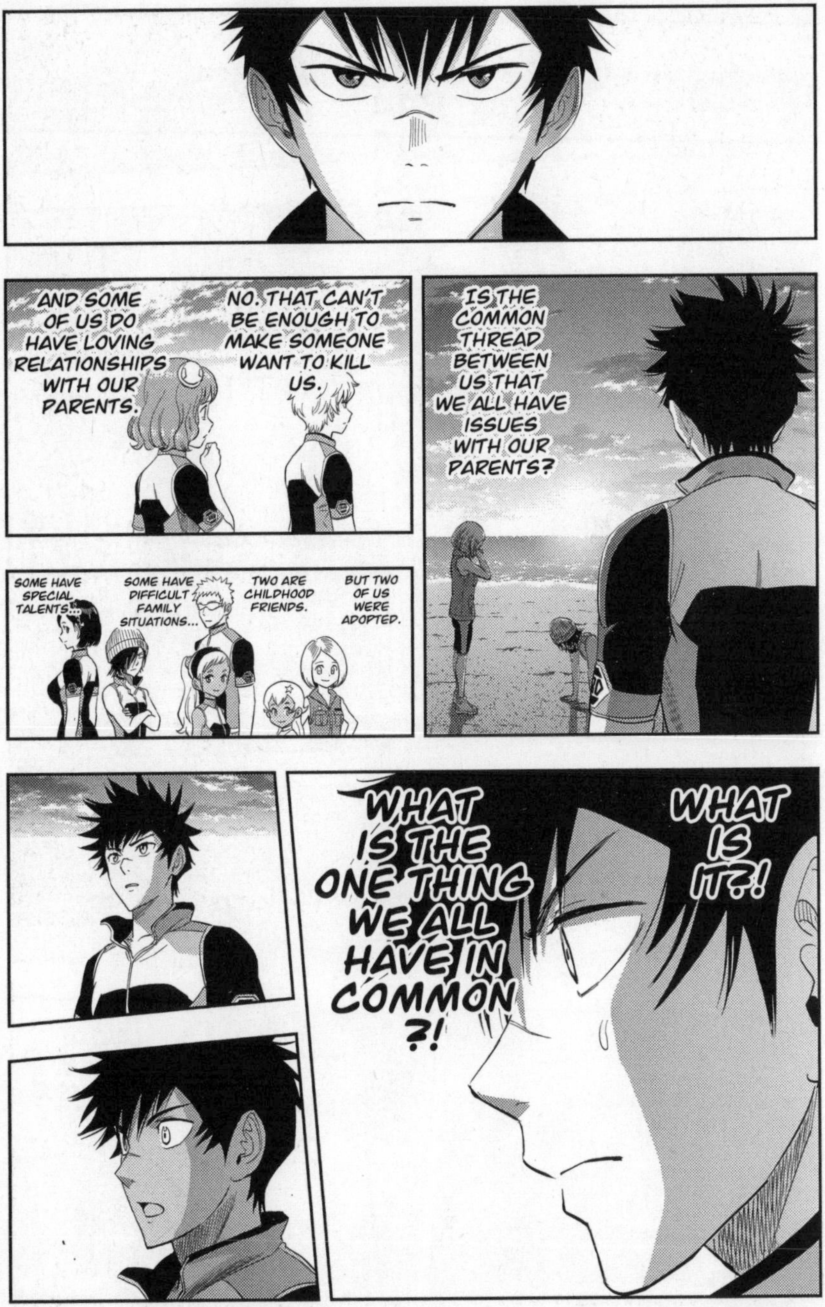
IS THE COMMON THREAD BETWEEN US THAT WE ALL HAVE ISSUES WITH OUR PARENTS?
NO. THAT CAN'T BE ENOUGH TO MAKE SOMEONE WANT TO KILL US.
AND SOME OF US DO HAVE LOVING RELATIONSHIPS WITH OUR PARENTS.
BUT TWO OF US WERE ADOPTED.
TWO ARE CHILDHOOD FRIENDS.
SOME HAVE DIFFICULT FAMILY SITUATIONS...
SOME HAVE SPECIAL TALENTS...
WHAT IS IT?!
WHAT IS THE ONE THING WE ALL HAVE IN COMMON?!

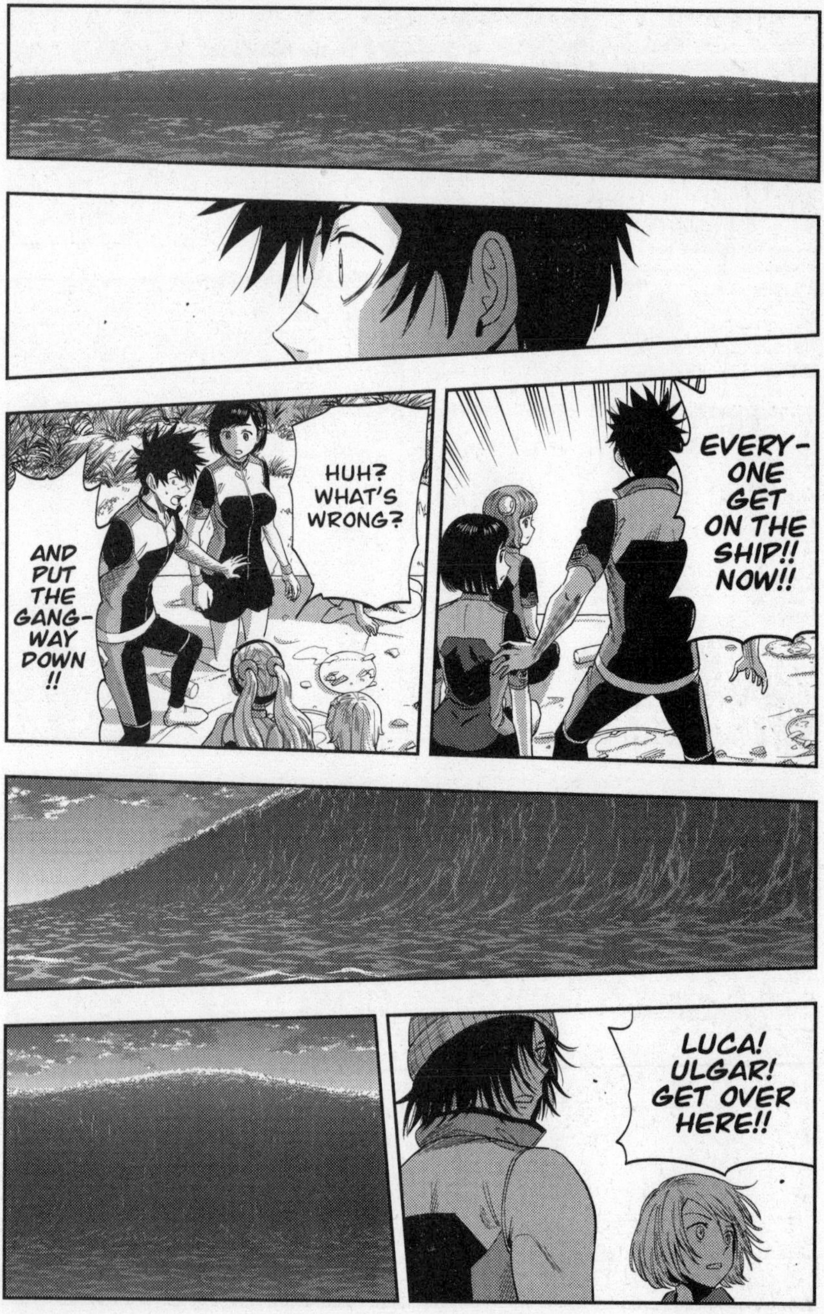
EVERY-ONE GET ON THE SHIP!! NOW!!
HUH? WHAT'S WRONG?
AND PUT THE GANG-WAY DOWN!!
LUCA! ULGAR! GET OVER HERE!!

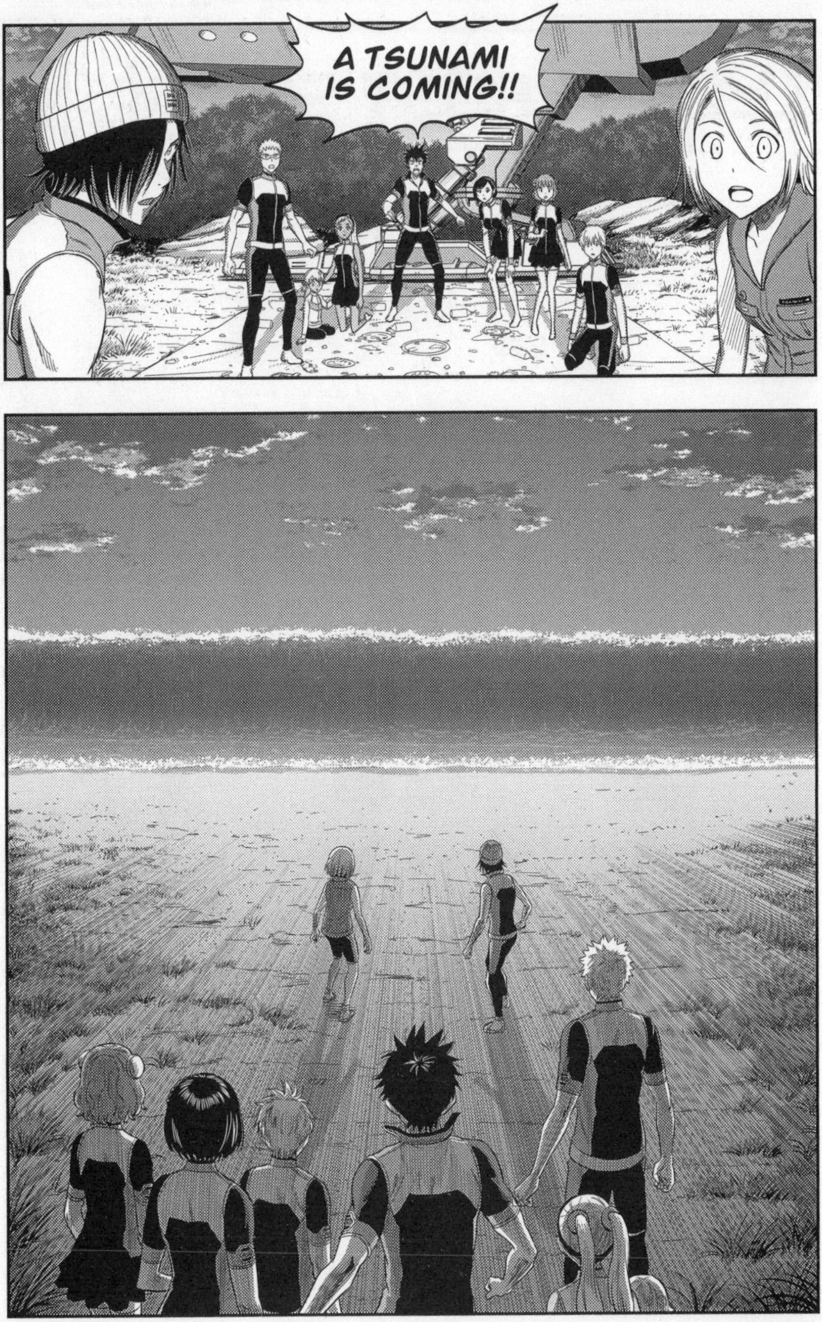
A TSUNAMI IS COMING!!

Material Collection Costume Design

LUCA'S CRUST SUIT

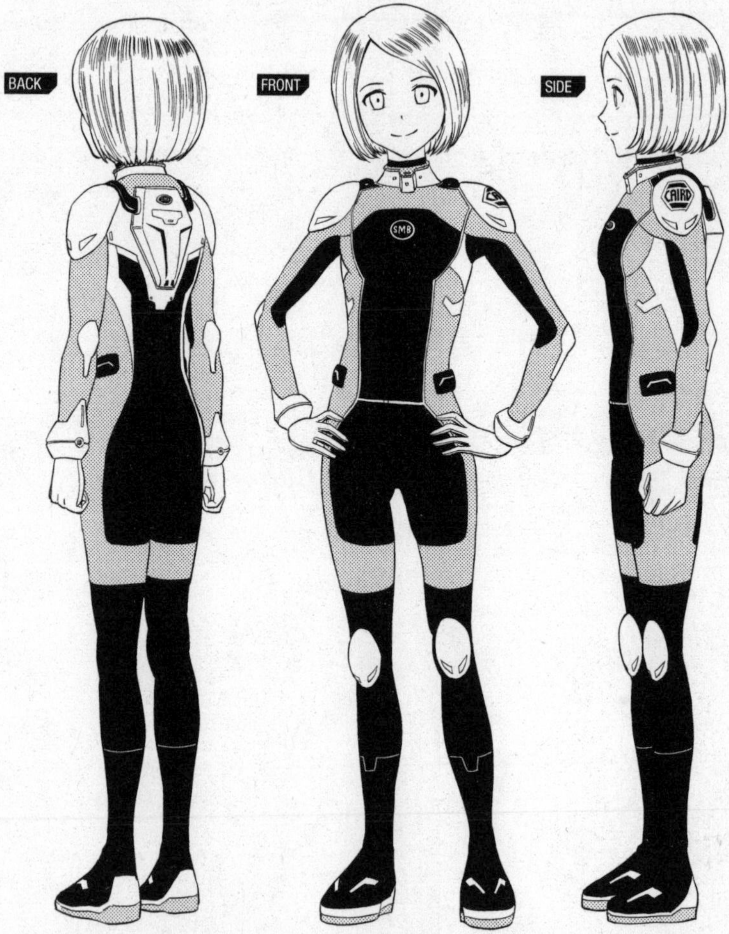
BACK
FRONT
SIDE
SMB
CAIRD

SMB men's crust suit.

Green and blue.

This is the generic model designed to fit any body type.

ASTRA LOST IN SPACE

#24

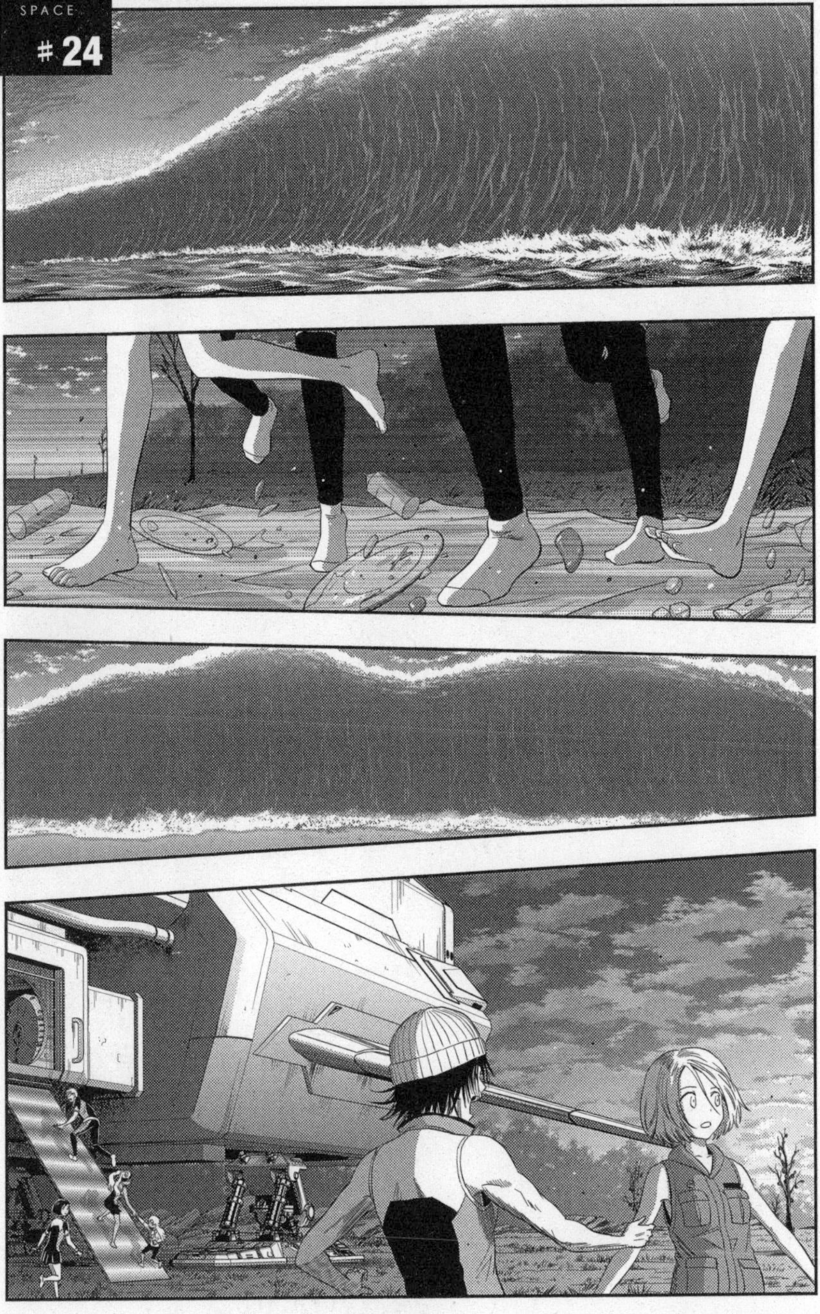

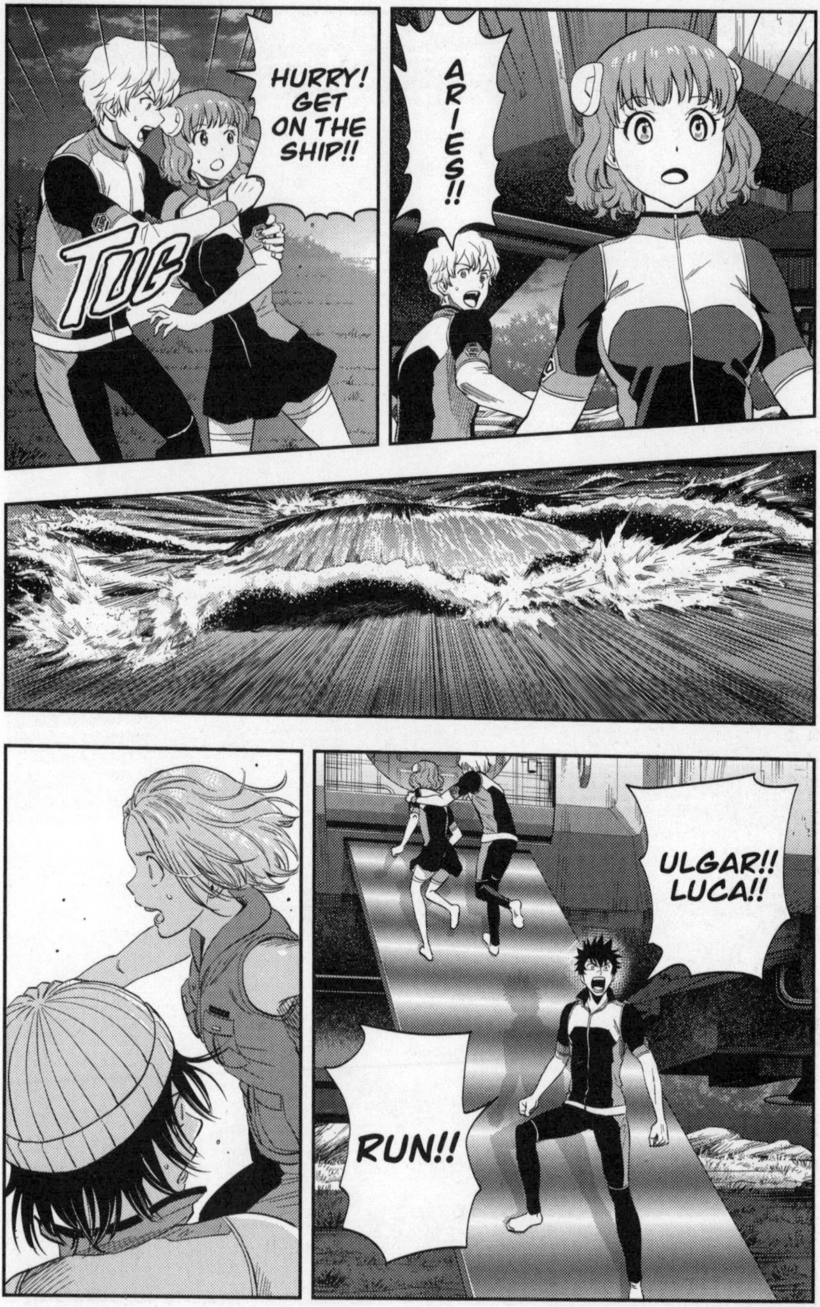
ARIES!!
HURRY! GET ON THE SHIP!!
TUG
ULGAR!! LUCA!!
RUN!!

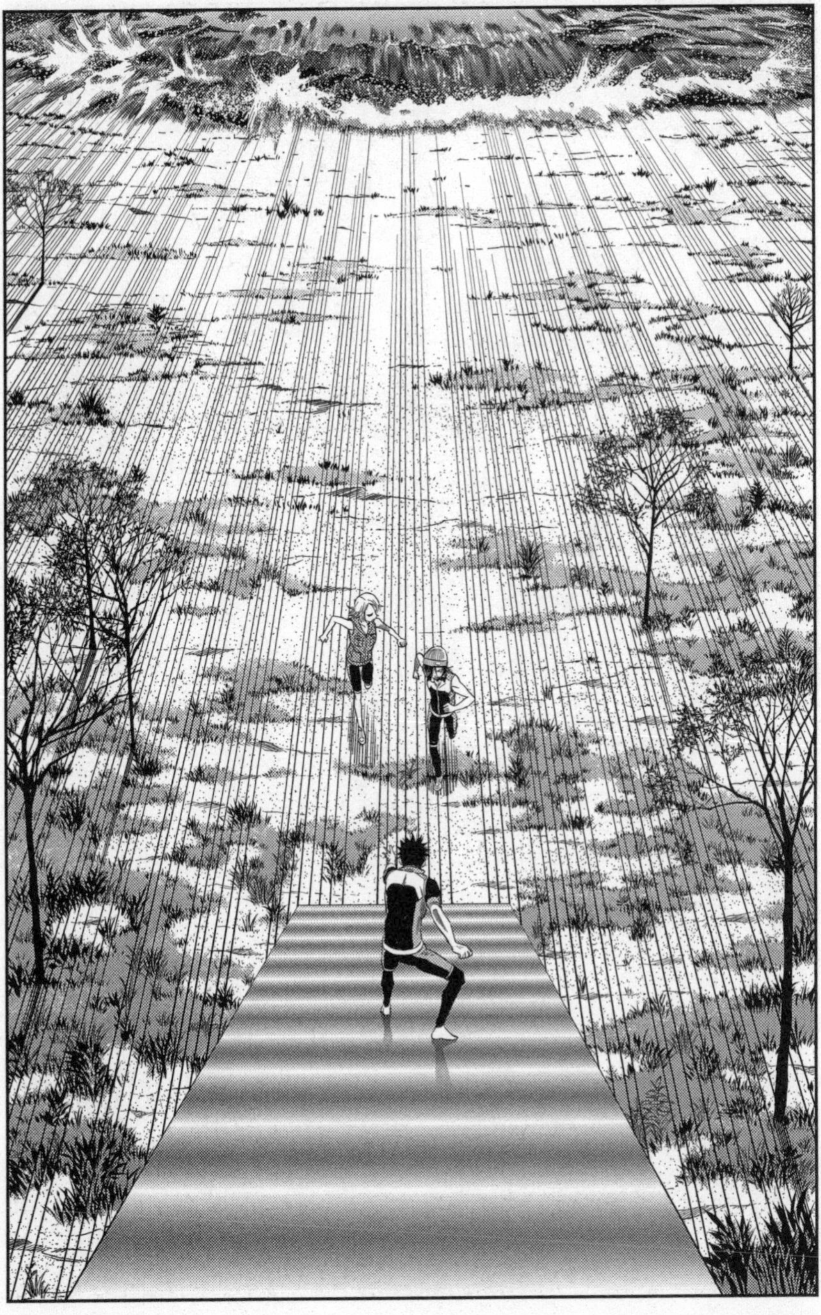

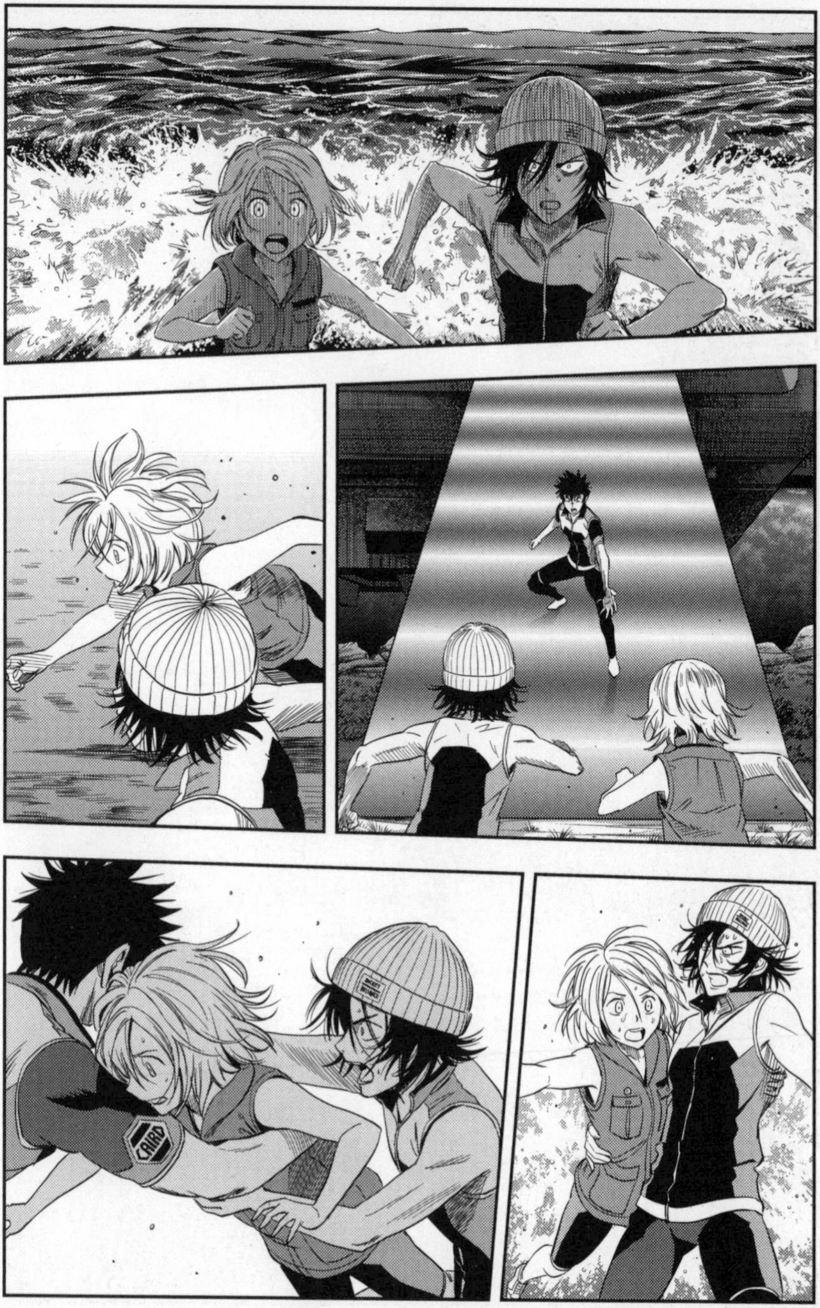
CAIRO

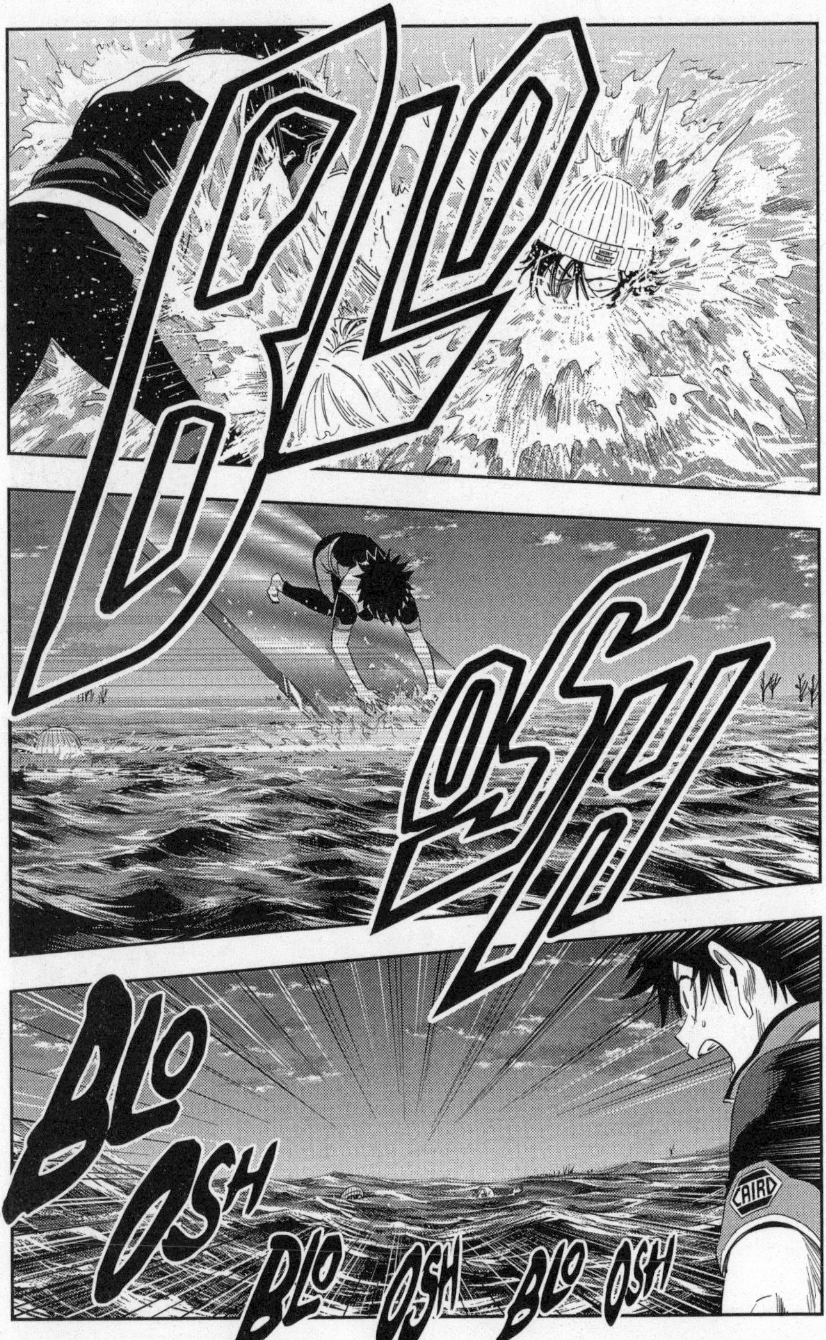
BLOOSH
CAIRD
BLO OSH
BLO OSH
BLO OSH

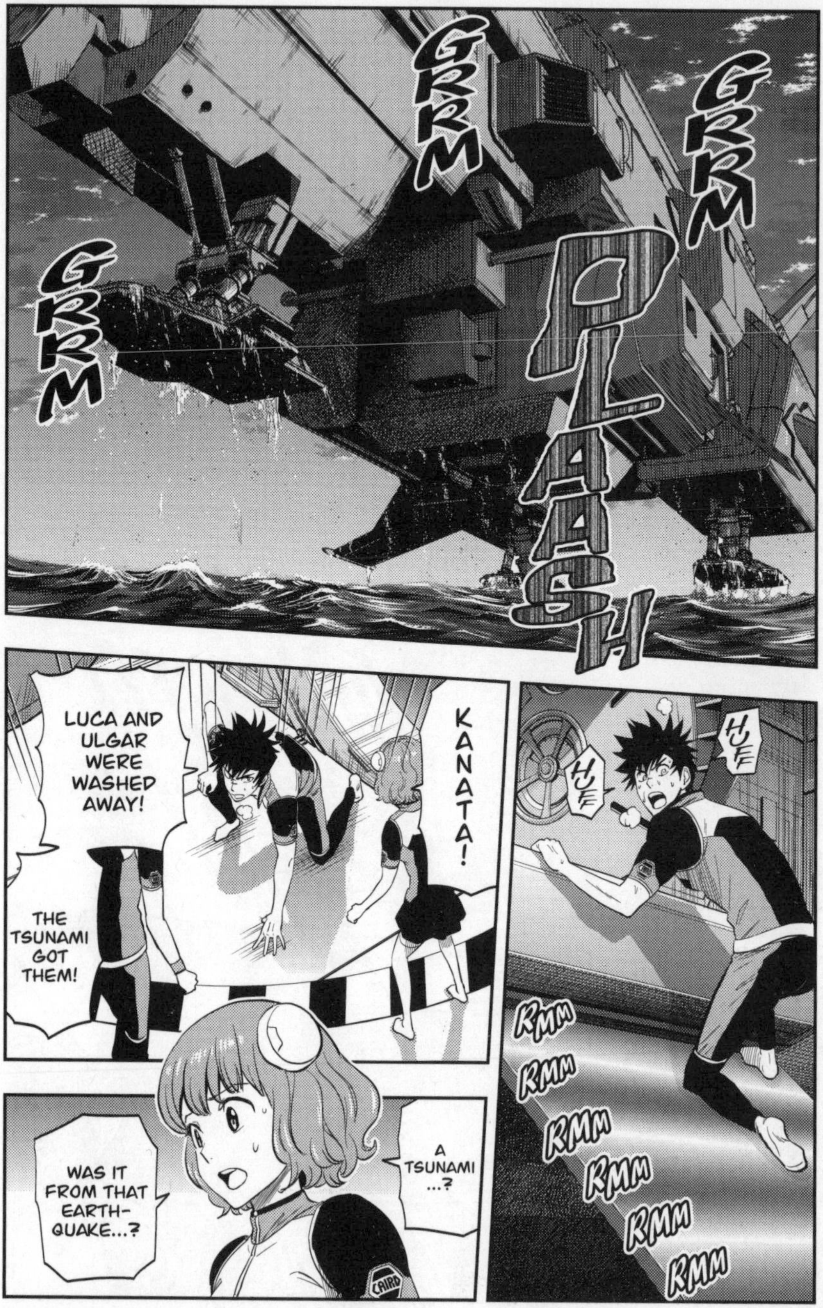
GRRM
GRRM
PLASH
GRRM
HUFF
HUFF
RMM
RMM
RMM
RMM
RMM
RMM
KANATA!
LUCA AND ULGAR WERE WASHED AWAY!
THE TSUNAMI GOT THEM!
A TSUNAMI ...?
WAS IT FROM THAT EARTH-QUAKE...?

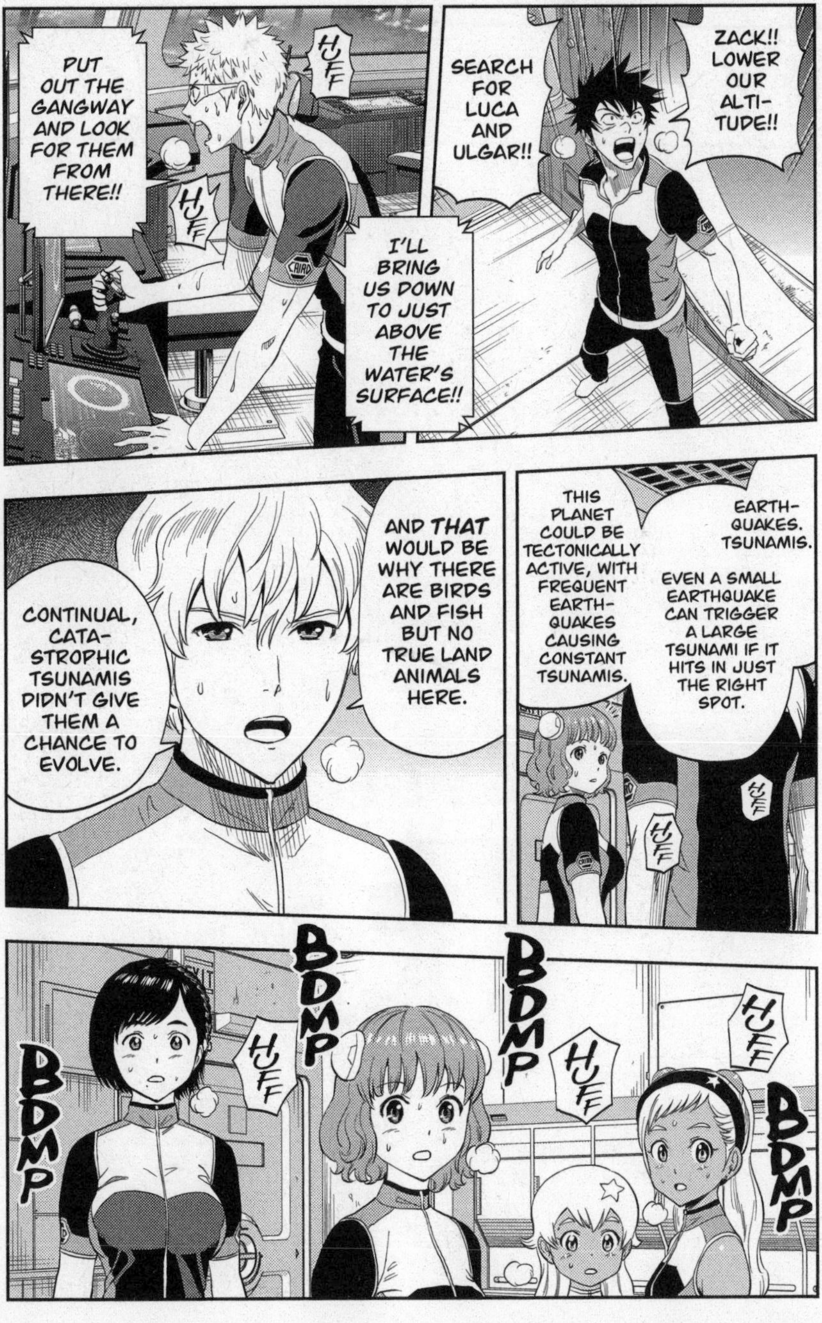
ZACK!! LOWER OUR ALTI-TUDE!!
SEARCH FOR LUCA AND ULGAR!!
HUFF
I'LL BRING US DOWN TO JUST ABOVE THE WATER'S SURFACE!!
PUT OUT THE GANGWAY AND LOOK FOR THEM FROM THERE!!
HUFF
EARTH-QUAKES. TSUNAMIS.
EVEN A SMALL EARTHQUAKE CAN TRIGGER A LARGE TSUNAMI IF IT HITS IN JUST THE RIGHT SPOT.
THIS PLANET COULD BE TECTONICALLY ACTIVE, WITH FREQUENT EARTH-QUAKES CAUSING CONSTANT TSUNAMIS.
HUFF
HUFF
AND THAT WOULD BE WHY THERE ARE BIRDS AND FISH BUT NO TRUE LAND ANIMALS HERE.
CONTINUAL, CATA-STROPHIC TSUNAMIS DIDN'T GIVE THEM A CHANCE TO EVOLVE.
BDMP
HUFF
BDMP
HUFF
BDMP
HUFF
BDMP
HUFF
BDMP

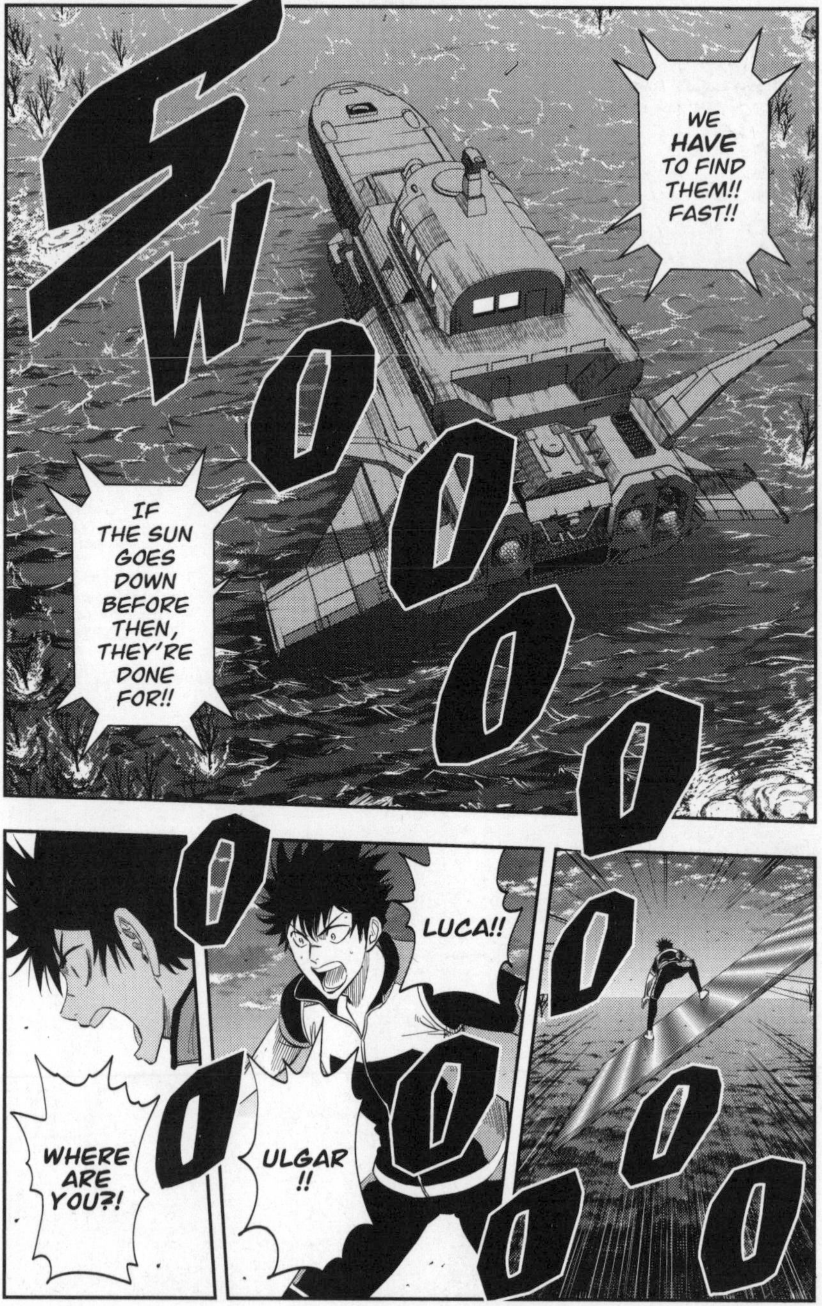
WE HAVE TO FIND THEM!! FAST!!
SWOOOOOOOOOOO
IF THE SUN GOES DOWN BEFORE THEN, THEY'RE DONE FOR!!
LUCA!!
ULGAR!!
WHERE ARE YOU?!

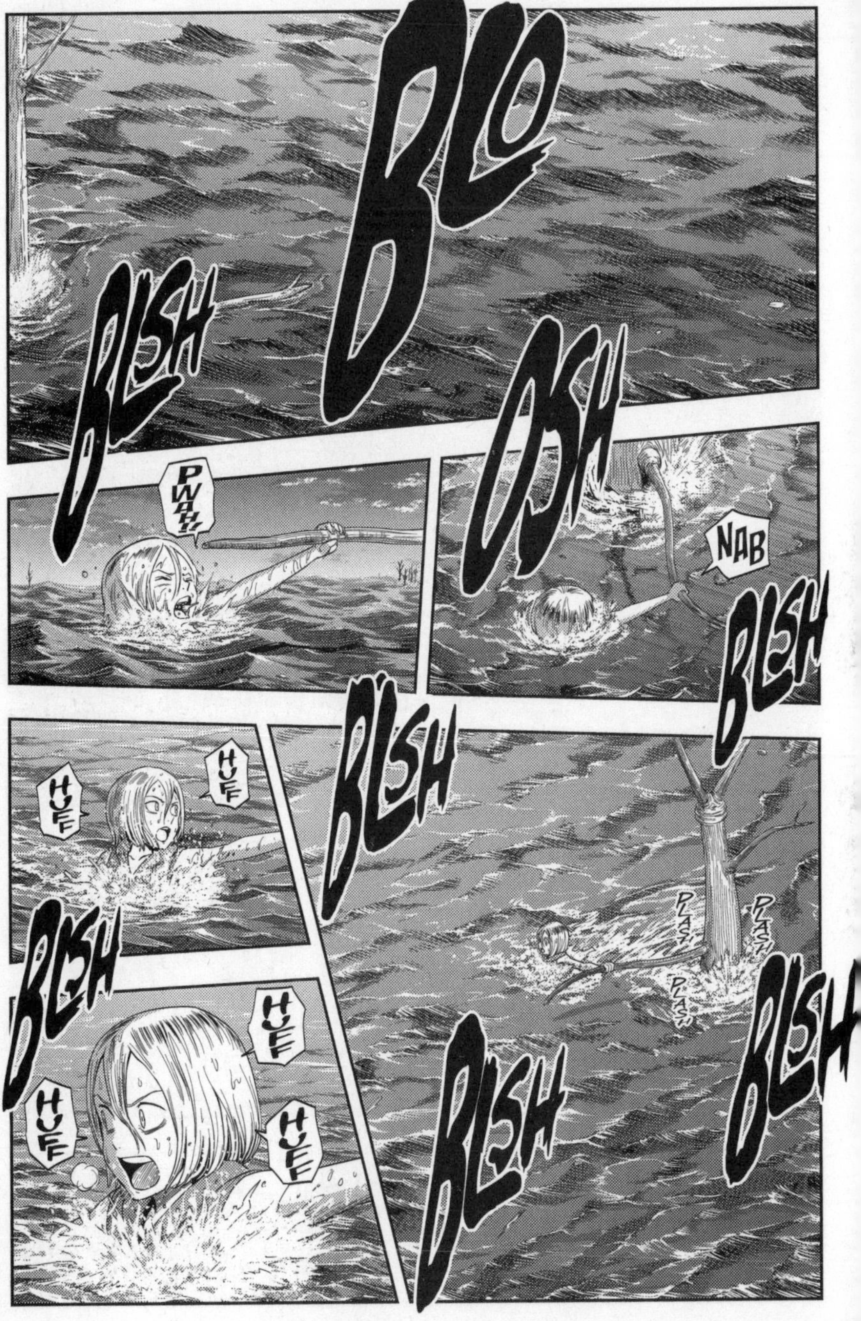
BLOOSH
BLISH
NAB
BLISH
PWAH!!
BLISH
PLASH
PLASH
PLASH
BLISH
BLISH
HUFF
HUFF
BLISH
HUFF
HUFF
HUFF

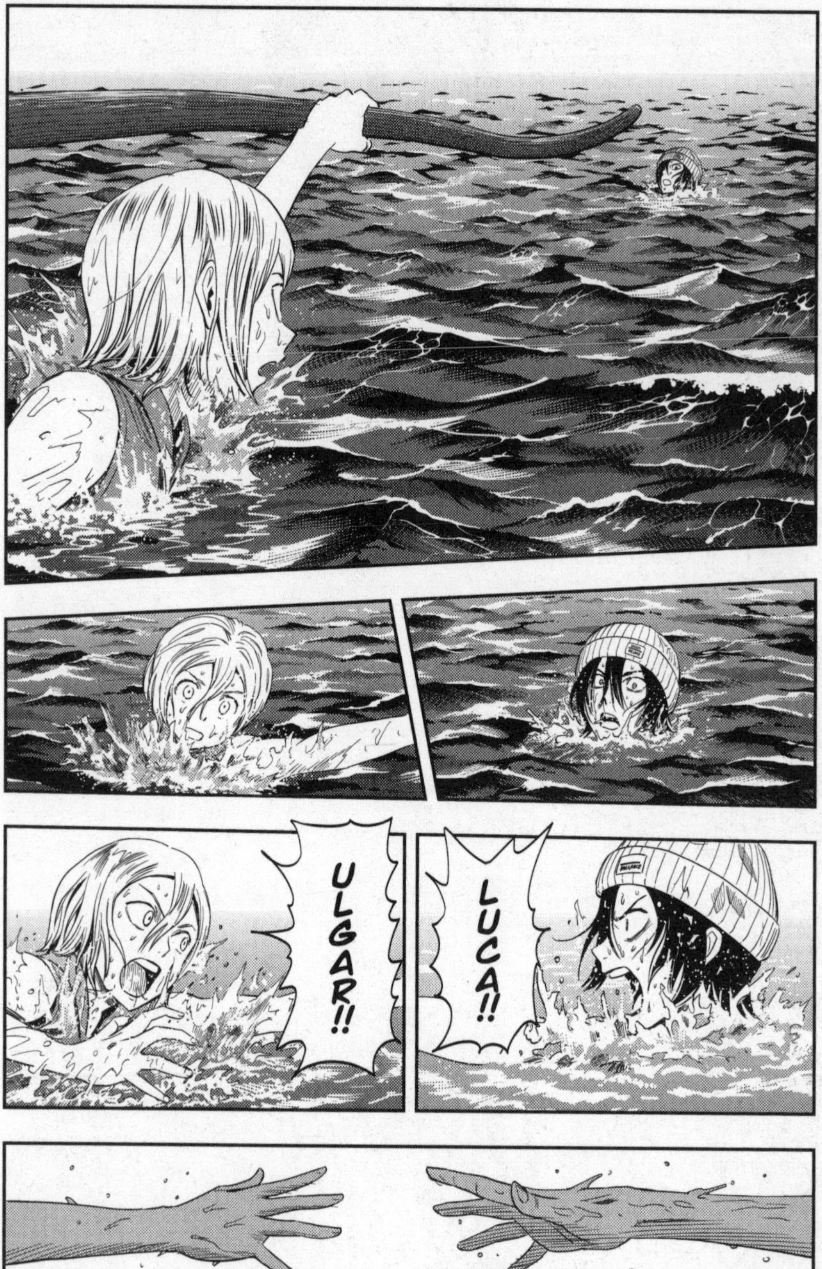
LUCA!!
ULGAR!!

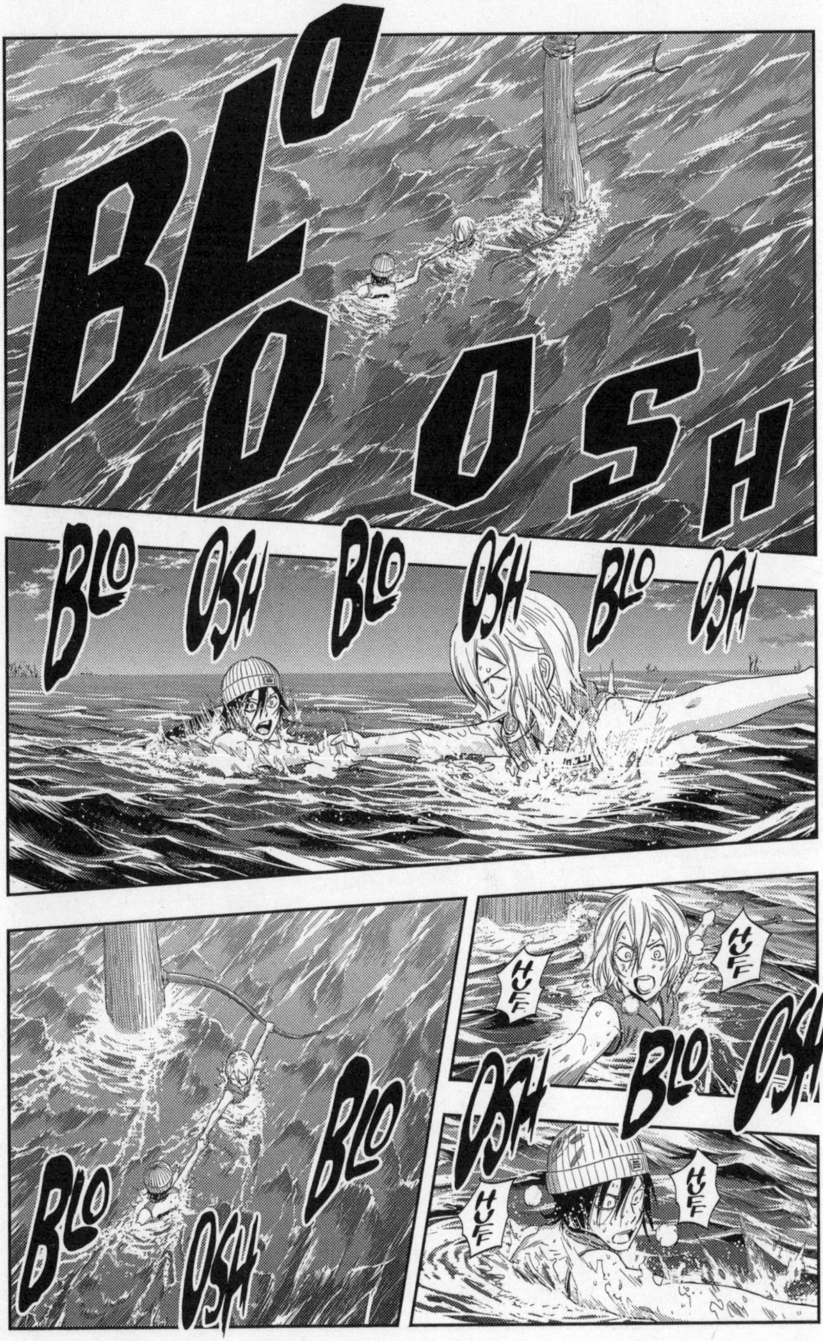
BLOOOOSH
BLOOSH BLOOSH BLOOSH
HUFF HUFF
BLOOSH OSH
HUFF HUFF
BLOOSH BLO

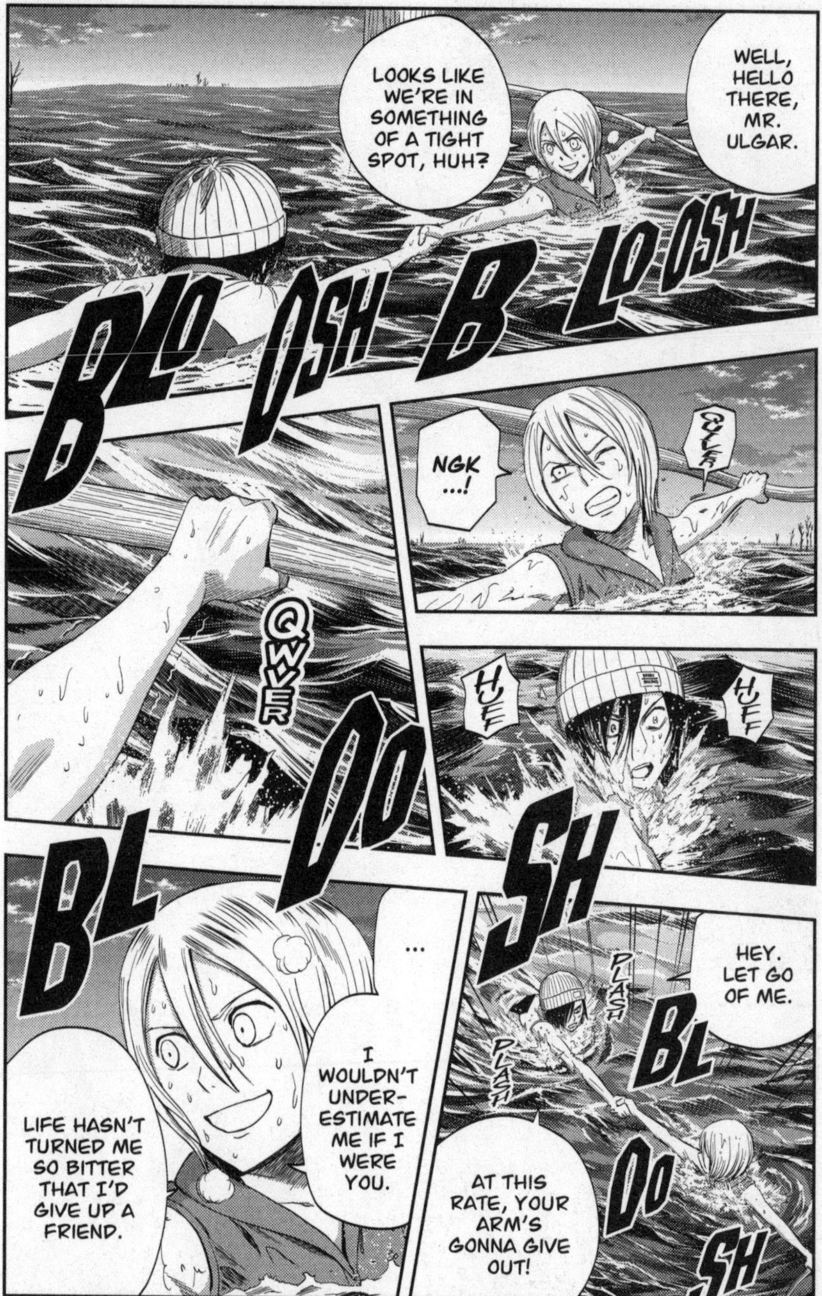
WELL, HELLO THERE, MR. ULGAR.
LOOKS LIKE WE'RE IN SOMETHING OF A TIGHT SPOT, HUH?
BLOOSH
BLOOSH
GULLER
NGK ...!
HUFF
HUFF
QWVER
BLOOSH
HEY. LET GO OF ME.
PLASH
PLASH
AT THIS RATE, YOUR ARM'S GONNA GIVE OUT!
BLOOSH
...
I WOULDN'T UNDER-ESTIMATE ME IF I WERE YOU.
LIFE HASN'T TURNED ME SO BITTER THAT I'D GIVE UP A FRIEND.

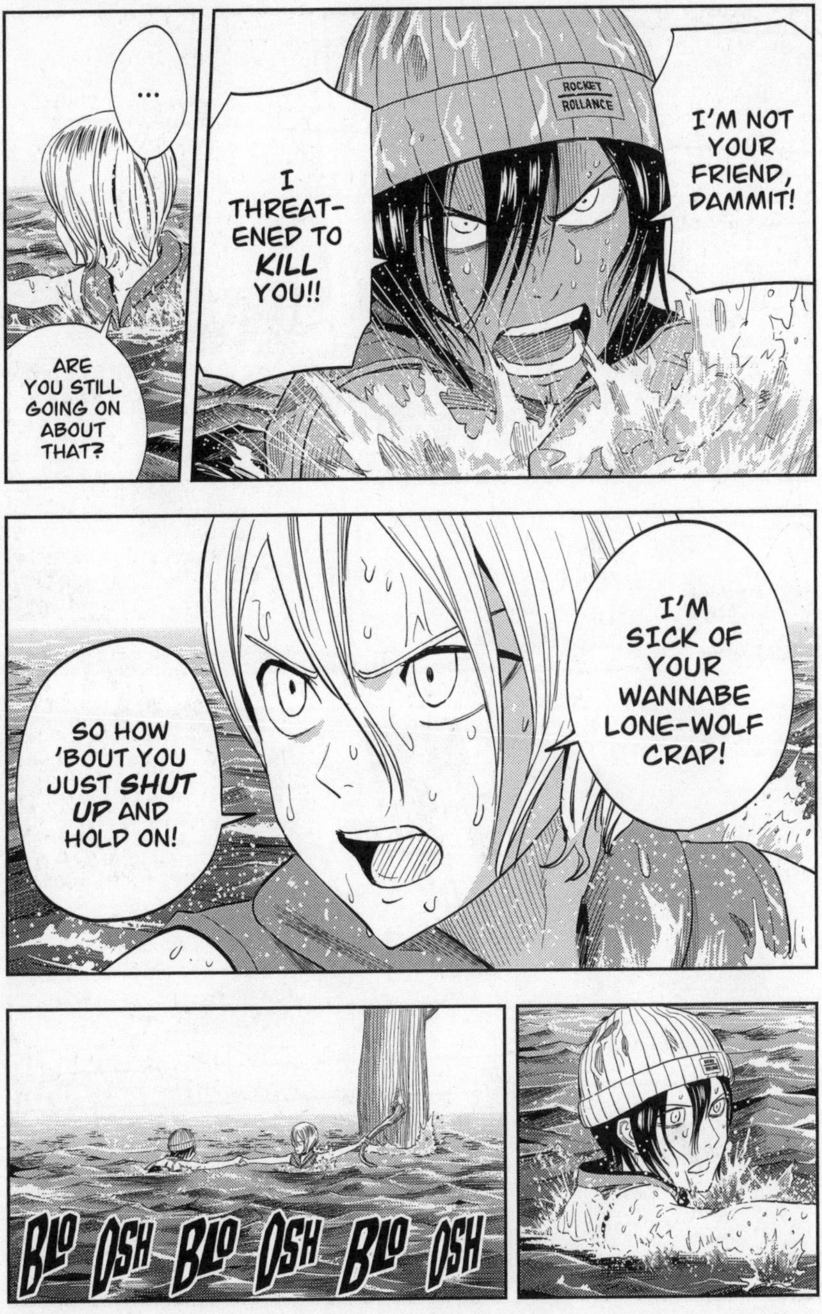
ROCKET ROLLANCE
I'M NOT YOUR FRIEND, DAMMIT!
I THREAT-ENED TO KILL YOU!!
...
ARE YOU STILL GOING ON ABOUT THAT?
I'M SICK OF YOUR WANNABE LONE-WOLF CRAP!
SO HOW 'BOUT YOU JUST SHUT UP AND HOLD ON!
BLOOSH BLOOSH BLOOSH

REMEM-BER THE CAPTAIN'S STORY?

Y'KNOW, THE ONE ABOUT WHEN HE WAS STRANDED ON THAT MOUNTAIN AND WAS SO WORN DOWN THAT HE COULDN'T SAVE HIS TEACHER?

...

NO WAY I'M MAKIN' ANYONE ELSE LUG THOSE KINDS OF REGRETS AROUND FOR THE REST OF THEIR LIFE BECAUSE OF ME.

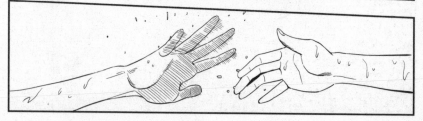

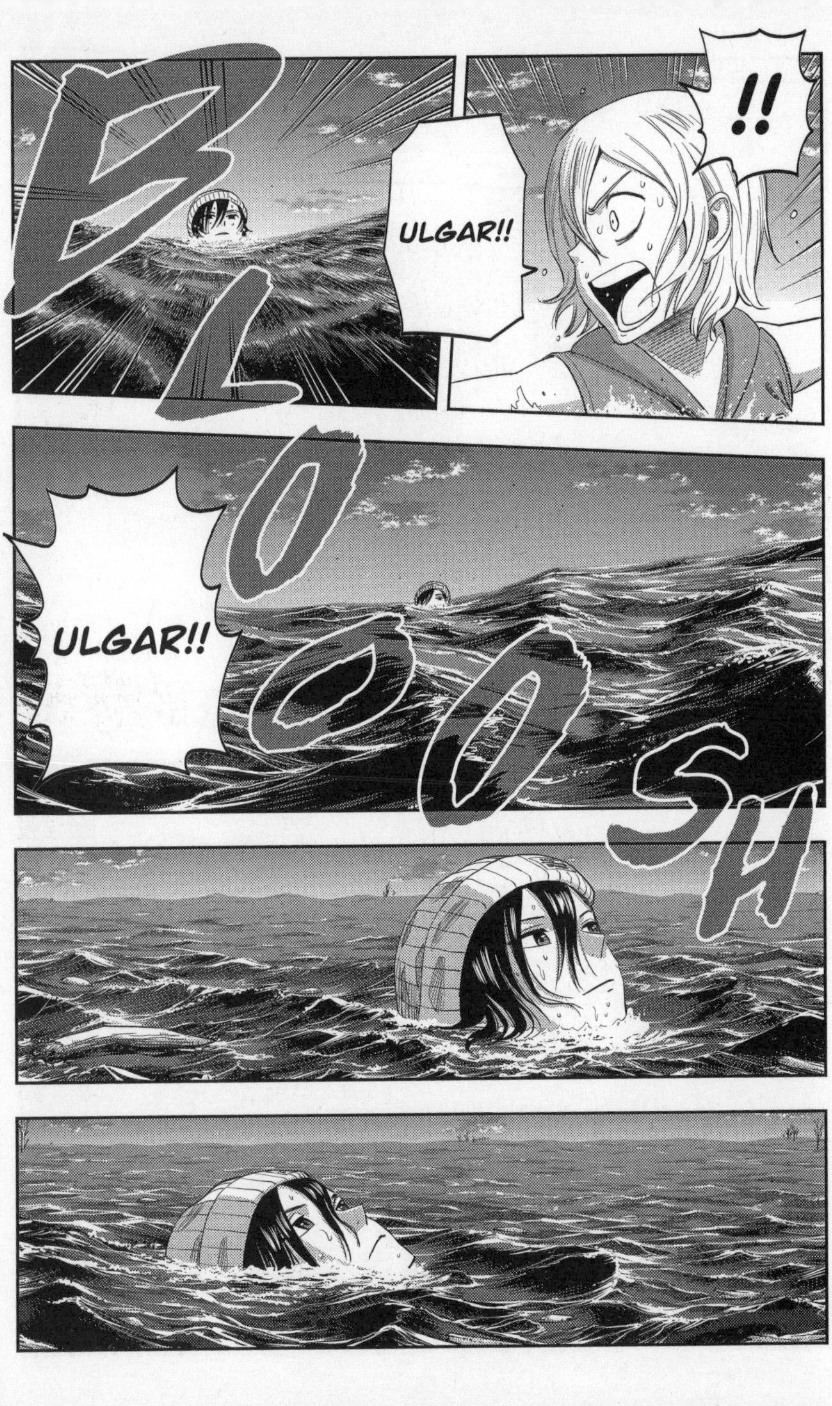
!!
ULGAR!!
SLOOOOSH
ULGAR!!

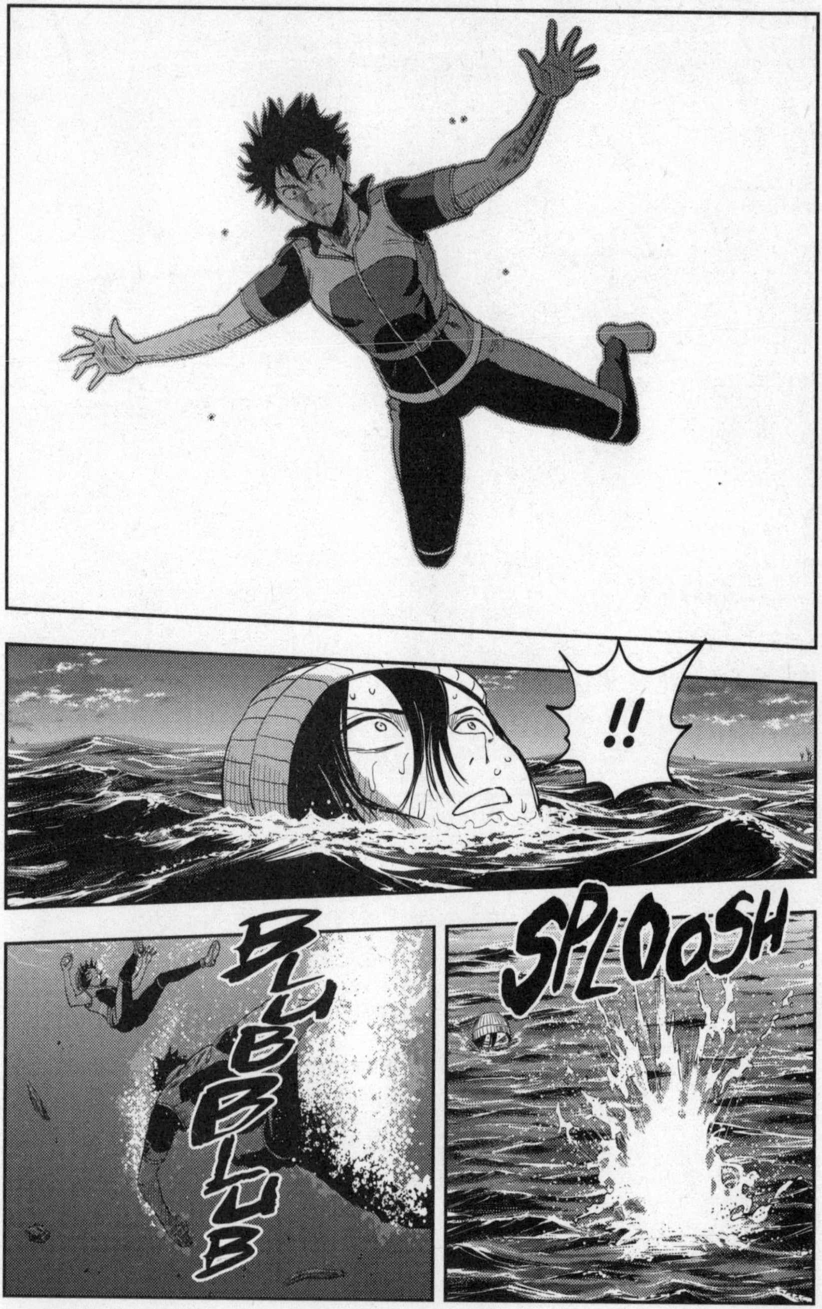
!!
SPLOOSH
BLUB BLUB

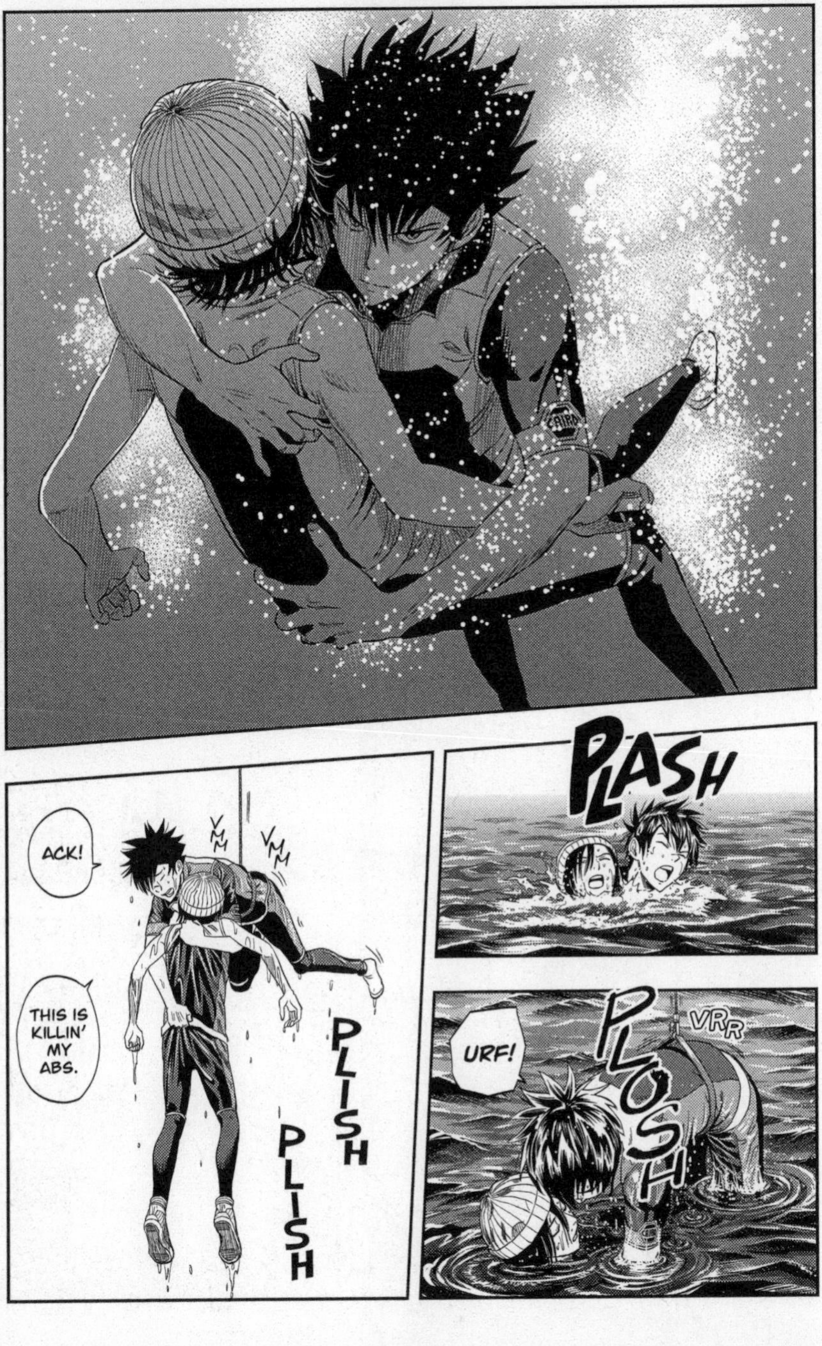
PLASH
VRR
PLOSH
URF!
VMM
VMM
ACK!
THIS IS KILLIN' MY ABS.
PLISH
PLISH

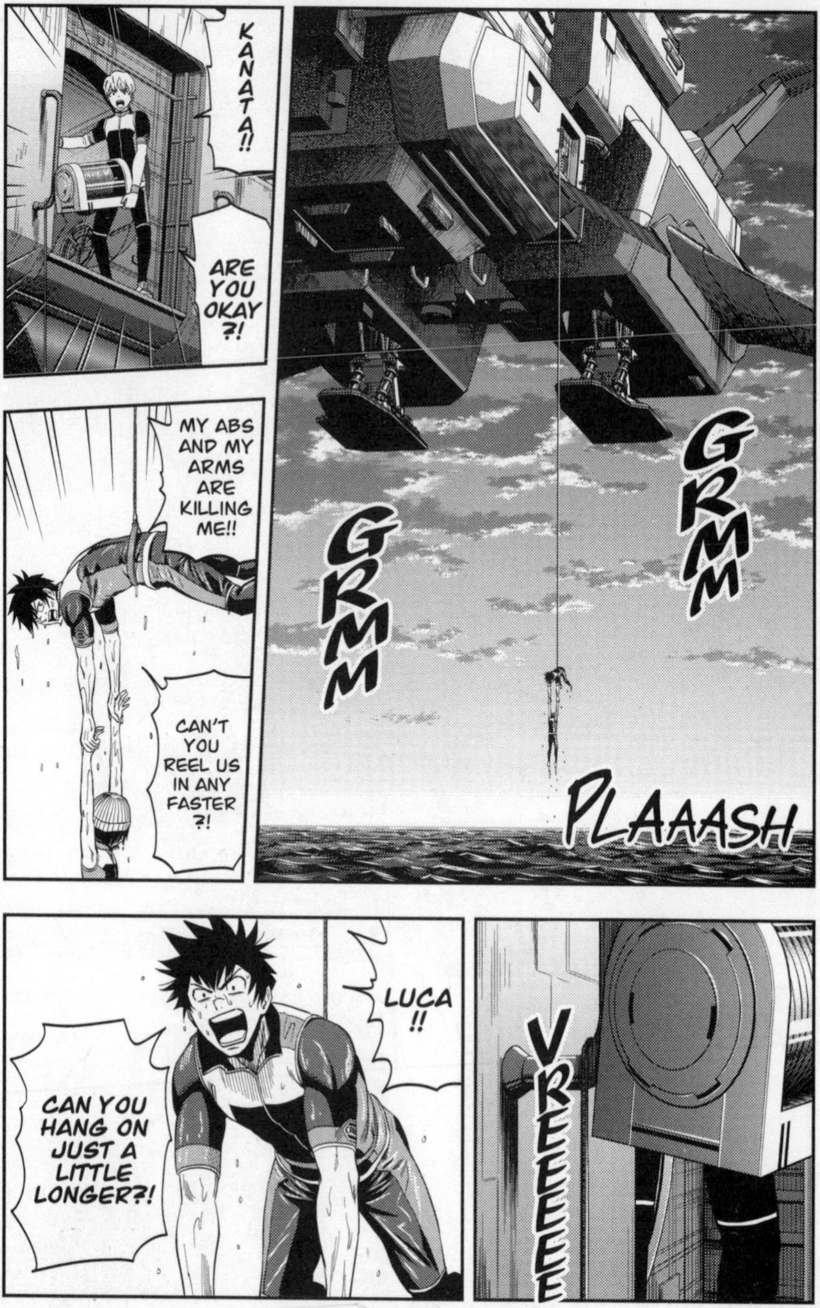
GRMM
GRMM
PLAASH
KANATA!!
ARE YOU OKAY?!
MY ABS AND MY ARMS ARE KILLING ME!!
CAN'T YOU REEL US IN ANY FASTER?!
VREEEEEE
LUCA!!
CAN YOU HANG ON JUST A LITTLE LONGER?!

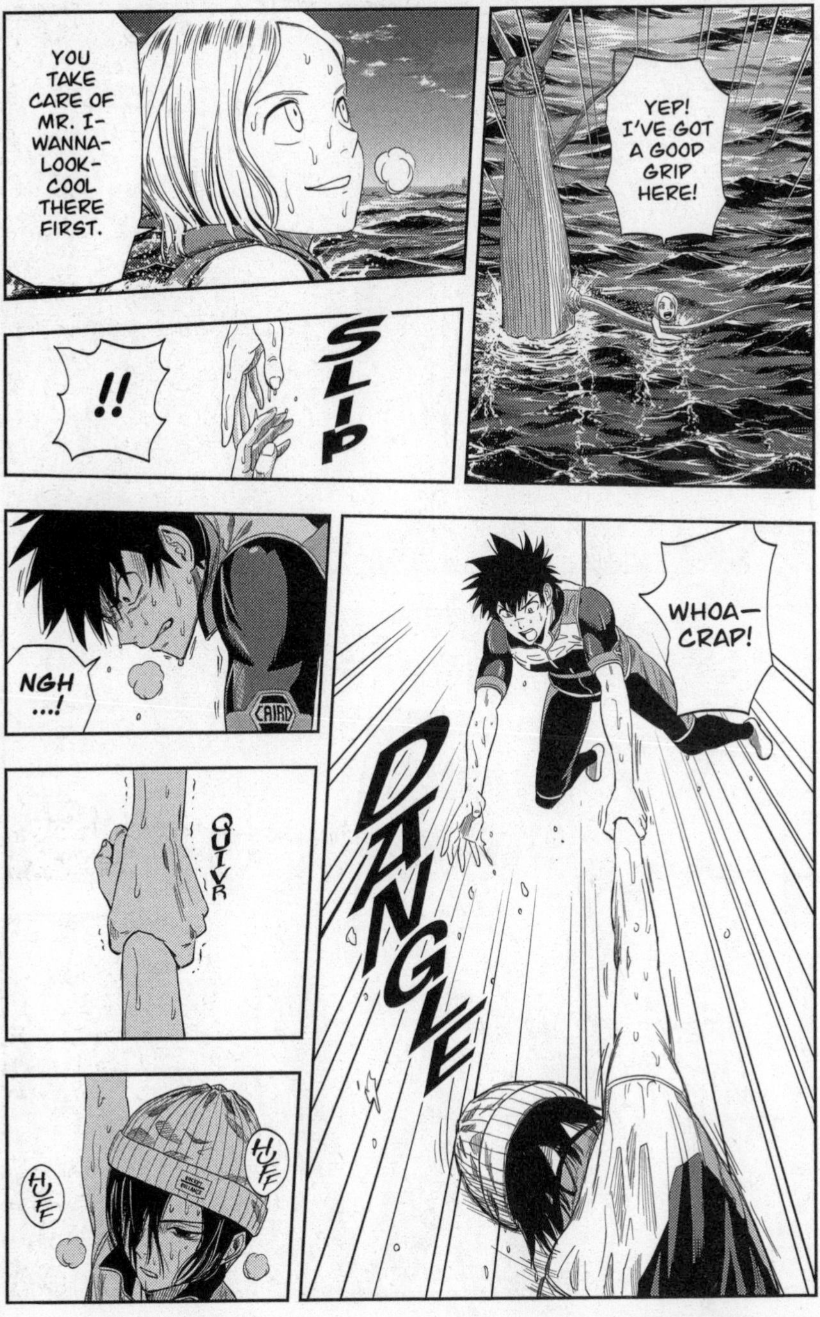
YEP! I'VE GOT A GOOD GRIP HERE!
YOU TAKE CARE OF MR. I-WANNA-LOOK-COOL THERE FIRST.
!!
SLIP
WHOA—CRAP!
DANGLE
NGH ...!
QUIVR
HUFF
HUFF

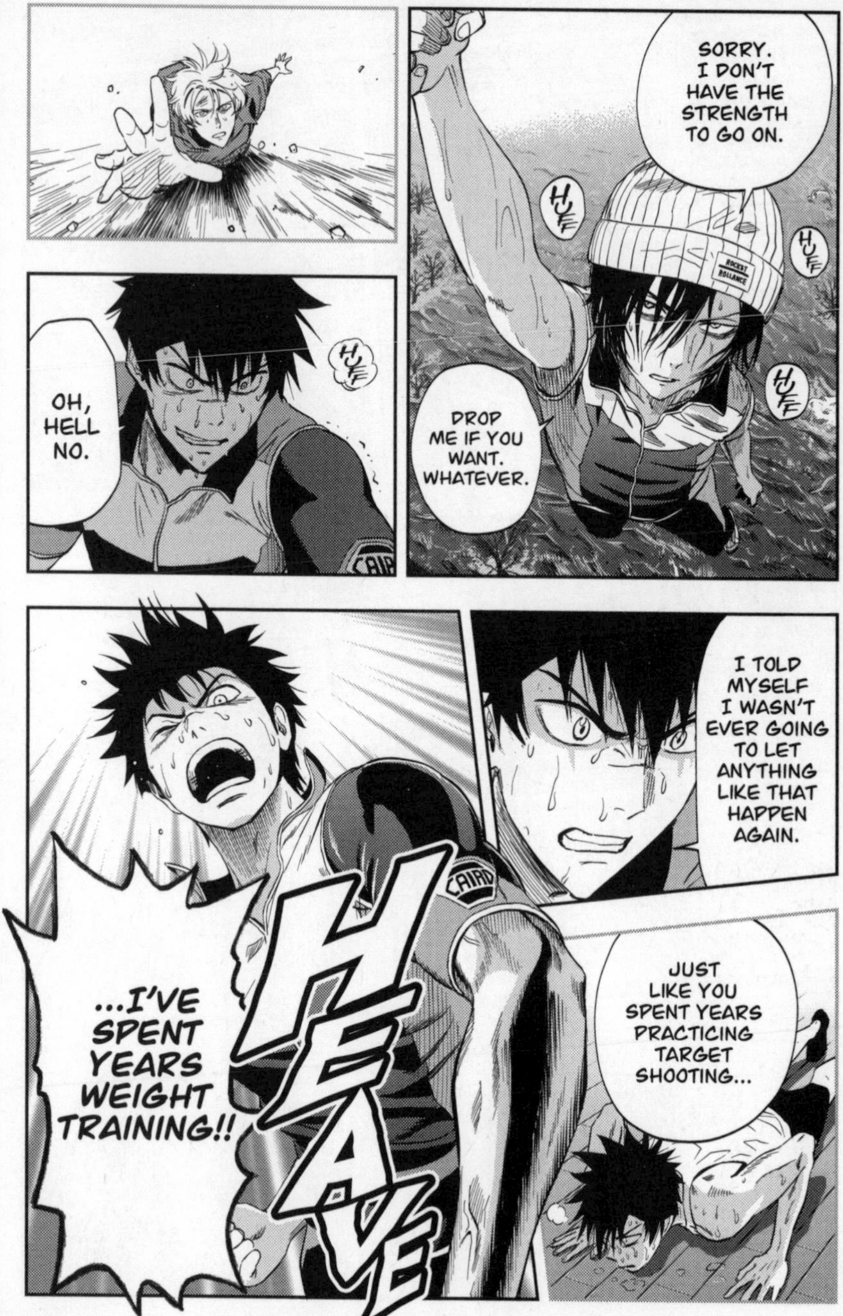
SORRY. I DON'T HAVE THE STRENGTH TO GO ON.
HUFF
HUFF
DROP ME IF YOU WANT. WHATEVER.
HUFF
HUFF
OH, HELL NO.
I TOLD MYSELF I WASN'T EVER GOING TO LET ANYTHING LIKE THAT HAPPEN AGAIN.
JUST LIKE YOU SPENT YEARS PRACTICING TARGET SHOOTING...
...I'VE SPENT YEARS WEIGHT TRAINING!!
HEAVE

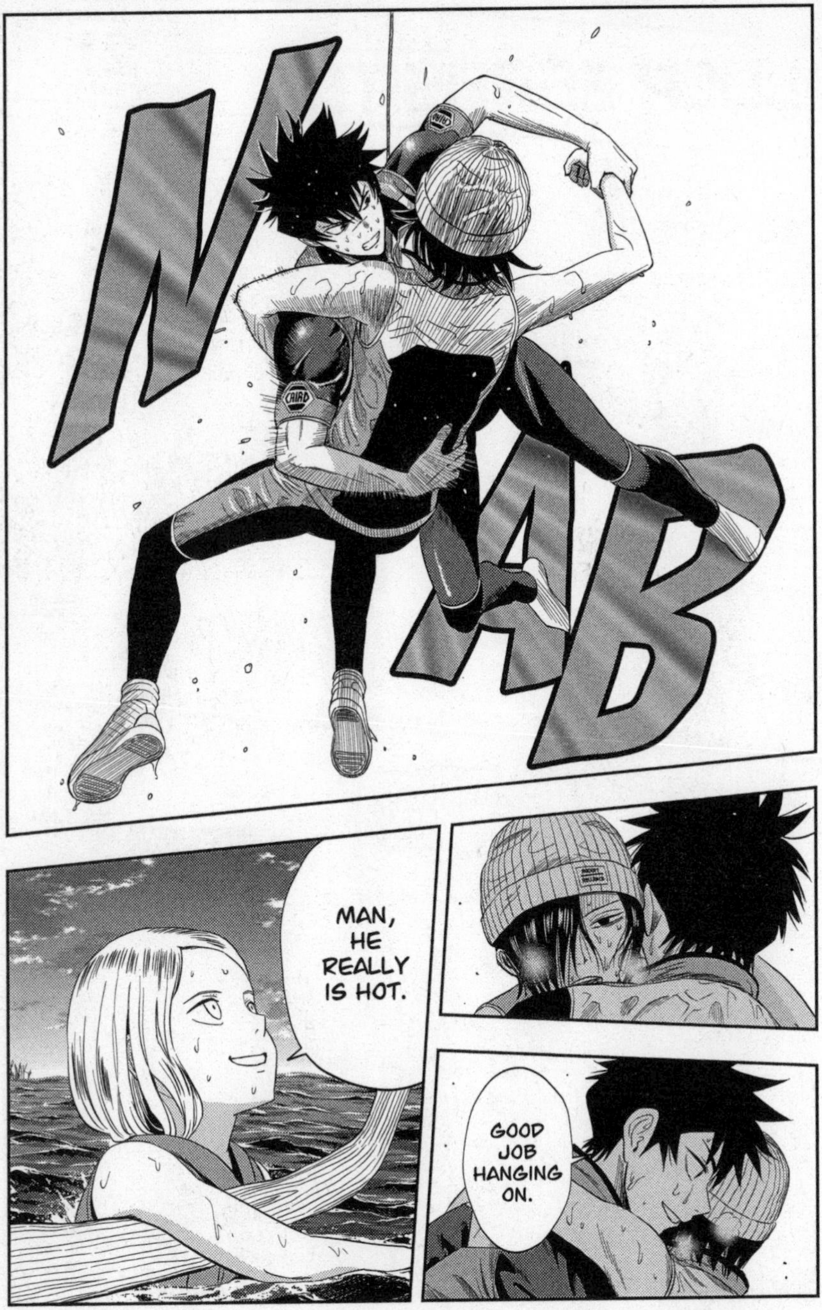
NAB
GOOD JOB HANGING ON.
MAN, HE REALLY IS HOT.

Material Collection **Characters**

Material Collection
Character Profile 21

LUCA ESPOSITO

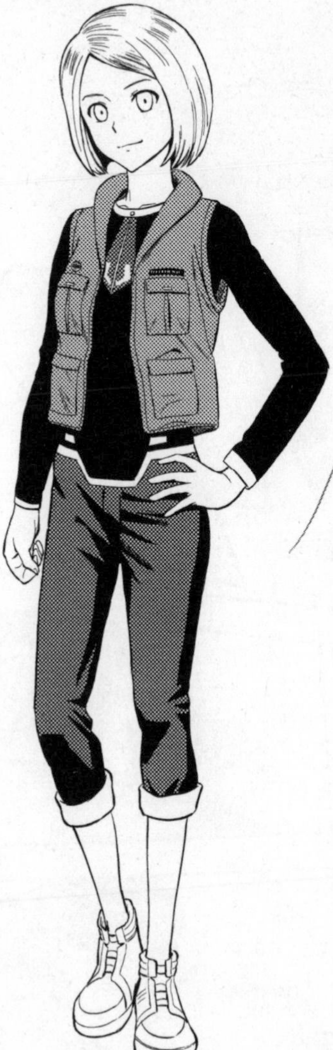

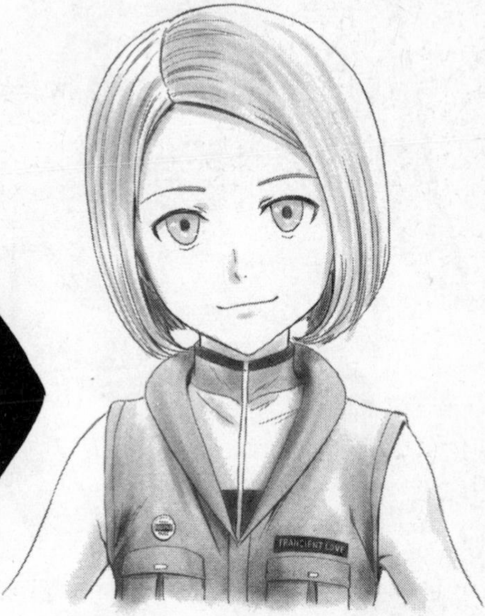
TRANSIENT LOVE

SINCE 2056
AUSPICE
TOOLS

TRANSIENT LOVE

DATA

Name: **Luca Esposito**

Age: **17**

Birthday: **August 19**

Height: **5'9"**

Weight: **104 lbs.**

Blood Type: **O**

Eye Color: **Gray**

Hometown: **Mousanish District**

As an intersex person, Luca possess both male and female sexual and reproductive organs. He currently identifies as male, but he explained how being male or female can feel fluid to him and can fluctuate by the day.

Deft with his hands, Luca has a strong artistic sense. He was adopted and raised by Senator Marco Esposito.

ASTRA
LOST IN SPACE

#25

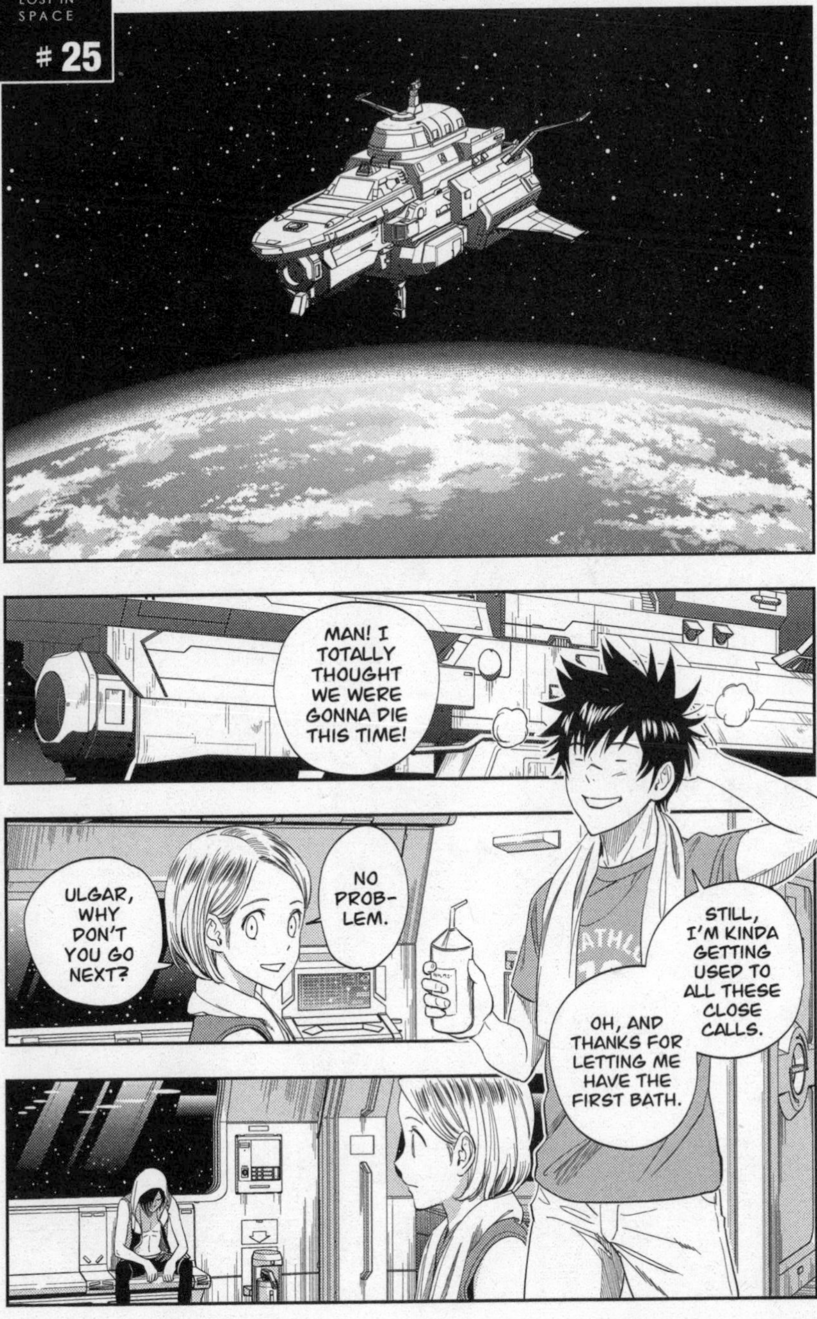
MAN! I TOTALLY THOUGHT WE WERE GONNA DIE THIS TIME!
STILL, I'M KINDA GETTING USED TO ALL THESE CLOSE CALLS.
OH, AND THANKS FOR LETTING ME HAVE THE FIRST BATH.
NO PROB-LEM.
ULGAR, WHY DON'T YOU GO NEXT?

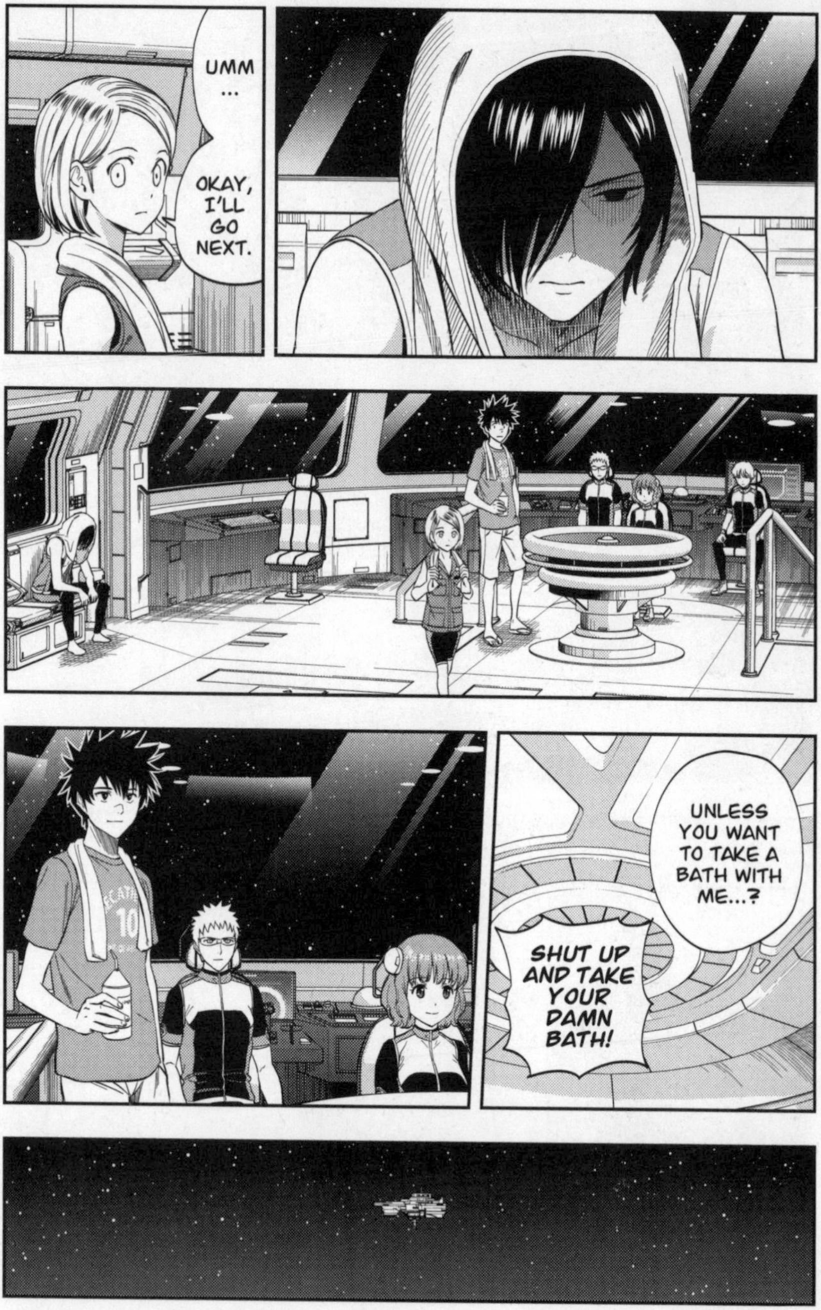
UMM ...
OKAY, I'LL GO NEXT.
UNLESS YOU WANT TO TAKE A BATH WITH ME...?
SHUT UP AND TAKE YOUR DAMN BATH!

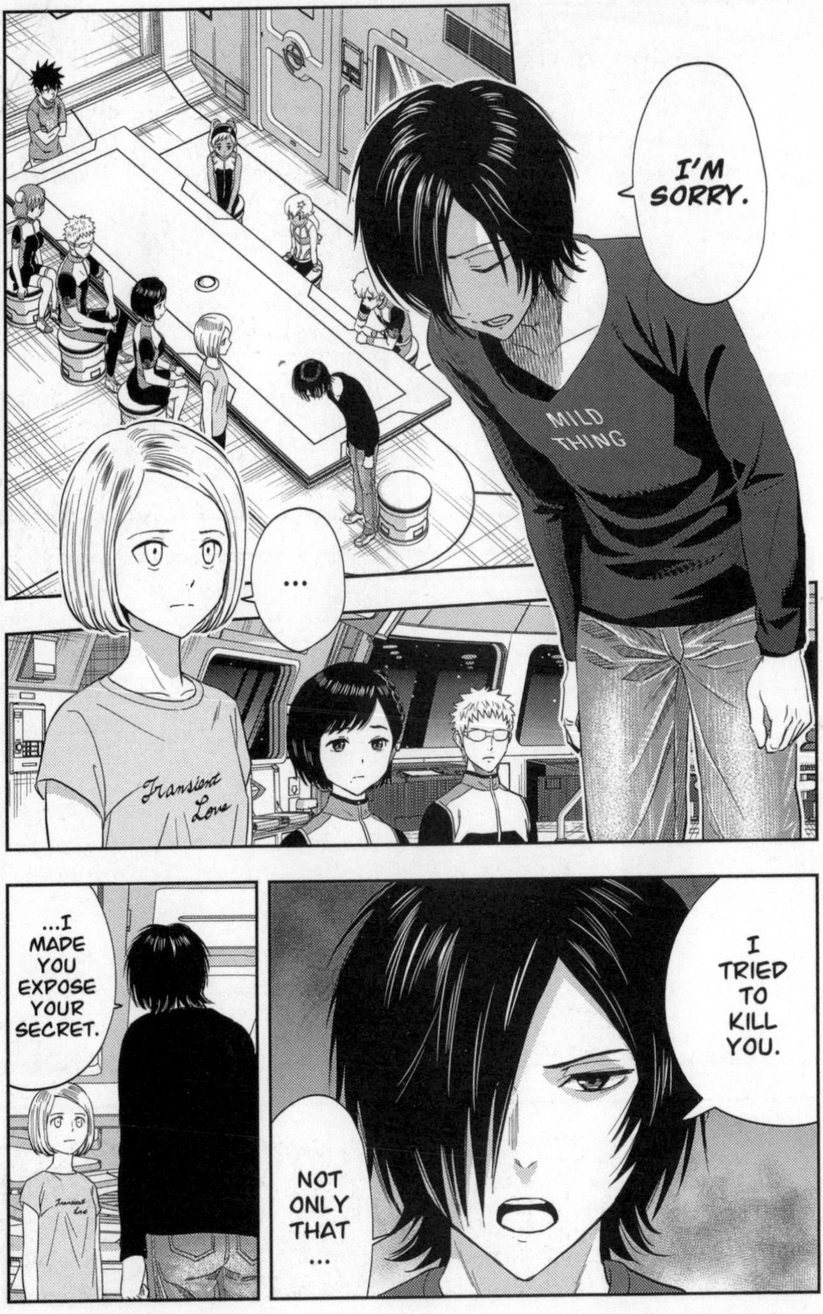
I'M SORRY.
MILD THING
...
Transient Love
I TRIED TO KILL YOU.
NOT ONLY THAT ...
...I MADE YOU EXPOSE YOUR SECRET.

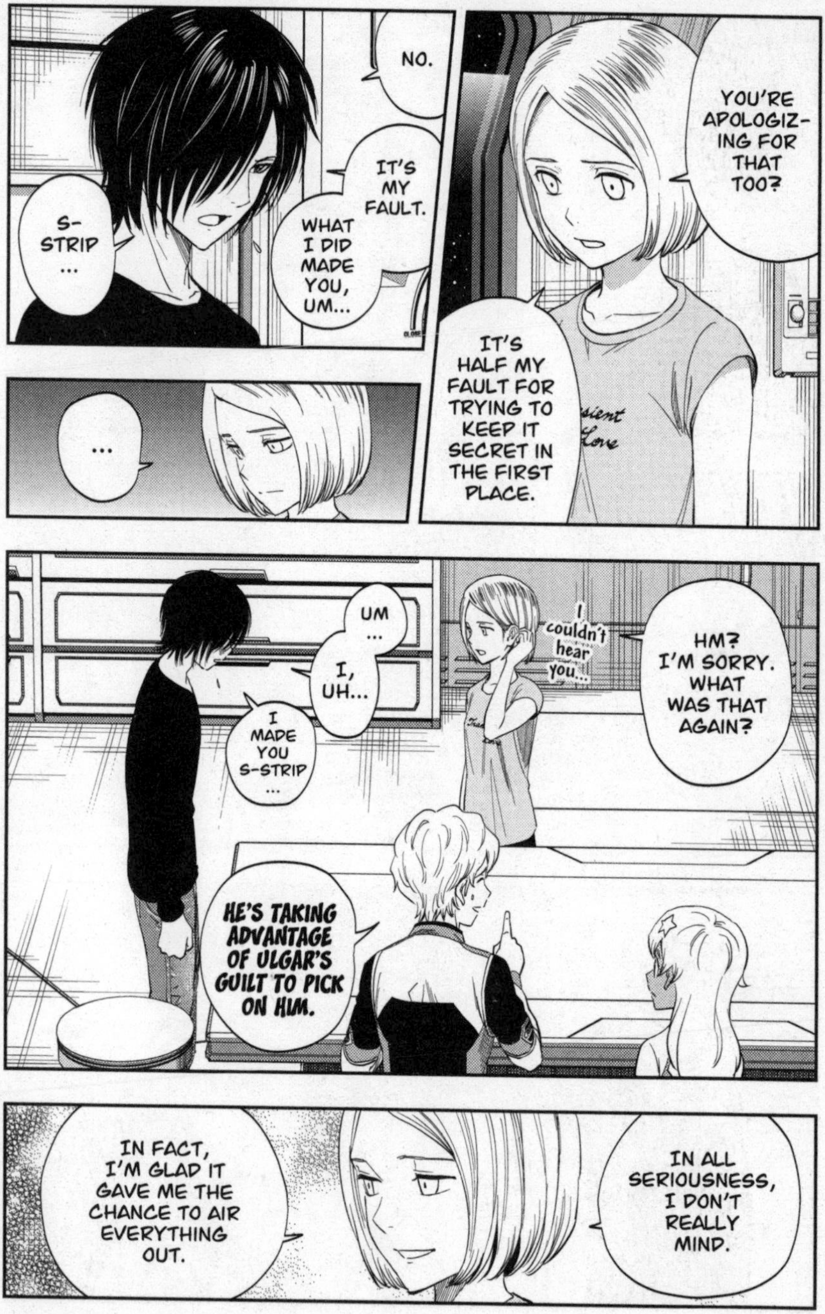
YOU'RE APOLOGIZING FOR THAT TOO?
IT'S HALF MY FAULT FOR TRYING TO KEEP IT SECRET IN THE FIRST PLACE.
NO.
IT'S MY FAULT.
WHAT I DID MADE YOU, UM...
S-STRIP...
...
HM? I'M SORRY. WHAT WAS THAT AGAIN?
I couldn't hear you...
UM...
I, UH...
I MADE YOU S-STRIP...
HE'S TAKING ADVANTAGE OF ULGAR'S GUILT TO PICK ON HIM.
IN ALL SERIOUSNESS, I DON'T REALLY MIND.
IN FACT, I'M GLAD IT GAVE ME THE CHANCE TO AIR EVERYTHING OUT.

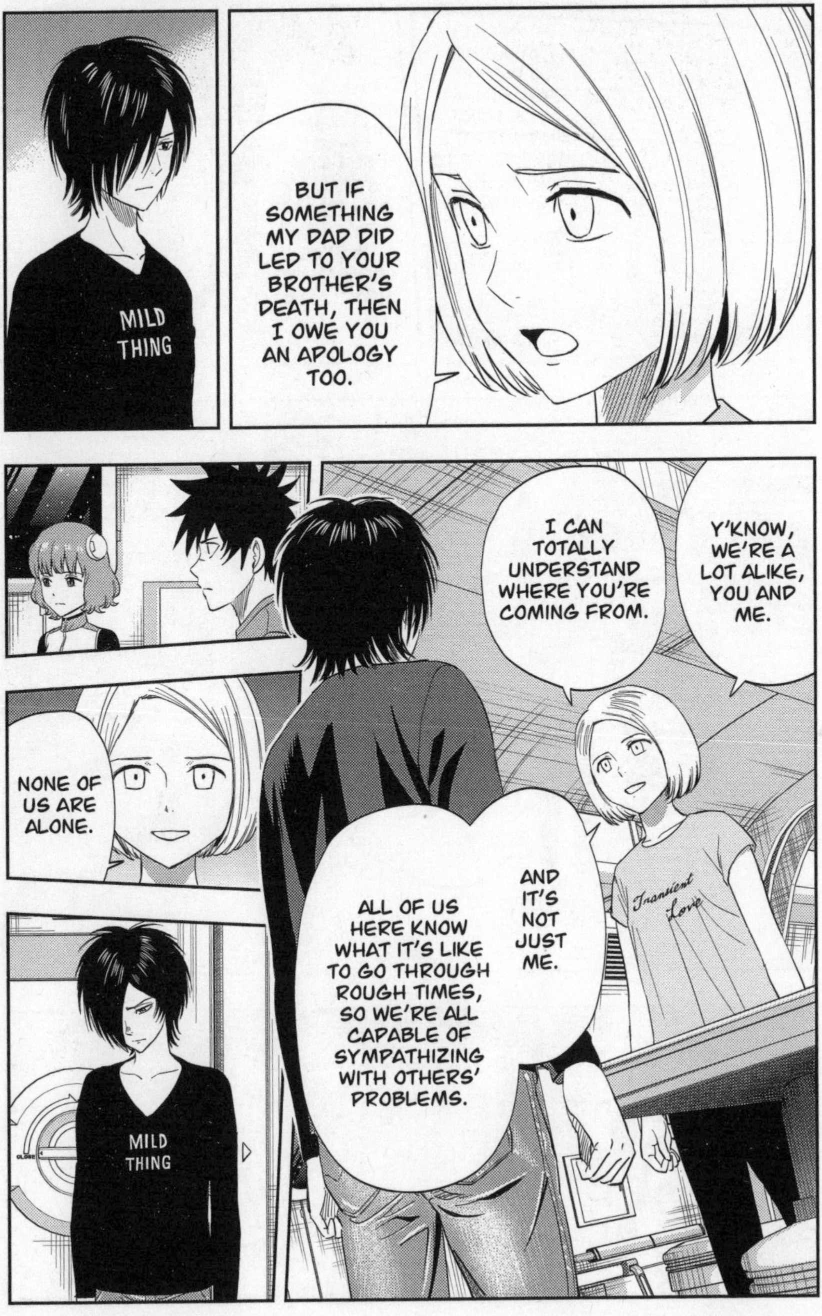
BUT IF SOMETHING MY DAD DID LED TO YOUR BROTHER'S DEATH, THEN I OWE YOU AN APOLOGY TOO.
MILD THING
Y'KNOW, WE'RE A LOT ALIKE, YOU AND ME.
I CAN TOTALLY UNDERSTAND WHERE YOU'RE COMING FROM.
Transient Love
AND IT'S NOT JUST ME.
ALL OF US HERE KNOW WHAT IT'S LIKE TO GO THROUGH ROUGH TIMES, SO WE'RE ALL CAPABLE OF SYMPATHIZING WITH OTHERS' PROBLEMS.
NONE OF US ARE ALONE.
MILD THING

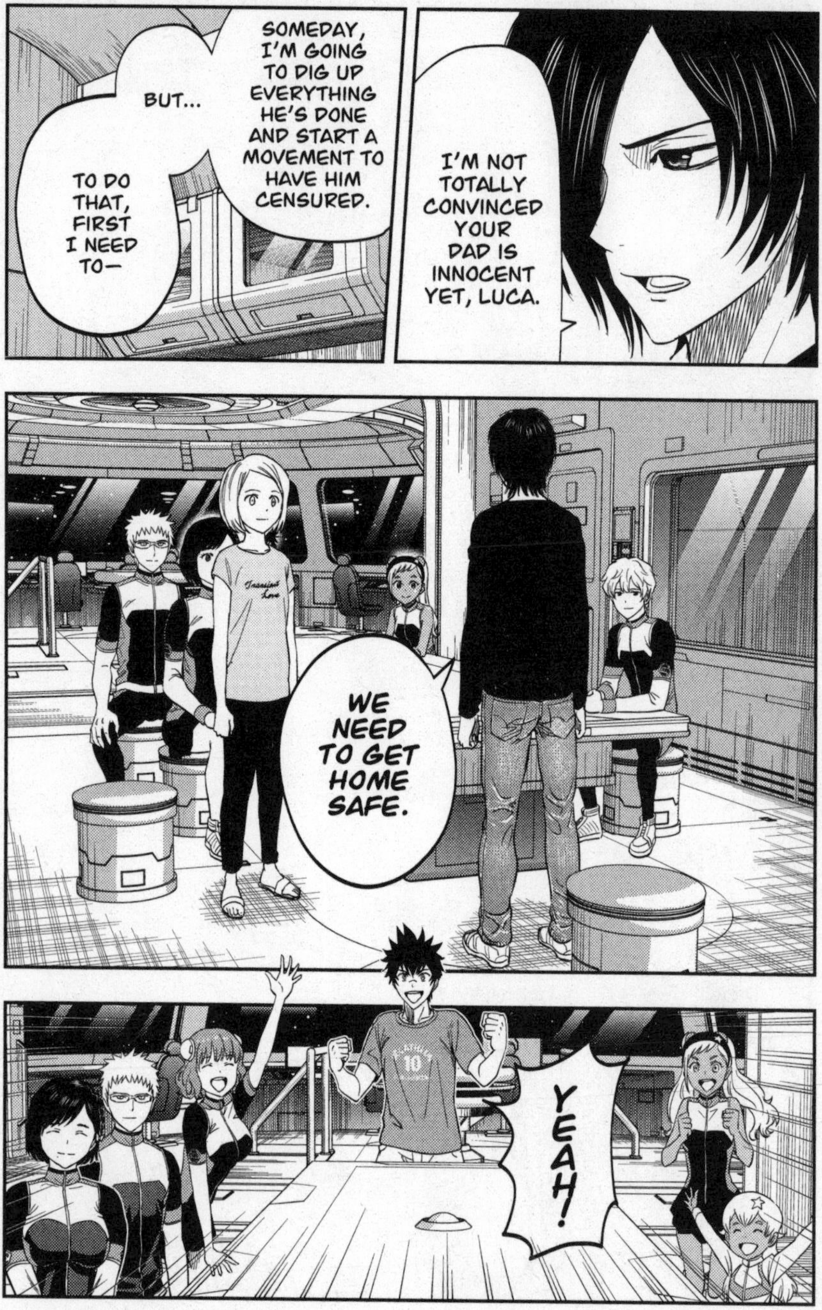
I'M NOT TOTALLY CONVINCED YOUR DAD IS INNOCENT YET, LUCA.
SOMEDAY, I'M GOING TO DIG UP EVERYTHING HE'S DONE AND START A MOVEMENT TO HAVE HIM CENSURED.
BUT...
TO DO THAT, FIRST I NEED TO—
WE NEED TO GET HOME SAFE.
YEAH!

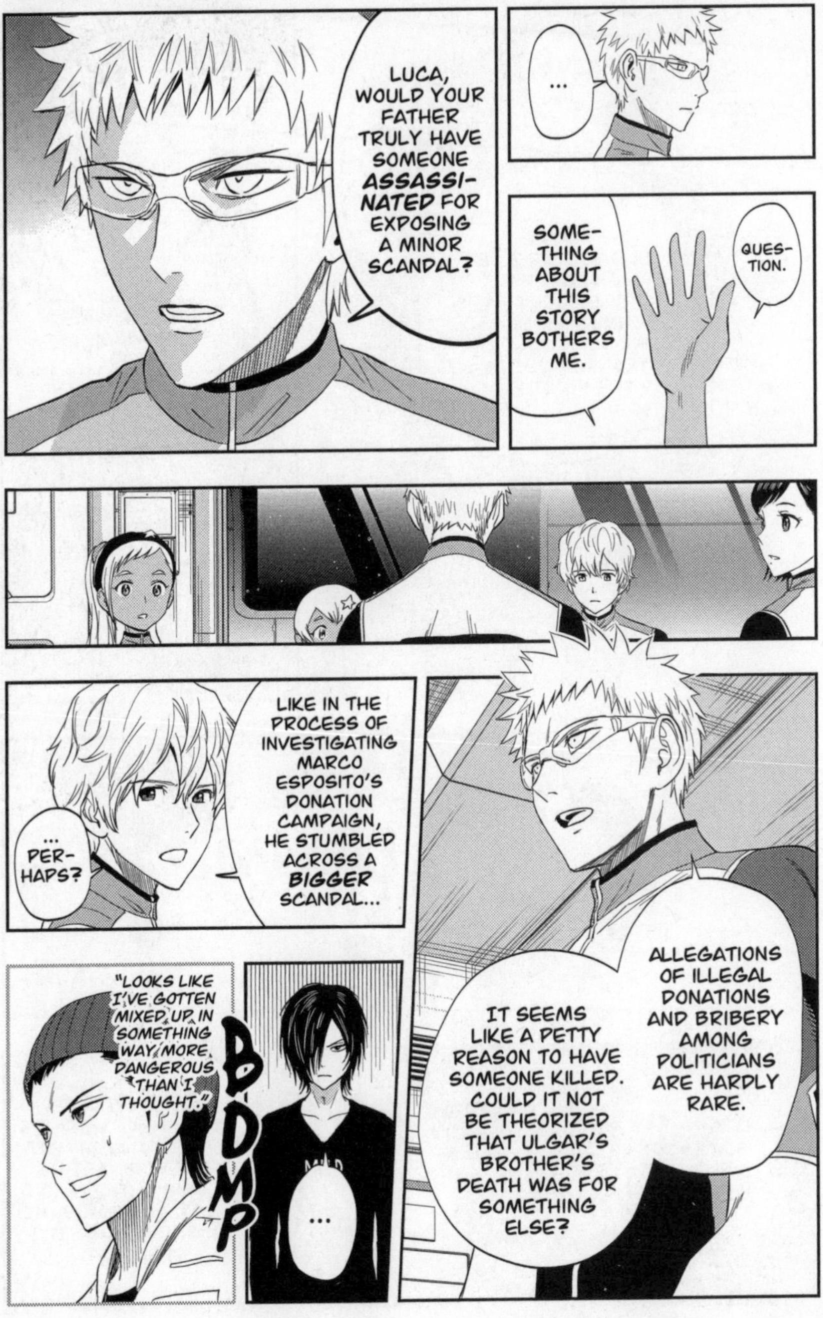
...
QUESTION.
SOMETHING ABOUT THIS STORY BOTHERS ME.
LUCA, WOULD YOUR FATHER TRULY HAVE SOMEONE **ASSASSINATED** FOR EXPOSING A MINOR SCANDAL?
ALLEGATIONS OF ILLEGAL DONATIONS AND BRIBERY AMONG POLITICIANS ARE HARDLY RARE.
IT SEEMS LIKE A PETTY REASON TO HAVE SOMEONE KILLED. COULD IT NOT BE THEORIZED THAT ULGAR'S BROTHER'S DEATH WAS FOR SOMETHING ELSE?
LIKE IN THE PROCESS OF INVESTIGATING MARCO ESPOSITO'S DONATION CAMPAIGN, HE STUMBLED ACROSS A **BIGGER** SCANDAL...
...PERHAPS?
...
BDMP
"LOOKS LIKE I'VE GOTTEN MIXED UP IN SOMETHING WAY MORE DANGEROUS THAN I THOUGHT."

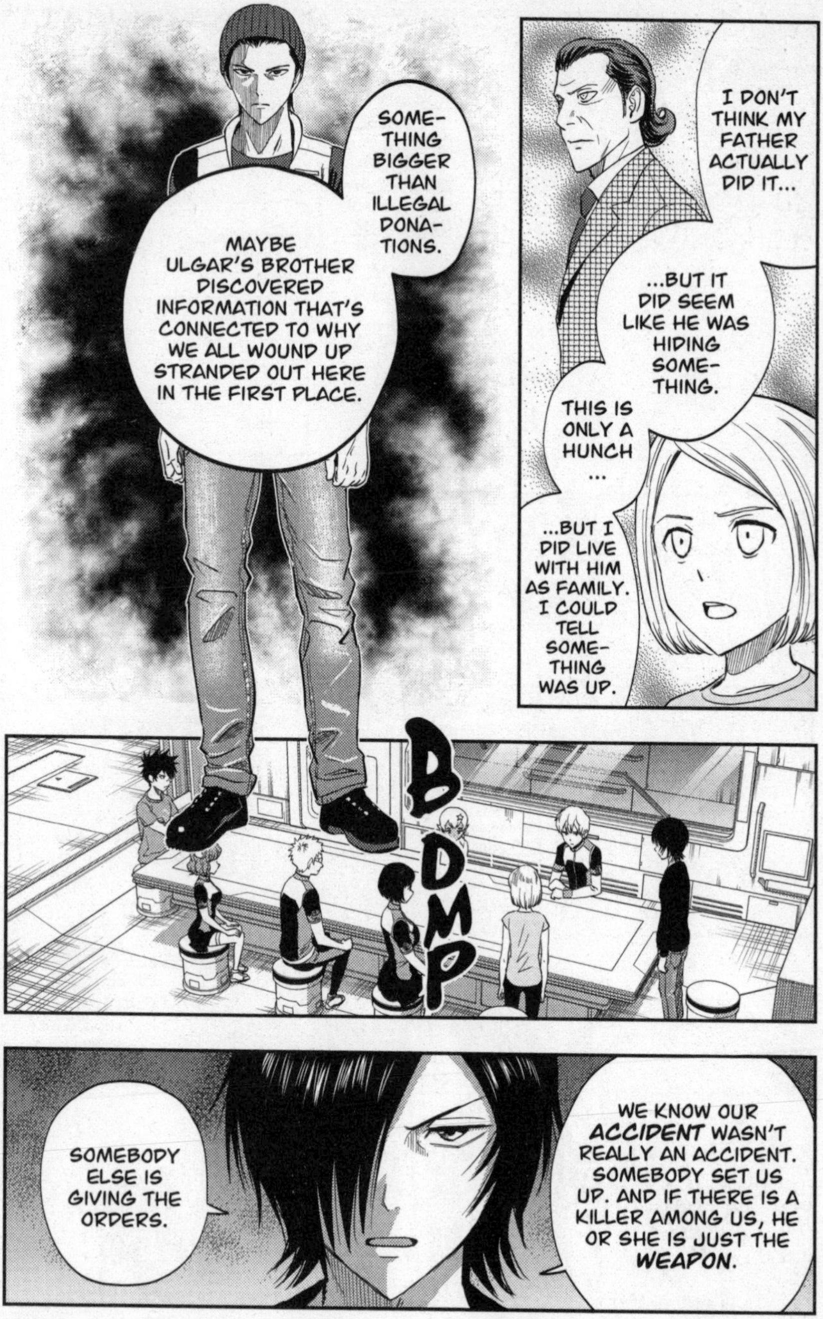
I DON'T THINK MY FATHER ACTUALLY DID IT...
...BUT IT DID SEEM LIKE HE WAS HIDING SOME-THING.
THIS IS ONLY A HUNCH ...
...BUT I DID LIVE WITH HIM AS FAMILY. I COULD TELL SOME-THING WAS UP.
SOME-THING BIGGER THAN ILLEGAL DONA-TIONS.
MAYBE ULGAR'S BROTHER DISCOVERED INFORMATION THAT'S CONNECTED TO WHY WE ALL WOUND UP STRANDED OUT HERE IN THE FIRST PLACE.
BDMP
WE KNOW OUR **ACCIDENT** WASN'T REALLY AN ACCIDENT. SOMEBODY SET US UP. AND IF THERE IS A KILLER AMONG US, HE OR SHE IS JUST THE **WEAPON**.
SOMEBODY ELSE IS GIVING THE ORDERS.

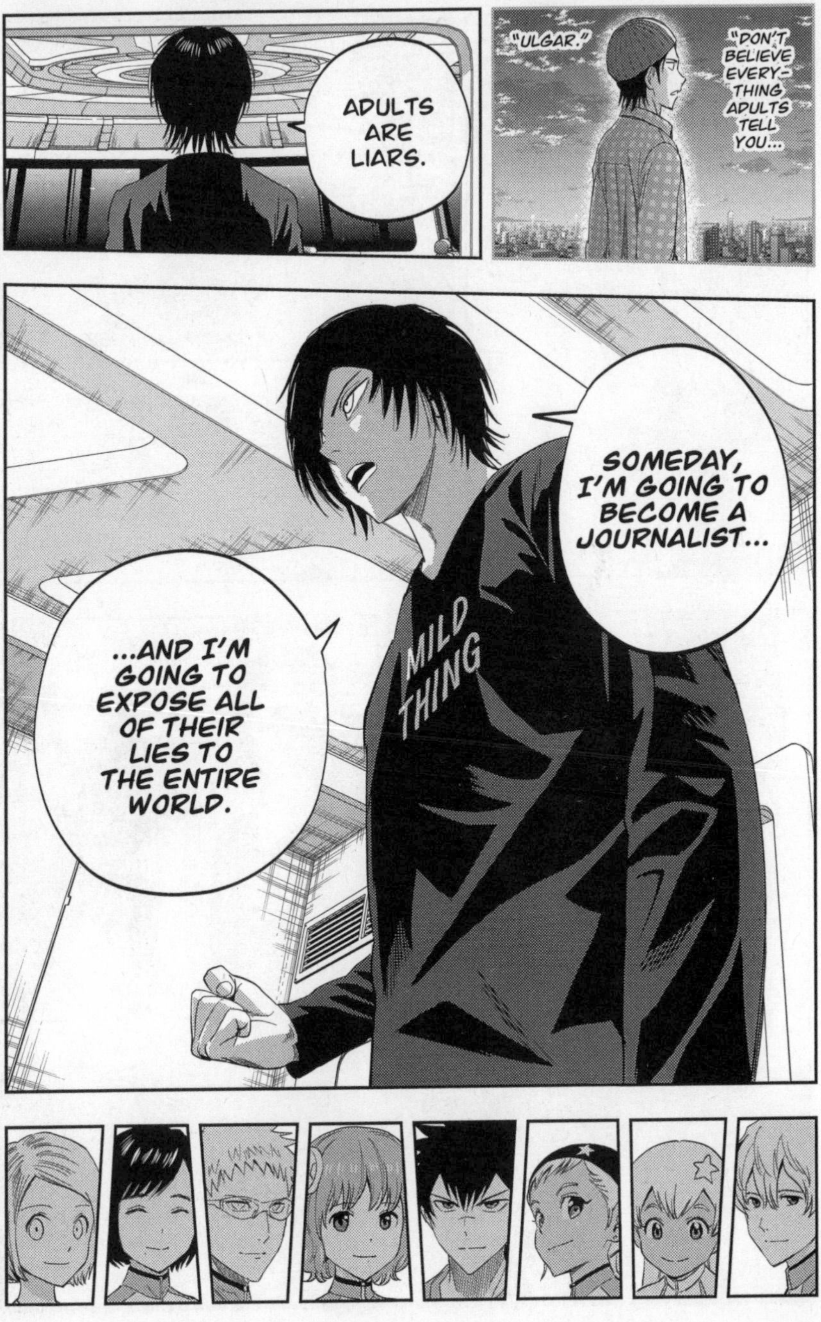
"DON'T BELIEVE EVERYTHING ADULTS TELL YOU...
"ULGAR."
ADULTS ARE LIARS.
SOMEDAY, I'M GOING TO BECOME A JOURNALIST...
MILD THING
...AND I'M GOING TO EXPOSE ALL OF THEIR LIES TO THE ENTIRE WORLD.

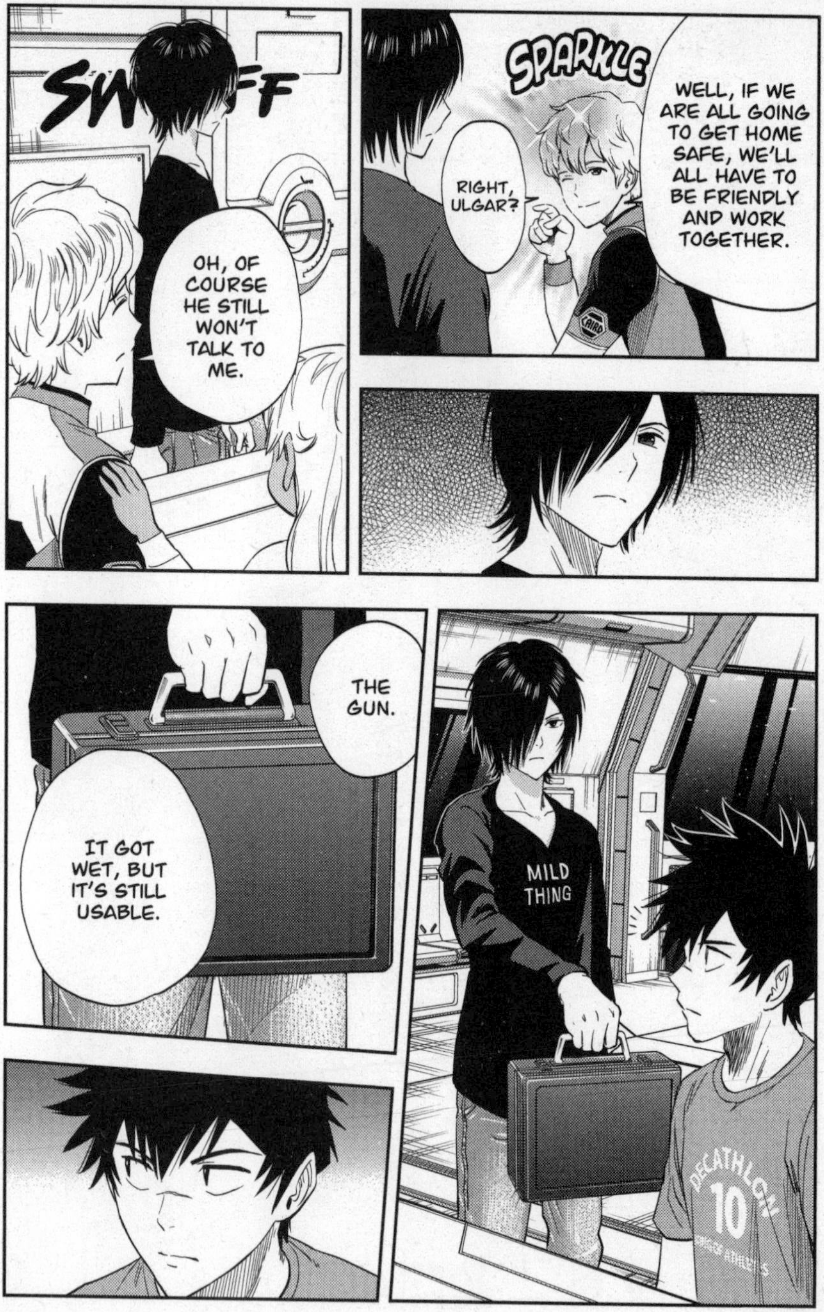
SPARKLE
WELL, IF WE ARE ALL GOING TO GET HOME SAFE, WE'LL ALL HAVE TO BE FRIENDLY AND WORK TOGETHER.
RIGHT, ULGAR?
OH, OF COURSE HE STILL WON'T TALK TO ME.
MILD THING
DECATHLON
10
THE GUN.
IT GOT WET, BUT IT'S STILL USABLE.

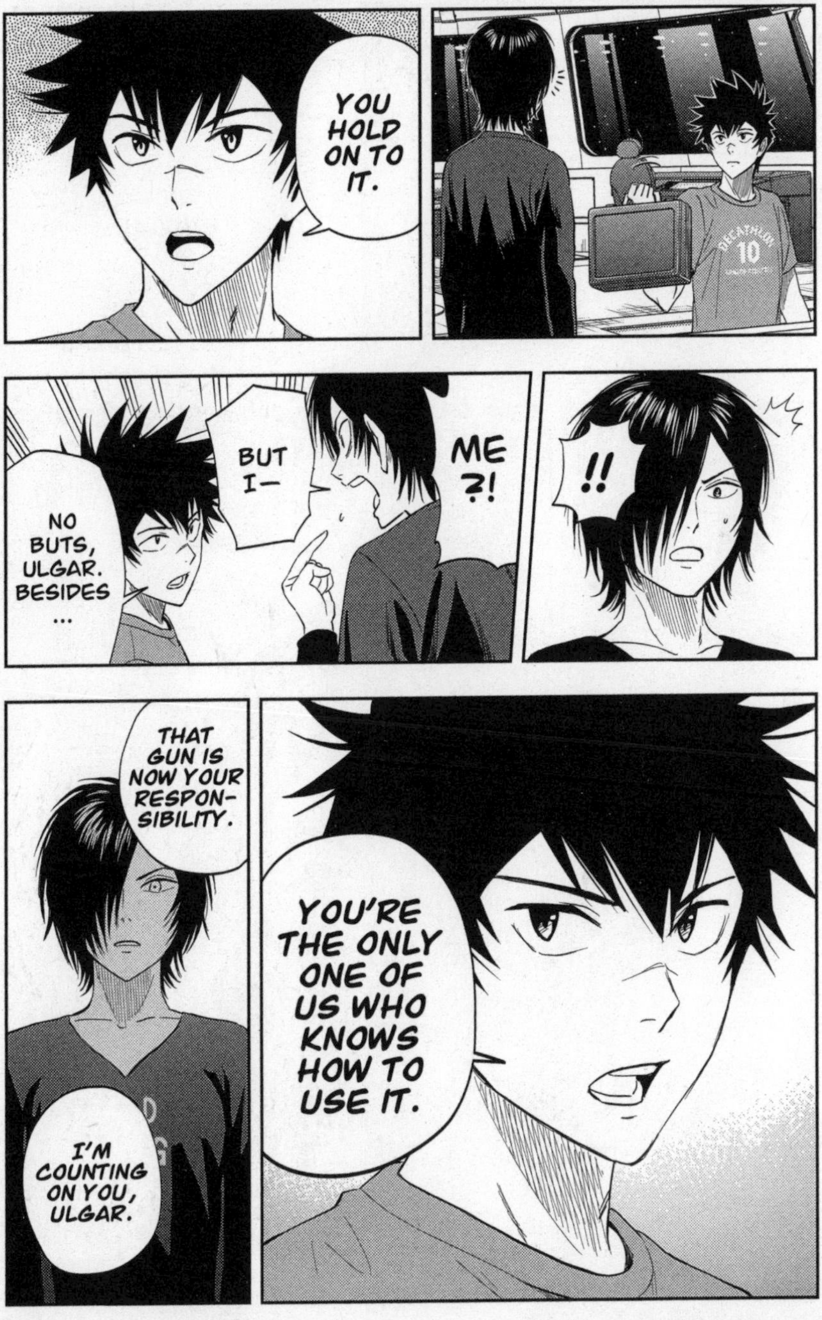
YOU HOLD ON TO IT.
!!
ME ?!
BUT I—
NO BUTS, ULGAR. BESIDES ...
YOU'RE THE ONLY ONE OF US WHO KNOWS HOW TO USE IT.
THAT GUN IS NOW YOUR RESPON-SIBILITY.
I'M COUNTING ON YOU, ULGAR.

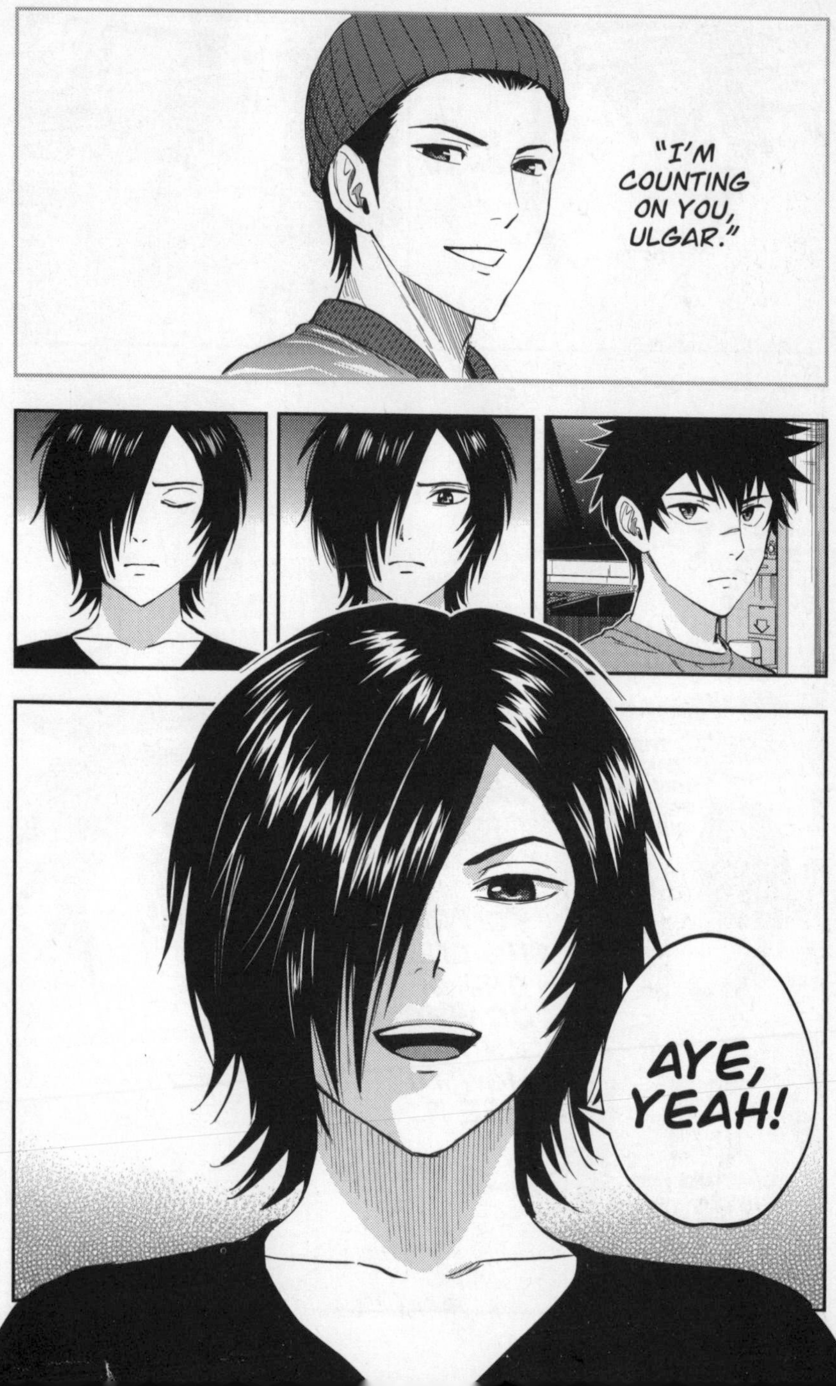
"I'M COUNTING ON YOU, ULGAR."
AYE, YEAH!

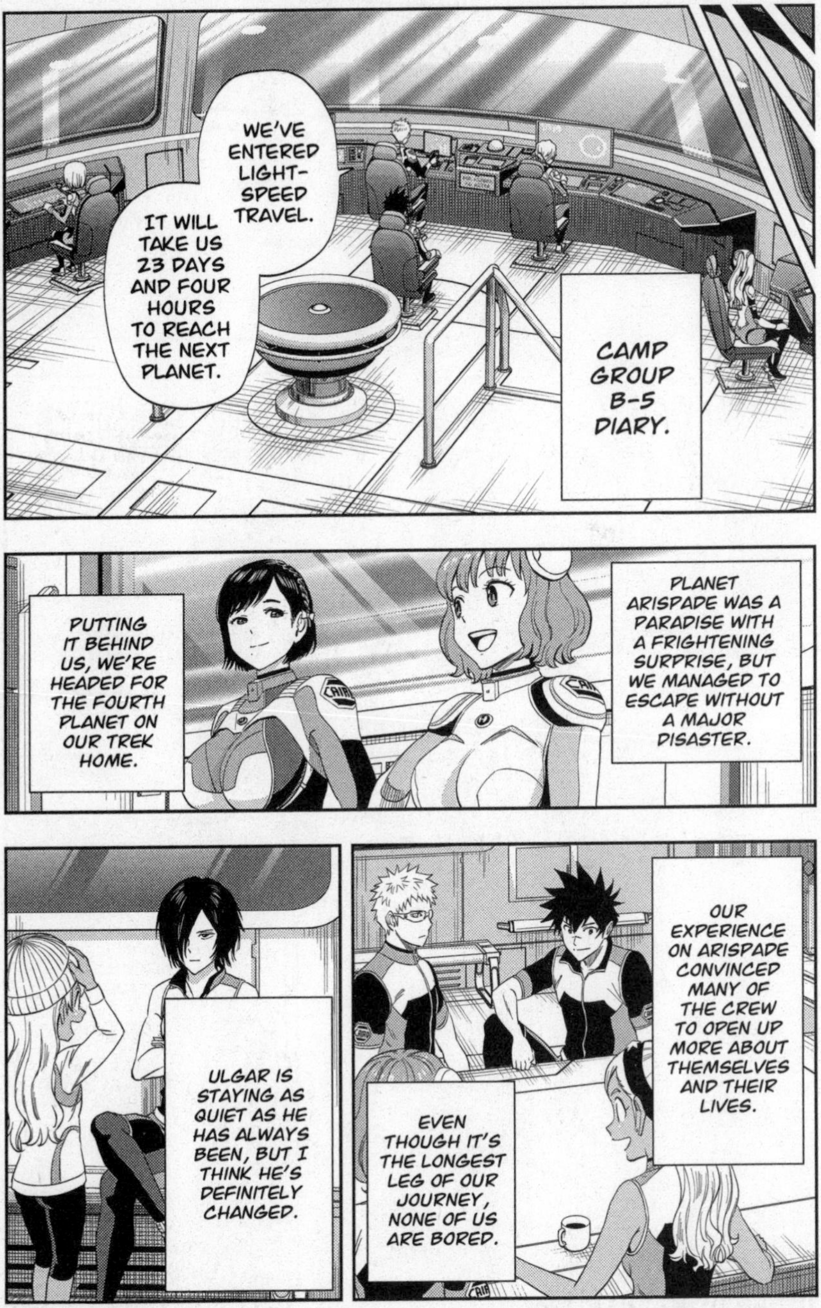
CAMP GROUP B-5 DIARY.
WE'VE ENTERED LIGHT-SPEED TRAVEL.
IT WILL TAKE US 23 DAYS AND FOUR HOURS TO REACH THE NEXT PLANET.
PLANET ARISPADE WAS A PARADISE WITH A FRIGHTENING SURPRISE, BUT WE MANAGED TO ESCAPE WITHOUT A MAJOR DISASTER.
PUTTING IT BEHIND US, WE'RE HEADED FOR THE FOURTH PLANET ON OUR TREK HOME.
OUR EXPERIENCE ON ARISPADE CONVINCED MANY OF THE CREW TO OPEN UP MORE ABOUT THEMSELVES AND THEIR LIVES.
EVEN THOUGH IT'S THE LONGEST LEG OF OUR JOURNEY, NONE OF US ARE BORED.
ULGAR IS STAYING AS QUIET AS HE HAS ALWAYS BEEN, BUT I THINK HE'S DEFINITELY CHANGED.

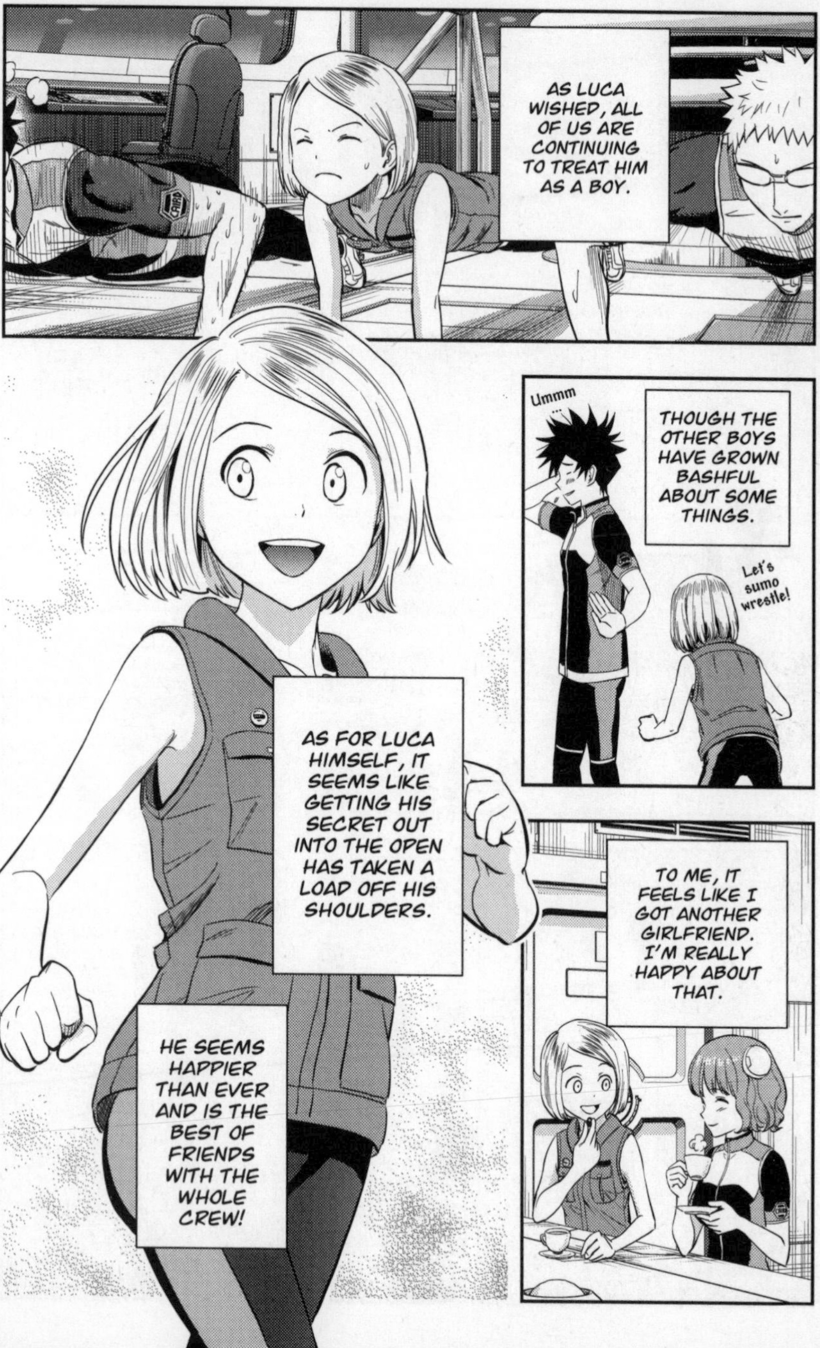
AS LUCA WISHED, ALL OF US ARE CONTINUING TO TREAT HIM AS A BOY.
THOUGH THE OTHER BOYS HAVE GROWN BASHFUL ABOUT SOME THINGS.
Ummm...
Let's sumo wrestle!
TO ME, IT FEELS LIKE I GOT ANOTHER GIRLFRIEND. I'M REALLY HAPPY ABOUT THAT.
AS FOR LUCA HIMSELF, IT SEEMS LIKE GETTING HIS SECRET OUT INTO THE OPEN HAS TAKEN A LOAD OFF HIS SHOULDERS.
HE SEEMS HAPPIER THAN EVER AND IS THE BEST OF FRIENDS WITH THE WHOLE CREW!

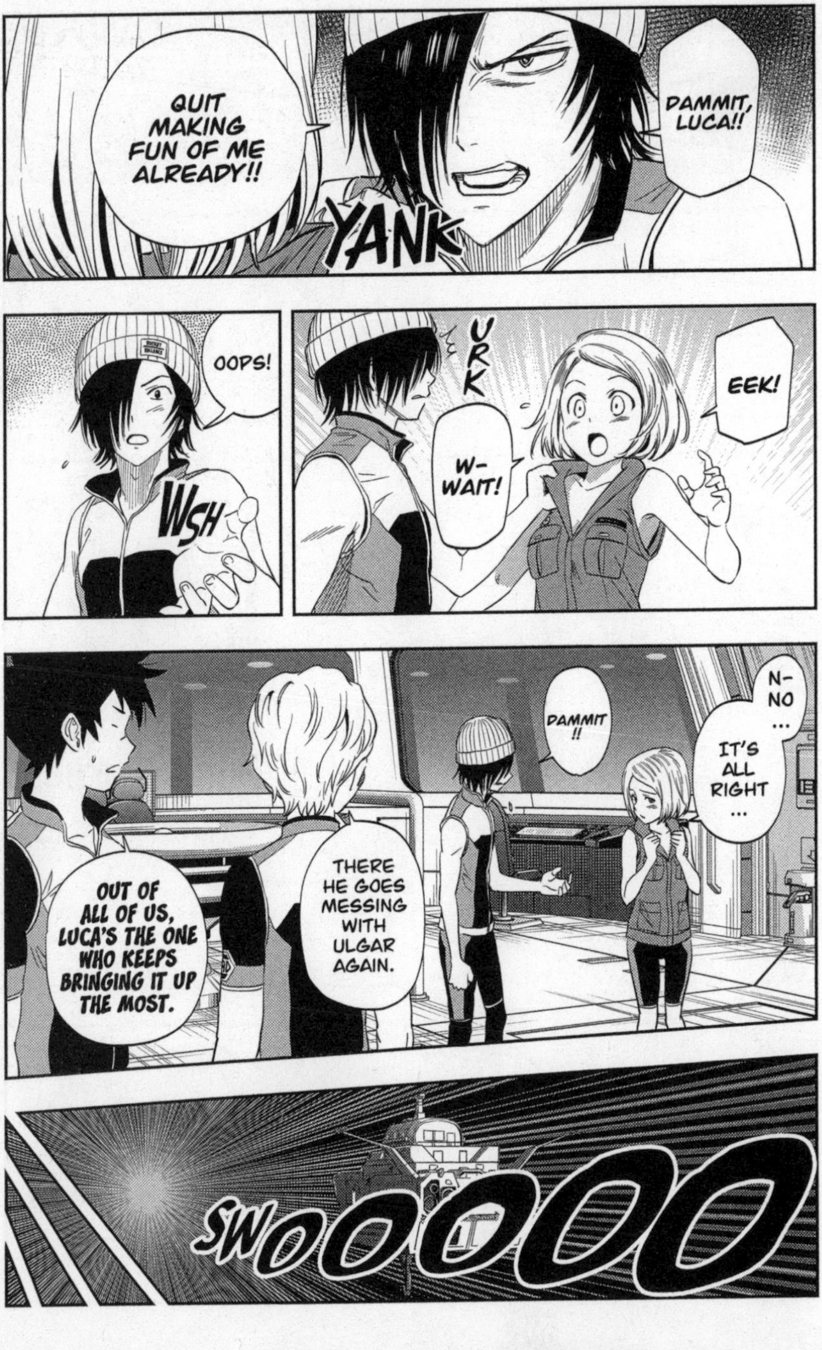
DAMMIT, LUCA!!
QUIT MAKING FUN OF ME ALREADY!!
YANK
EEK!
URK
W-WAIT!
OOPS!
WSH
N-NO ... IT'S ALL RIGHT ...
DAMMIT !!
THERE HE GOES MESSING WITH ULGAR AGAIN.
OUT OF ALL OF US, LUCA'S THE ONE WHO KEEPS BRINGING IT UP THE MOST.
SWOOOOOO

Light-Speed Journey: 20 Days Aboard the Ship (71 days since initial stranding)

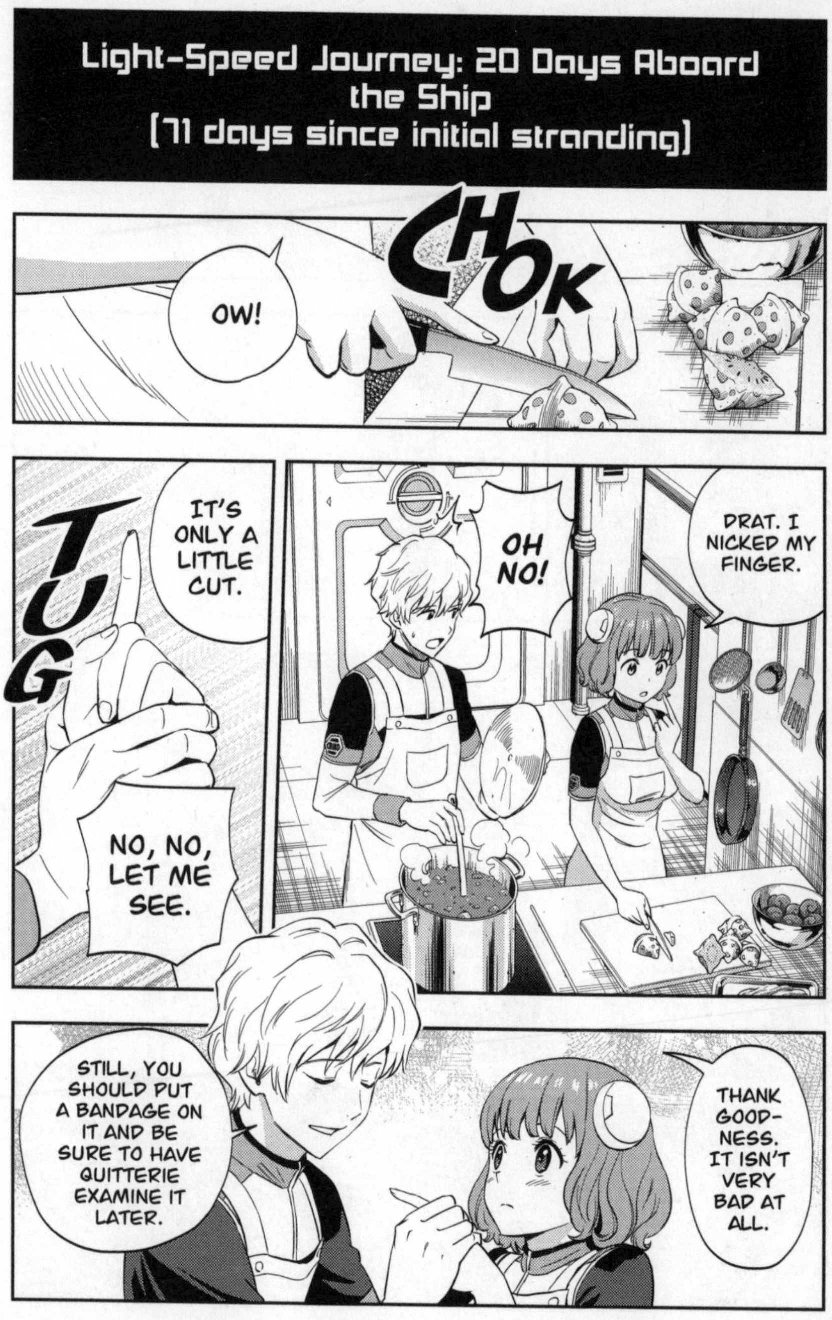
CHOK
OW!
DRAT. I NICKED MY FINGER.
OH NO!
IT'S ONLY A LITTLE CUT.
TUG
NO, NO, LET ME SEE.
THANK GOODNESS. IT ISN'T VERY BAD AT ALL.
STILL, YOU SHOULD PUT A BANDAGE ON IT AND BE SURE TO HAVE QUITTERIE EXAMINE IT LATER.

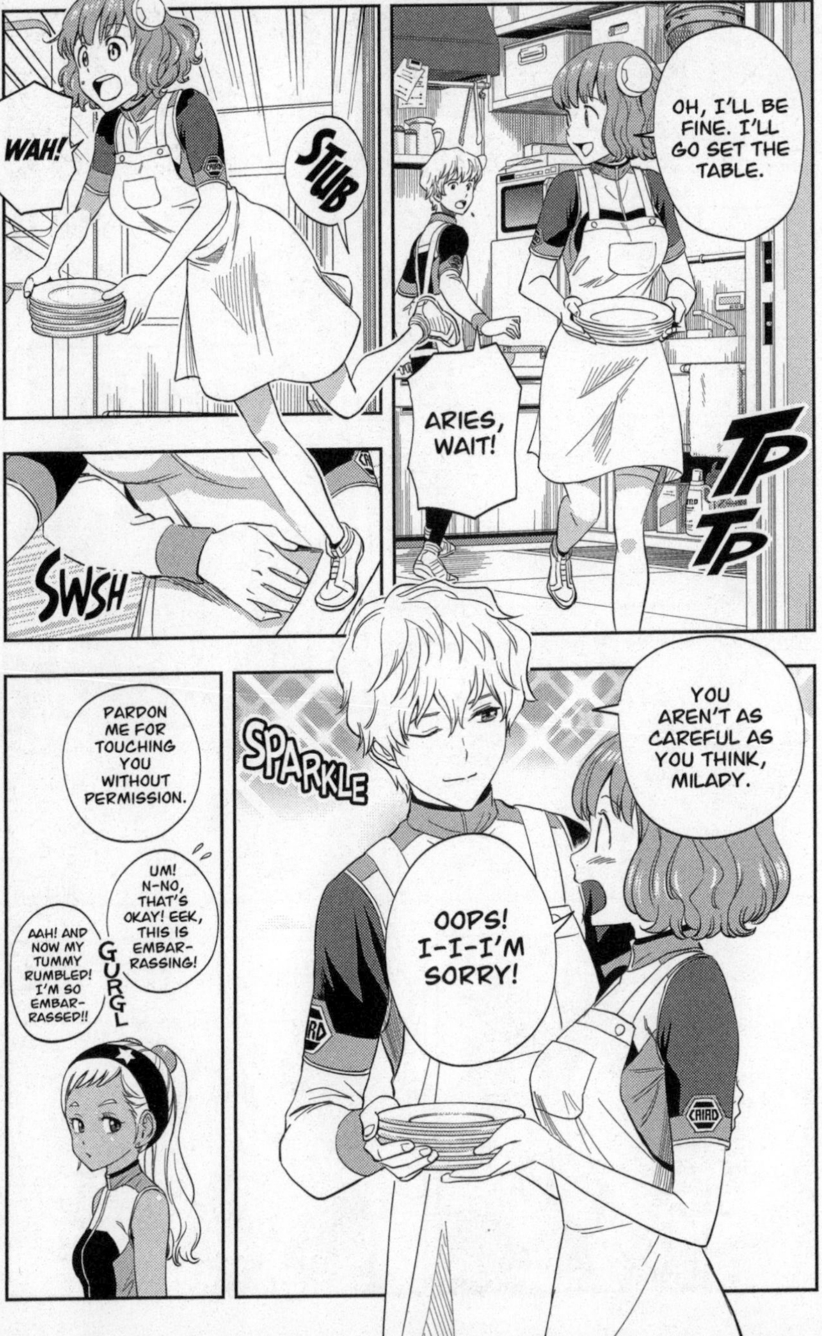
OH, I'LL BE FINE. I'LL GO SET THE TABLE.
ARIES, WAIT!
TP TP
STUB
WAH!
SWSH
YOU AREN'T AS CAREFUL AS YOU THINK, MILADY.
SPARKLE
OOPS! I-I-I'M SORRY!
PARDON ME FOR TOUCHING YOU WITHOUT PERMISSION.
UM! N-NO, THAT'S OKAY! EEK, THIS IS EMBAR-RASSING!
GURGL
AAH! AND NOW MY TUMMY RUMBLED! I'M SO EMBAR-RASSED!!

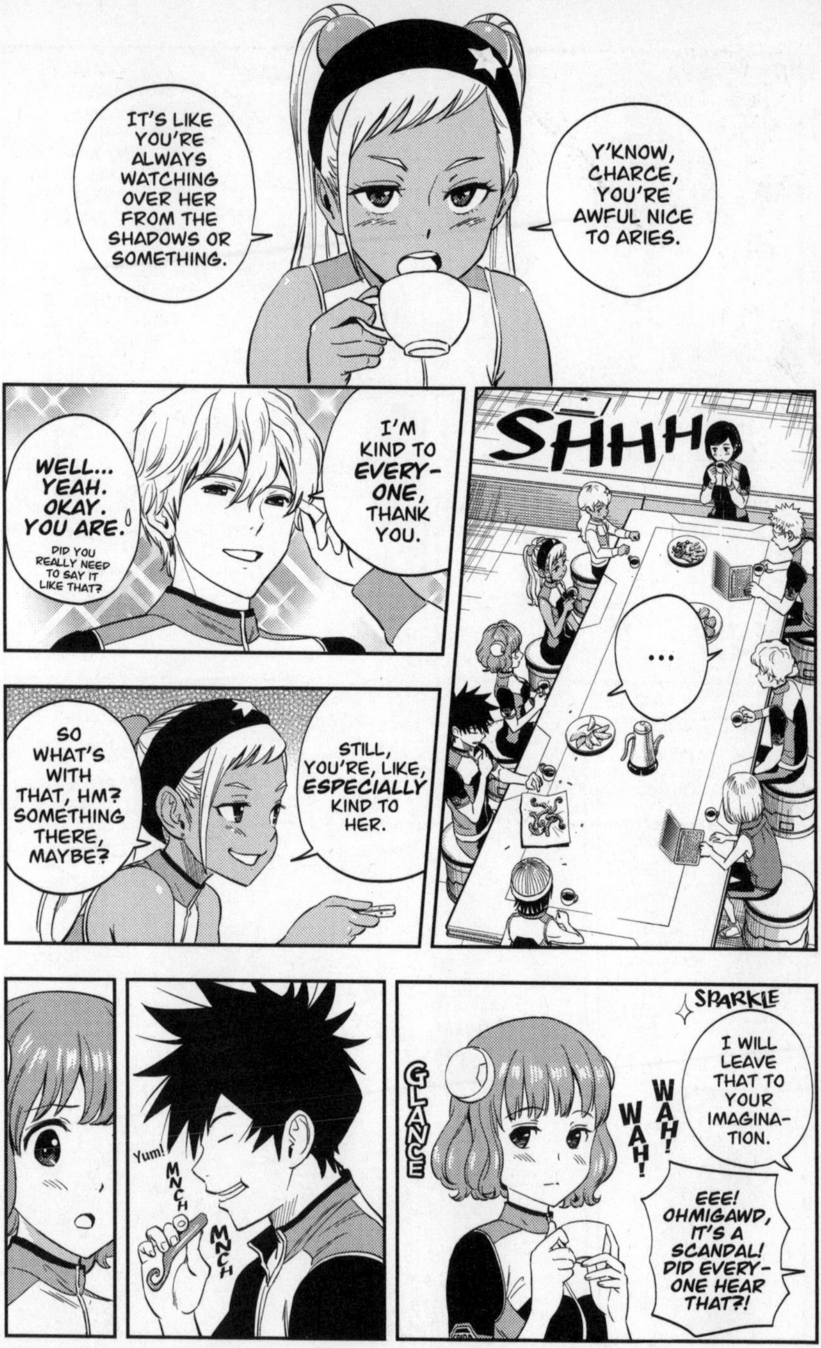
Y'KNOW, CHARCE, YOU'RE AWFUL NICE TO ARIES.
IT'S LIKE YOU'RE ALWAYS WATCHING OVER HER FROM THE SHADOWS OR SOMETHING.
SHHH
...
I'M KIND TO EVERYONE, THANK YOU.
WELL... YEAH. OKAY. YOU ARE.
DID YOU REALLY NEED TO SAY IT LIKE THAT?
STILL, YOU'RE, LIKE, ESPECIALLY KIND TO HER.
SO WHAT'S WITH THAT, HM? SOMETHING THERE, MAYBE?
SPARKLE
I WILL LEAVE THAT TO YOUR IMAGINATION.
WAH! WAH!
GLANCE
EEE! OHMIGAWD, IT'S A SCANDAL! DID EVERYONE HEAR THAT?!
Yum!
MNCH
MNCH

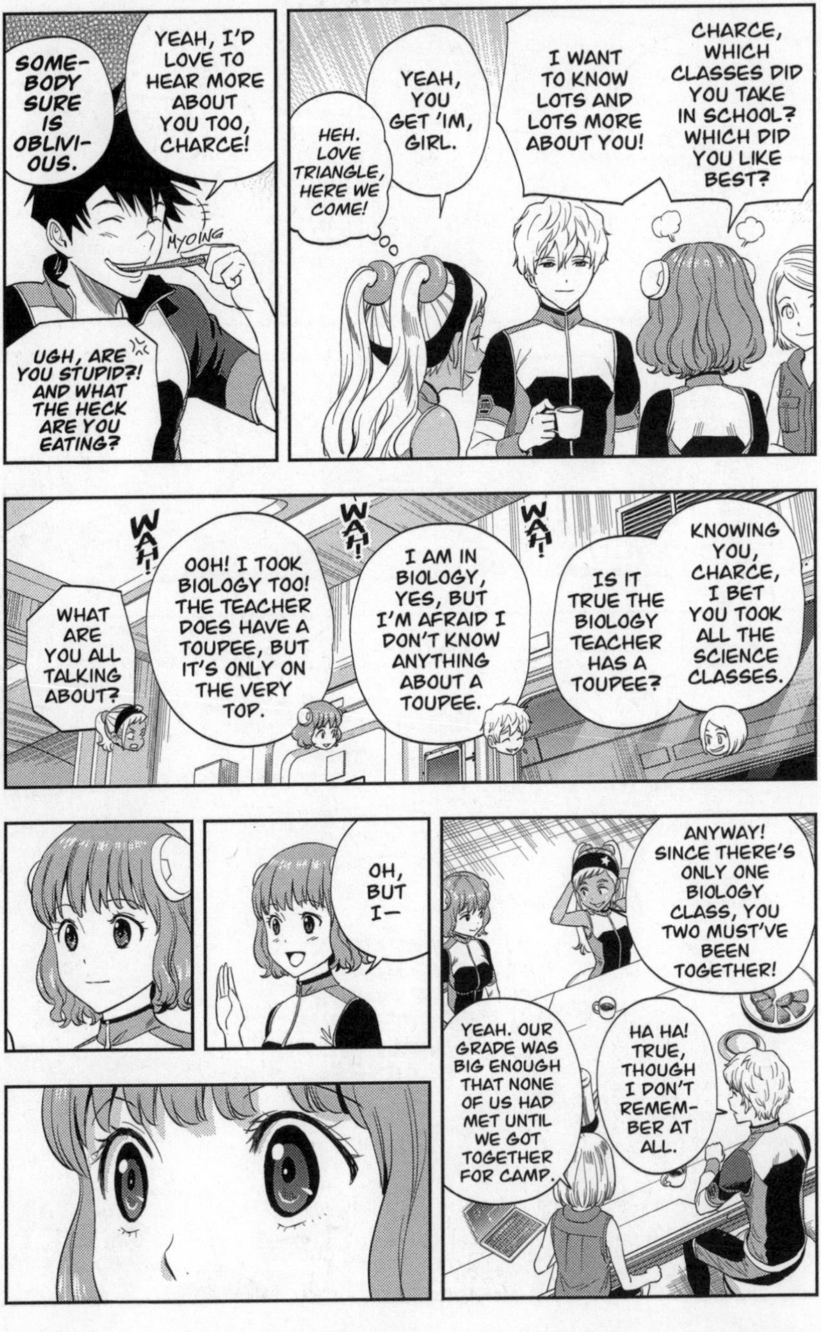
CHARCE, WHICH CLASSES DID YOU TAKE IN SCHOOL? WHICH DID YOU LIKE BEST?
I WANT TO KNOW LOTS AND LOTS MORE ABOUT YOU!
YEAH, YOU GET 'IM, GIRL.
HEH. LOVE TRIANGLE, HERE WE COME!
YEAH, I'D LOVE TO HEAR MORE ABOUT YOU TOO, CHARCE!
SOMEBODY SURE IS OBLIVIOUS.
MYOING
UGH, ARE YOU STUPID?! AND WHAT THE HECK ARE YOU EATING?
KNOWING YOU, CHARCE, I BET YOU TOOK ALL THE SCIENCE CLASSES.
WAH!
IS IT TRUE THE BIOLOGY TEACHER HAS A TOUPEE?
WAH!
I AM IN BIOLOGY, YES, BUT I'M AFRAID I DON'T KNOW ANYTHING ABOUT A TOUPEE.
WAH!
OOH! I TOOK BIOLOGY TOO! THE TEACHER DOES HAVE A TOUPEE, BUT IT'S ONLY ON THE VERY TOP.
WHAT ARE YOU ALL TALKING ABOUT?
ANYWAY! SINCE THERE'S ONLY ONE BIOLOGY CLASS, YOU TWO MUST'VE BEEN TOGETHER!
HA HA! TRUE, THOUGH I DON'T REMEMBER AT ALL.
YEAH. OUR GRADE WAS BIG ENOUGH THAT NONE OF US HAD MET UNTIL WE GOT TOGETHER FOR CAMP.
OH, BUT I—

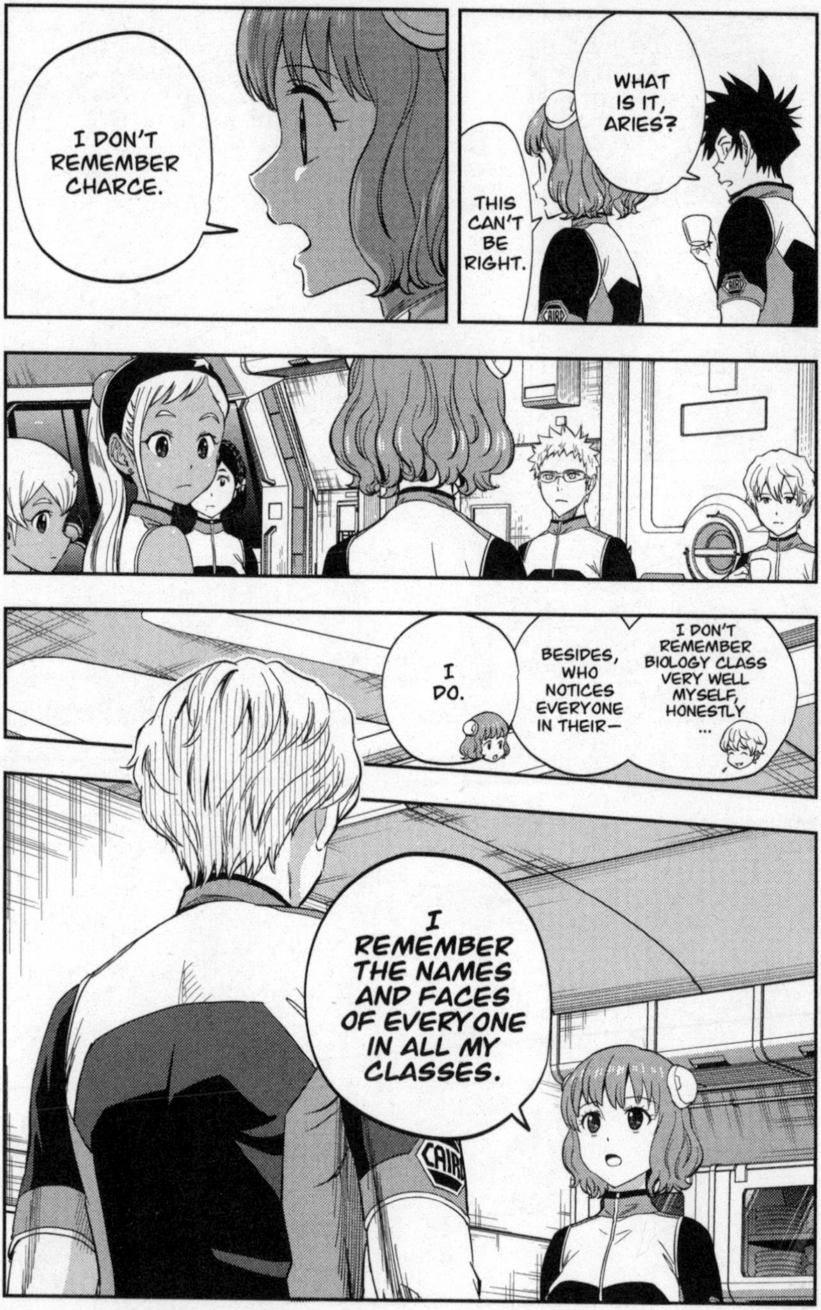
WHAT IS IT, ARIES?
THIS CAN'T BE RIGHT.
I DON'T REMEMBER CHARCE.
I DON'T REMEMBER BIOLOGY CLASS VERY WELL MYSELF, HONESTLY...
BESIDES, WHO NOTICES EVERYONE IN THEIR—
I DO.
I REMEMBER THE NAMES AND FACES OF EVERYONE IN ALL MY CLASSES.

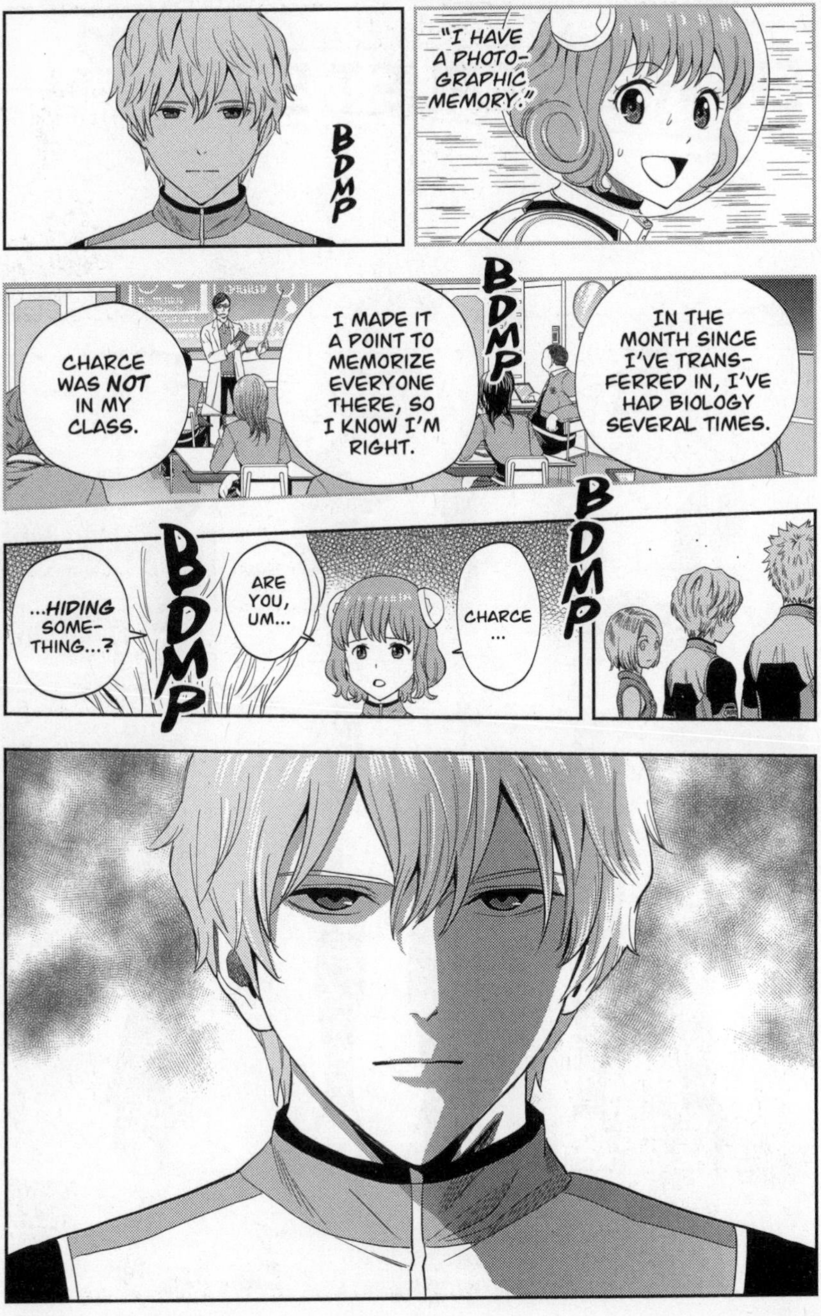
"I HAVE A PHOTO-GRAPHIC MEMORY."
BDMP
BDMP
IN THE MONTH SINCE I'VE TRANS-FERRED IN, I'VE HAD BIOLOGY SEVERAL TIMES.
I MADE IT A POINT TO MEMORIZE EVERYONE THERE, SO I KNOW I'M RIGHT.
CHARCE WAS **NOT** IN MY CLASS.
BDMP
CHARCE...
ARE YOU, UM...
BDMP
...HIDING SOME-THING...?

Material Collection   Costume Design

CHARCE'S CRUST SUIT

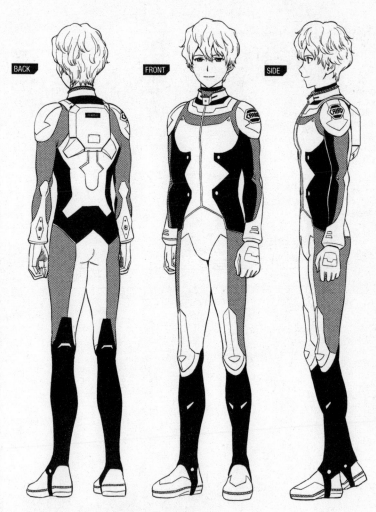

BACK

FRONT

SIDE

A Genesis men's crust suit.

Navy blue and white.

A classy design by Genesis, one of the oldest and most upscale crust suit manufacturers. Since it takes just the right person to wear it well, it's also known as the Prince Suit.

ASTRA LOST IN SPACE

#26

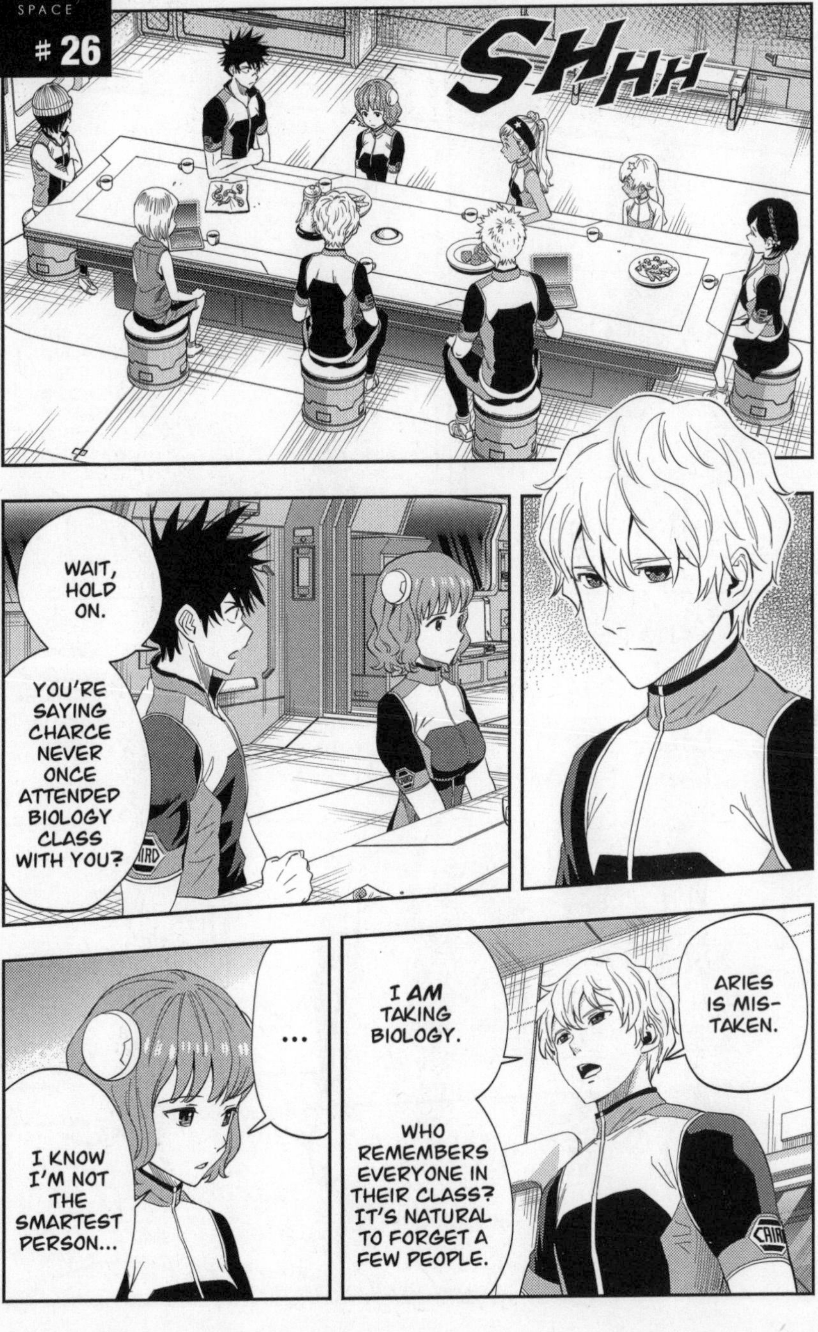
SHHH
WAIT, HOLD ON.
YOU'RE SAYING CHARCE NEVER ONCE ATTENDED BIOLOGY CLASS WITH YOU?
ARIES IS MIS-TAKEN.
I AM TAKING BIOLOGY.
WHO REMEMBERS EVERYONE IN THEIR CLASS? IT'S NATURAL TO FORGET A FEW PEOPLE.
...
I KNOW I'M NOT THE SMARTEST PERSON...

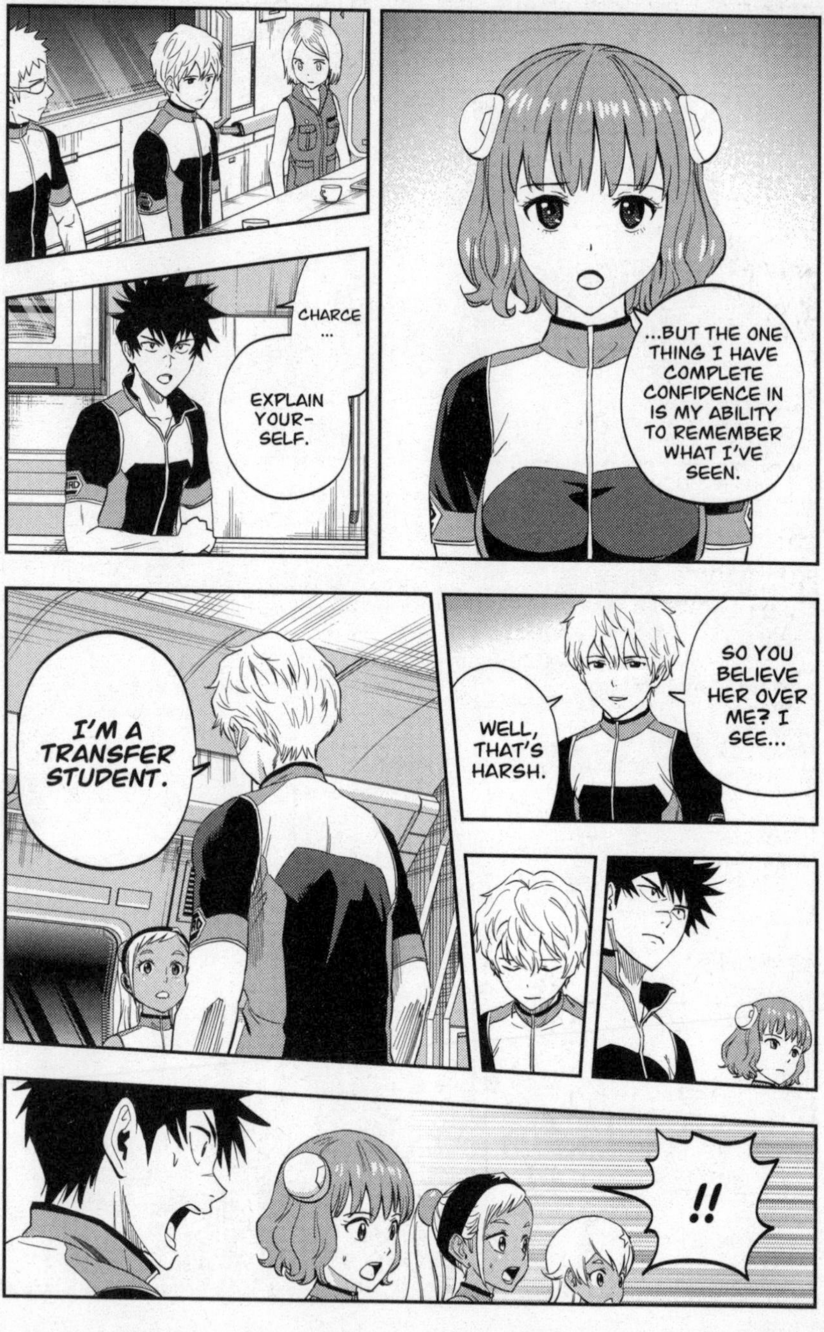
...BUT THE ONE THING I HAVE COMPLETE CONFIDENCE IN IS MY ABILITY TO REMEMBER WHAT I'VE SEEN.
CHARCE ...
EXPLAIN YOUR-SELF.
SO YOU BELIEVE HER OVER ME? I SEE...
WELL, THAT'S HARSH.
I'M A TRANSFER STUDENT.
!!

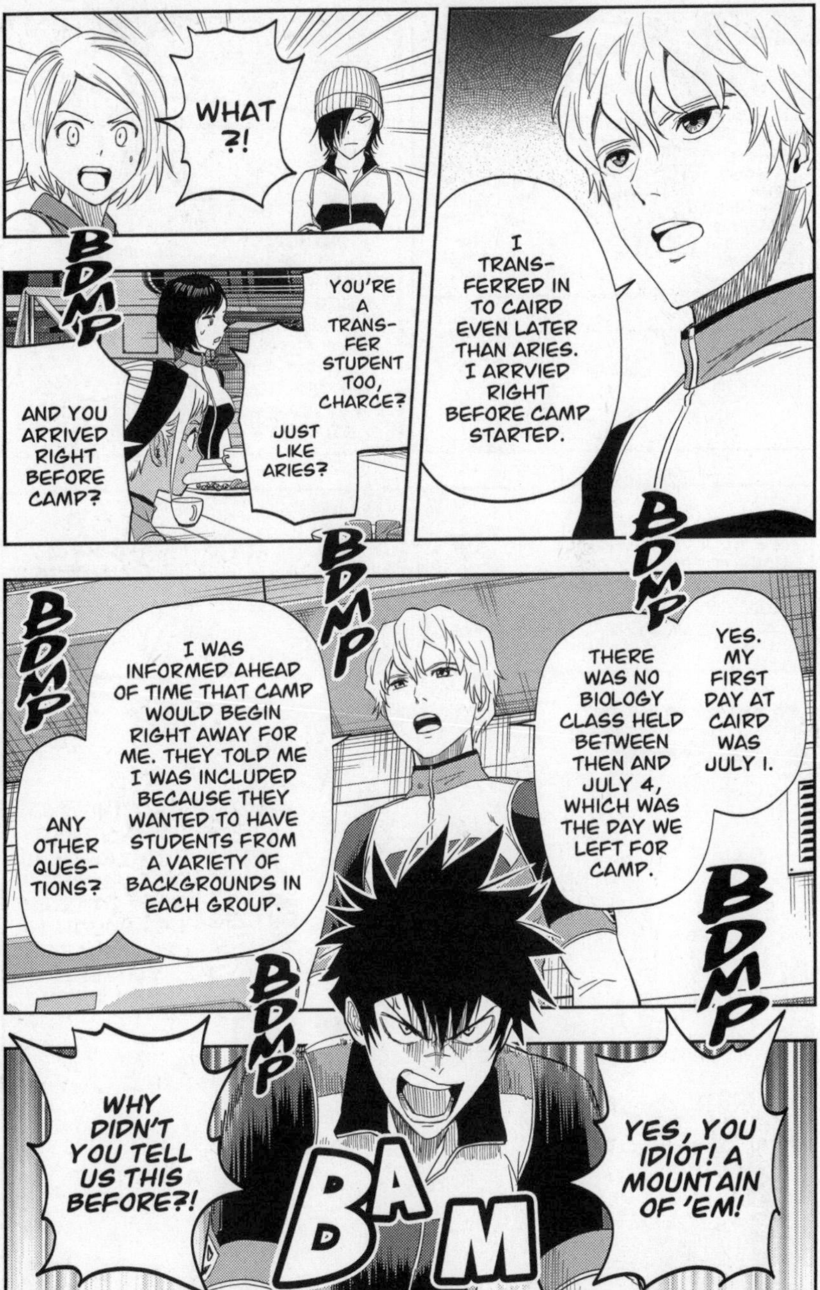
I TRANS-FERRED IN TO CAIRD EVEN LATER THAN ARIES. I ARRVIED RIGHT BEFORE CAMP STARTED.
WHAT ?!
BDMP
YOU'RE A TRANS-FER STUDENT TOO, CHARCE?
JUST LIKE ARIES?
AND YOU ARRIVED RIGHT BEFORE CAMP?
BDMP
BDMP
YES. MY FIRST DAY AT CAIRD WAS JULY 1.
THERE WAS NO BIOLOGY CLASS HELD BETWEEN THEN AND JULY 4, WHICH WAS THE DAY WE LEFT FOR CAMP.
I WAS INFORMED AHEAD OF TIME THAT CAMP WOULD BEGIN RIGHT AWAY FOR ME. THEY TOLD ME I WAS INCLUDED BECAUSE THEY WANTED TO HAVE STUDENTS FROM A VARIETY OF BACKGROUNDS IN EACH GROUP.
ANY OTHER QUES-TIONS?
BDMP
BDMP
BDMP
YES, YOU IDIOT! A MOUNTAIN OF 'EM!
BAM
WHY DIDN'T YOU TELL US THIS BEFORE?!

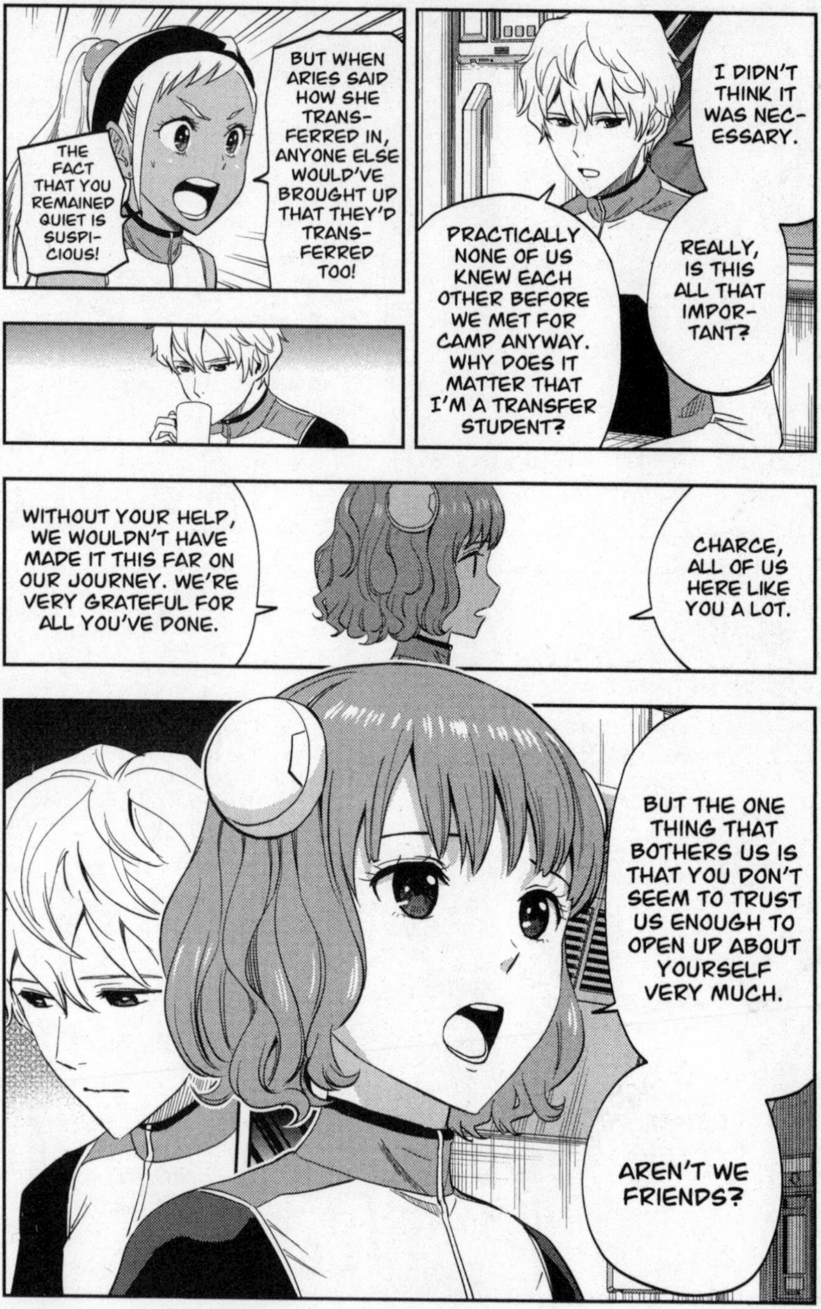
I DIDN'T THINK IT WAS NECESSARY.
REALLY, IS THIS ALL THAT IMPORTANT?
PRACTICALLY NONE OF US KNEW EACH OTHER BEFORE WE MET FOR CAMP ANYWAY. WHY DOES IT MATTER THAT I'M A TRANSFER STUDENT?
BUT WHEN ARIES SAID HOW SHE TRANSFERRED IN, ANYONE ELSE WOULD'VE BROUGHT UP THAT THEY'D TRANSFERRED TOO!
THE FACT THAT YOU REMAINED QUIET IS SUSPICIOUS!
CHARCE, ALL OF US HERE LIKE YOU A LOT.
WITHOUT YOUR HELP, WE WOULDN'T HAVE MADE IT THIS FAR ON OUR JOURNEY. WE'RE VERY GRATEFUL FOR ALL YOU'VE DONE.
BUT THE ONE THING THAT BOTHERS US IS THAT YOU DON'T SEEM TO TRUST US ENOUGH TO OPEN UP ABOUT YOURSELF VERY MUCH.
AREN'T WE FRIENDS?

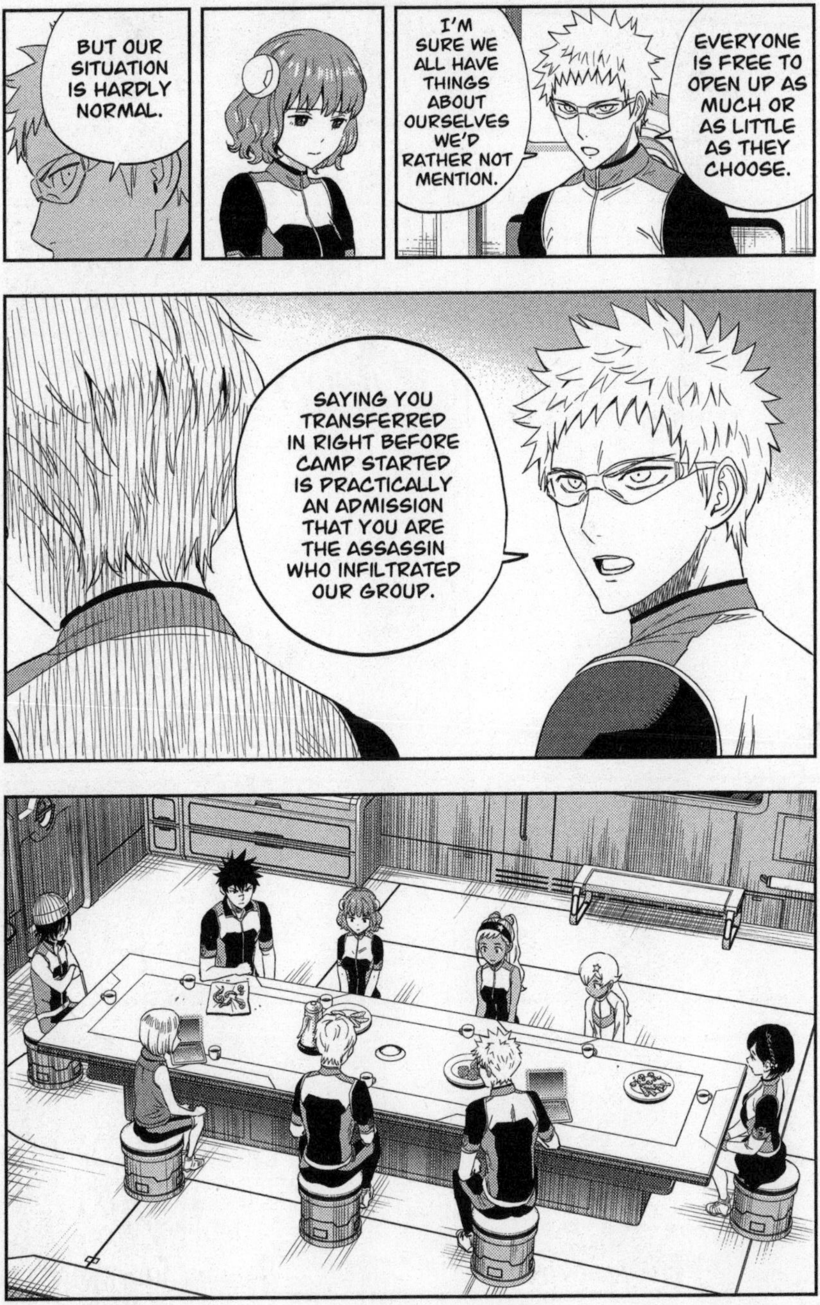
EVERYONE IS FREE TO OPEN UP AS MUCH OR AS LITTLE AS THEY CHOOSE.
I'M SURE WE ALL HAVE THINGS ABOUT OURSELVES WE'D RATHER NOT MENTION.
BUT OUR SITUATION IS HARDLY NORMAL.
SAYING YOU TRANSFERRED IN RIGHT BEFORE CAMP STARTED IS PRACTICALLY AN ADMISSION THAT YOU ARE THE ASSASSIN WHO INFILTRATED OUR GROUP.

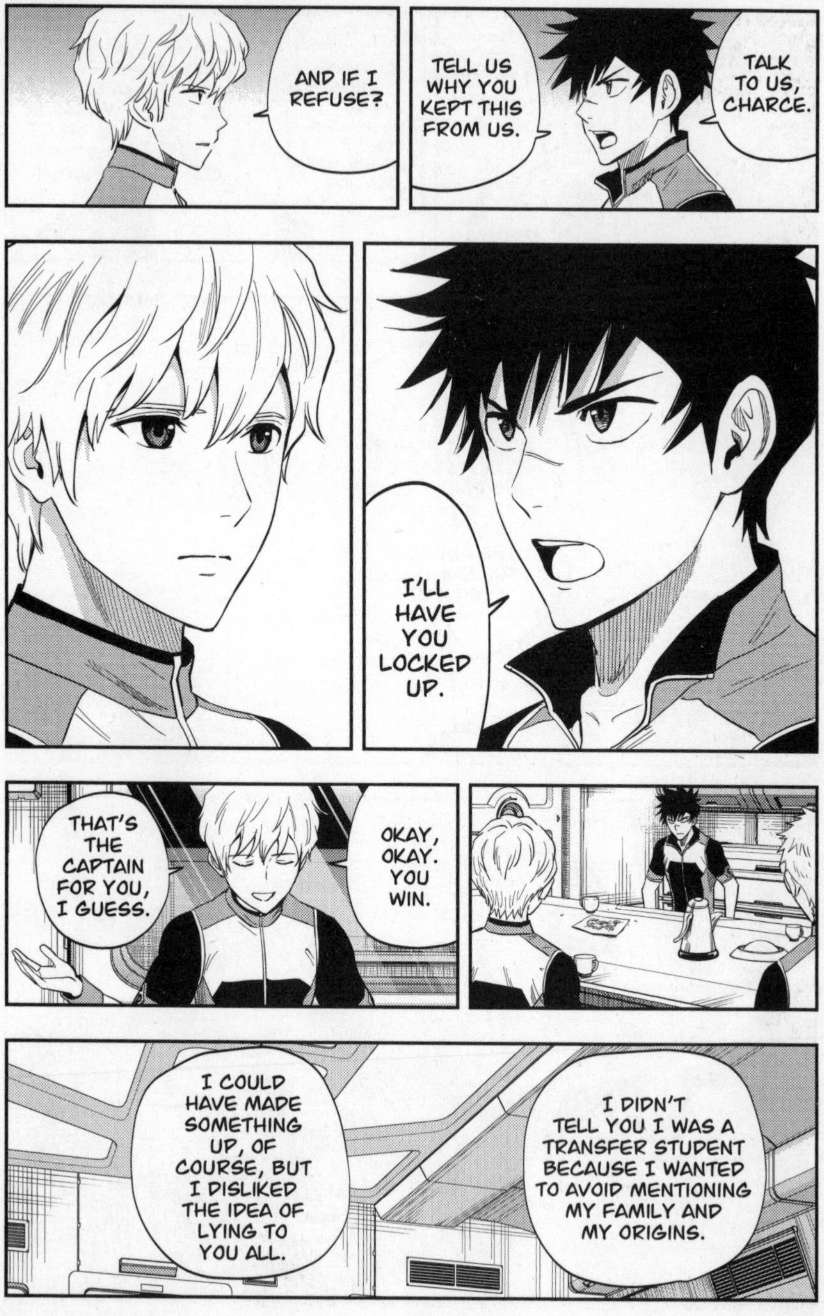
TALK TO US, CHARCE.
TELL US WHY YOU KEPT THIS FROM US.
AND IF I REFUSE?
I'LL HAVE YOU LOCKED UP.
OKAY, OKAY. YOU WIN.
THAT'S THE CAPTAIN FOR YOU, I GUESS.
I DIDN'T TELL YOU I WAS A TRANSFER STUDENT BECAUSE I WANTED TO AVOID MENTIONING MY FAMILY AND MY ORIGINS.
I COULD HAVE MADE SOMETHING UP, OF COURSE, BUT I DISLIKED THE IDEA OF LYING TO YOU ALL.

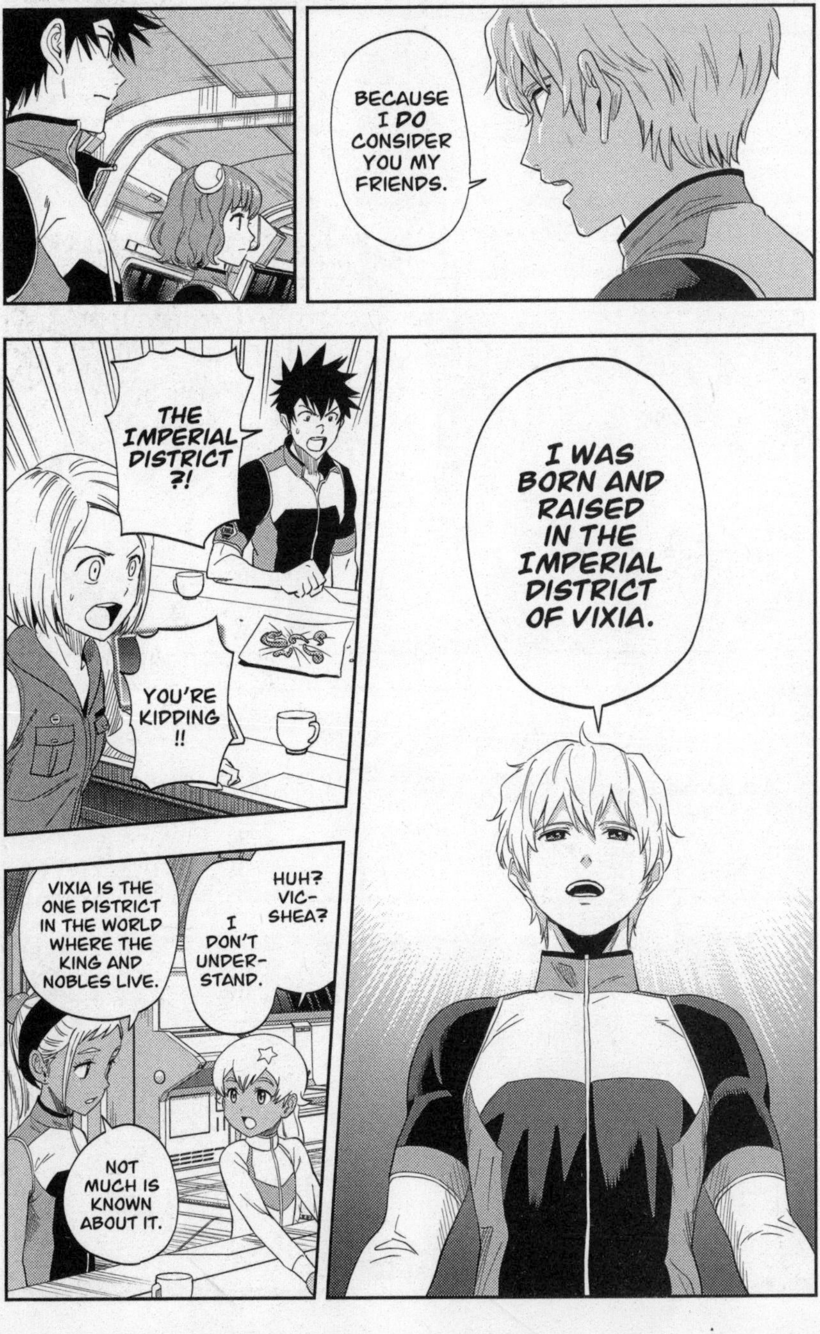
BECAUSE I DO CONSIDER YOU MY FRIENDS.
I WAS BORN AND RAISED IN THE IMPERIAL DISTRICT OF VIXIA.
THE IMPERIAL DISTRICT ?!
YOU'RE KIDDING !!
HUH? VIC-SHEA?
I DON'T UNDER-STAND.
VIXIA IS THE ONE DISTRICT IN THE WORLD WHERE THE KING AND NOBLES LIVE.
NOT MUCH IS KNOWN ABOUT IT.

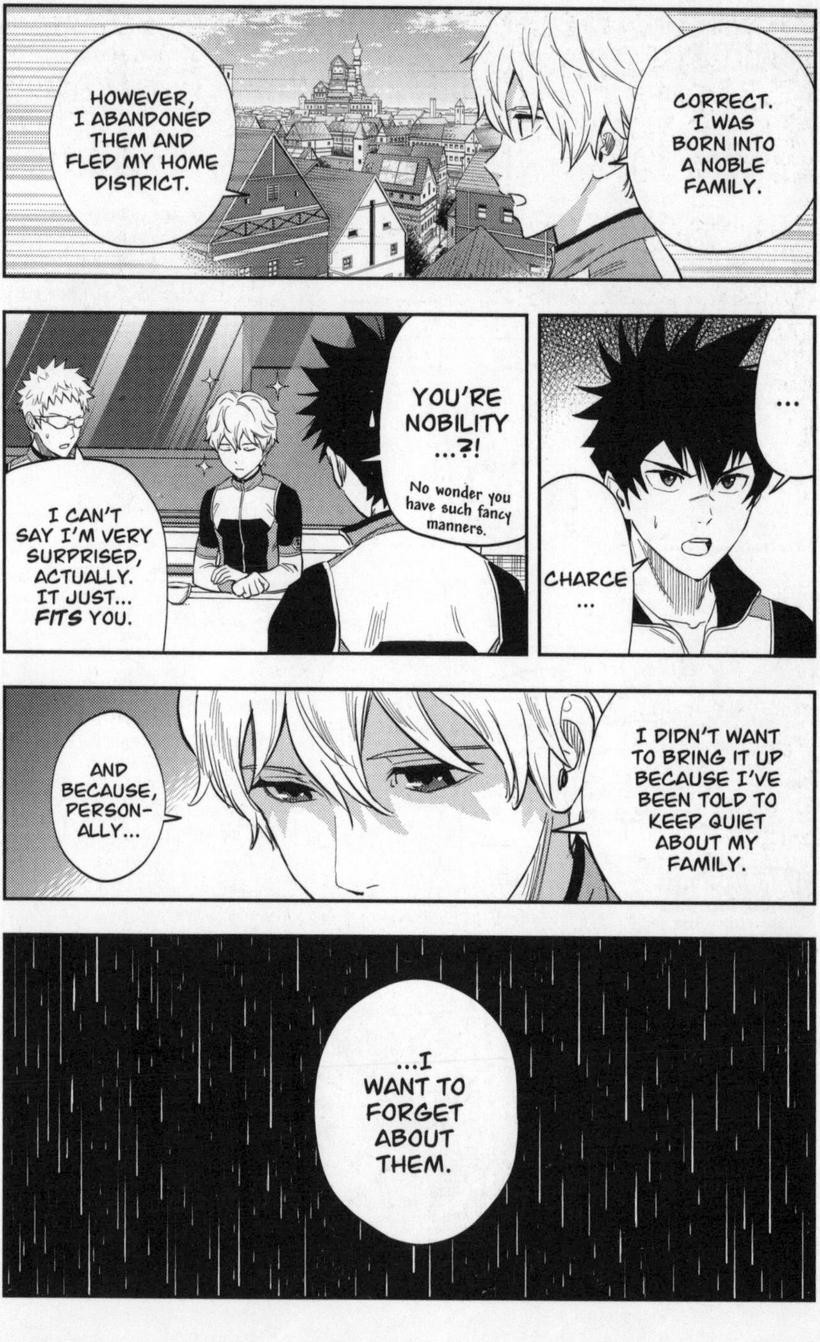
CORRECT. I WAS BORN INTO A NOBLE FAMILY.
HOWEVER, I ABANDONED THEM AND FLED MY HOME DISTRICT.
...
CHARCE ...
YOU'RE NOBILITY ...?!
No wonder you have such fancy manners.
I CAN'T SAY I'M VERY SURPRISED, ACTUALLY. IT JUST... FITS YOU.
I DIDN'T WANT TO BRING IT UP BECAUSE I'VE BEEN TOLD TO KEEP QUIET ABOUT MY FAMILY.
AND BECAUSE, PERSONALLY...
...I WANT TO FORGET ABOUT THEM.

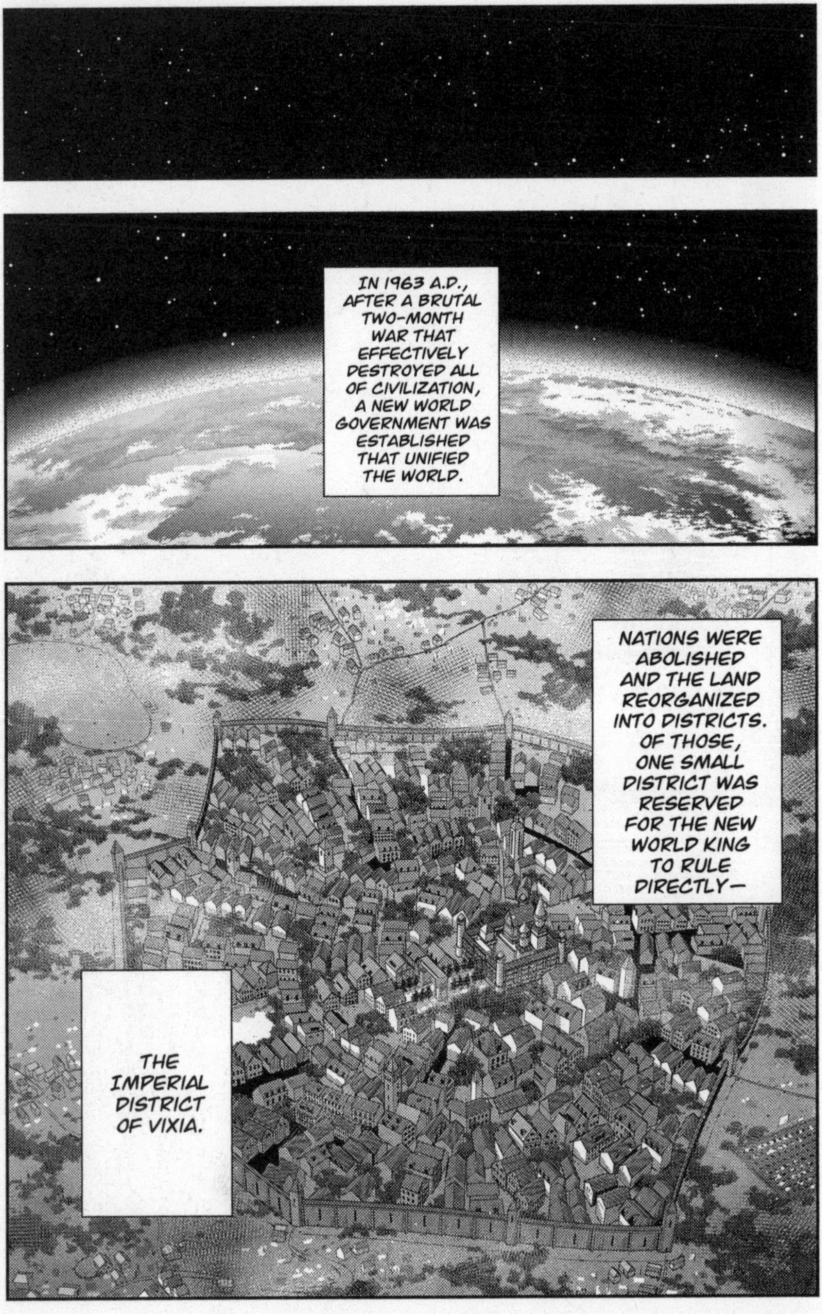
IN 1963 A.D., AFTER A BRUTAL TWO-MONTH WAR THAT EFFECTIVELY DESTROYED ALL OF CIVILIZATION, A NEW WORLD GOVERNMENT WAS ESTABLISHED THAT UNIFIED THE WORLD.
NATIONS WERE ABOLISHED AND THE LAND REORGANIZED INTO DISTRICTS. OF THOSE, ONE SMALL DISTRICT WAS RESERVED FOR THE NEW WORLD KING TO RULE DIRECTLY—
THE IMPERIAL DISTRICT OF VIXIA.

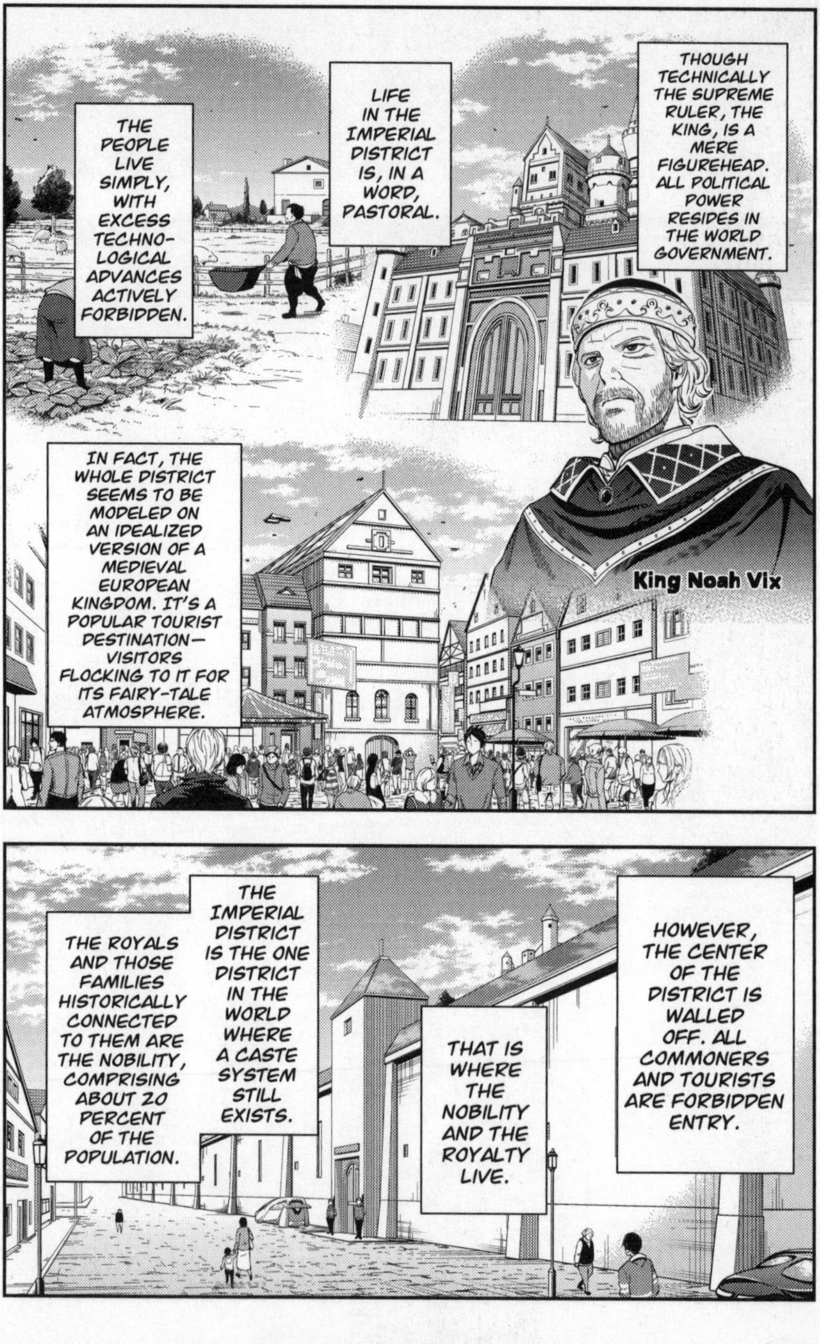
THOUGH TECHNICALLY THE SUPREME RULER, THE KING, IS A MERE FIGUREHEAD. ALL POLITICAL POWER RESIDES IN THE WORLD GOVERNMENT.
LIFE IN THE IMPERIAL DISTRICT IS, IN A WORD, PASTORAL.
THE PEOPLE LIVE SIMPLY, WITH EXCESS TECHNOLOGICAL ADVANCES ACTIVELY FORBIDDEN.
King Noah Vix
IN FACT, THE WHOLE DISTRICT SEEMS TO BE MODELED ON AN IDEALIZED VERSION OF A MEDIEVAL EUROPEAN KINGDOM. IT'S A POPULAR TOURIST DESTINATION—VISITORS FLOCKING TO IT FOR ITS FAIRY-TALE ATMOSPHERE.
HOWEVER, THE CENTER OF THE DISTRICT IS WALLED OFF. ALL COMMONERS AND TOURISTS ARE FORBIDDEN ENTRY.
THAT IS WHERE THE NOBILITY AND THE ROYALTY LIVE.
THE IMPERIAL DISTRICT IS THE ONE DISTRICT IN THE WORLD WHERE A CASTE SYSTEM STILL EXISTS.
THE ROYALS AND THOSE FAMILIES HISTORICALLY CONNECTED TO THEM ARE THE NOBILITY, COMPRISING ABOUT 20 PERCENT OF THE POPULATION.

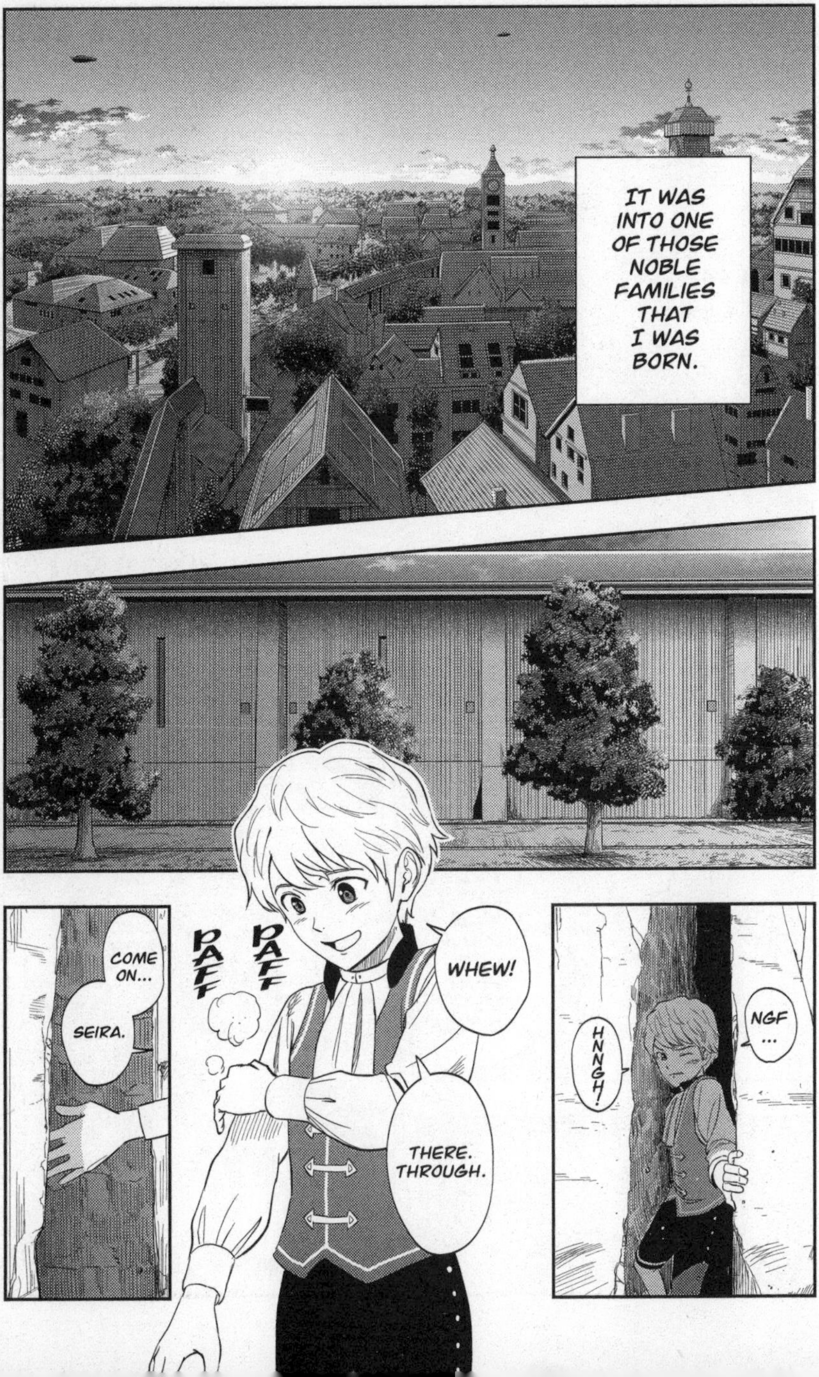
IT WAS INTO ONE OF THOSE NOBLE FAMILIES THAT I WAS BORN.
NGF...
HNNGH!
WHEW!
PAFF PAFF
THERE. THROUGH.
COME ON...
SEIRA.

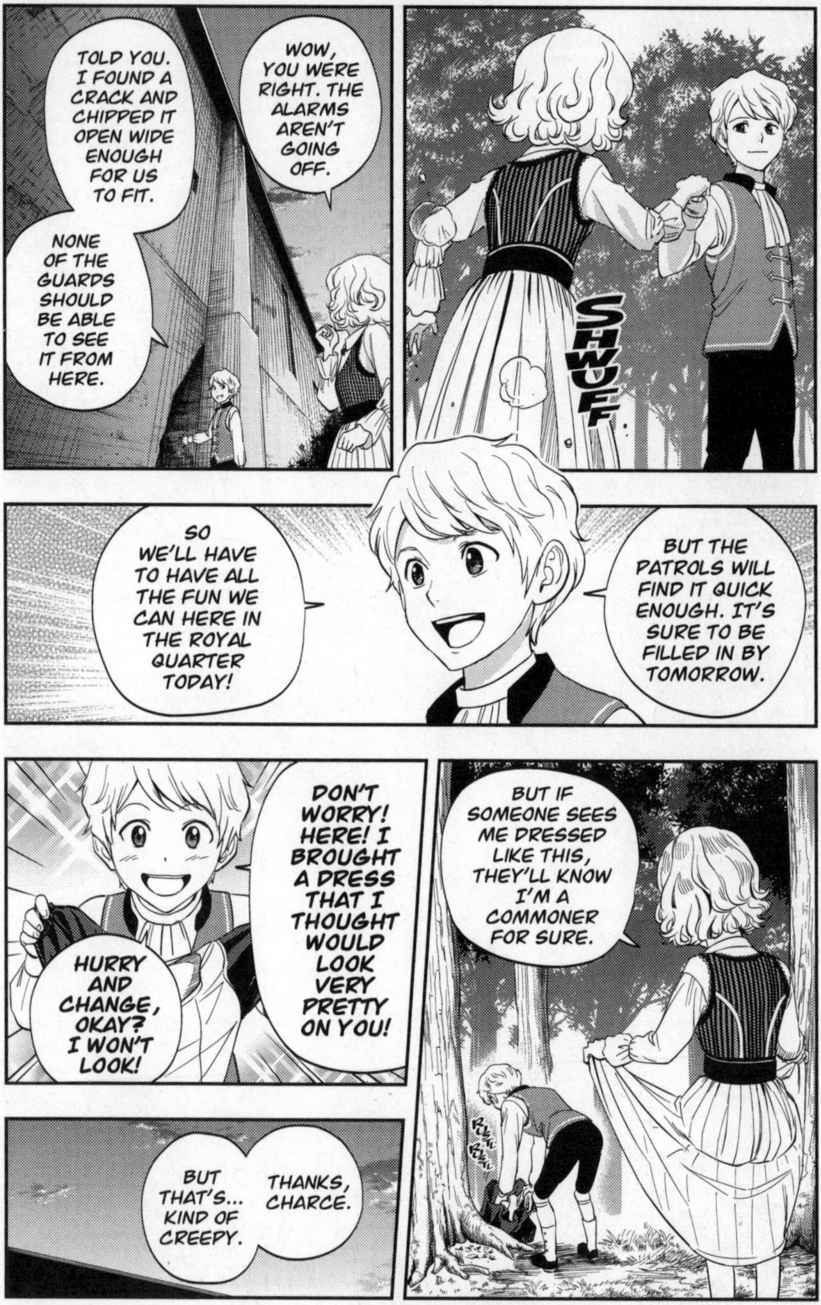
SHWUFF
WOW, YOU WERE RIGHT. THE ALARMS AREN'T GOING OFF.
TOLD YOU. I FOUND A CRACK AND CHIPPED IT OPEN WIDE ENOUGH FOR US TO FIT.
NONE OF THE GUARDS SHOULD BE ABLE TO SEE IT FROM HERE.
BUT THE PATROLS WILL FIND IT QUICK ENOUGH. IT'S SURE TO BE FILLED IN BY TOMORROW.
SO WE'LL HAVE TO HAVE ALL THE FUN WE CAN HERE IN THE ROYAL QUARTER TODAY!
BUT IF SOMEONE SEES ME DRESSED LIKE THIS, THEY'LL KNOW I'M A COMMONER FOR SURE.
DON'T WORRY! HERE! I BROUGHT A DRESS THAT I THOUGHT WOULD LOOK VERY PRETTY ON YOU!
HURRY AND CHANGE, OKAY? I WON'T LOOK!
THANKS, CHARCE.
BUT THAT'S... KIND OF CREEPY.

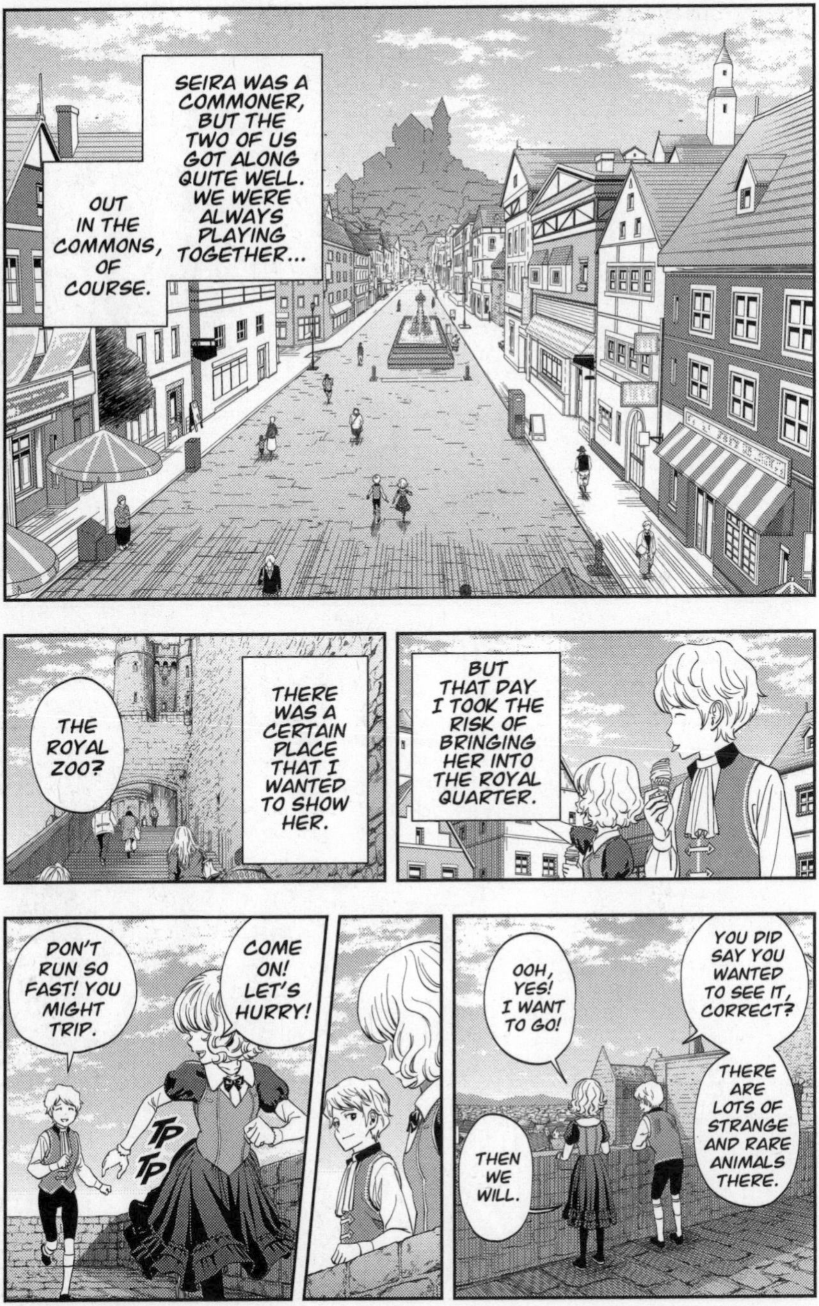
SEIRA WAS A COMMONER, BUT THE TWO OF US GOT ALONG QUITE WELL. WE WERE ALWAYS PLAYING TOGETHER...
OUT IN THE COMMONS, OF COURSE.
BUT THAT DAY I TOOK THE RISK OF BRINGING HER INTO THE ROYAL QUARTER.
THERE WAS A CERTAIN PLACE THAT I WANTED TO SHOW HER.
THE ROYAL ZOO?
YOU DID SAY YOU WANTED TO SEE IT, CORRECT?
THERE ARE LOTS OF STRANGE AND RARE ANIMALS THERE.
OOH, YES! I WANT TO GO!
THEN WE WILL.
COME ON! LET'S HURRY!
TP TP
DON'T RUN SO FAST! YOU MIGHT TRIP.

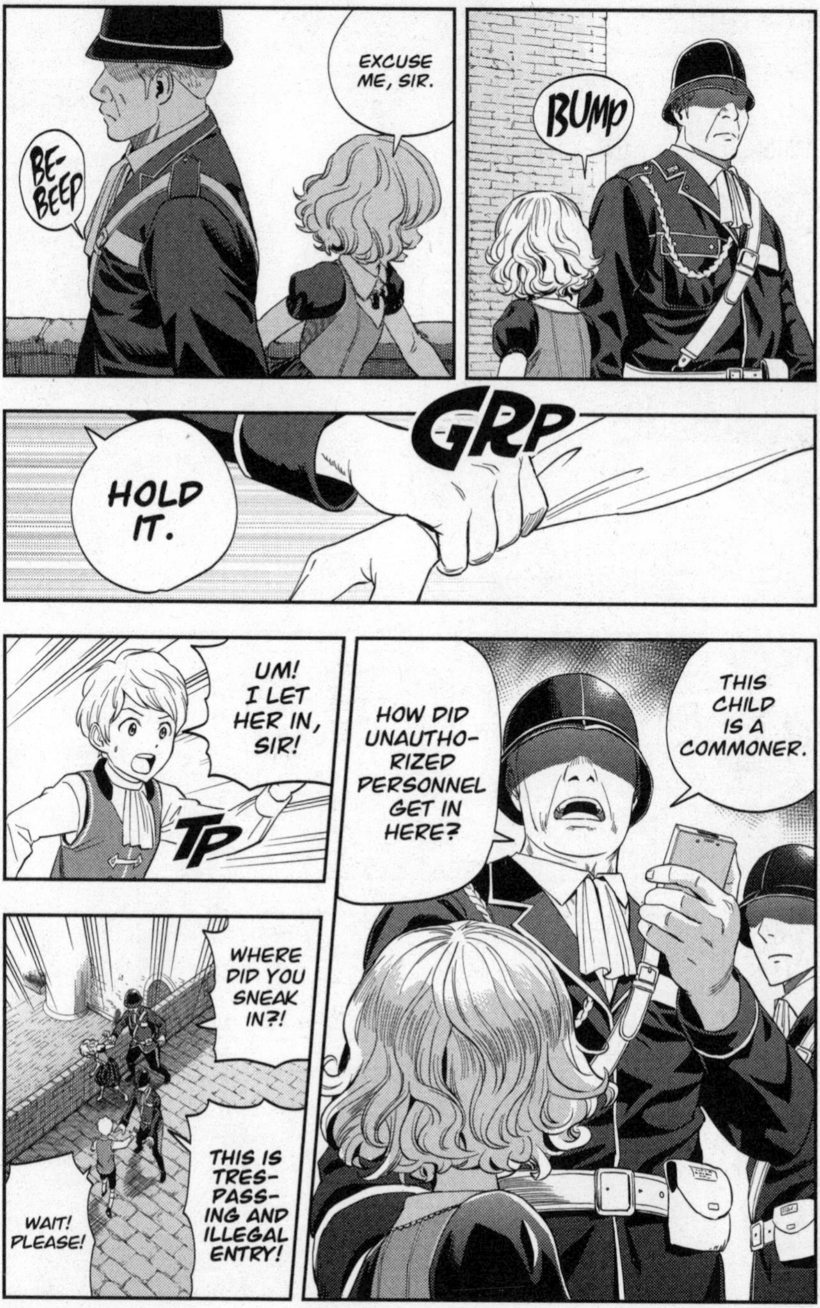
BUMP
EXCUSE ME, SIR.
BE-BEEP
GRP
HOLD IT.
THIS CHILD IS A COMMONER.
HOW DID UNAUTHO-RIZED PERSONNEL GET IN HERE?
UM! I LET HER IN, SIR!
TP
WHERE DID YOU SNEAK IN?!
THIS IS TRES-PASS-ING AND ILLEGAL ENTRY!
WAIT! PLEASE!

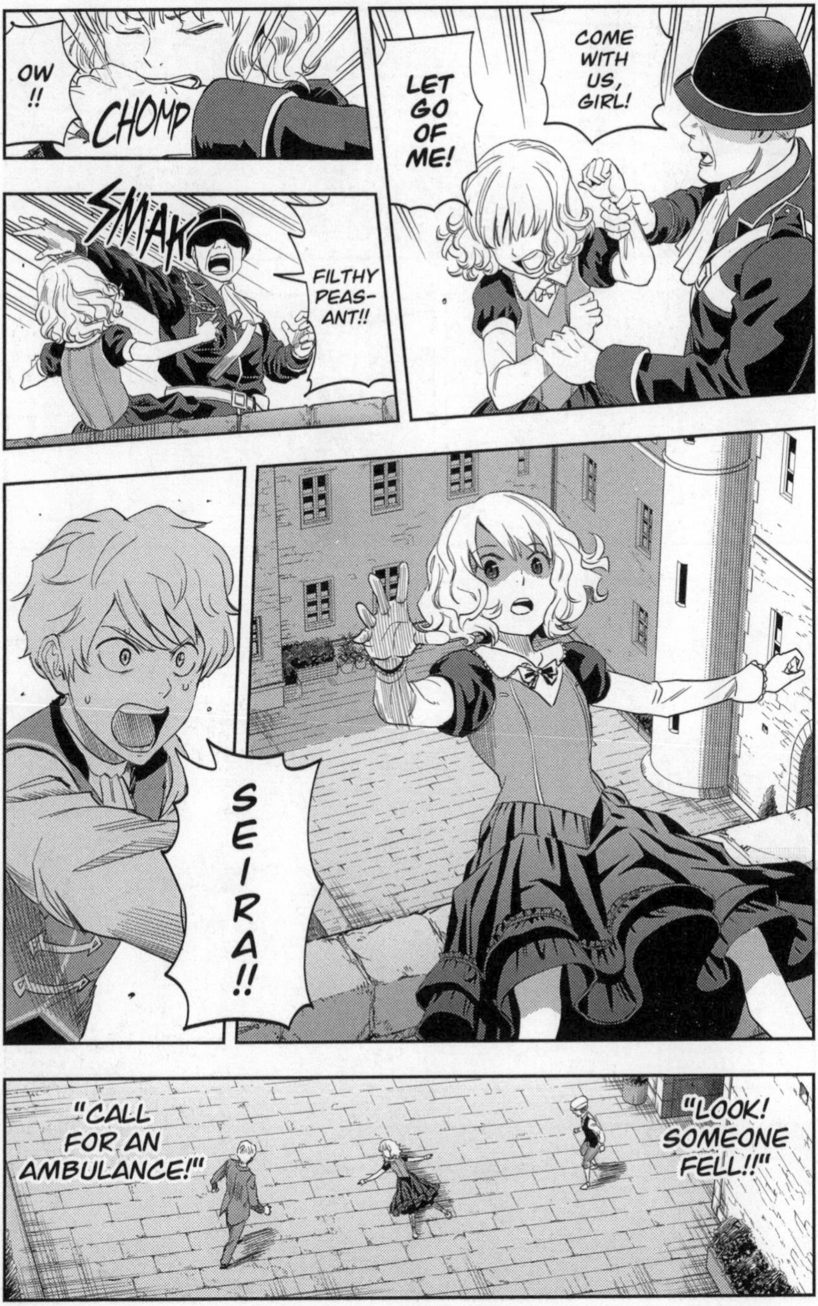
COME WITH US, GIRL!
LET GO OF ME!
OW!!
CHOMP
SMAK
FILTHY PEAS-ANT!!
SEIRA!!
"LOOK! SOMEONE FELL!!"
"CALL FOR AN AMBULANCE!"

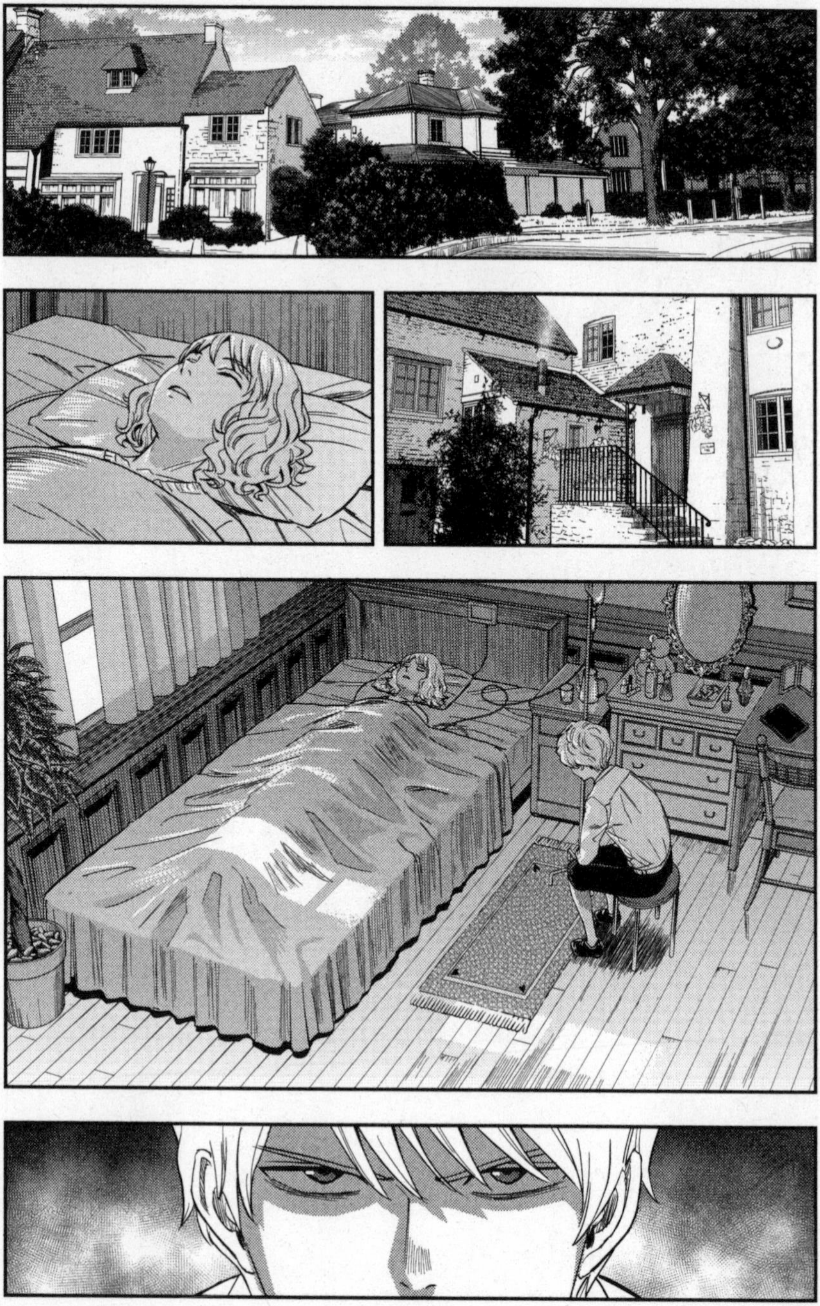

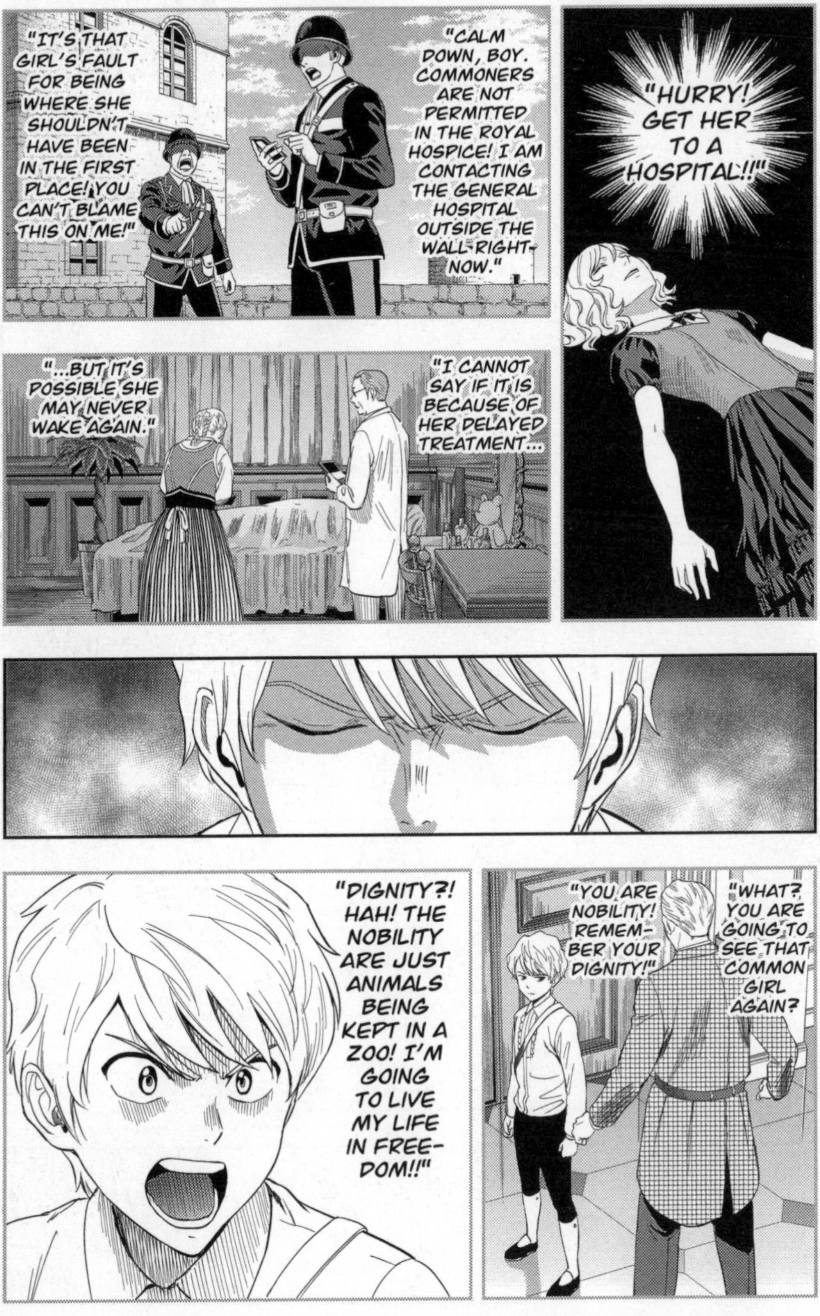
"HURRY! GET HER TO A HOSPITAL!!"
"CALM DOWN, BOY. COMMONERS ARE NOT PERMITTED IN THE ROYAL HOSPICE! I AM CONTACTING THE GENERAL HOSPITAL OUTSIDE THE WALL RIGHT NOW."
"IT'S THAT GIRL'S FAULT FOR BEING WHERE SHE SHOULDN'T HAVE BEEN IN THE FIRST PLACE! YOU CAN'T BLAME THIS ON ME!"
"I CANNOT SAY IF IT IS BECAUSE OF HER DELAYED TREATMENT...
"...BUT IT'S POSSIBLE SHE MAY NEVER WAKE AGAIN."
"WHAT? YOU ARE GOING TO SEE THAT COMMON GIRL AGAIN?
"YOU ARE NOBILITY! REMEM-BER YOUR DIGNITY!"
"DIGNITY?! HAH! THE NOBILITY ARE JUST ANIMALS BEING KEPT IN A ZOO! I'M GOING TO LIVE MY LIFE IN FREE-DOM!!"

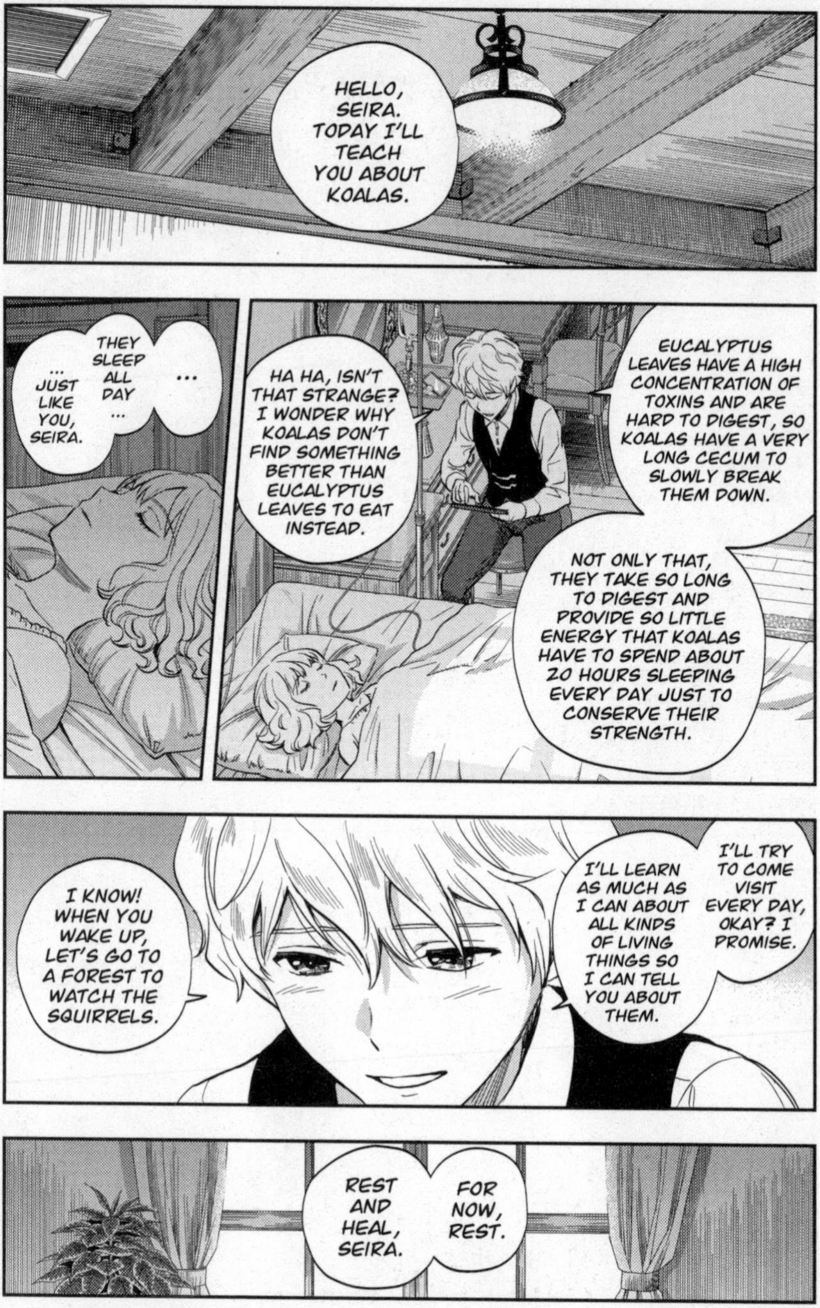
HELLO, SEIRA. TODAY I'LL TEACH YOU ABOUT KOALAS.
EUCALYPTUS LEAVES HAVE A HIGH CONCENTRATION OF TOXINS AND ARE HARD TO DIGEST, SO KOALAS HAVE A VERY LONG CECUM TO SLOWLY BREAK THEM DOWN.
NOT ONLY THAT, THEY TAKE SO LONG TO DIGEST AND PROVIDE SO LITTLE ENERGY THAT KOALAS HAVE TO SPEND ABOUT 20 HOURS SLEEPING EVERY DAY JUST TO CONSERVE THEIR STRENGTH.
HA HA, ISN'T THAT STRANGE? I WONDER WHY KOALAS DON'T FIND SOMETHING BETTER THAN EUCALYPTUS LEAVES TO EAT INSTEAD.
...
THEY SLEEP ALL DAY ...
... JUST LIKE YOU, SEIRA.
I'LL TRY TO COME VISIT EVERY DAY, OKAY? I PROMISE.
I'LL LEARN AS MUCH AS I CAN ABOUT ALL KINDS OF LIVING THINGS SO I CAN TELL YOU ABOUT THEM.
I KNOW! WHEN YOU WAKE UP, LET'S GO TO A FOREST TO WATCH THE SQUIRRELS.
FOR NOW, REST.
REST AND HEAL, SEIRA.

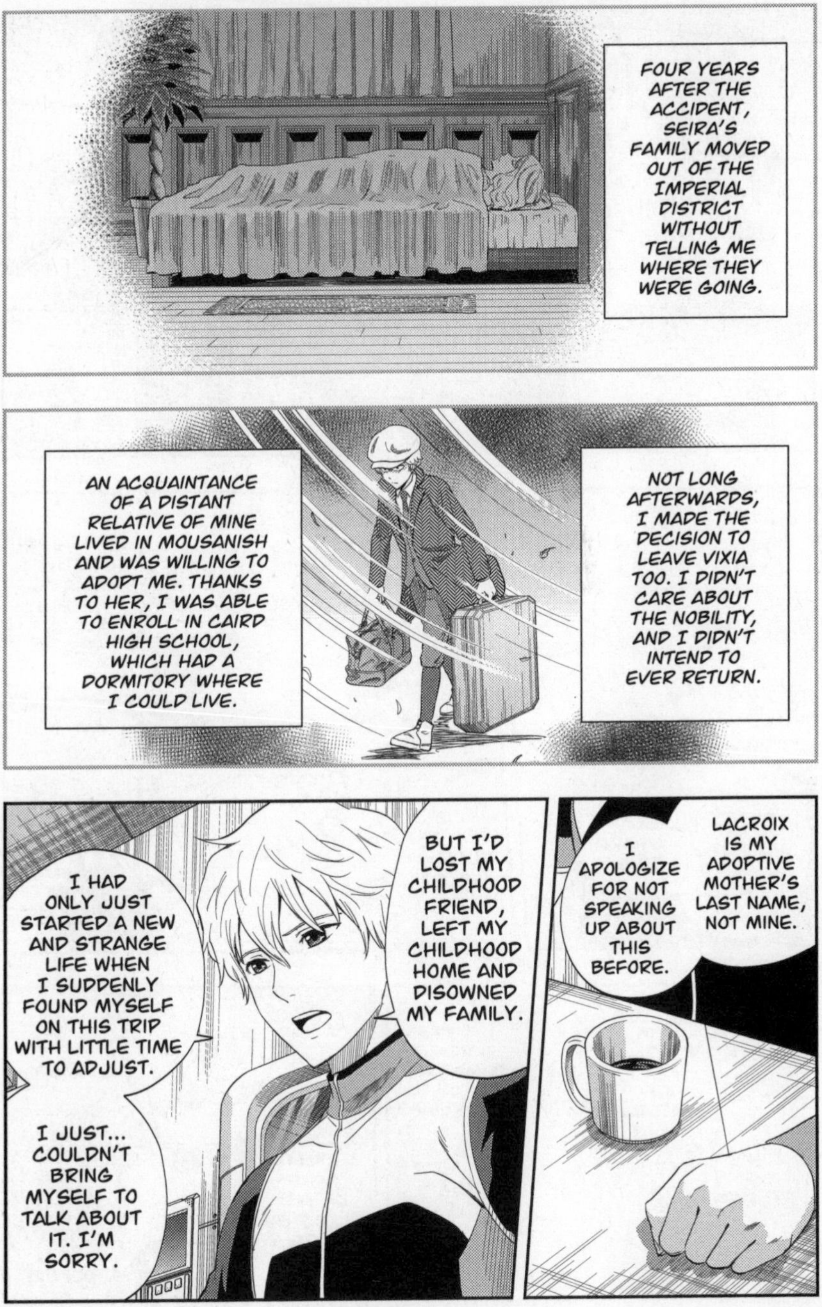
FOUR YEARS AFTER THE ACCIDENT, SEIRA'S FAMILY MOVED OUT OF THE IMPERIAL DISTRICT WITHOUT TELLING ME WHERE THEY WERE GOING.
NOT LONG AFTERWARDS, I MADE THE DECISION TO LEAVE VIXIA TOO. I DIDN'T CARE ABOUT THE NOBILITY, AND I DIDN'T INTEND TO EVER RETURN.
AN ACQUAINTANCE OF A DISTANT RELATIVE OF MINE LIVED IN MOUSANISH AND WAS WILLING TO ADOPT ME. THANKS TO HER, I WAS ABLE TO ENROLL IN CAIRD HIGH SCHOOL, WHICH HAD A DORMITORY WHERE I COULD LIVE.
LACROIX IS MY ADOPTIVE MOTHER'S LAST NAME, NOT MINE.
I APOLOGIZE FOR NOT SPEAKING UP ABOUT THIS BEFORE.
BUT I'D LOST MY CHILDHOOD FRIEND, LEFT MY CHILDHOOD HOME AND DISOWNED MY FAMILY.
I HAD ONLY JUST STARTED A NEW AND STRANGE LIFE WHEN I SUDDENLY FOUND MYSELF ON THIS TRIP WITH LITTLE TIME TO ADJUST.
I JUST... COULDN'T BRING MYSELF TO TALK ABOUT IT. I'M SORRY.

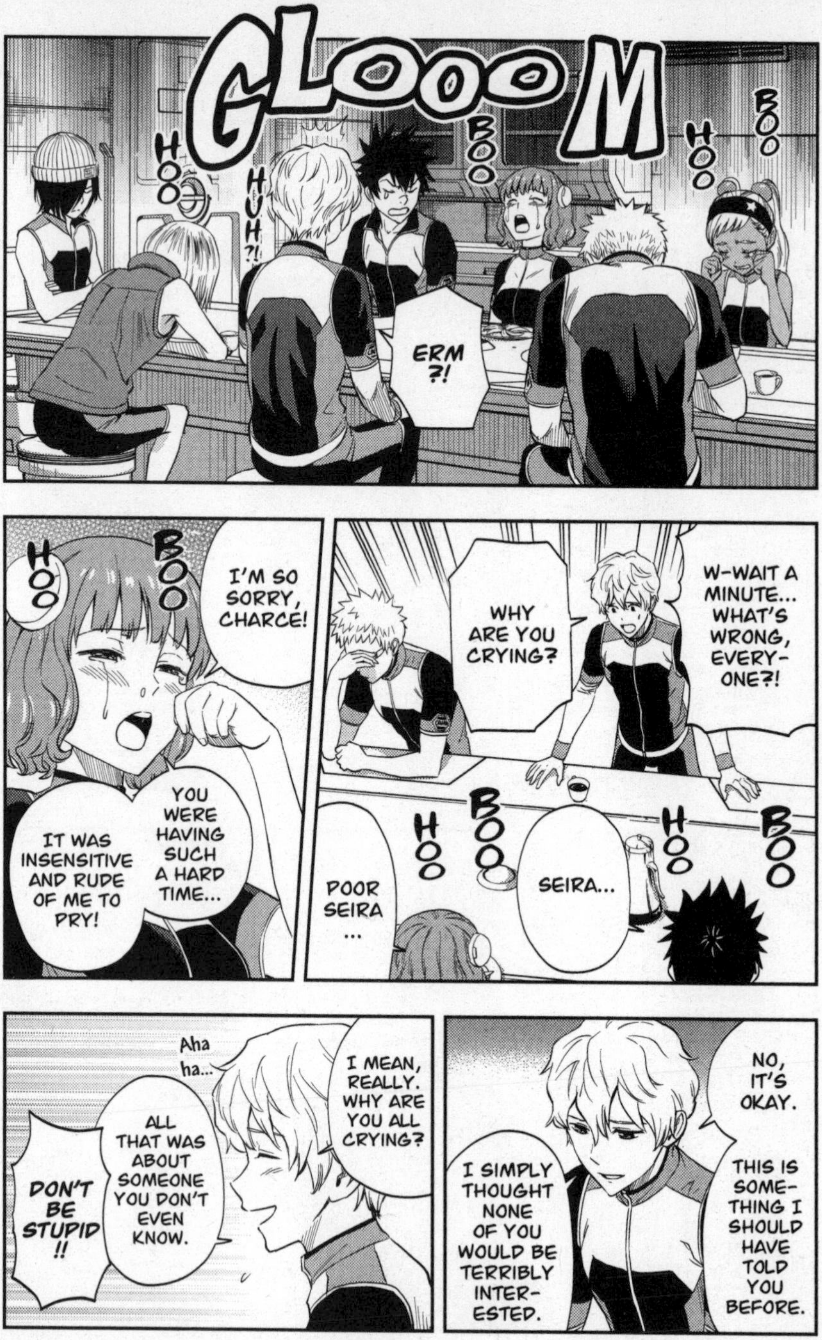
GLOOOM
BOO HOO
ERM?!
BOO HOO
HUH?!
HOO
W-WAIT A MINUTE... WHAT'S WRONG, EVERYONE?!
WHY ARE YOU CRYING?
BOO HOO
SEIRA...
BOO HOO
POOR SEIRA...
BOO HOO
I'M SO SORRY, CHARCE!
YOU WERE HAVING SUCH A HARD TIME...
IT WAS INSENSITIVE AND RUDE OF ME TO PRY!
NO, IT'S OKAY.
THIS IS SOMETHING I SHOULD HAVE TOLD YOU BEFORE.
I SIMPLY THOUGHT NONE OF YOU WOULD BE TERRIBLY INTERESTED.
I MEAN, REALLY. WHY ARE YOU ALL CRYING?
Aha ha...
ALL THAT WAS ABOUT SOMEONE YOU DON'T EVEN KNOW.
DON'T BE STUPID!!

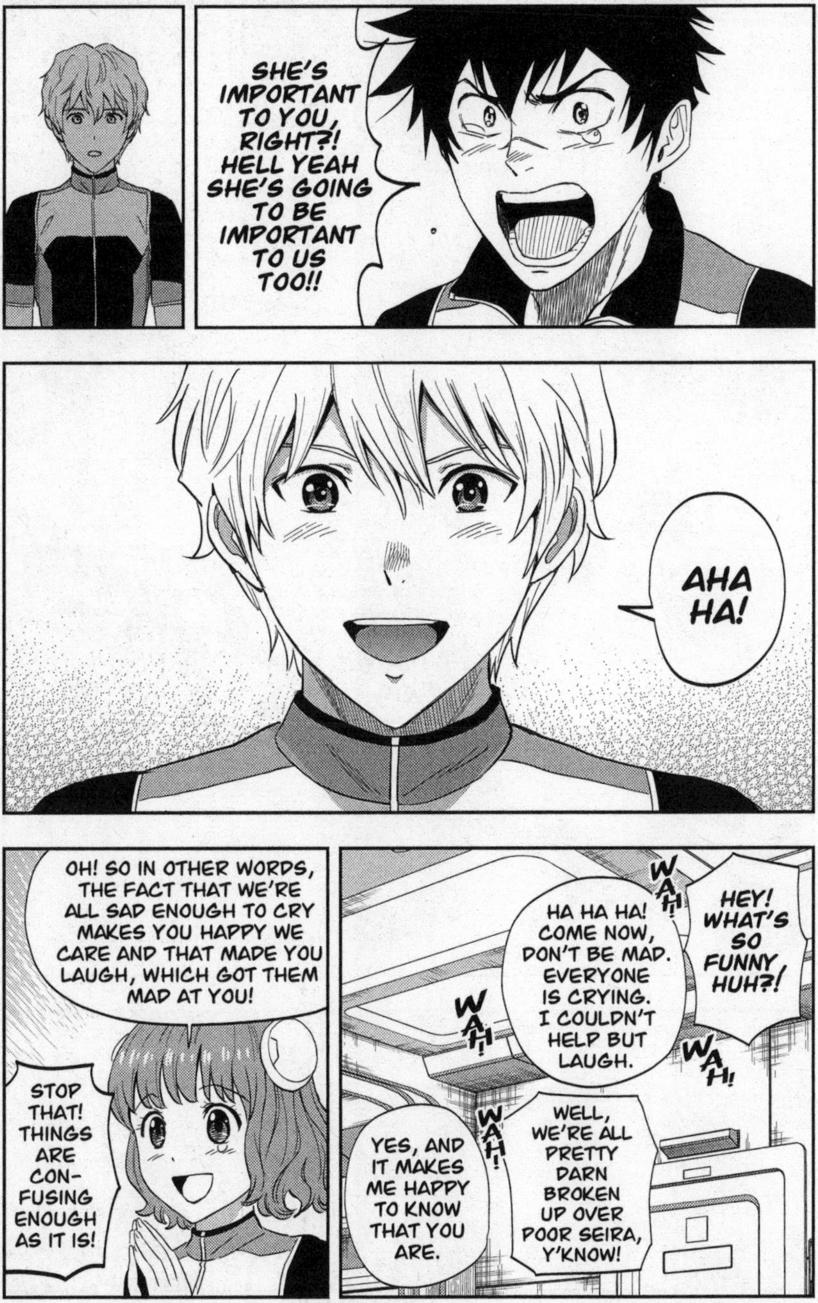
SHE'S IMPORTANT TO YOU, RIGHT?! HELL YEAH SHE'S GOING TO BE IMPORTANT TO US TOO!!
AHA HA!
HEY! WHAT'S SO FUNNY, HUH?!
WAH!
HA HA HA! COME NOW, DON'T BE MAD. EVERYONE IS CRYING. I COULDN'T HELP BUT LAUGH.
WAH!
WAH!
WELL, WE'RE ALL PRETTY DARN BROKEN UP OVER POOR SEIRA, Y'KNOW!
WAH!
YES, AND IT MAKES ME HAPPY TO KNOW THAT YOU ARE.
OH! SO IN OTHER WORDS, THE FACT THAT WE'RE ALL SAD ENOUGH TO CRY MAKES YOU HAPPY WE CARE AND THAT MADE YOU LAUGH, WHICH GOT THEM MAD AT YOU!
STOP THAT! THINGS ARE CON-FUSING ENOUGH AS IT IS!

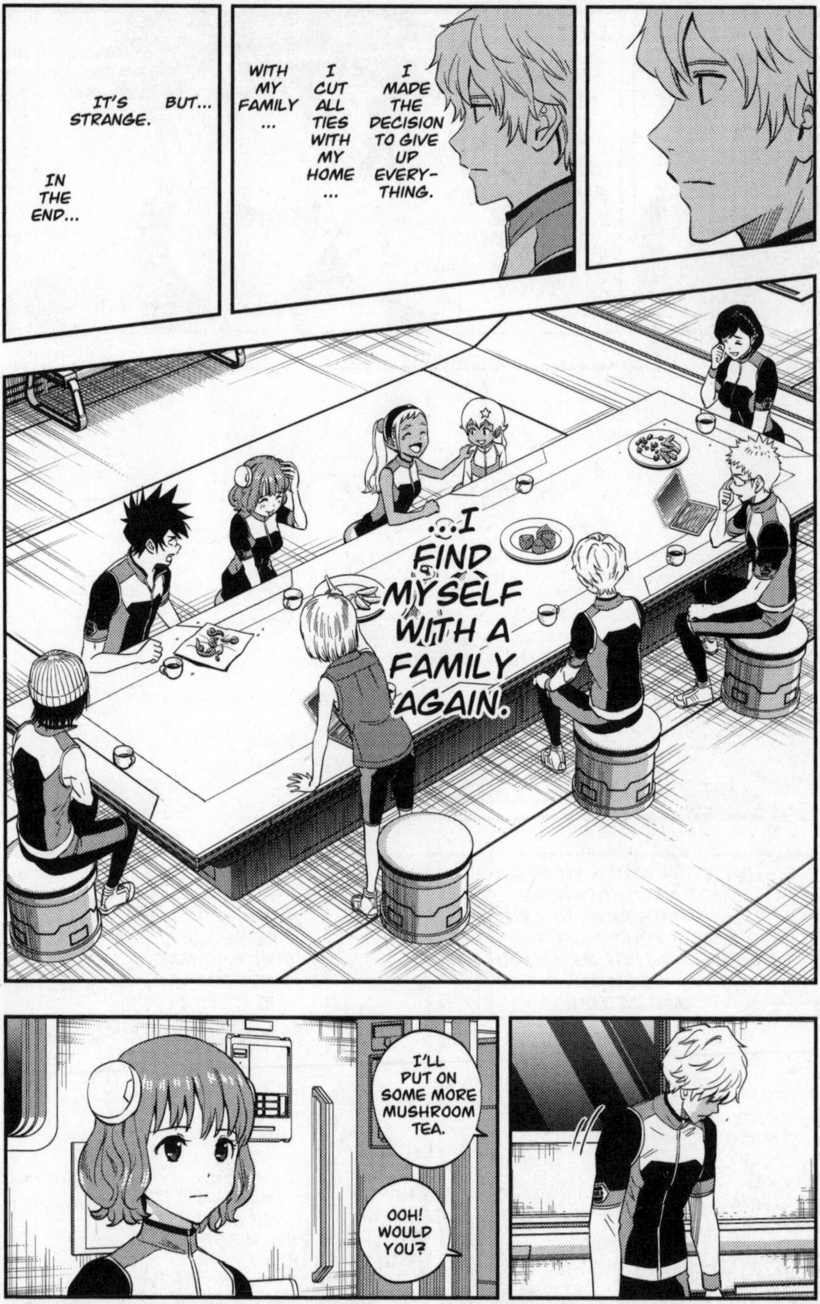
I MADE THE DECISION TO GIVE UP EVERYTHING.
I CUT ALL TIES WITH MY HOME...
WITH MY FAMILY...
BUT...
IT'S STRANGE.
IN THE END...
...I FIND MYSELF WITH A FAMILY AGAIN.
I'LL PUT ON SOME MORE MUSHROOM TEA.
OOH! WOULD YOU?

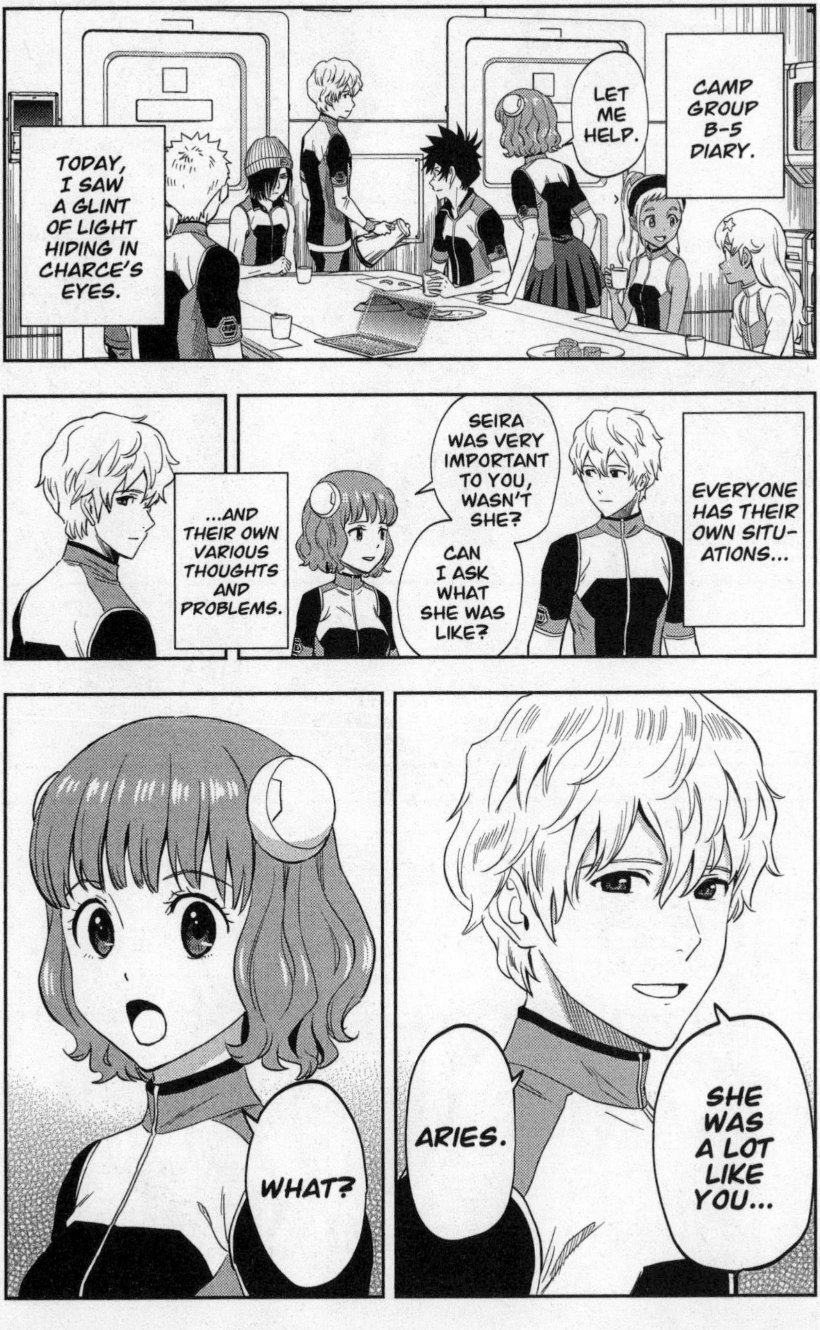
CAMP GROUP B-5 DIARY.
LET ME HELP.
TODAY, I SAW A GLINT OF LIGHT HIDING IN CHARCE'S EYES.
EVERYONE HAS THEIR OWN SITU-ATIONS...
SEIRA WAS VERY IMPORTANT TO YOU, WASN'T SHE?
CAN I ASK WHAT SHE WAS LIKE?
...AND THEIR OWN VARIOUS THOUGHTS AND PROBLEMS.
SHE WAS A LOT LIKE YOU...
ARIES.
WHAT?

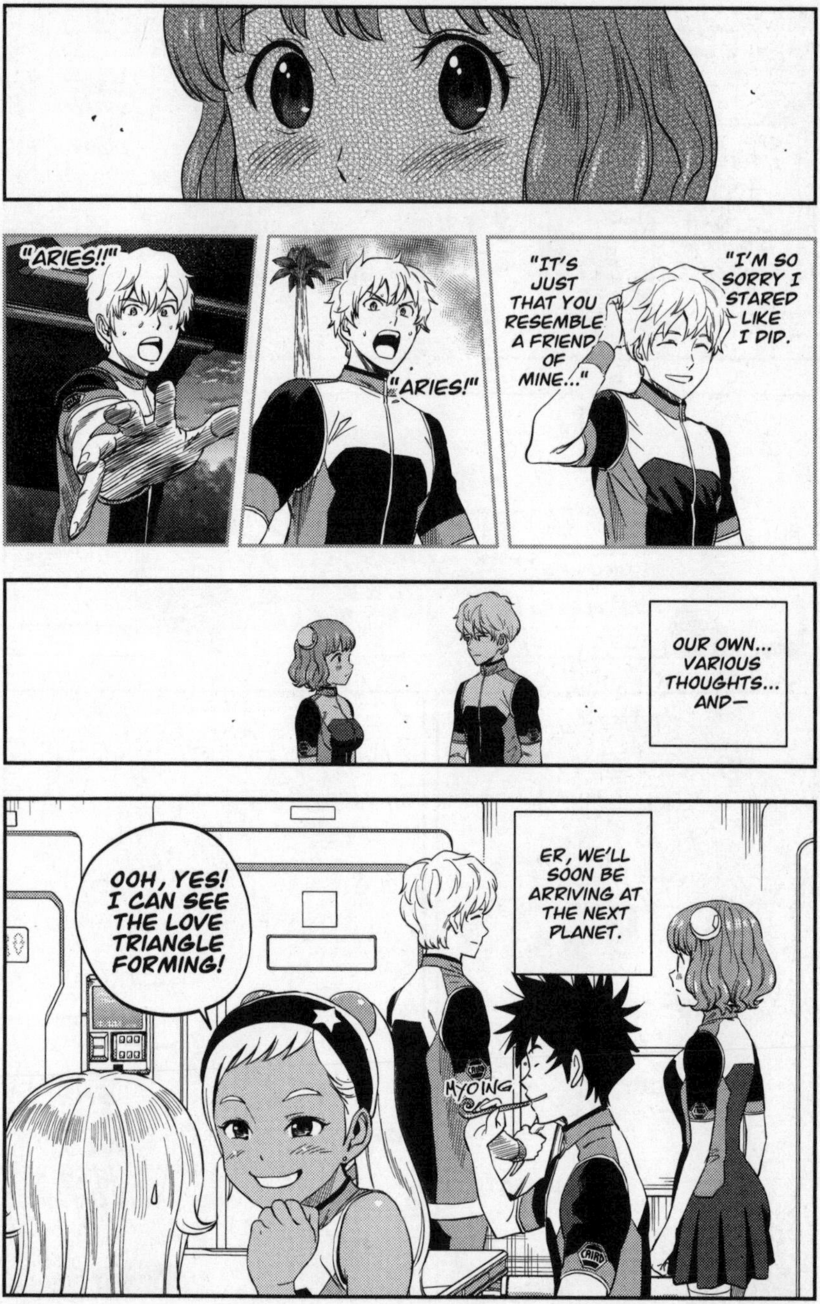
"I'M SO SORRY I STARED LIKE I DID.
"IT'S JUST THAT YOU RESEMBLE A FRIEND OF MINE..."
"ARIES!"
"ARIES!!"
OUR OWN... VARIOUS THOUGHTS... AND—
ER, WE'LL SOON BE ARRIVING AT THE NEXT PLANET.
OOH, YES! I CAN SEE THE LOVE TRIANGLE FORMING!
MYOING

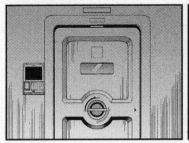

SEIRA... I'M SORRY.

Material Collection Characters

Material Collection
Character Profile 23

CHARCE LACROIX

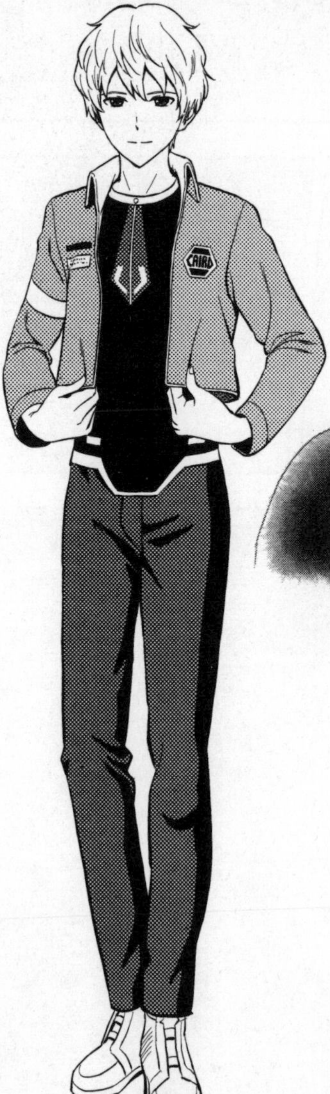
CAIRD

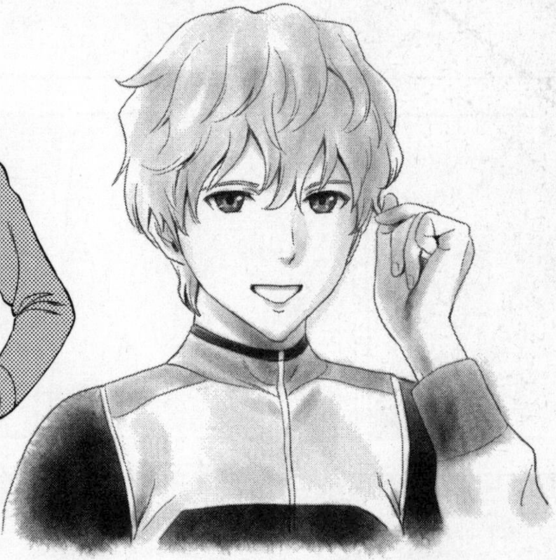

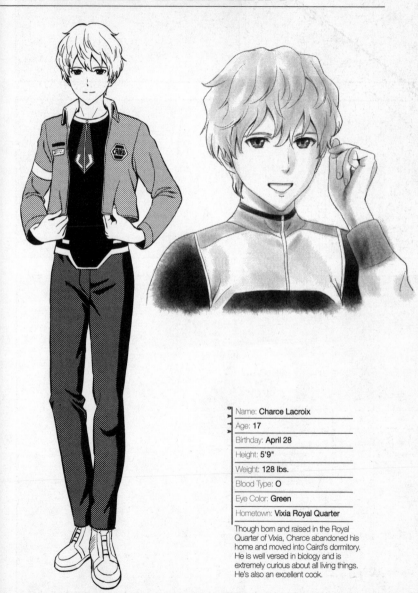

DATA

Name: **Charce Lacroix**

Age: **17**

Birthday: **April 28**

Height: **5'9"**

Weight: **128 lbs.**

Blood Type: **O**

Eye Color: **Green**

Hometown: **Vixia Royal Quarter**

Though born and raised in the Royal Quarter of Vixia, Charce abandoned his home and moved into Caird's dormitory. He is well versed in biology and is extremely curious about all living things. He's also an excellent cook.

ASTRA LOST IN SPACE

#27

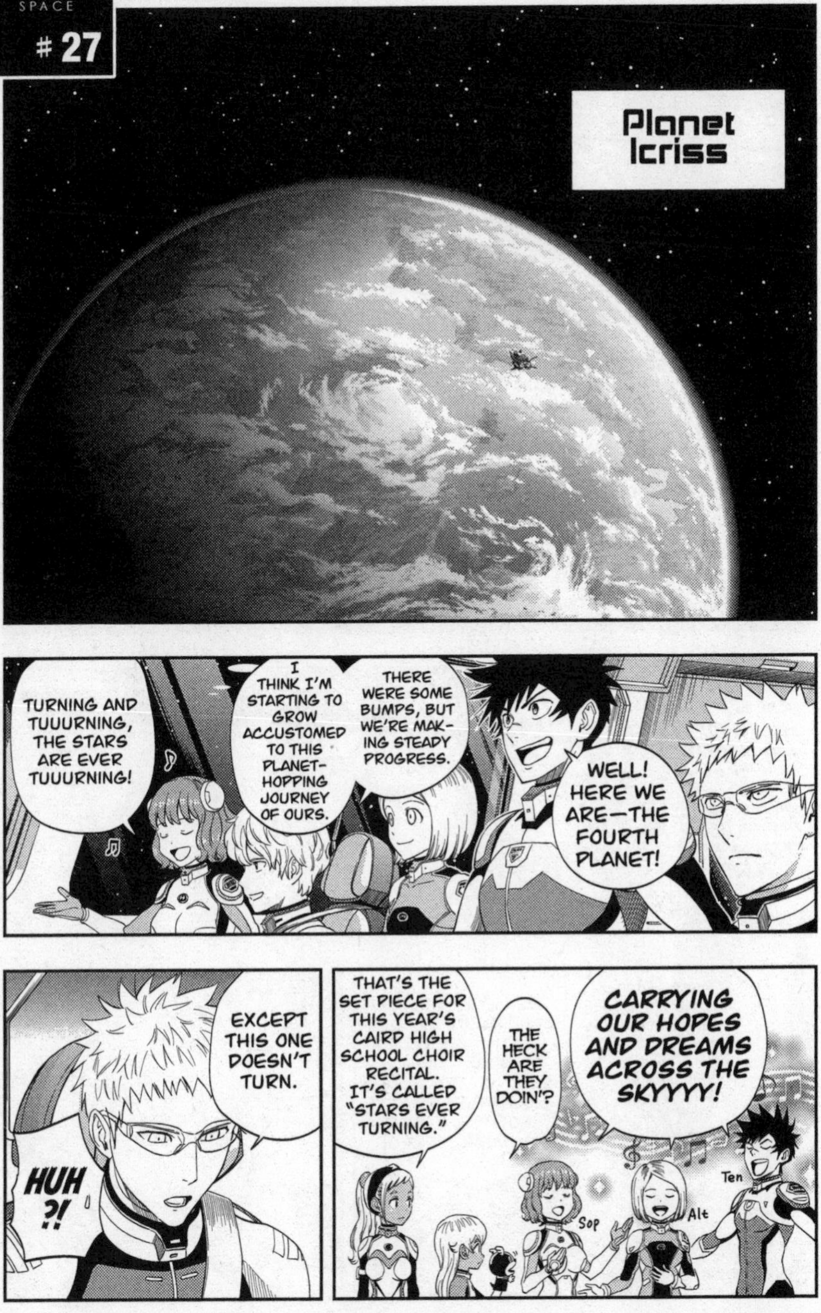

Planet Icriss
WELL! HERE WE ARE—THE FOURTH PLANET!
THERE WERE SOME BUMPS, BUT WE'RE MAKING STEADY PROGRESS.
I THINK I'M STARTING TO GROW ACCUSTOMED TO THIS PLANET-HOPPING JOURNEY OF OURS.
TURNING AND TUUURNING, THE STARS ARE EVER TUUURNING!
CARRYING OUR HOPES AND DREAMS ACROSS THE SKYYYY!
Ten
Alt
Sop
THE HECK ARE THEY DOIN'?
THAT'S THE SET PIECE FOR THIS YEAR'S CAIRD HIGH SCHOOL CHOIR RECITAL. IT'S CALLED "STARS EVER TURNING."
EXCEPT THIS ONE DOESN'T TURN.
HUH?!

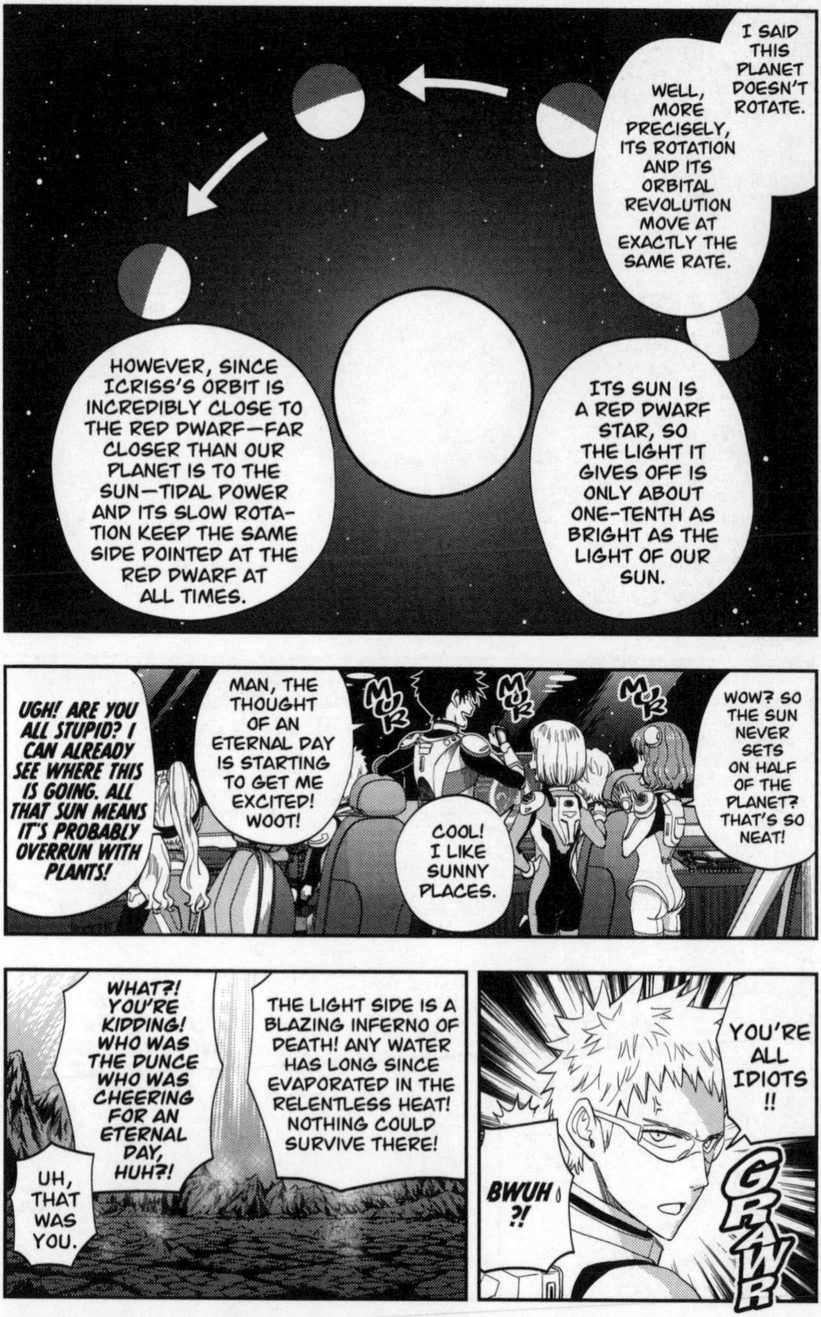
I SAID THIS PLANET DOESN'T ROTATE.
WELL, MORE PRECISELY, ITS ROTATION AND ITS ORBITAL REVOLUTION MOVE AT EXACTLY THE SAME RATE.
ITS SUN IS A RED DWARF STAR, SO THE LIGHT IT GIVES OFF IS ONLY ABOUT ONE-TENTH AS BRIGHT AS THE LIGHT OF OUR SUN.
HOWEVER, SINCE ICRISS'S ORBIT IS INCREDIBLY CLOSE TO THE RED DWARF—FAR CLOSER THAN OUR PLANET IS TO THE SUN—TIDAL POWER AND ITS SLOW ROTATION KEEP THE SAME SIDE POINTED AT THE RED DWARF AT ALL TIMES.
WOW? SO THE SUN NEVER SETS ON HALF OF THE PLANET? THAT'S SO NEAT!
MUR
MUR
MUR
COOL! I LIKE SUNNY PLACES.
MAN, THE THOUGHT OF AN ETERNAL DAY IS STARTING TO GET ME EXCITED! WOOT!
UGH! ARE YOU ALL STUPID? I CAN ALREADY SEE WHERE THIS IS GOING. ALL THAT SUN MEANS IT'S PROBABLY OVERRUN WITH PLANTS!
YOU'RE ALL IDIOTS !!
GRAWR
BWUH ?!
THE LIGHT SIDE IS A BLAZING INFERNO OF DEATH! ANY WATER HAS LONG SINCE EVAPORATED IN THE RELENTLESS HEAT! NOTHING COULD SURVIVE THERE!
WHAT?! YOU'RE KIDDING! WHO WAS THE DUNCE WHO WAS CHEERING FOR AN ETERNAL DAY, HUH?!
UH, THAT WAS YOU.

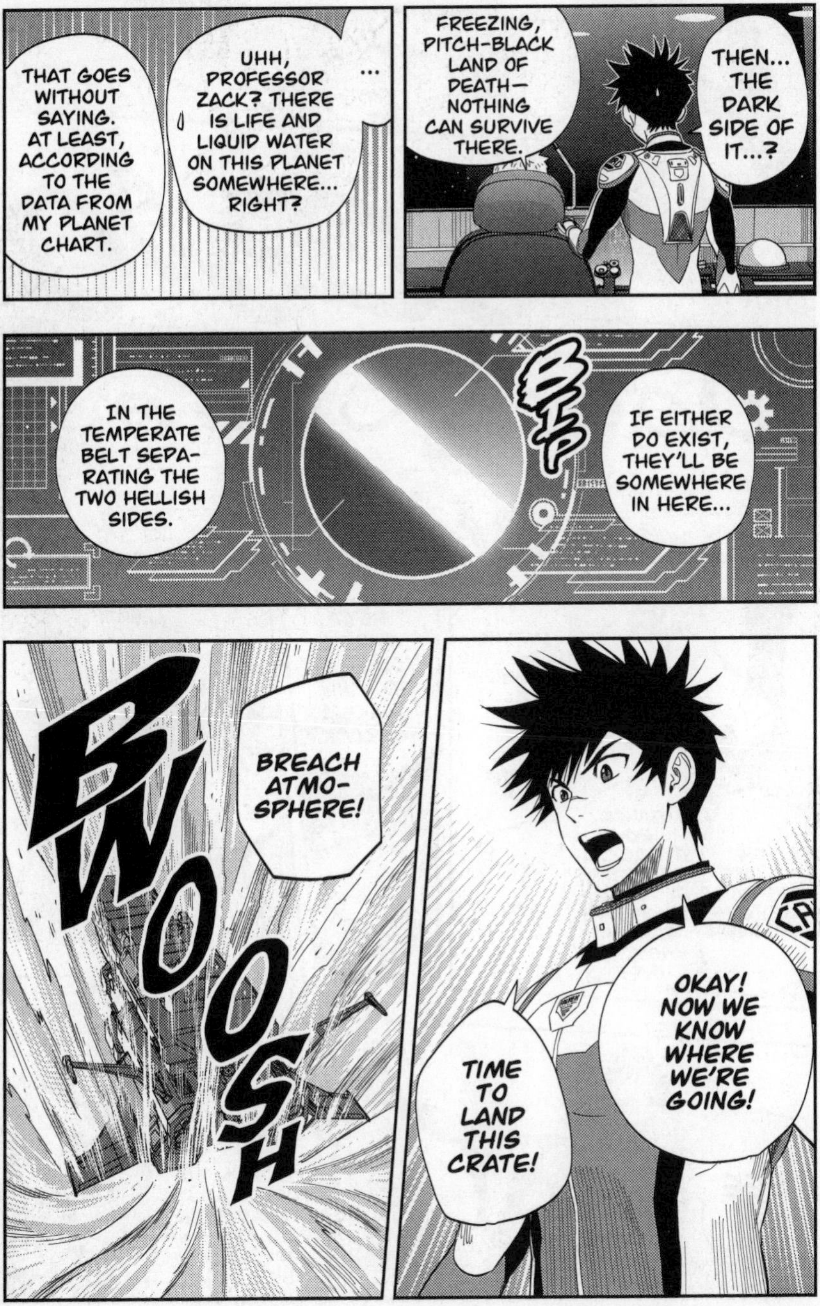
THEN... THE DARK SIDE OF IT...?
FREEZING, PITCH-BLACK LAND OF DEATH— NOTHING CAN SURVIVE THERE.
...
UHH, PROFESSOR ZACK? THERE IS LIFE AND LIQUID WATER ON THIS PLANET SOMEWHERE... RIGHT?
THAT GOES WITHOUT SAYING. AT LEAST, ACCORDING TO THE DATA FROM MY PLANET CHART.
BIP
IF EITHER DO EXIST, THEY'LL BE SOMEWHERE IN HERE...
IN THE TEMPERATE BELT SEPA-RATING THE TWO HELLISH SIDES.
OKAY! NOW WE KNOW WHERE WE'RE GOING!
TIME TO LAND THIS CRATE!
BREACH ATMO-SPHERE!
BWOOSH

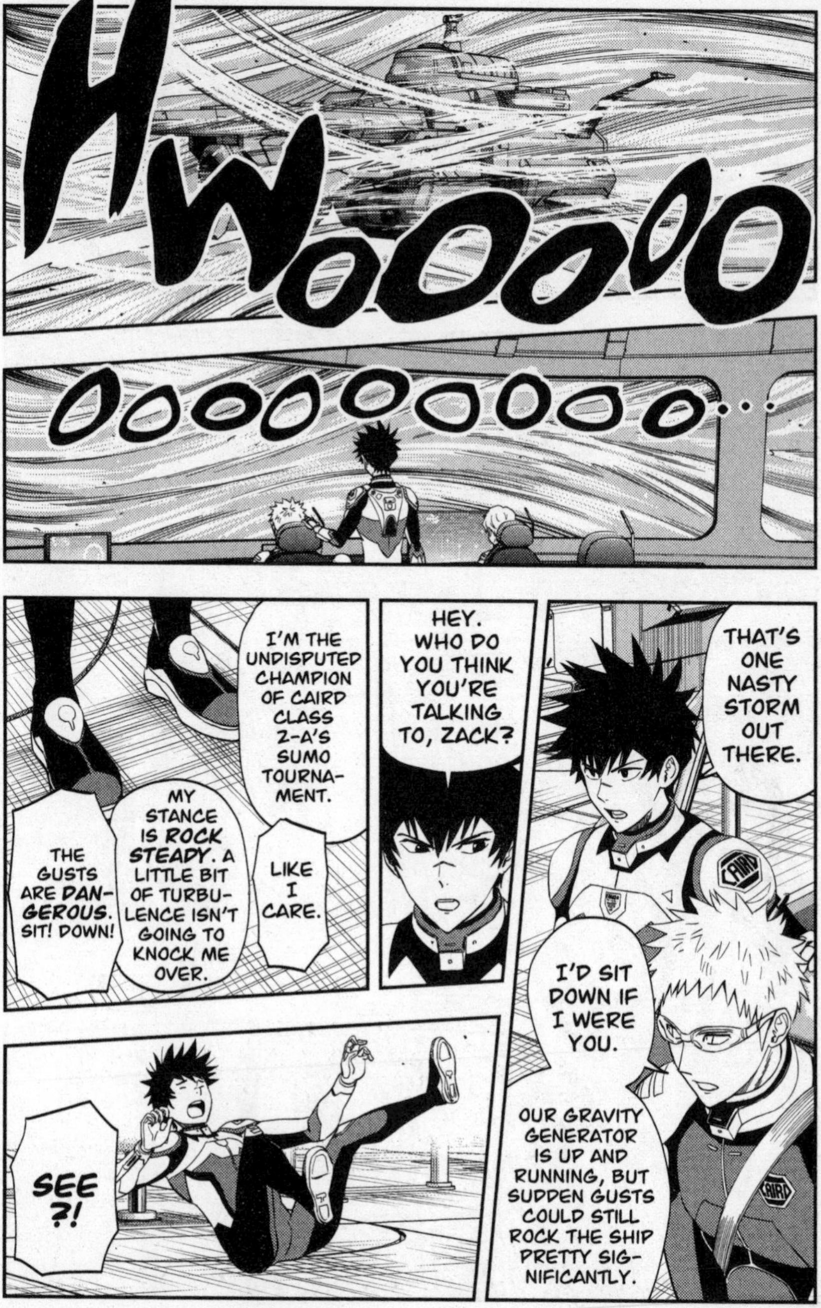
HWOOOOO
OOOOOOOOO...
THAT'S ONE NASTY STORM OUT THERE.
HEY. WHO DO YOU THINK YOU'RE TALKING TO, ZACK?
I'D SIT DOWN IF I WERE YOU.
OUR GRAVITY GENERATOR IS UP AND RUNNING, BUT SUDDEN GUSTS COULD STILL ROCK THE SHIP PRETTY SIGNIFICANTLY.
I'M THE UNDISPUTED CHAMPION OF CAIRD CLASS 2-A'S SUMO TOURNAMENT.
LIKE I CARE.
MY STANCE IS **ROCK STEADY**. A LITTLE BIT OF TURBULENCE ISN'T GOING TO KNOCK ME OVER.
THE GUSTS ARE **DANGEROUS**. SIT! DOWN!
SEE?!

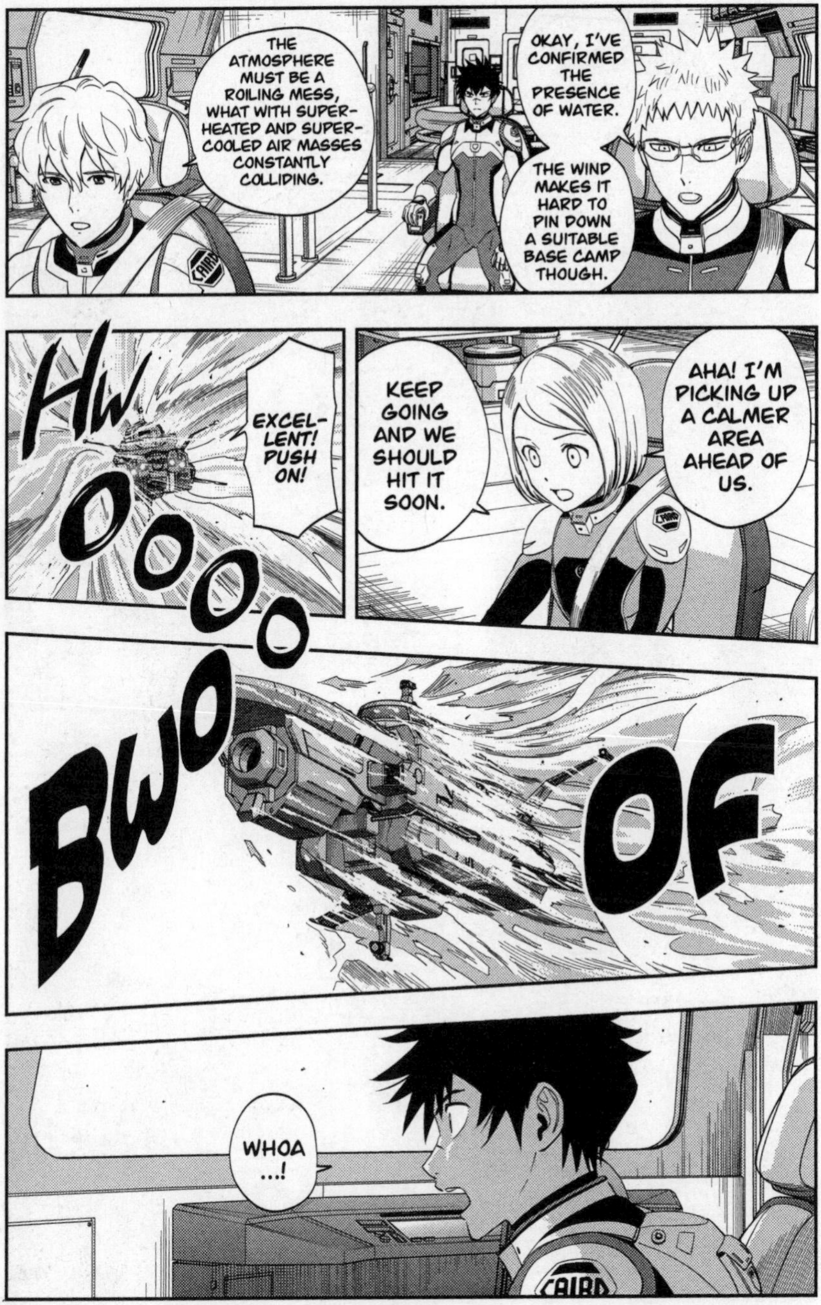
OKAY, I'VE CONFIRMED THE PRESENCE OF WATER.
THE WIND MAKES IT HARD TO PIN DOWN A SUITABLE BASE CAMP THOUGH.
THE ATMOSPHERE MUST BE A ROILING MESS, WHAT WITH SUPER-HEATED AND SUPER-COOLED AIR MASSES CONSTANTLY COLLIDING.
AHA! I'M PICKING UP A CALMER AREA AHEAD OF US.
KEEP GOING AND WE SHOULD HIT IT SOON.
HWOOOO
EXCEL-LENT! PUSH ON!
BWOOF
WHOA ...!

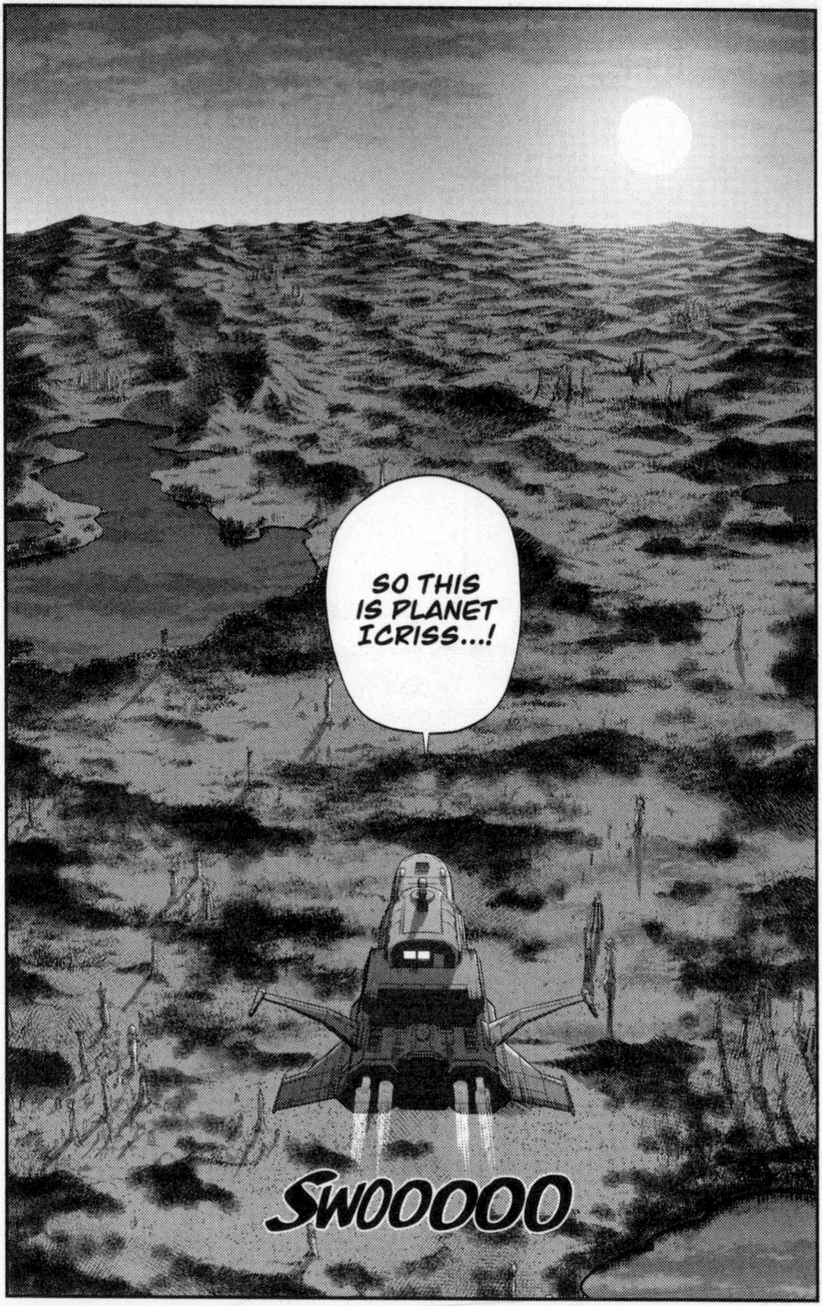
SO THIS IS PLANET ICRISS...!
SWOOOOO

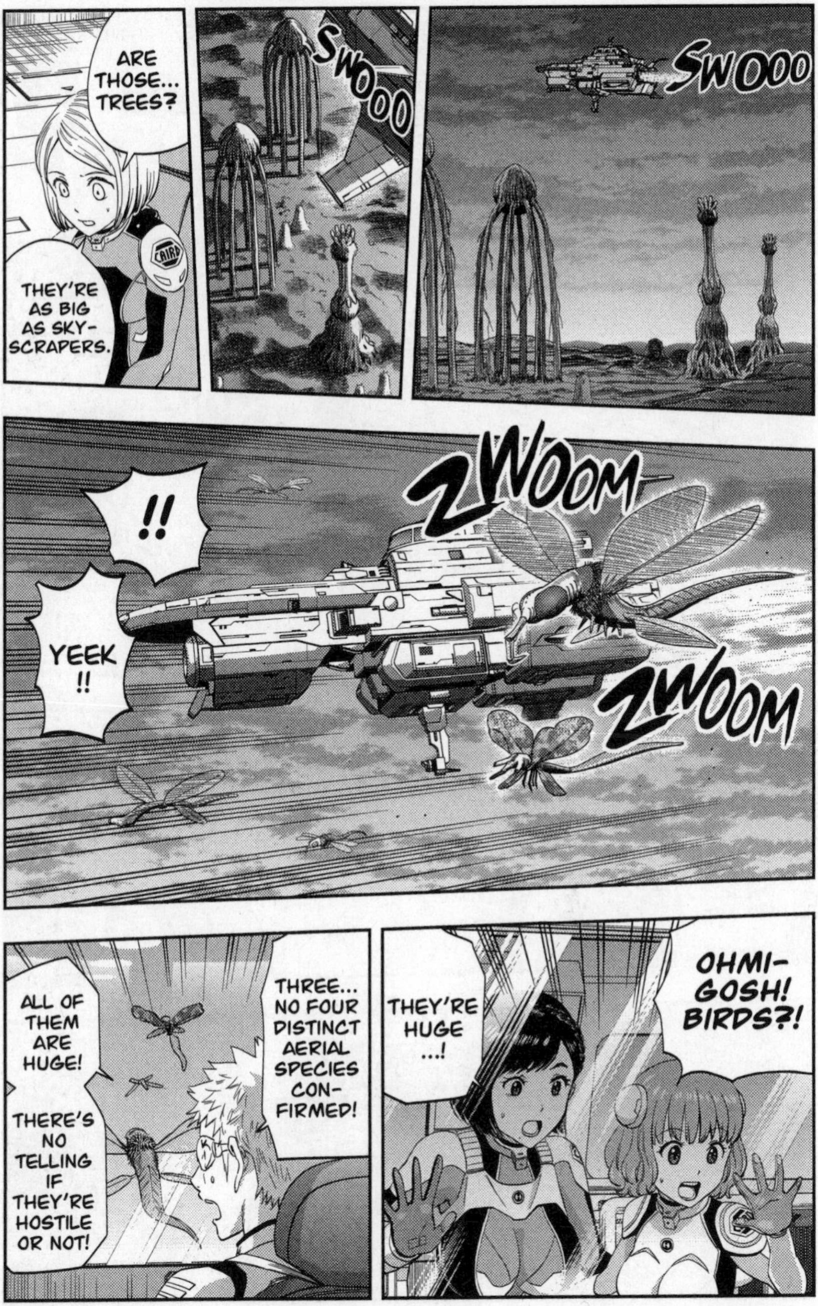
SWOOO
SWOOOO
ARE THOSE... TREES?
THEY'RE AS BIG AS SKY-SCRAPERS.
ZWOOM
!!
YEEK !!
ZWOOM
OHMI-GOSH! BIRDS?!
THEY'RE HUGE ...!
THREE... NO FOUR DISTINCT AERIAL SPECIES CON-FIRMED!
ALL OF THEM ARE HUGE!
THERE'S NO TELLING IF THEY'RE HOSTILE OR NOT!

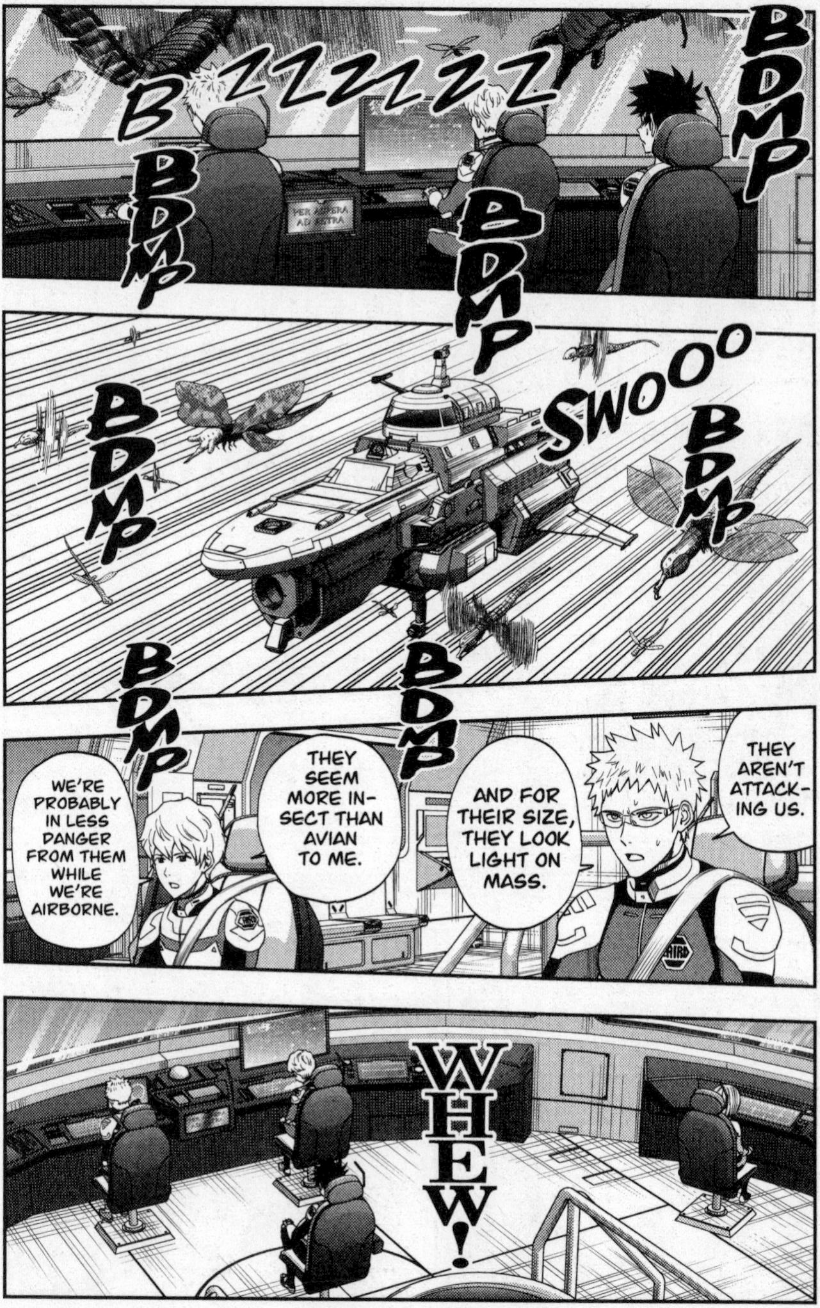
BDMP
BZZZZZZZ
BDMP
BDMP
SWOOO
BDMP
BDMP
BDMP
BDMP
THEY AREN'T ATTACK-ING US.
AND FOR THEIR SIZE, THEY LOOK LIGHT ON MASS.
THEY SEEM MORE IN-SECT THAN AVIAN TO ME.
WE'RE PROBABLY IN LESS DANGER FROM THEM WHILE WE'RE AIRBORNE.
WHEW!

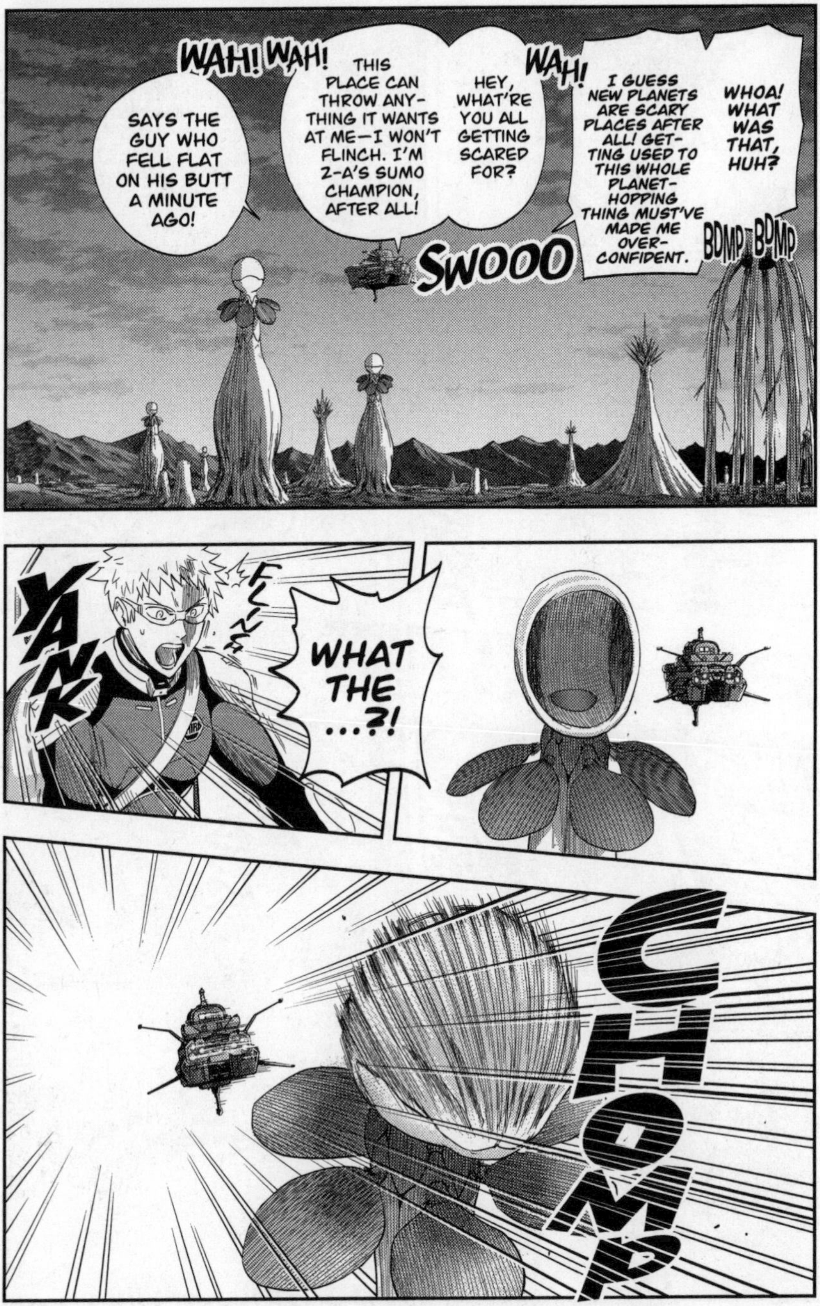
WHOA! WHAT WAS THAT, HUH?
BDMP BDMP
I GUESS NEW PLANETS ARE SCARY PLACES AFTER ALL! GETTING USED TO THIS WHOLE PLANET-HOPPING THING MUST'VE MADE ME OVERCONFIDENT.
WAH!
SWOOO
HEY, WHAT'RE YOU ALL GETTING SCARED FOR?
THIS PLACE CAN THROW ANYTHING IT WANTS AT ME—I WON'T FLINCH. I'M 2-A'S SUMO CHAMPION, AFTER ALL!
WAH! WAH!
SAYS THE GUY WHO FELL FLAT ON HIS BUTT A MINUTE AGO!
WHAT THE ...?!
FLING
YANK
CHOMP

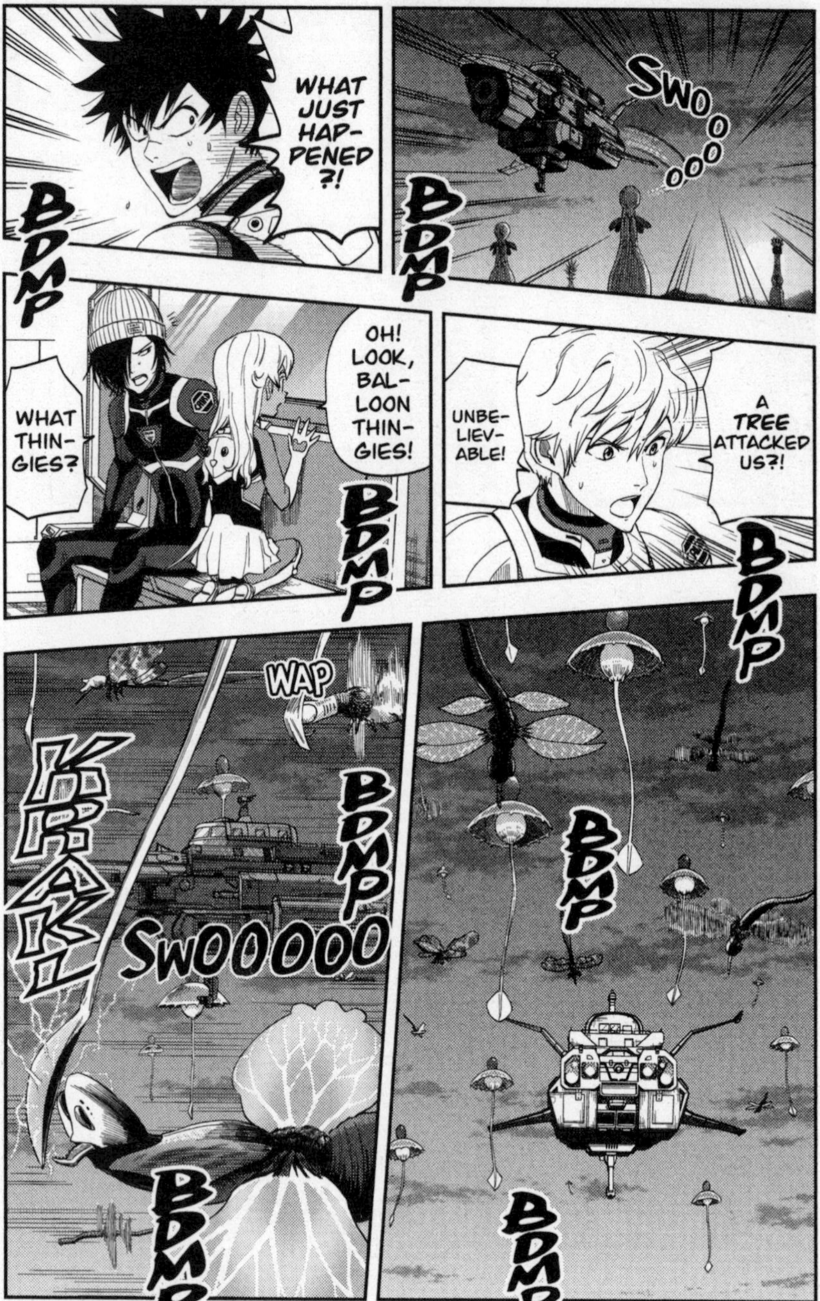
SWOOOOOOOO
BDMP
WHAT JUST HAPPENED?!
BDMP
A TREE ATTACKED US?!
UNBELIEVABLE!
BDMP
OH! LOOK, BALLOON THINGIES!
WHAT THINGIES?
BDMP
BDMP
BDMP
WAP
BDMP
KRAK
SWOOOOOO
BDMP

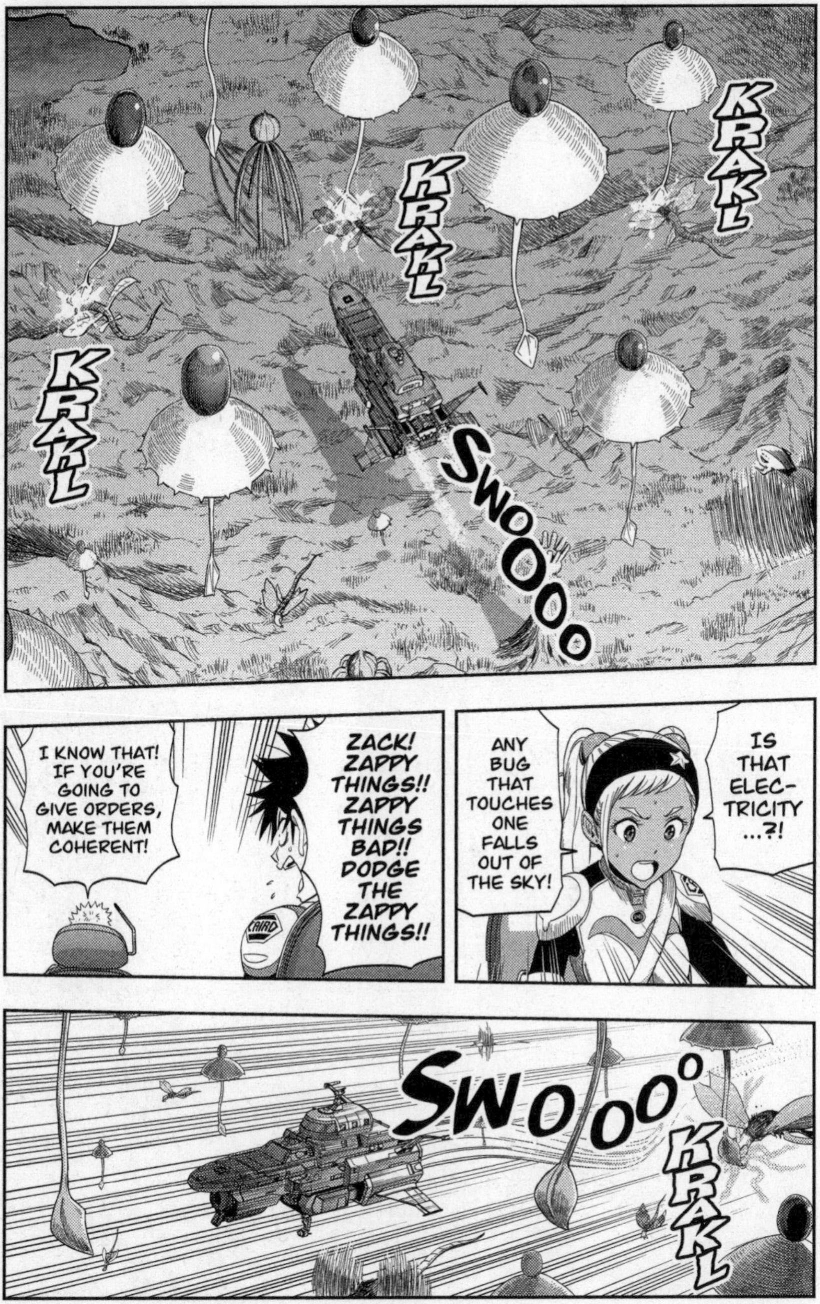
KRAKL
KRAKL
KRAKL
SWOOOOO
IS THAT ELEC-TRICITY ...?!
ANY BUG THAT TOUCHES ONE FALLS OUT OF THE SKY!
ZACK! ZAPPY THINGS!! ZAPPY THINGS BAD!! DODGE THE ZAPPY THINGS!!
I KNOW THAT! IF YOU'RE GOING TO GIVE ORDERS, MAKE THEM COHERENT!
SWOOOO
KRAKL

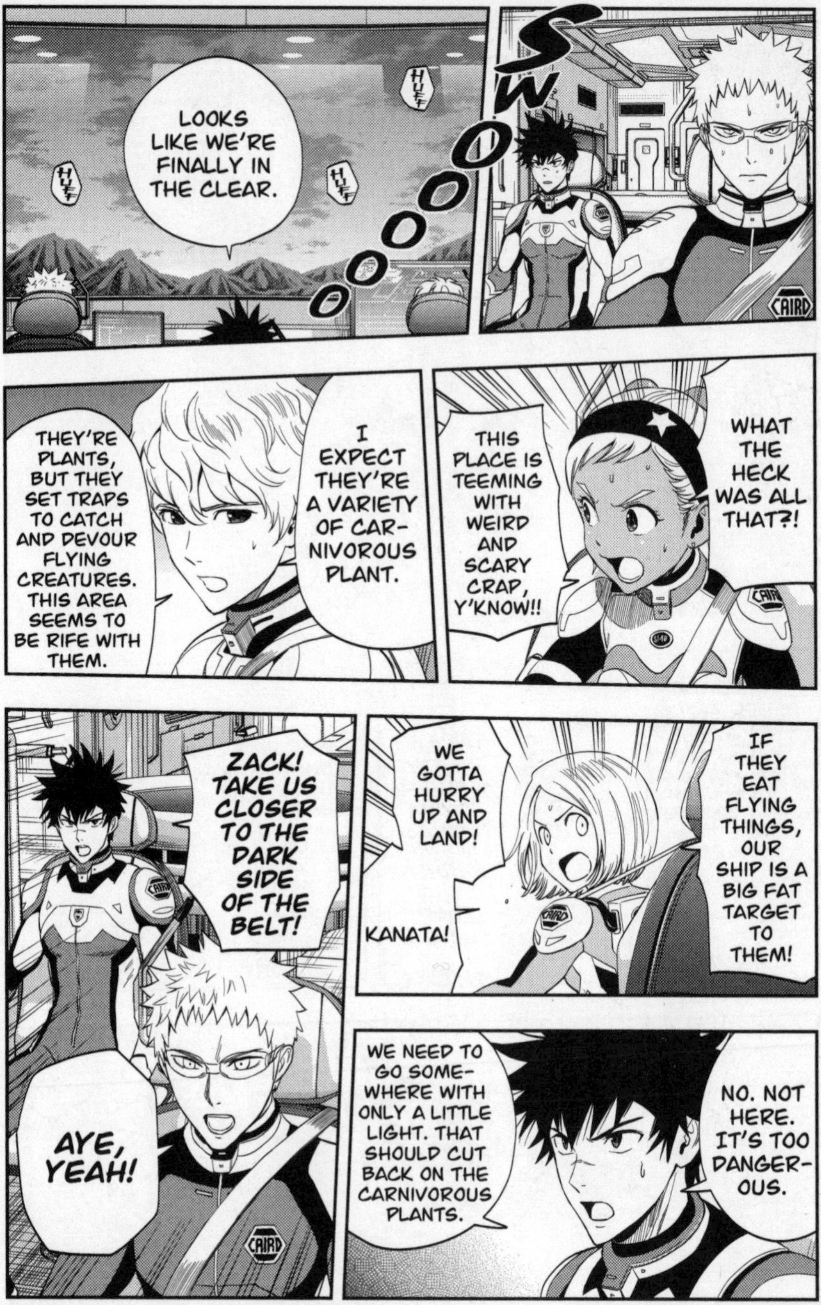
SWOOOOOO
HUFF
HUFF
HUFF
LOOKS LIKE WE'RE FINALLY IN THE CLEAR.
WHAT THE HECK WAS ALL THAT?!
THIS PLACE IS TEEMING WITH WEIRD AND SCARY CRAP, Y'KNOW!!
I EXPECT THEY'RE A VARIETY OF CAR-NIVOROUS PLANT.
THEY'RE PLANTS, BUT THEY SET TRAPS TO CATCH AND DEVOUR FLYING CREATURES. THIS AREA SEEMS TO BE RIFE WITH THEM.
IF THEY EAT FLYING THINGS, OUR SHIP IS A BIG FAT TARGET TO THEM!
WE GOTTA HURRY UP AND LAND!
KANATA!
NO. NOT HERE. IT'S TOO DANGER-OUS.
WE NEED TO GO SOME-WHERE WITH ONLY A LITTLE LIGHT. THAT SHOULD CUT BACK ON THE CARNIVOROUS PLANTS.
ZACK! TAKE US CLOSER TO THE DARK SIDE OF THE BELT!
AYE, YEAH!

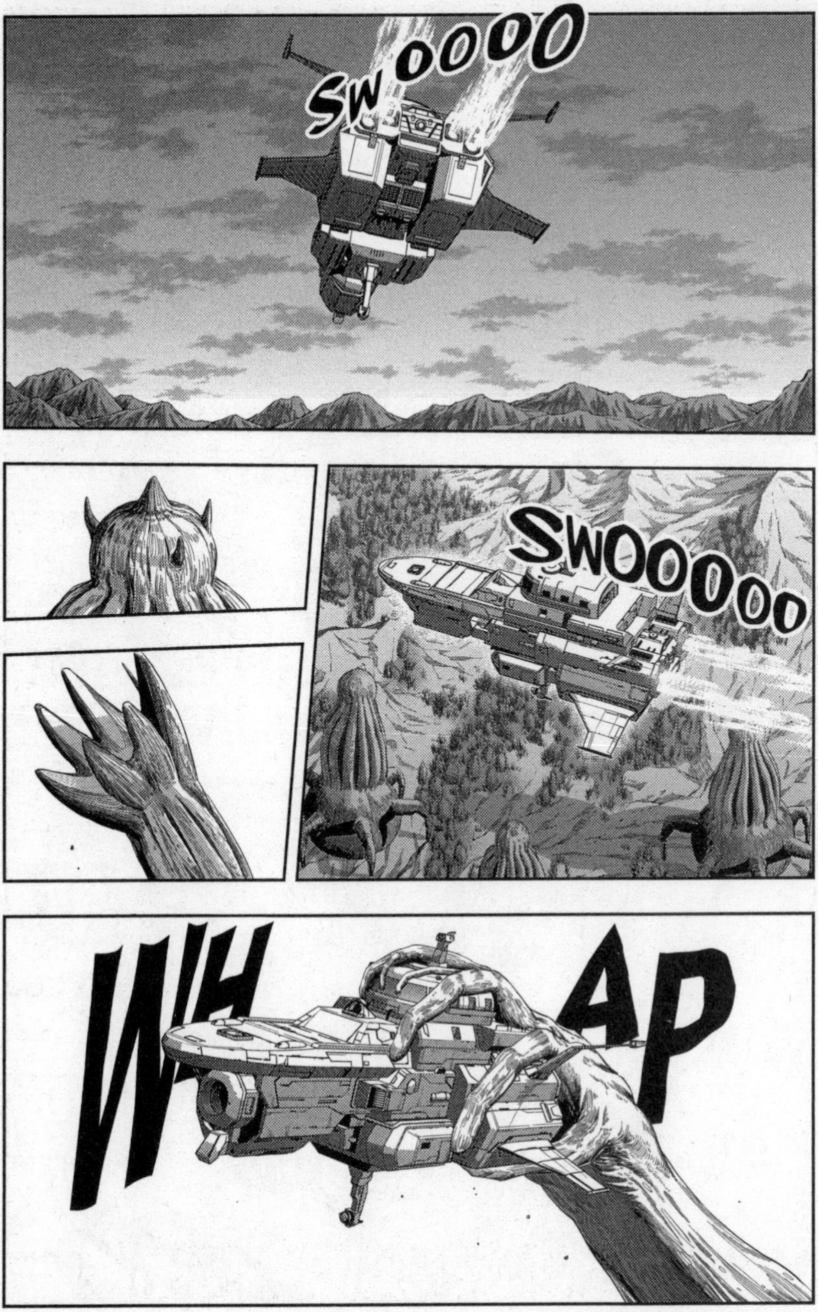
SWOOOO
SWOOOOOO
WHAP

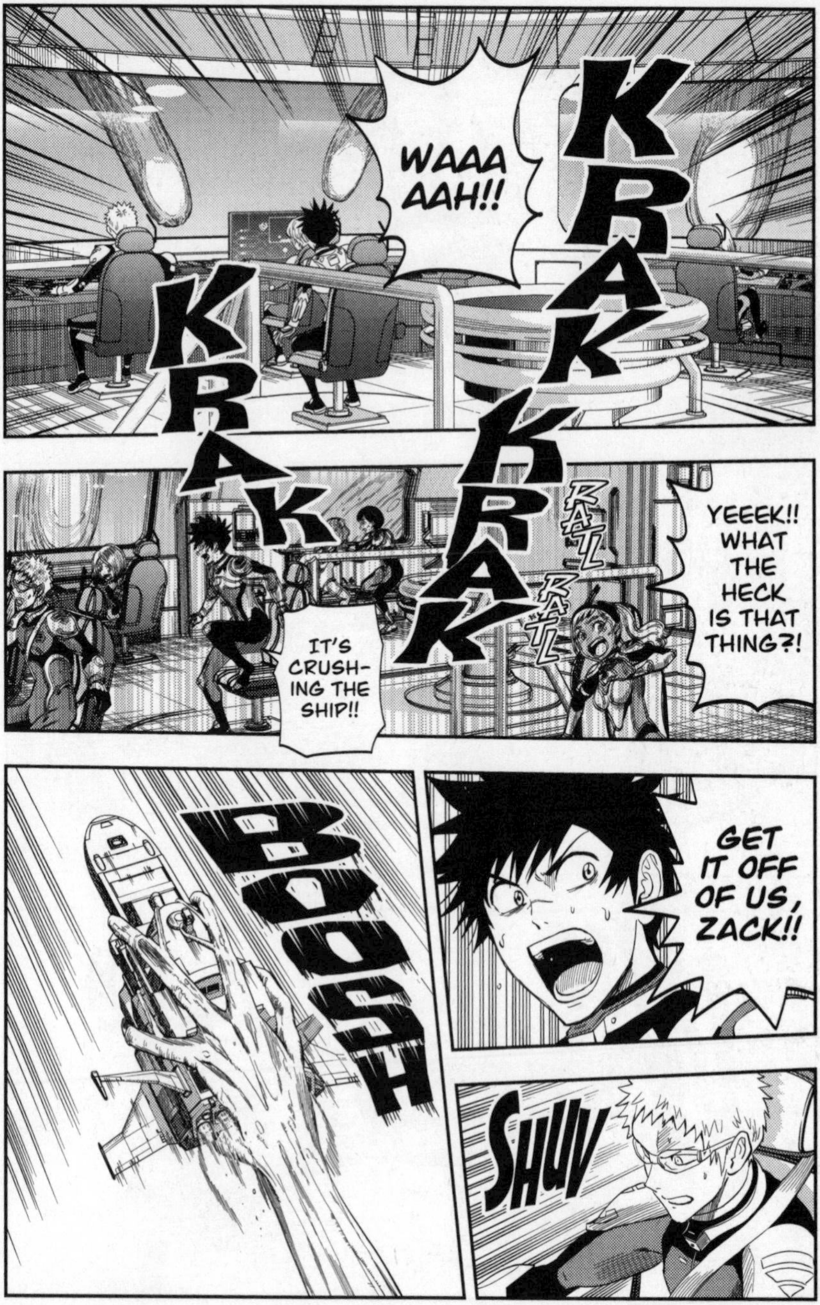
KRAK
KRAK
WAAAA AAH!!
KRAK
YEEEK!! WHAT THE HECK IS THAT THING?!
RATL
RATL
IT'S CRUSHING THE SHIP!!
GET IT OFF OF US, ZACK!!
SHUV
BOOSH

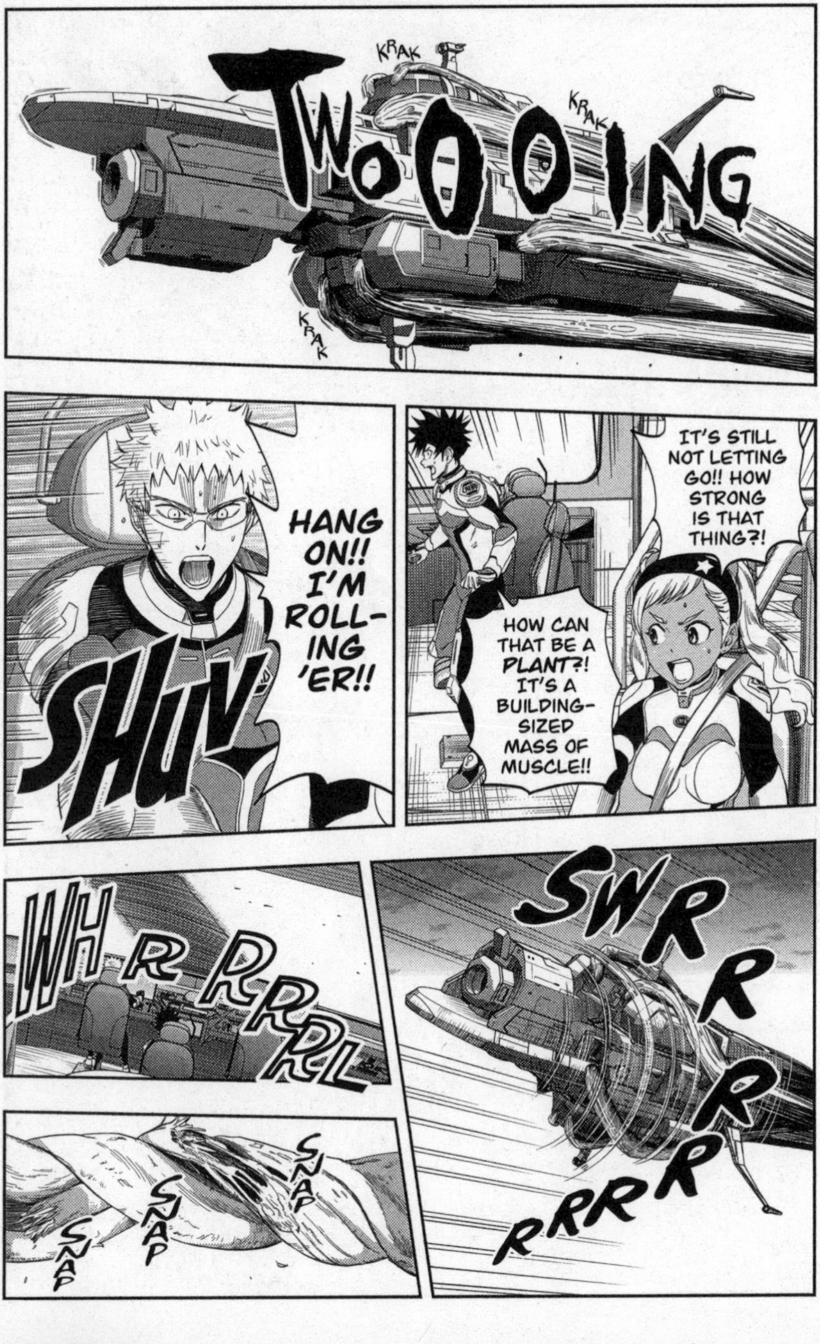
KRAK
TWOOOING
KRAK
KRAK
IT'S STILL NOT LETTING GO!! HOW STRONG IS THAT THING?!
HOW CAN THAT BE A PLANT?! IT'S A BUILDING-SIZED MASS OF MUSCLE!!
HANG ON!! I'M ROLLING 'ER!!
SHUV
SWRRRRRRR
WHRRRRL
SNAP
SNAP
SNAP

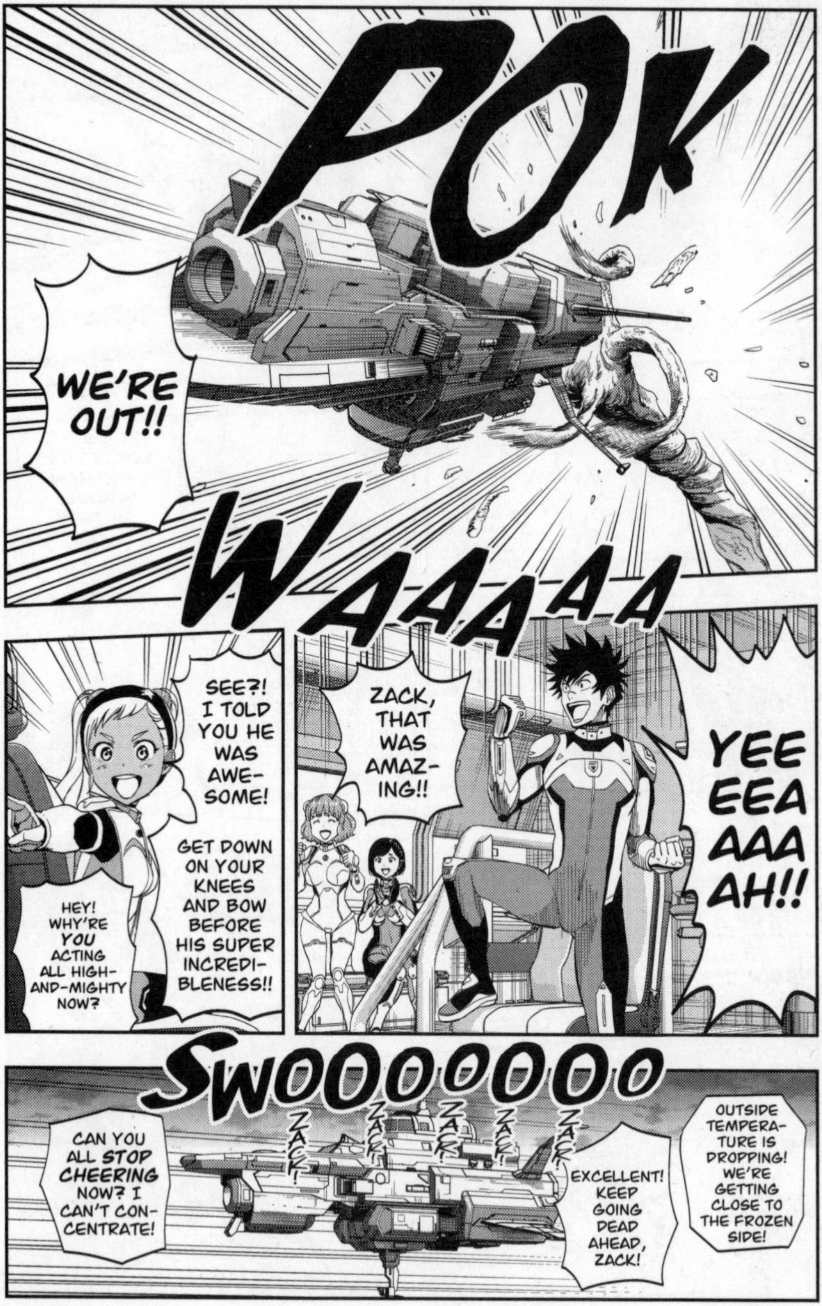
POK
WE'RE OUT!!
WAAAAAA
YEEEEAAAAAAH!!
ZACK, THAT WAS AMAZ-ING!!
SEE?! I TOLD YOU HE WAS AWE-SOME!
GET DOWN ON YOUR KNEES AND BOW BEFORE HIS SUPER INCREDI-BLENESS!!
HEY! WHY'RE YOU ACTING ALL HIGH-AND-MIGHTY NOW?
SWOOOOOOOO
OUTSIDE TEMPERA-TURE IS DROPPING! WE'RE GETTING CLOSE TO THE FROZEN SIDE!
ZACK!
ZACK!
ZACK!
ZACK!
ZACK!
EXCELLENT! KEEP GOING DEAD AHEAD, ZACK!
CAN YOU ALL STOP CHEERING NOW? I CAN'T CON-CENTRATE!

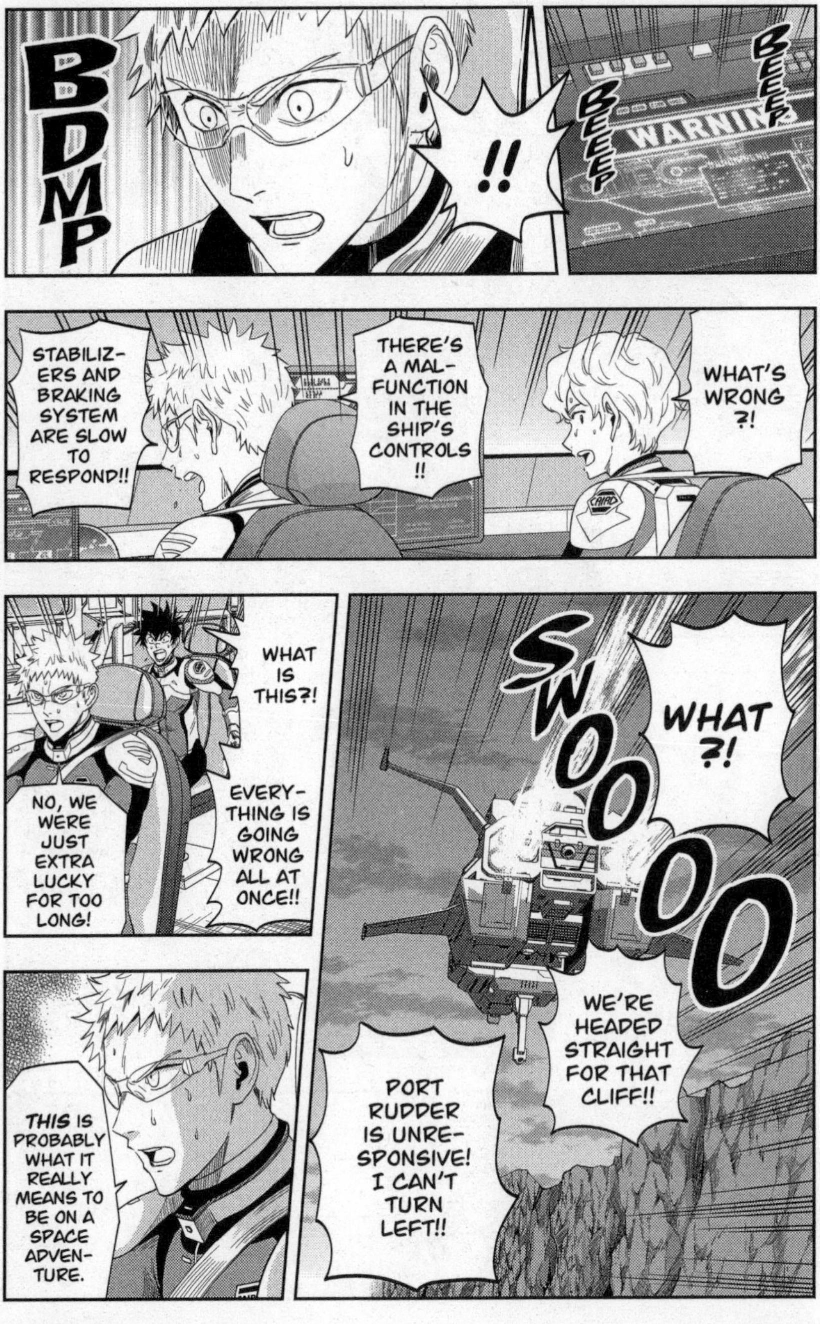
BEEEP
BEEEP
WARNING
!!
BDMP
WHAT'S WRONG?!
THERE'S A MALFUNCTION IN THE SHIP'S CONTROLS!!
STABILIZERS AND BRAKING SYSTEM ARE SLOW TO RESPOND!!
WHAT?!
SWOOOO
WE'RE HEADED STRAIGHT FOR THAT CLIFF!!
PORT RUDDER IS UNRESPONSIVE! I CAN'T TURN LEFT!!
WHAT IS THIS?!
EVERYTHING IS GOING WRONG ALL AT ONCE!!
NO, WE WERE JUST EXTRA LUCKY FOR TOO LONG!
THIS IS PROBABLY WHAT IT REALLY MEANS TO BE ON A SPACE ADVENTURE.

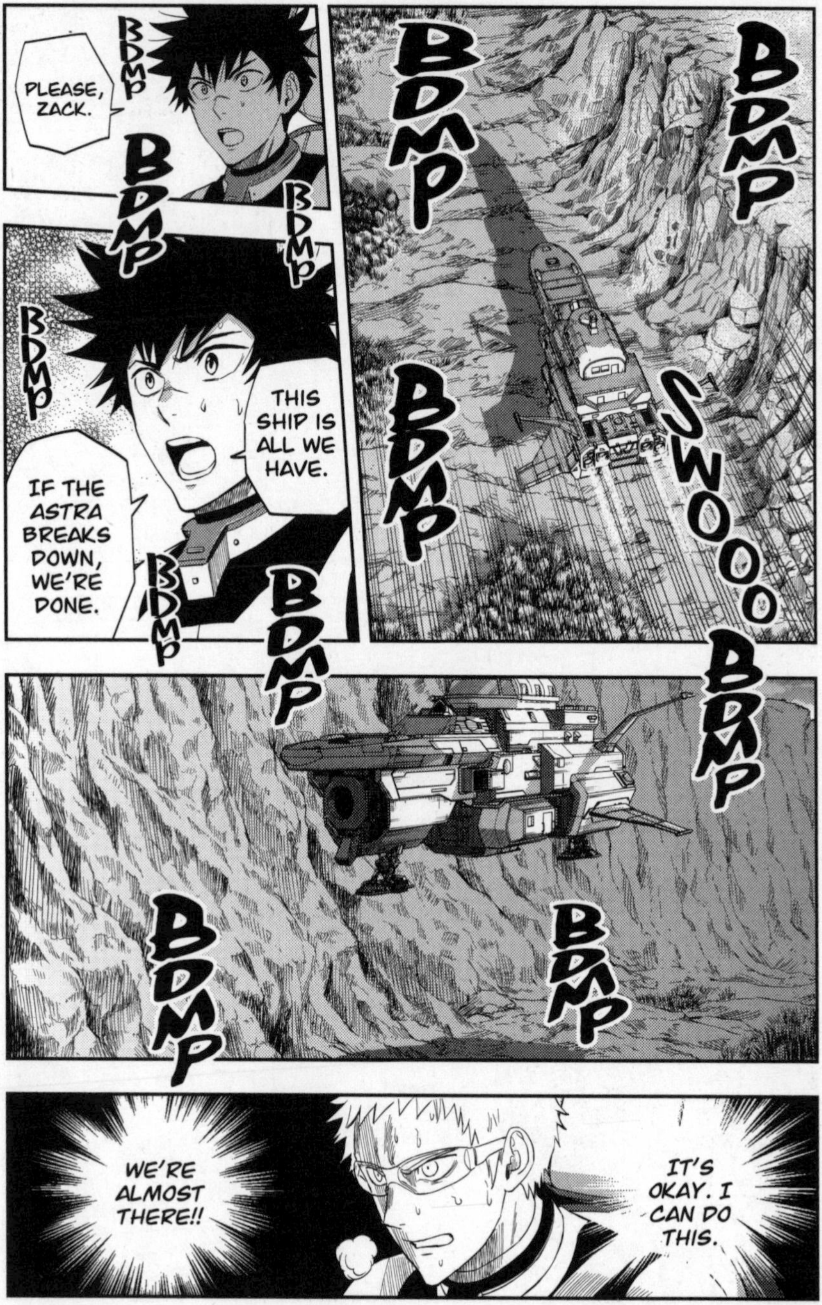
BDMP
BDMP
SWOOO
BDMP
PLEASE, ZACK.
BDMP
BDMP
BDMP
BDMP
THIS SHIP IS ALL WE HAVE.
IF THE ASTRA BREAKS DOWN, WE'RE DONE.
BDMP
BDMP
BDMP
BDMP
BDMP
IT'S OKAY. I CAN DO THIS.
WE'RE ALMOST THERE!!

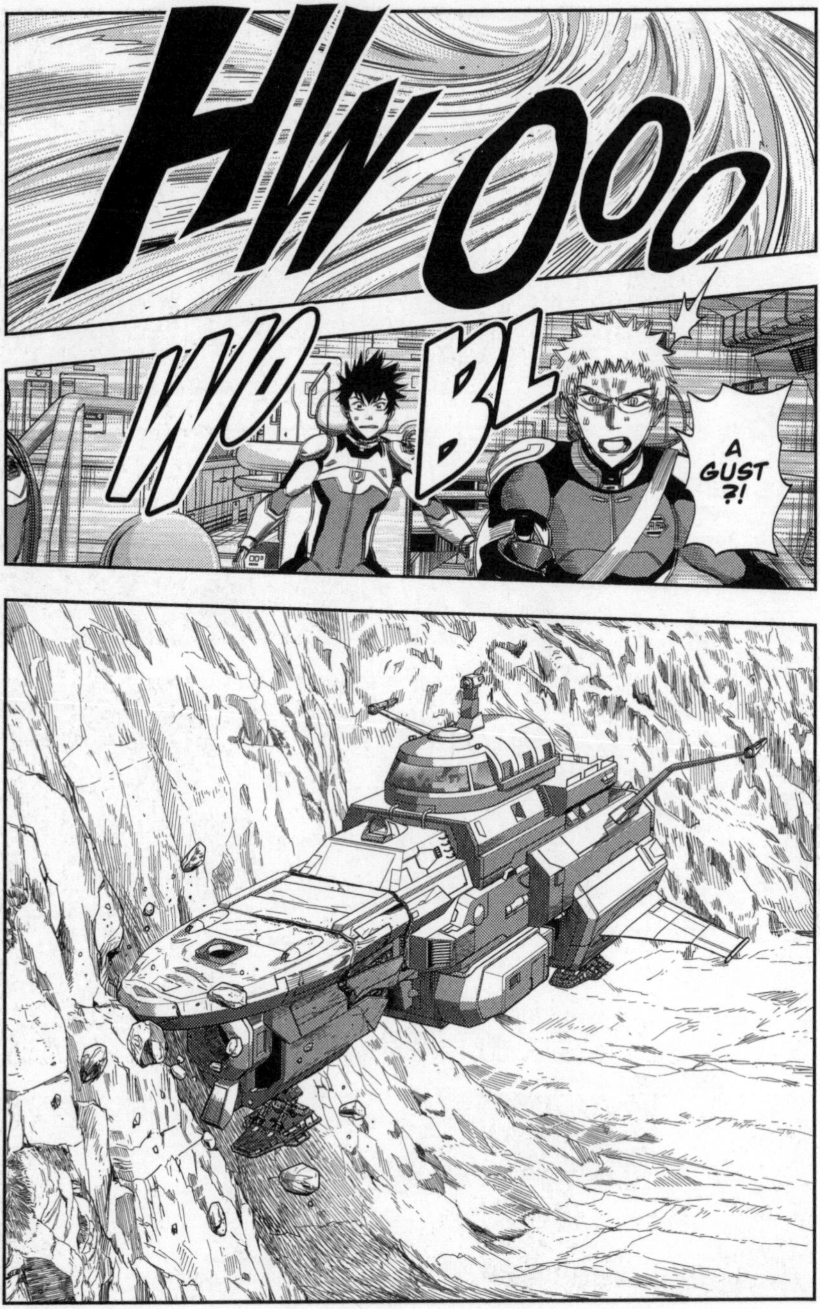
HWOOO
A GUST ?!
WO BL

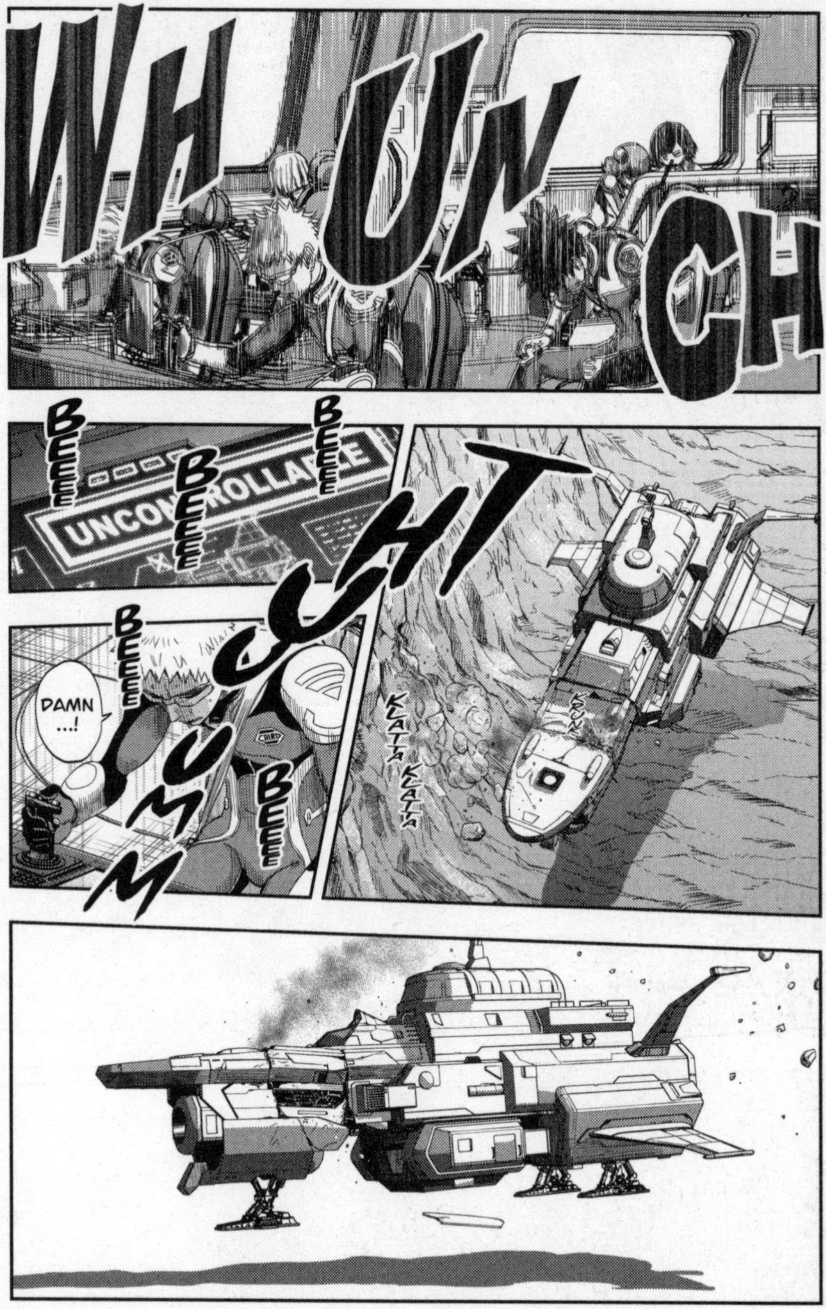
WHUNCH
KRUNK
KLATTA KLATTA
BEEEE
BEEEE
BEEEE
BEEEE
DAMN ...!
BEEEE

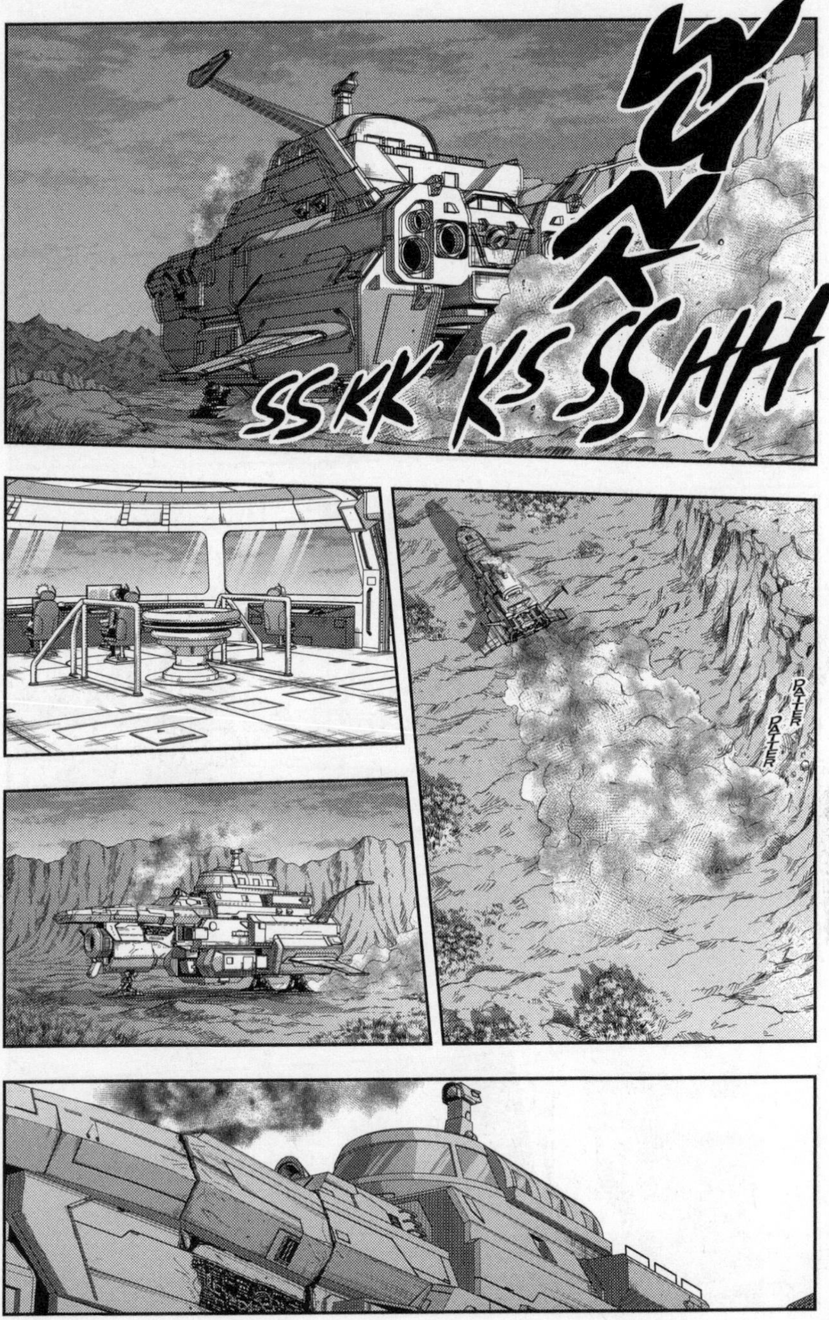
SSKK KSSSHH
PATTER
PATTER

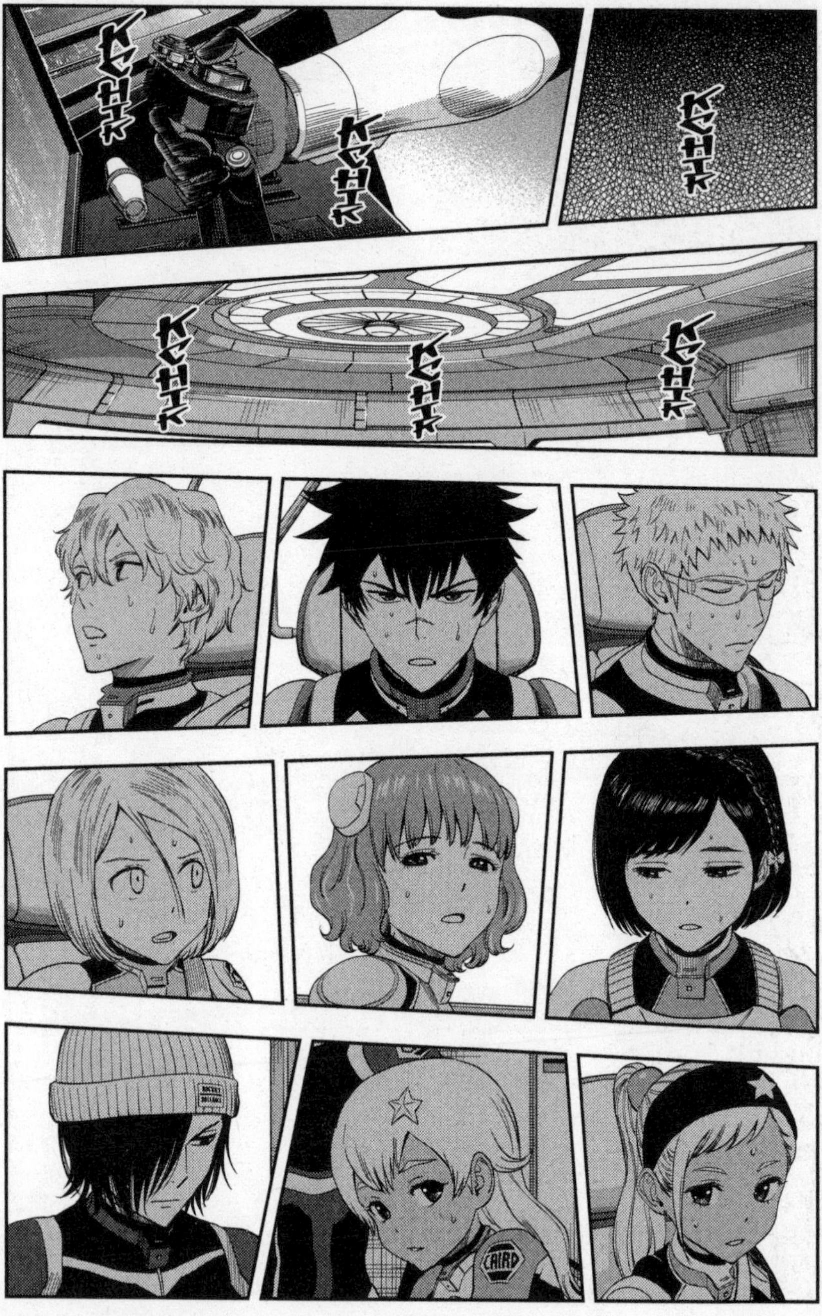
KCHIK
KCHIK
KCHIK
KCHIK
KCHIK
KCHIK
CAIRD

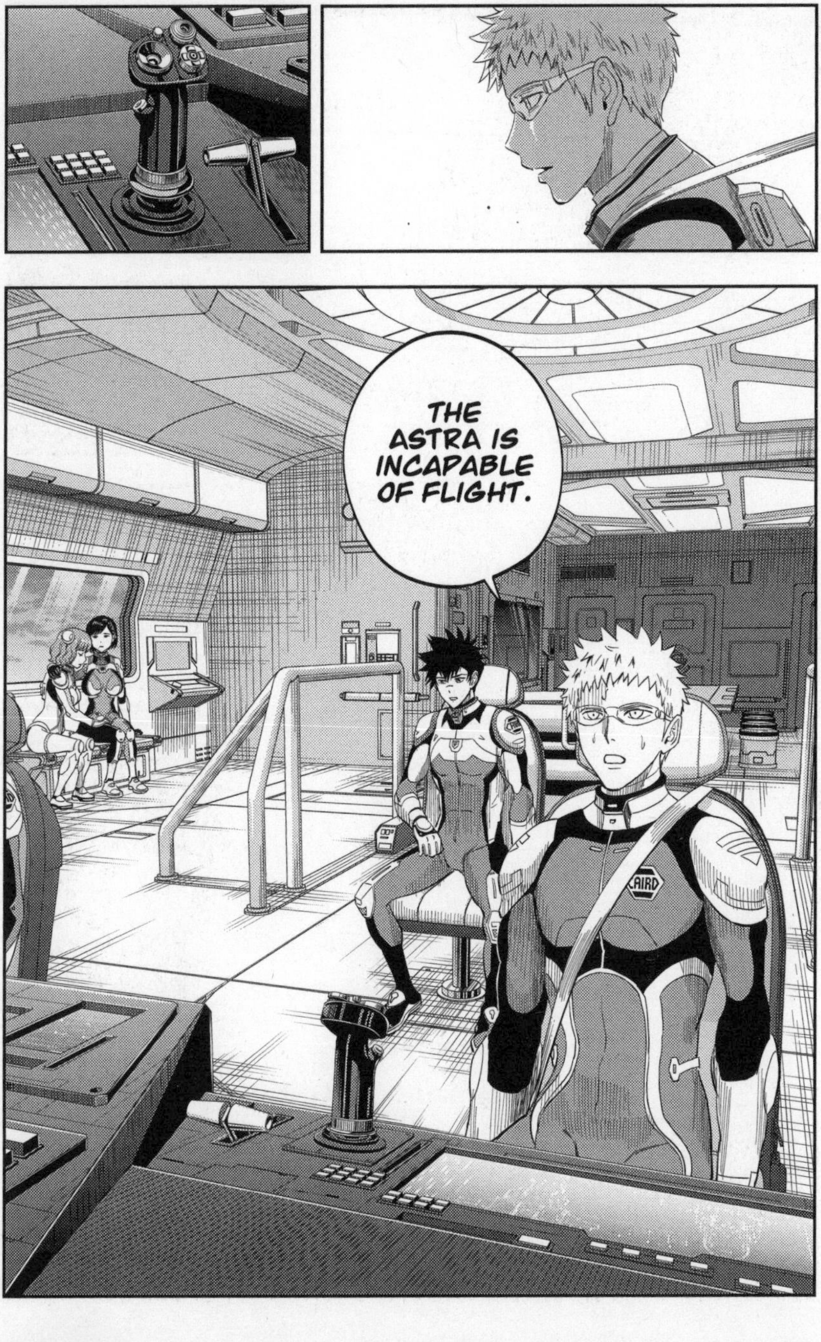
. . .
THE ASTRA IS INCAPABLE OF FLIGHT.
AIRD

ASTRA
LOST IN SPACE

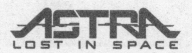

ASTRA LOST IN SPACE

28

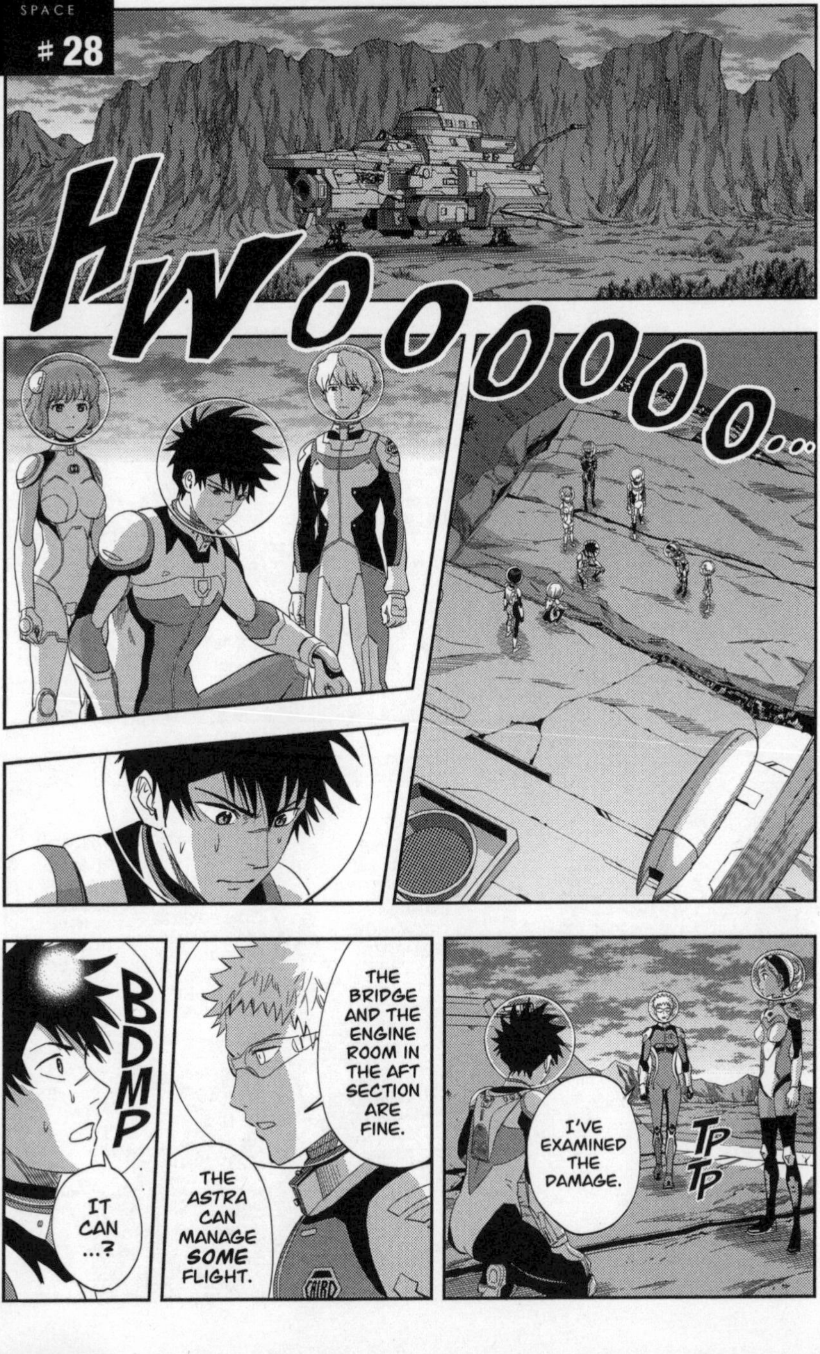
HWOOOOOO...
TP TP
I'VE EXAMINED THE DAMAGE.
THE BRIDGE AND THE ENGINE ROOM IN THE AFT SECTION ARE FINE.
THE ASTRA CAN MANAGE **SOME** FLIGHT.
BDMP
IT CAN ...?

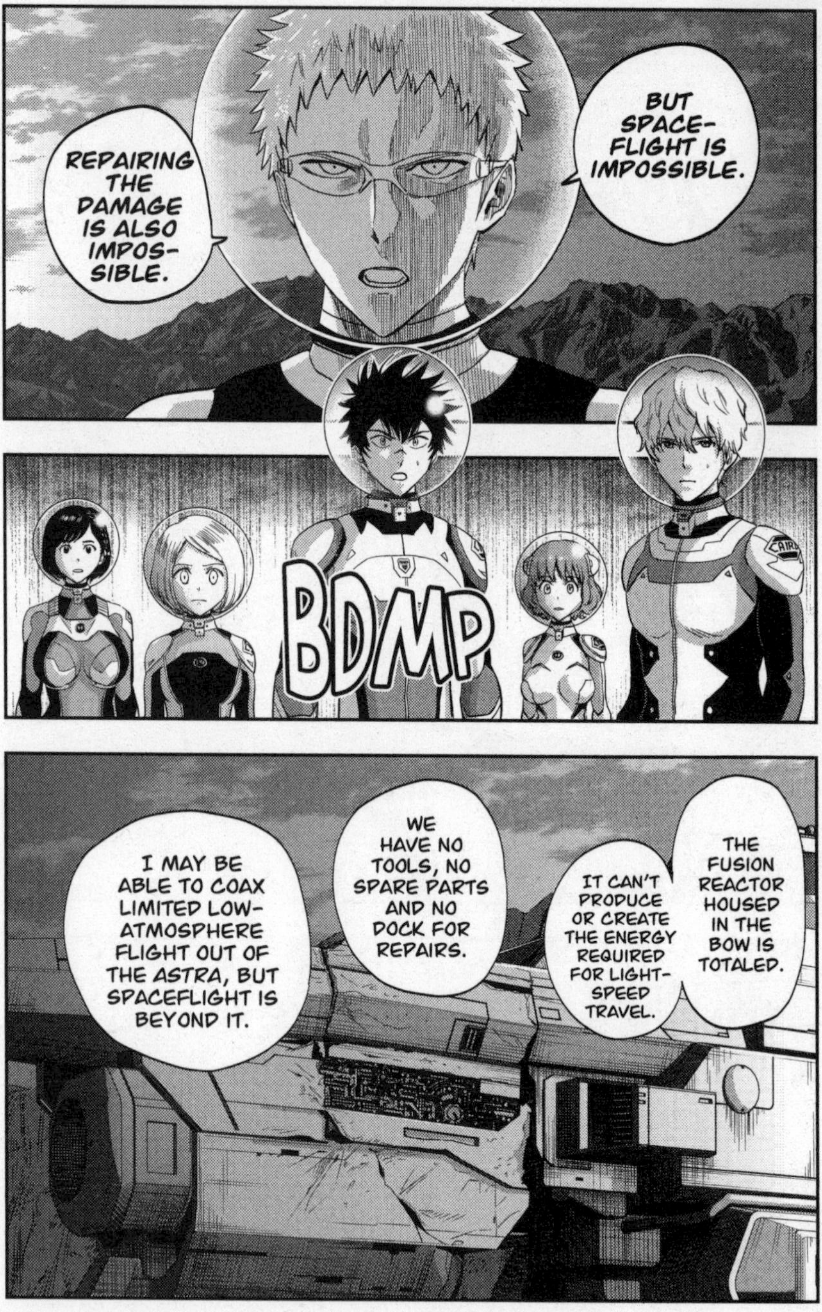
BUT SPACE-FLIGHT IS IMPOSSIBLE.
REPAIRING THE DAMAGE IS ALSO IMPOS-SIBLE.
BDMP
THE FUSION REACTOR HOUSED IN THE BOW IS TOTALED.
IT CAN'T PRODUCE OR CREATE THE ENERGY REQUIRED FOR LIGHT-SPEED TRAVEL.
WE HAVE NO TOOLS, NO SPARE PARTS AND NO DOCK FOR REPAIRS.
I MAY BE ABLE TO COAX LIMITED LOW-ATMOSPHERE FLIGHT OUT OF THE ASTRA, BUT SPACEFLIGHT IS BEYOND IT.

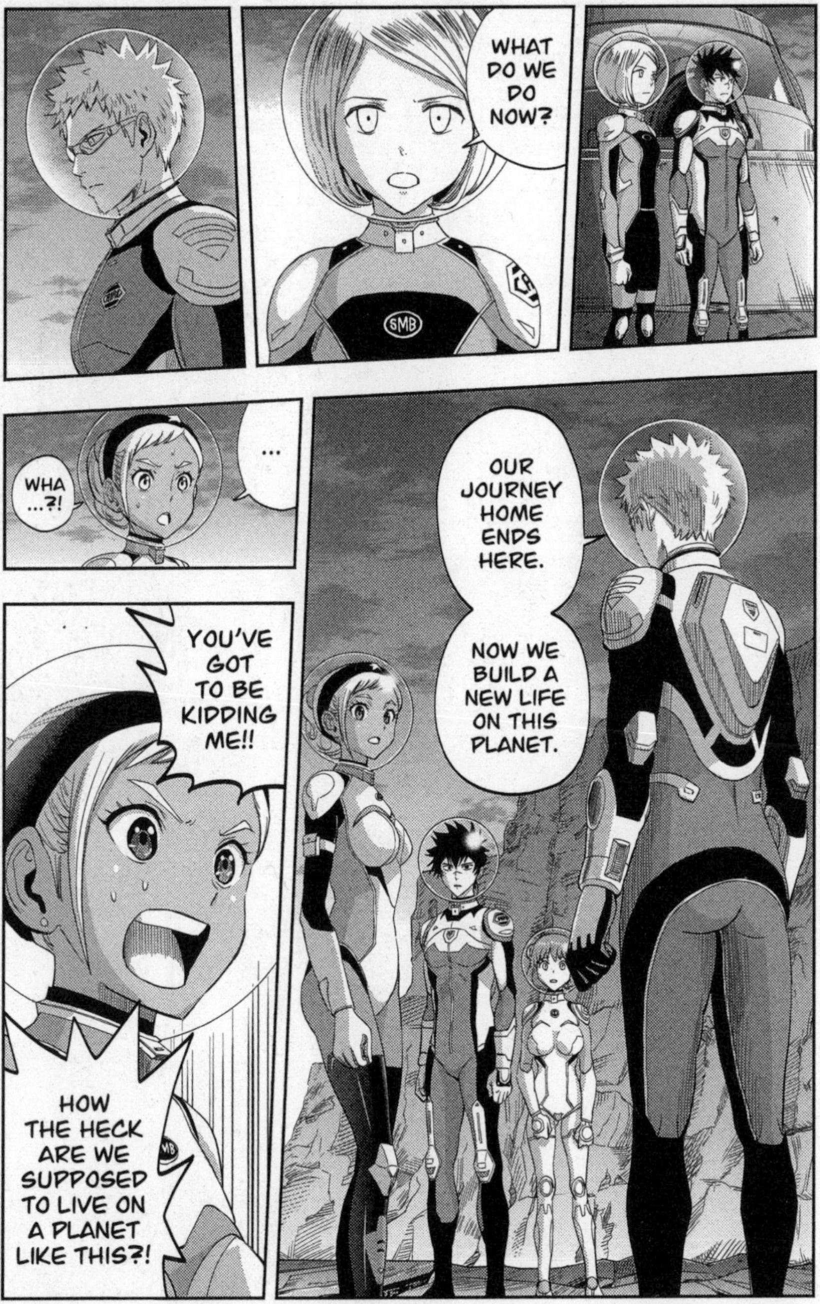
WHAT DO WE DO NOW?
OUR JOURNEY HOME ENDS HERE.
NOW WE BUILD A NEW LIFE ON THIS PLANET.
...
WHA ...?!
YOU'VE GOT TO BE KIDDING ME!!
HOW THE HECK ARE WE SUPPOSED TO LIVE ON A PLANET LIKE THIS?!

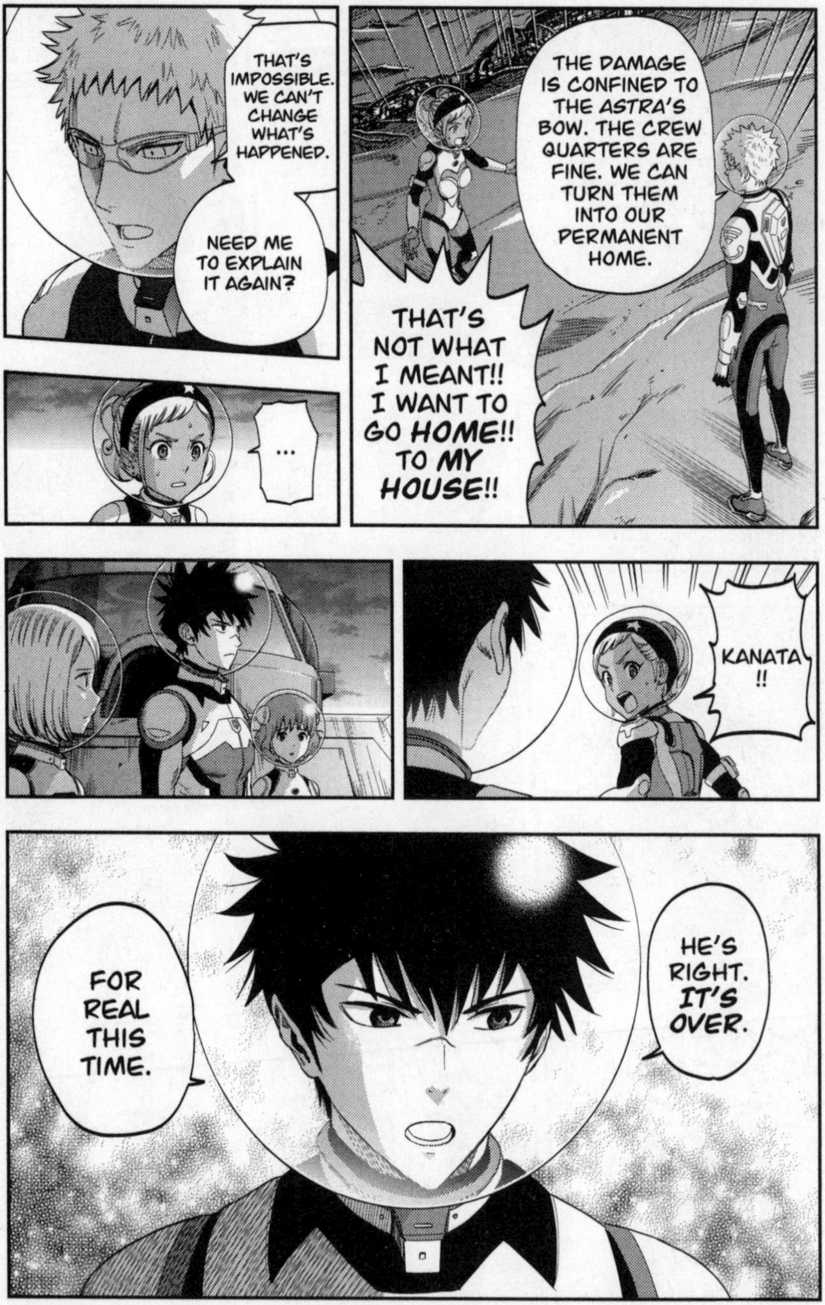
THE DAMAGE IS CONFINED TO THE ASTRA'S BOW. THE CREW QUARTERS ARE FINE. WE CAN TURN THEM INTO OUR PERMANENT HOME.
THAT'S NOT WHAT I MEANT!! I WANT TO GO HOME!! TO MY HOUSE!!
THAT'S IMPOSSIBLE. WE CAN'T CHANGE WHAT'S HAPPENED.
NEED ME TO EXPLAIN IT AGAIN?
...
KANATA!!
HE'S RIGHT. IT'S OVER.
FOR REAL THIS TIME.

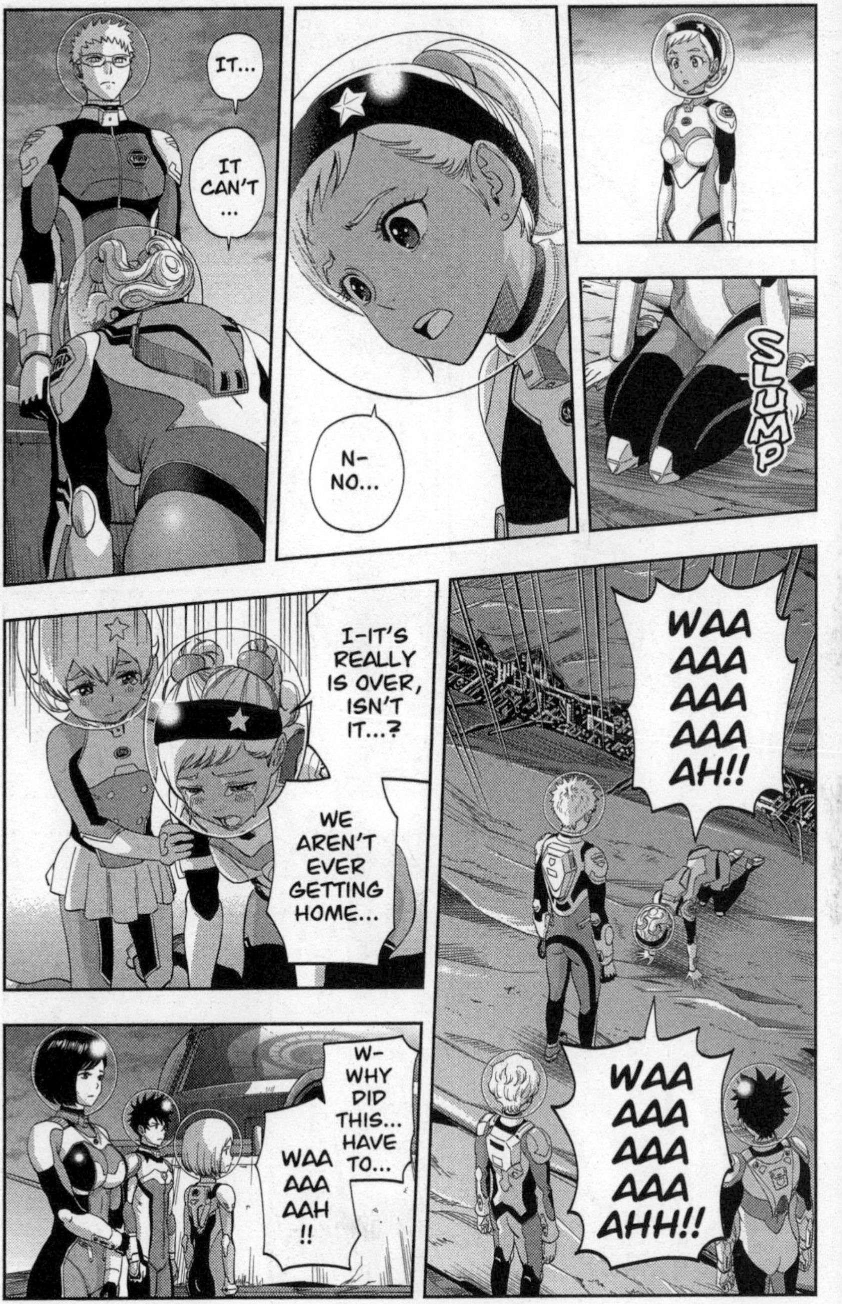
SLUMP
N-NO...
IT...
IT CAN'T...
WAAAAAAAAAAAAAH!!
WAAAAAAAAAAAAAAHH!!
I-IT'S REALLY IS OVER, ISN'T IT...?
WE AREN'T EVER GETTING HOME...
W-WHY DID THIS... HAVE TO...
WAAAAAAAH!!

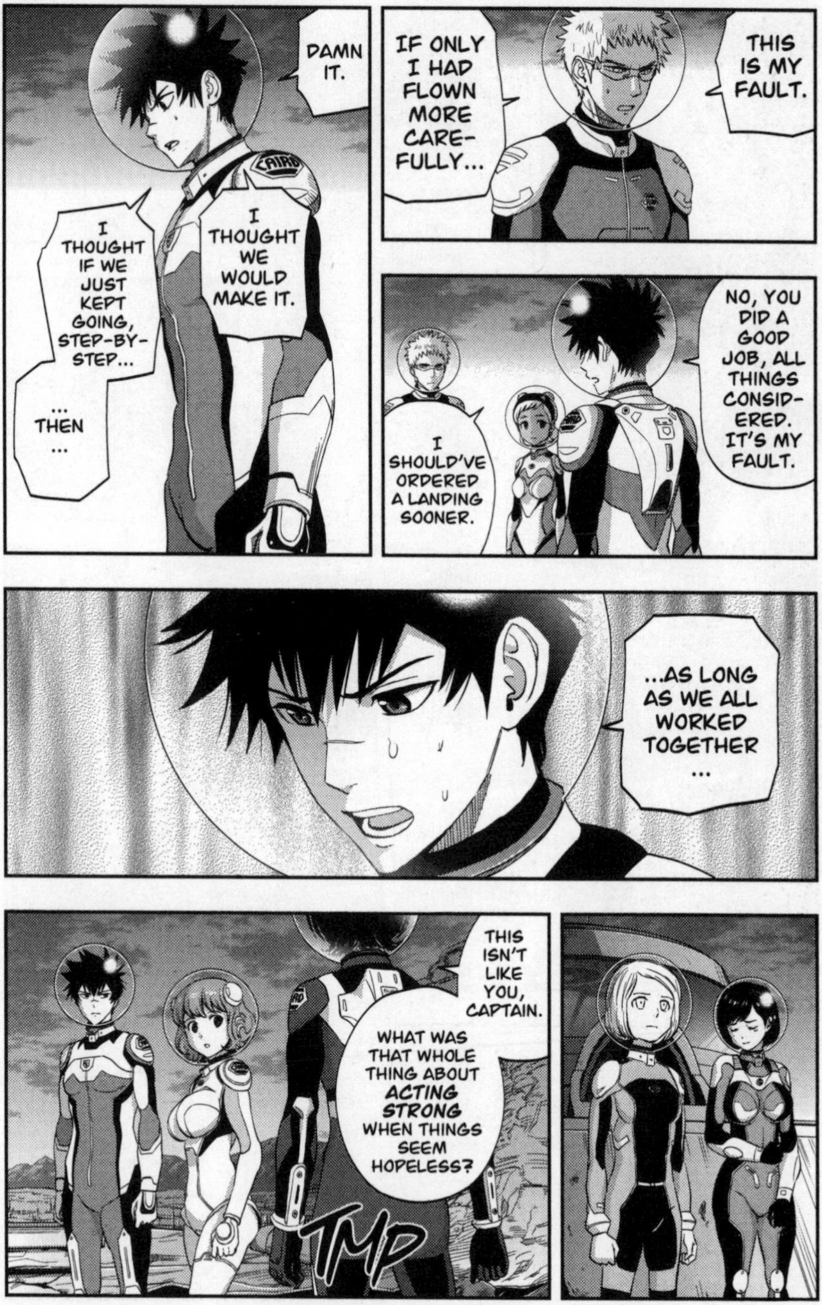
THIS IS MY FAULT.
IF ONLY I HAD FLOWN MORE CAREFULLY...
NO, YOU DID A GOOD JOB, ALL THINGS CONSIDERED. IT'S MY FAULT.
I SHOULD'VE ORDERED A LANDING SOONER.
DAMN IT.
I THOUGHT WE WOULD MAKE IT.
I THOUGHT IF WE JUST KEPT GOING, STEP-BY-STEP...
...THEN...
...AS LONG AS WE ALL WORKED TOGETHER...
THIS ISN'T LIKE YOU, CAPTAIN.
WHAT WAS THAT WHOLE THING ABOUT ACTING STRONG WHEN THINGS SEEM HOPELESS?
TMP

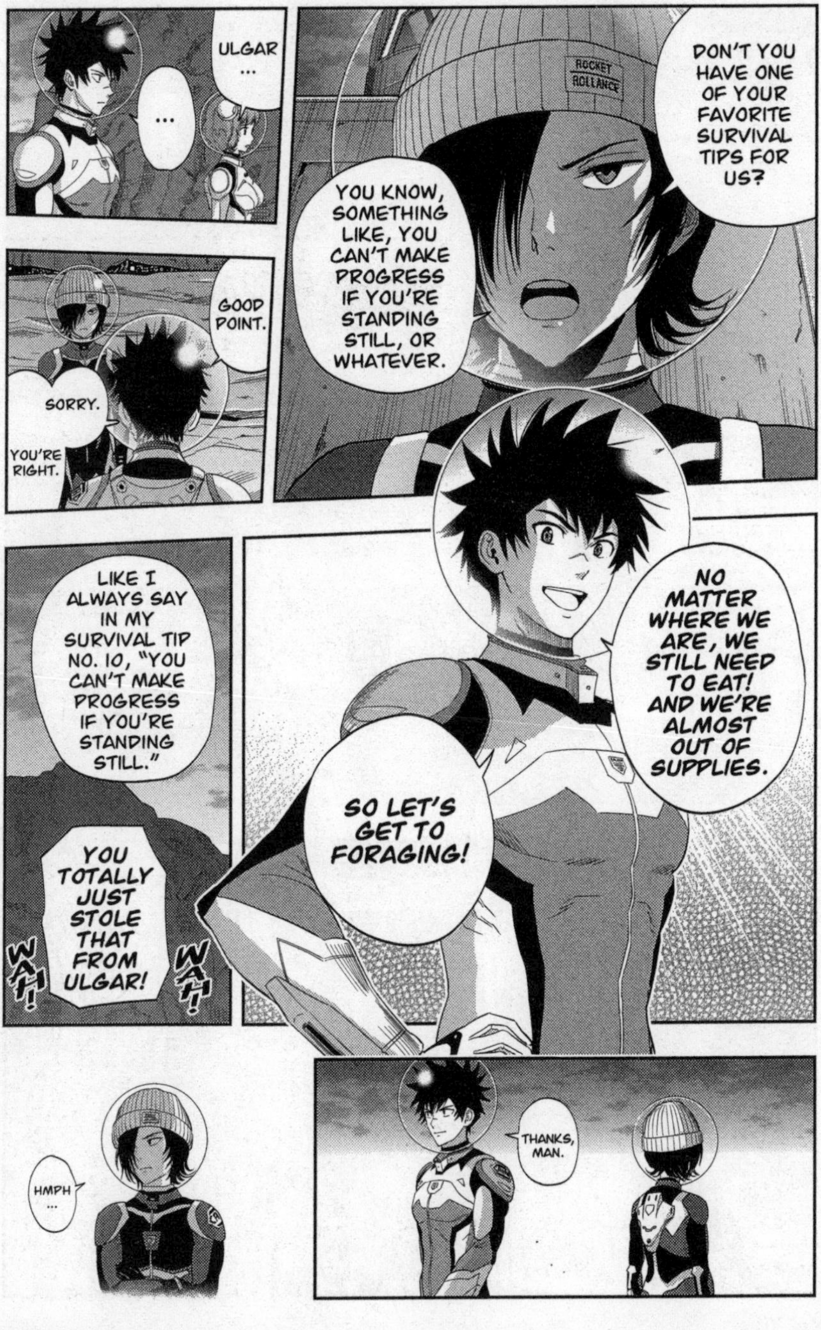
DON'T YOU HAVE ONE OF YOUR FAVORITE SURVIVAL TIPS FOR US?
YOU KNOW, SOMETHING LIKE, YOU CAN'T MAKE PROGRESS IF YOU'RE STANDING STILL, OR WHATEVER.
ULGAR ...
...
GOOD POINT.
SORRY.
YOU'RE RIGHT.
NO MATTER WHERE WE ARE, WE STILL NEED TO EAT! AND WE'RE ALMOST OUT OF SUPPLIES.
SO LET'S GET TO FORAGING!
LIKE I ALWAYS SAY IN MY SURVIVAL TIP NO. 10, "YOU CAN'T MAKE PROGRESS IF YOU'RE STANDING STILL."
YOU TOTALLY JUST STOLE THAT FROM ULGAR!
WAH!
WAH!
THANKS, MAN.
HMPH ...

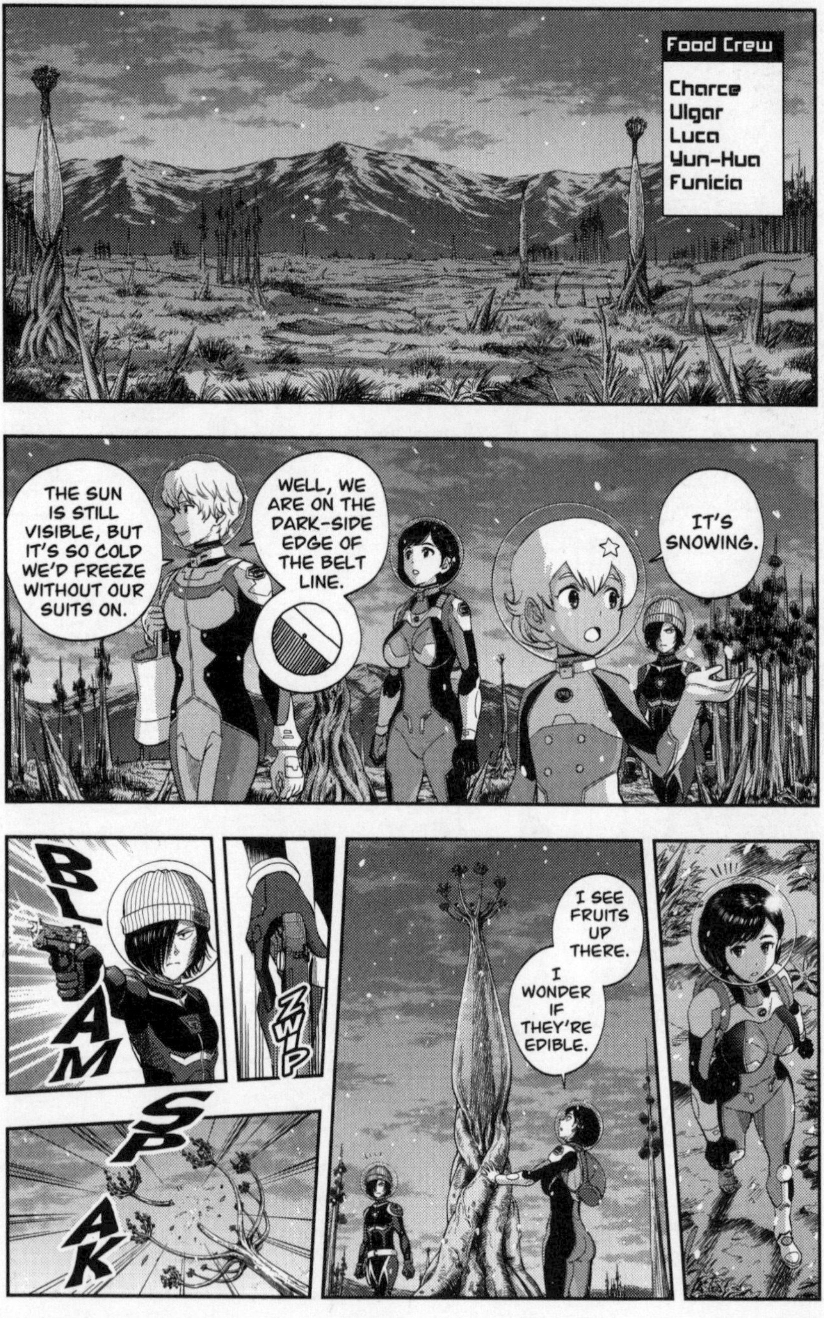
Food Crew
Charce
Ulgar
Luca
Yun-Hua
Funicia
IT'S SNOWING.
WELL, WE ARE ON THE DARK-SIDE EDGE OF THE BELT LINE.
THE SUN IS STILL VISIBLE, BUT IT'S SO COLD WE'D FREEZE WITHOUT OUR SUITS ON.
I SEE FRUITS UP THERE.
I WONDER IF THEY'RE EDIBLE.
ZWIP
BLAM
SPAK

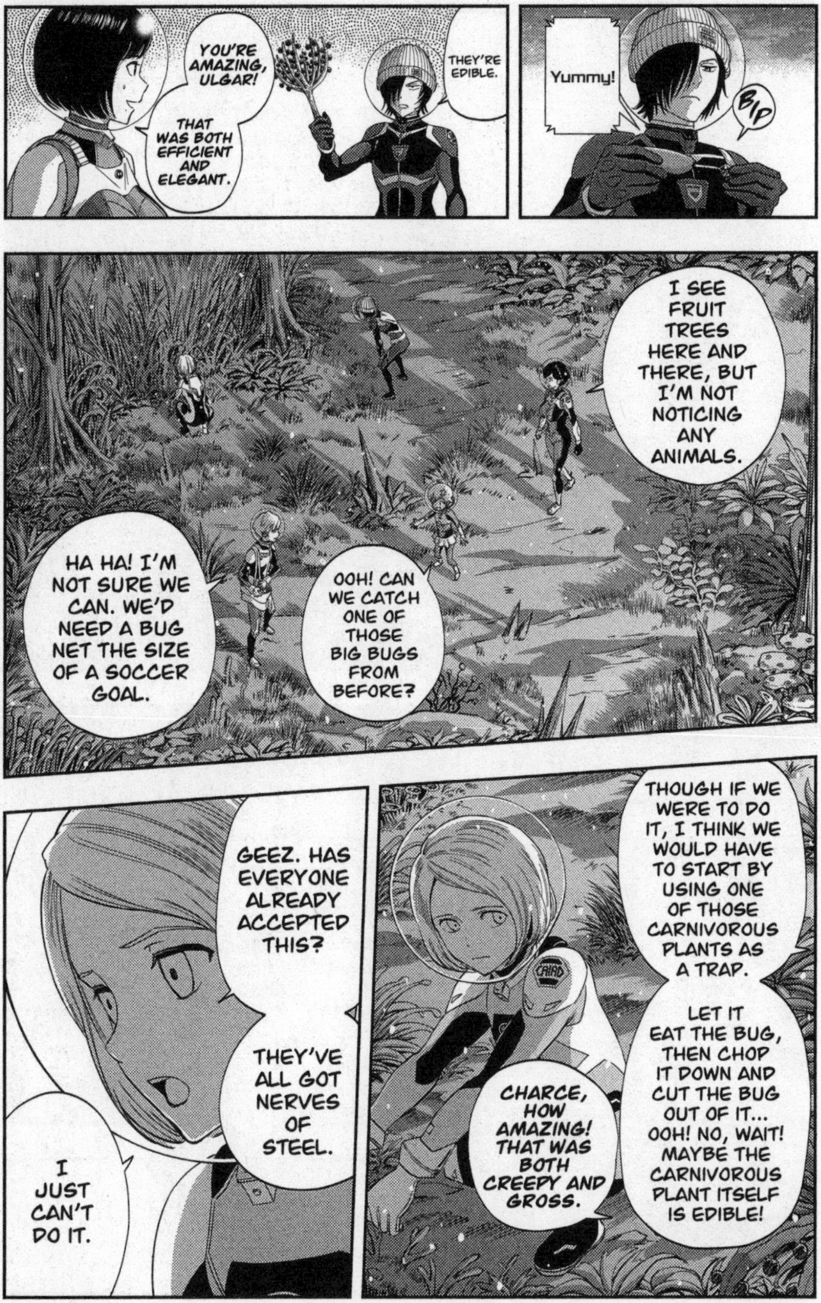

Yummy!
BIP
THEY'RE EDIBLE.
YOU'RE AMAZING, ULGAR!
THAT WAS BOTH EFFICIENT AND ELEGANT.
I SEE FRUIT TREES HERE AND THERE, BUT I'M NOT NOTICING ANY ANIMALS.
OOH! CAN WE CATCH ONE OF THOSE BIG BUGS FROM BEFORE?
HA HA! I'M NOT SURE WE CAN. WE'D NEED A BUG NET THE SIZE OF A SOCCER GOAL.
THOUGH IF WE WERE TO DO IT, I THINK WE WOULD HAVE TO START BY USING ONE OF THOSE CARNIVOROUS PLANTS AS A TRAP.
LET IT EAT THE BUG, THEN CHOP IT DOWN AND CUT THE BUG OUT OF IT... OOH! NO, WAIT! MAYBE THE CARNIVOROUS PLANT ITSELF IS EDIBLE!
CHARCE, HOW AMAZING! THAT WAS BOTH CREEPY AND GROSS.
GEEZ. HAS EVERYONE ALREADY ACCEPTED THIS?
THEY'VE ALL GOT NERVES OF STEEL.
I JUST CAN'T DO IT.

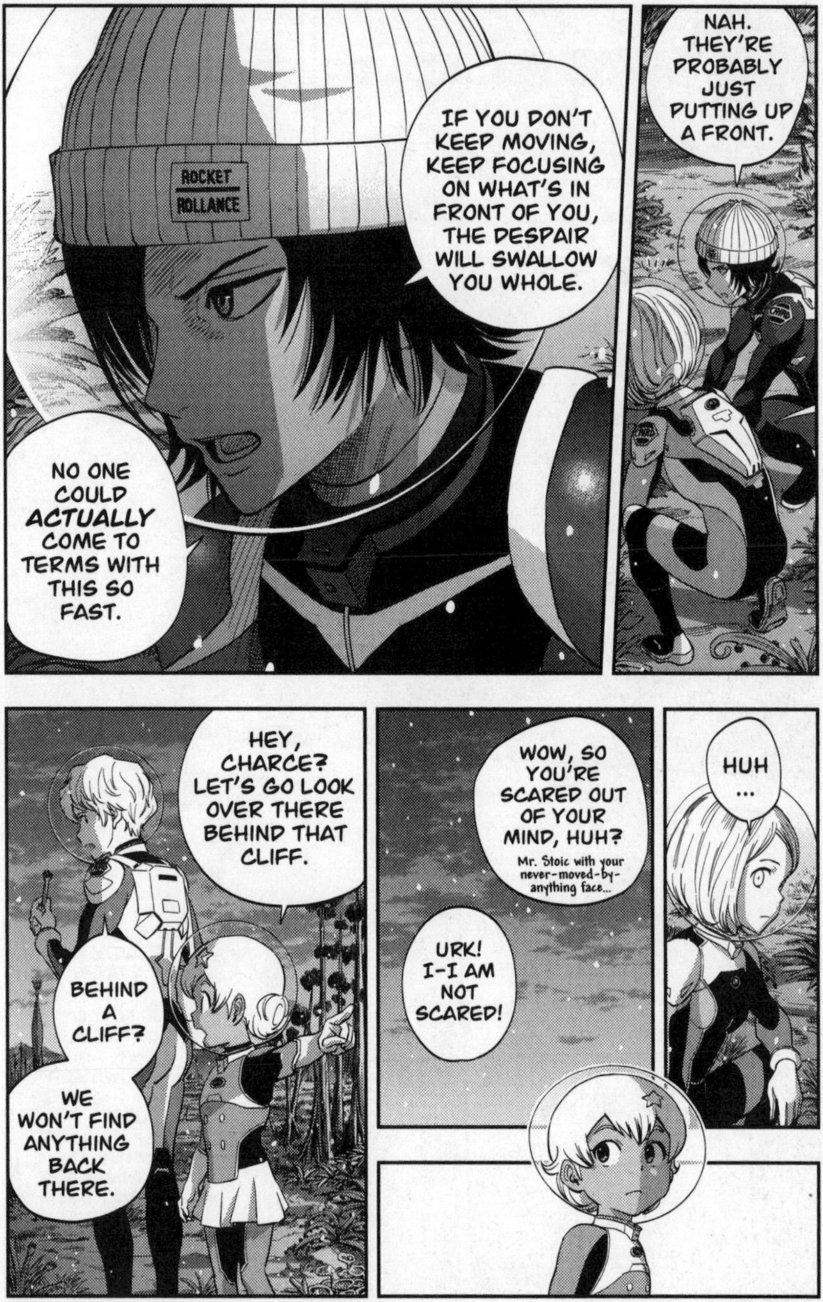
NAH. THEY'RE PROBABLY JUST PUTTING UP A FRONT.
ROCKET ROLLANCE
IF YOU DON'T KEEP MOVING, KEEP FOCUSING ON WHAT'S IN FRONT OF YOU, THE DESPAIR WILL SWALLOW YOU WHOLE.
NO ONE COULD ACTUALLY COME TO TERMS WITH THIS SO FAST.
HUH ...
WOW, SO YOU'RE SCARED OUT OF YOUR MIND, HUH?
Mr. Stoic with your never-moved-by-anything face...
URK! I-I AM NOT SCARED!
HEY, CHARCE? LET'S GO LOOK OVER THERE BEHIND THAT CLIFF.
BEHIND A CLIFF?
WE WON'T FIND ANYTHING BACK THERE.

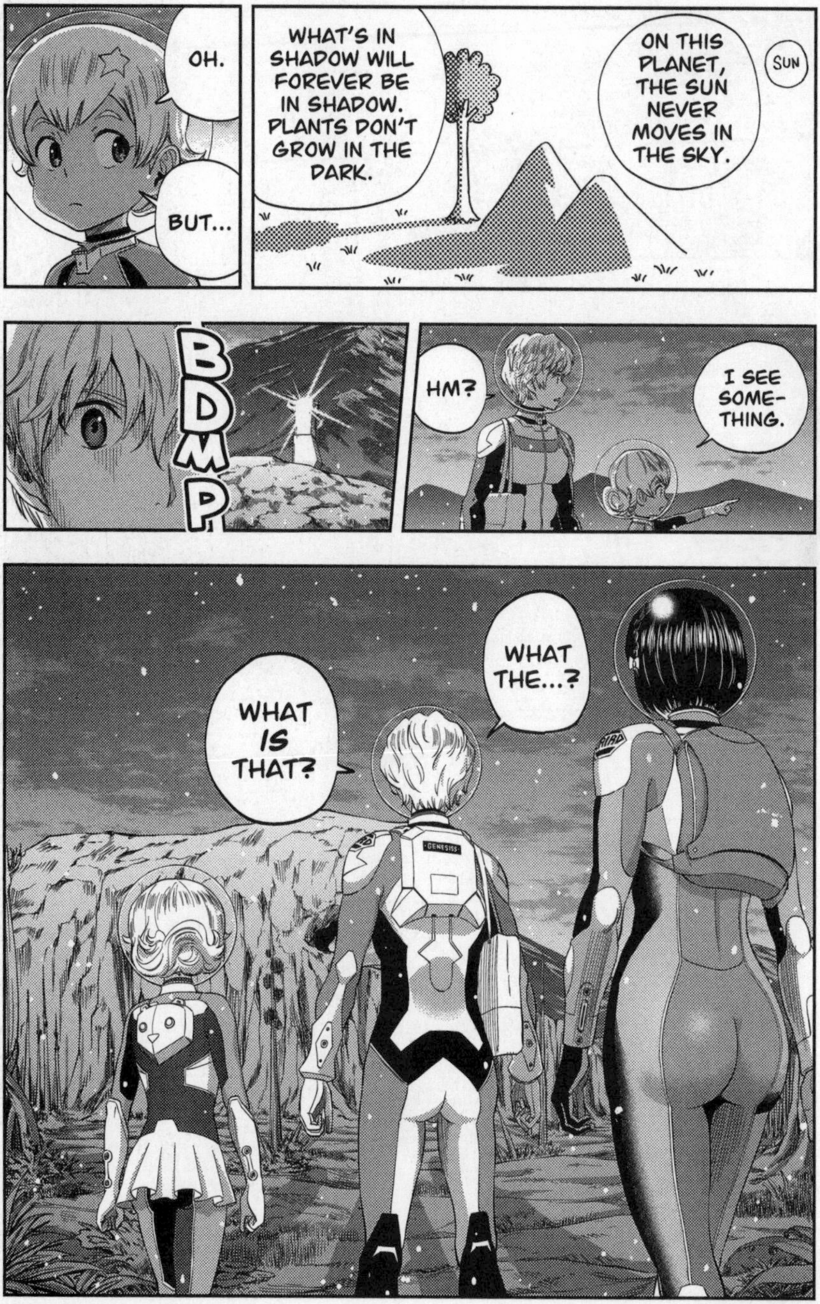
SUN
ON THIS PLANET, THE SUN NEVER MOVES IN THE SKY.
WHAT'S IN SHADOW WILL FOREVER BE IN SHADOW. PLANTS DON'T GROW IN THE DARK.
OH.
BUT...
I SEE SOME-THING.
HM?
BDMP
WHAT THE...?
WHAT IS THAT?

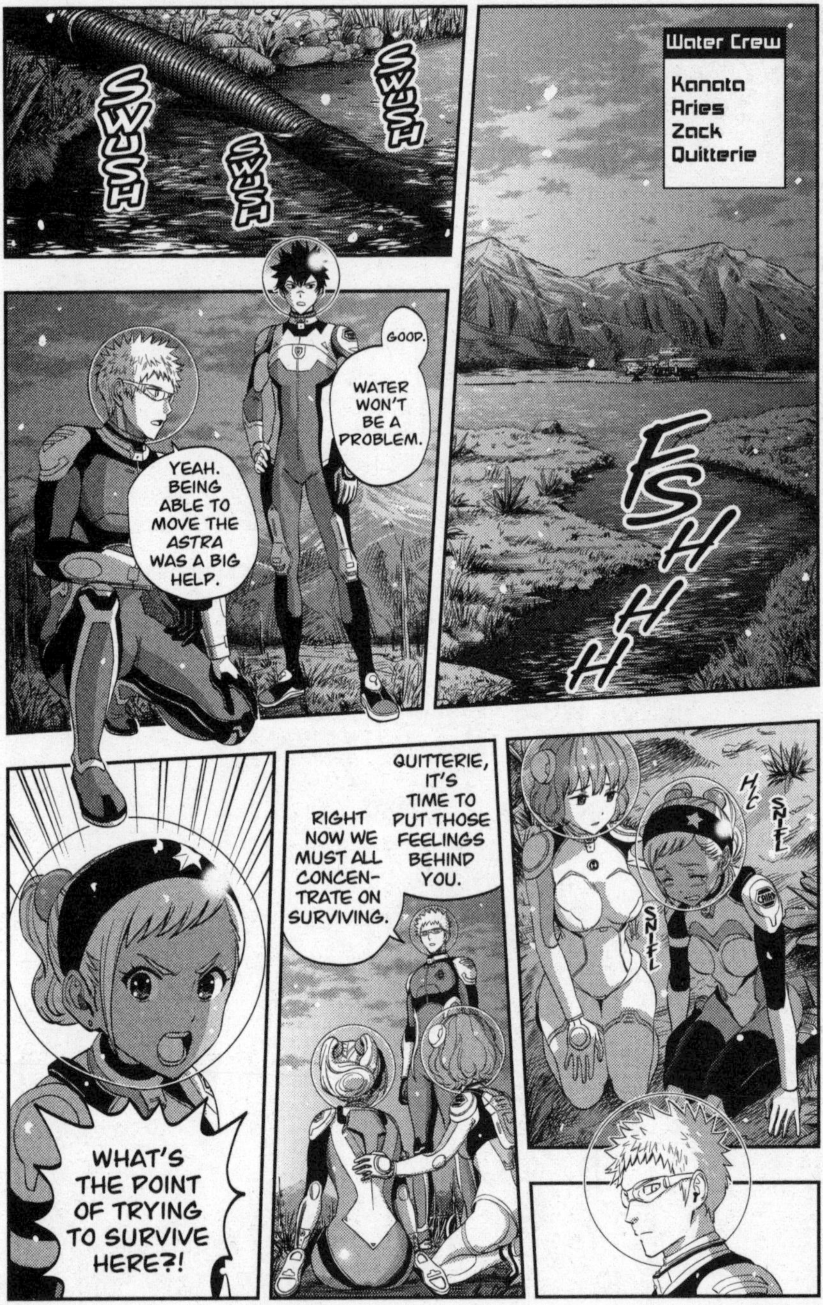
Water Crew
Kanata
Aries
Zack
Quitterie
FSHHHH
SWUSH
SWUSH
SWUSH
GOOD.
WATER WON'T BE A PROBLEM.
YEAH. BEING ABLE TO MOVE THE ASTRA WAS A BIG HELP.
SNIFL
HIC
SNIFL
QUITTERIE, IT'S TIME TO PUT THOSE FEELINGS BEHIND YOU.
RIGHT NOW WE MUST ALL CONCEN-TRATE ON SURVIVING.
WHAT'S THE POINT OF TRYING TO SURVIVE HERE?!

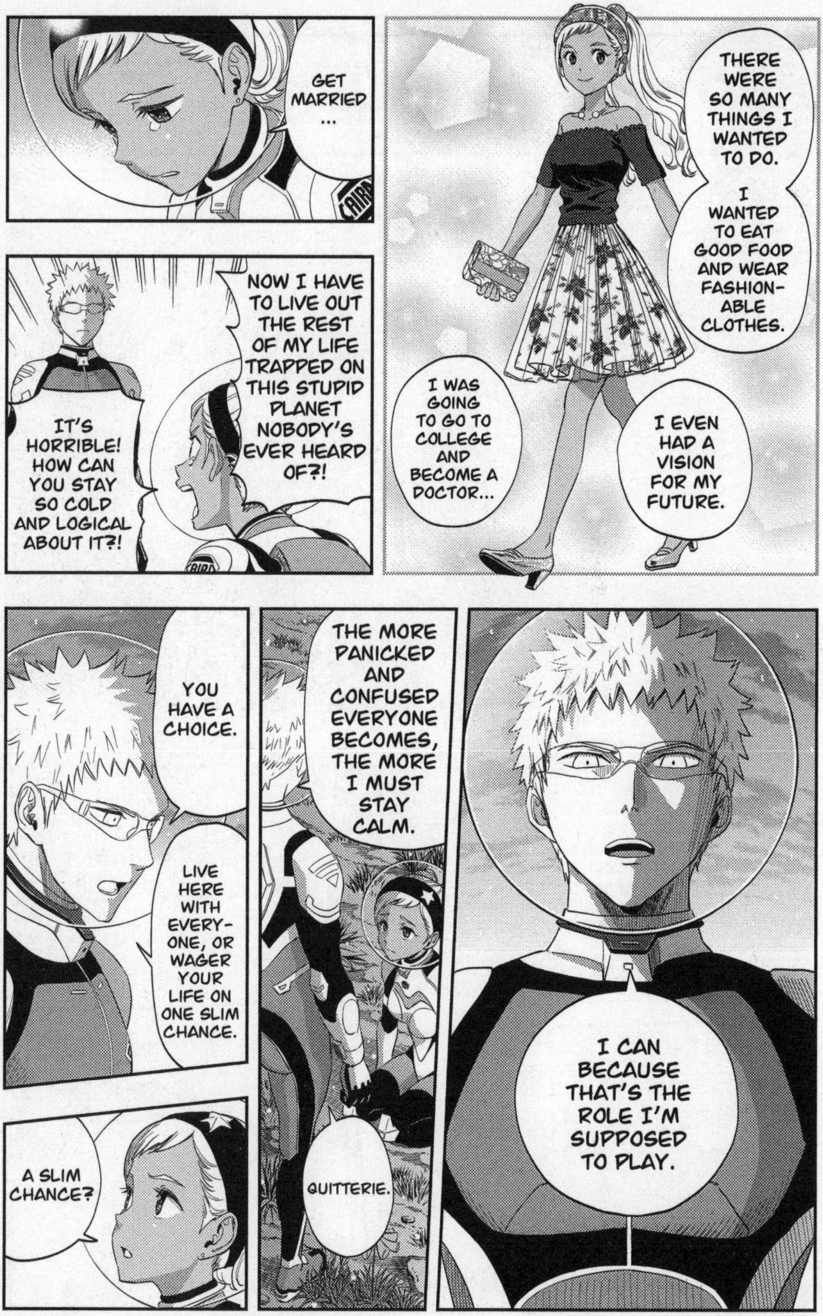
THERE WERE SO MANY THINGS I WANTED TO DO.
I WANTED TO EAT GOOD FOOD AND WEAR FASHION-ABLE CLOTHES.
I EVEN HAD A VISION FOR MY FUTURE.
I WAS GOING TO GO TO COLLEGE AND BECOME A DOCTOR...
GET MARRIED ...
NOW I HAVE TO LIVE OUT THE REST OF MY LIFE TRAPPED ON THIS STUPID PLANET NOBODY'S EVER HEARD OF?!
IT'S HORRIBLE! HOW CAN YOU STAY SO COLD AND LOGICAL ABOUT IT?!
I CAN BECAUSE THAT'S THE ROLE I'M SUPPOSED TO PLAY.
THE MORE PANICKED AND CONFUSED EVERYONE BECOMES, THE MORE I MUST STAY CALM.
QUITTERIE.
YOU HAVE A CHOICE.
LIVE HERE WITH EVERY-ONE, OR WAGER YOUR LIFE ON ONE SLIM CHANCE.
A SLIM CHANCE?

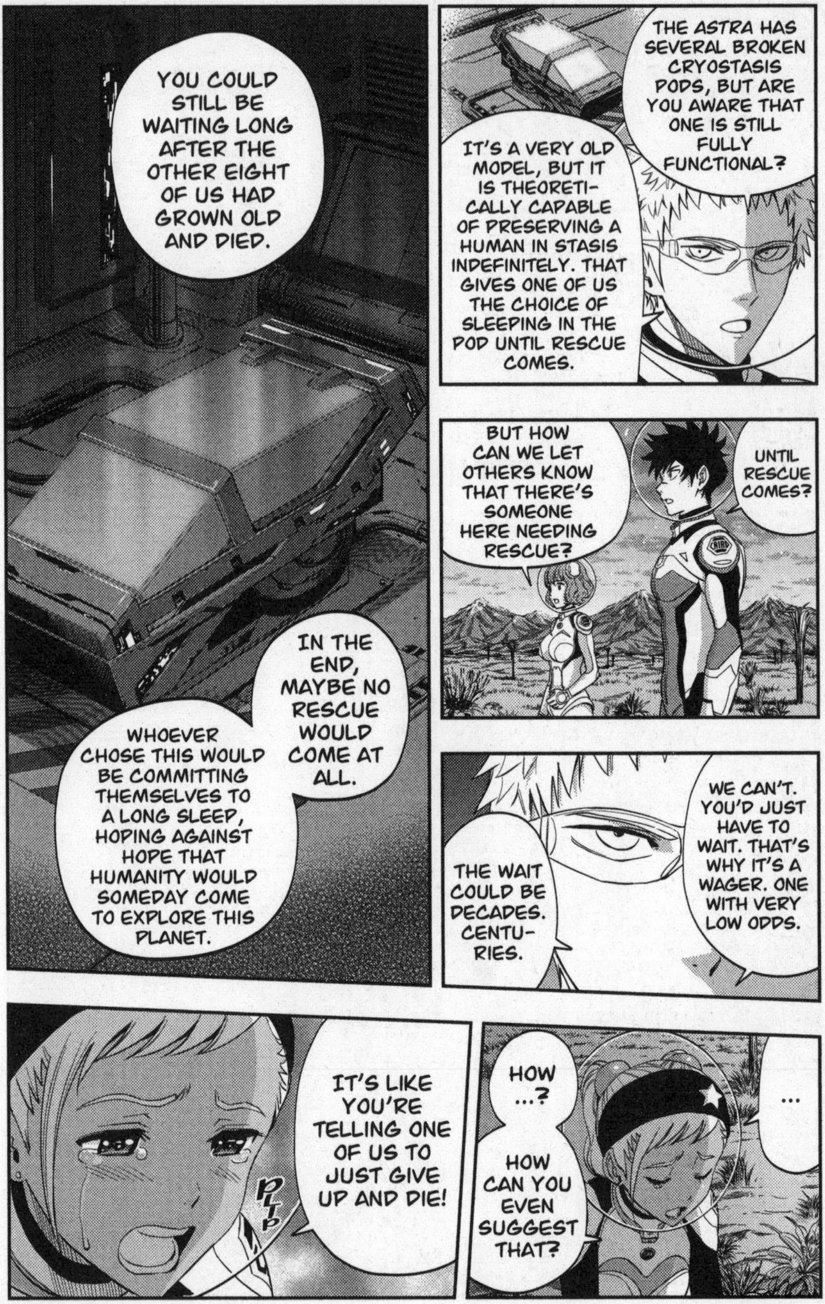
THE ASTRA HAS SEVERAL BROKEN CRYOSTASIS PODS, BUT ARE YOU AWARE THAT ONE IS STILL FULLY FUNCTIONAL?
IT'S A VERY OLD MODEL, BUT IT IS THEORETI-CALLY CAPABLE OF PRESERVING A HUMAN IN STASIS INDEFINITELY. THAT GIVES ONE OF US THE CHOICE OF SLEEPING IN THE POD UNTIL RESCUE COMES.
UNTIL RESCUE COMES?
BUT HOW CAN WE LET OTHERS KNOW THAT THERE'S SOMEONE HERE NEEDING RESCUE?
WE CAN'T. YOU'D JUST HAVE TO WAIT. THAT'S WHY IT'S A WAGER. ONE WITH VERY LOW ODDS.
THE WAIT COULD BE DECADES. CENTU-RIES.
YOU COULD STILL BE WAITING LONG AFTER THE OTHER EIGHT OF US HAD GROWN OLD AND DIED.
IN THE END, MAYBE NO RESCUE WOULD COME AT ALL.
WHOEVER CHOSE THIS WOULD BE COMMITTING THEMSELVES TO A LONG SLEEP, HOPING AGAINST HOPE THAT HUMANITY WOULD SOMEDAY COME TO EXPLORE THIS PLANET.
...
HOW ...?
HOW CAN YOU EVEN SUGGEST THAT?
IT'S LIKE YOU'RE TELLING ONE OF US TO JUST GIVE UP AND DIE!
PLIP

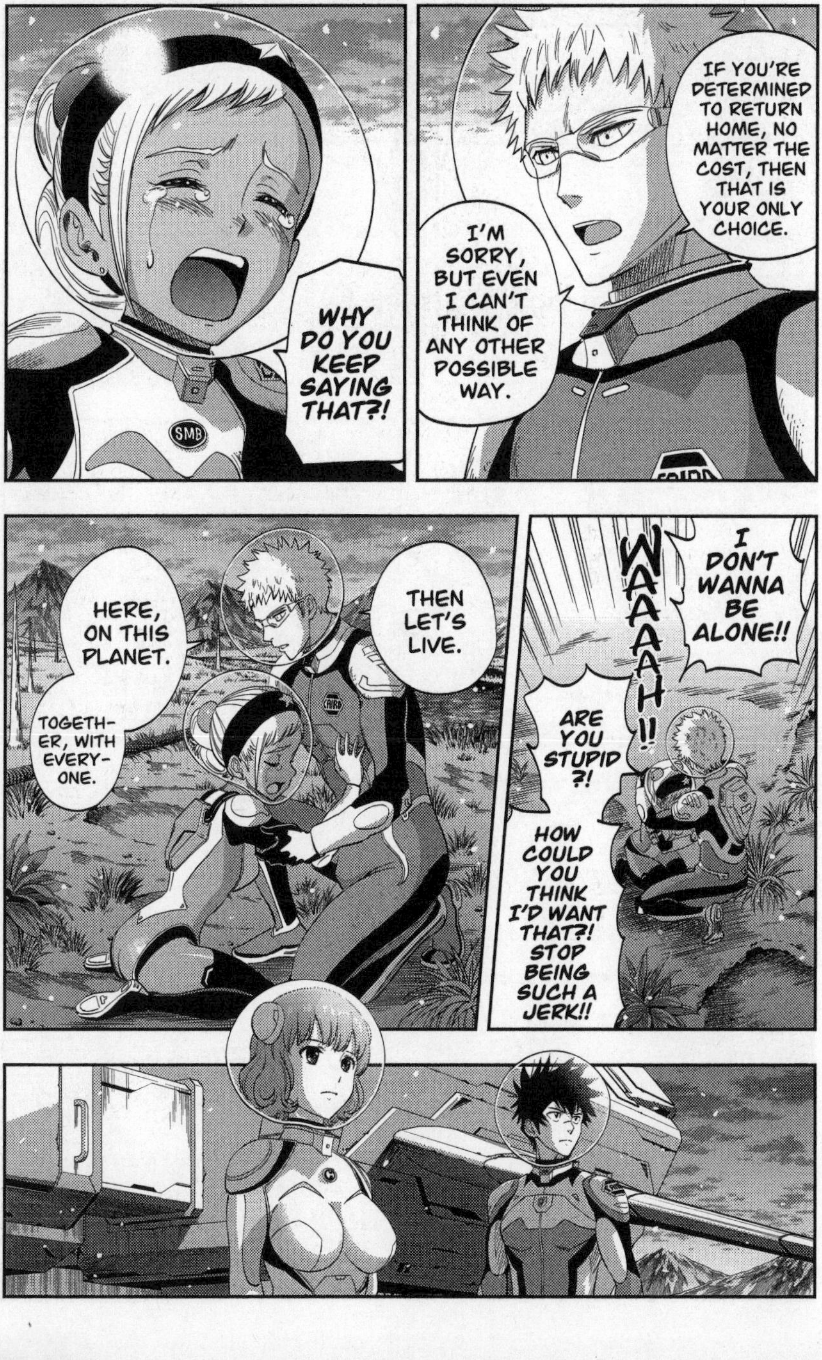
IF YOU'RE DETERMINED TO RETURN HOME, NO MATTER THE COST, THEN THAT IS YOUR ONLY CHOICE.
I'M SORRY, BUT EVEN I CAN'T THINK OF ANY OTHER POSSIBLE WAY.
WHY DO YOU KEEP SAYING THAT?!
I DON'T WANNA BE ALONE!!
WAAAAH!!
ARE YOU STUPID?!
HOW COULD YOU THINK I'D WANT THAT?! STOP BEING SUCH A JERK!!
THEN LET'S LIVE.
HERE, ON THIS PLANET.
TOGETH-ER, WITH EVERY-ONE.

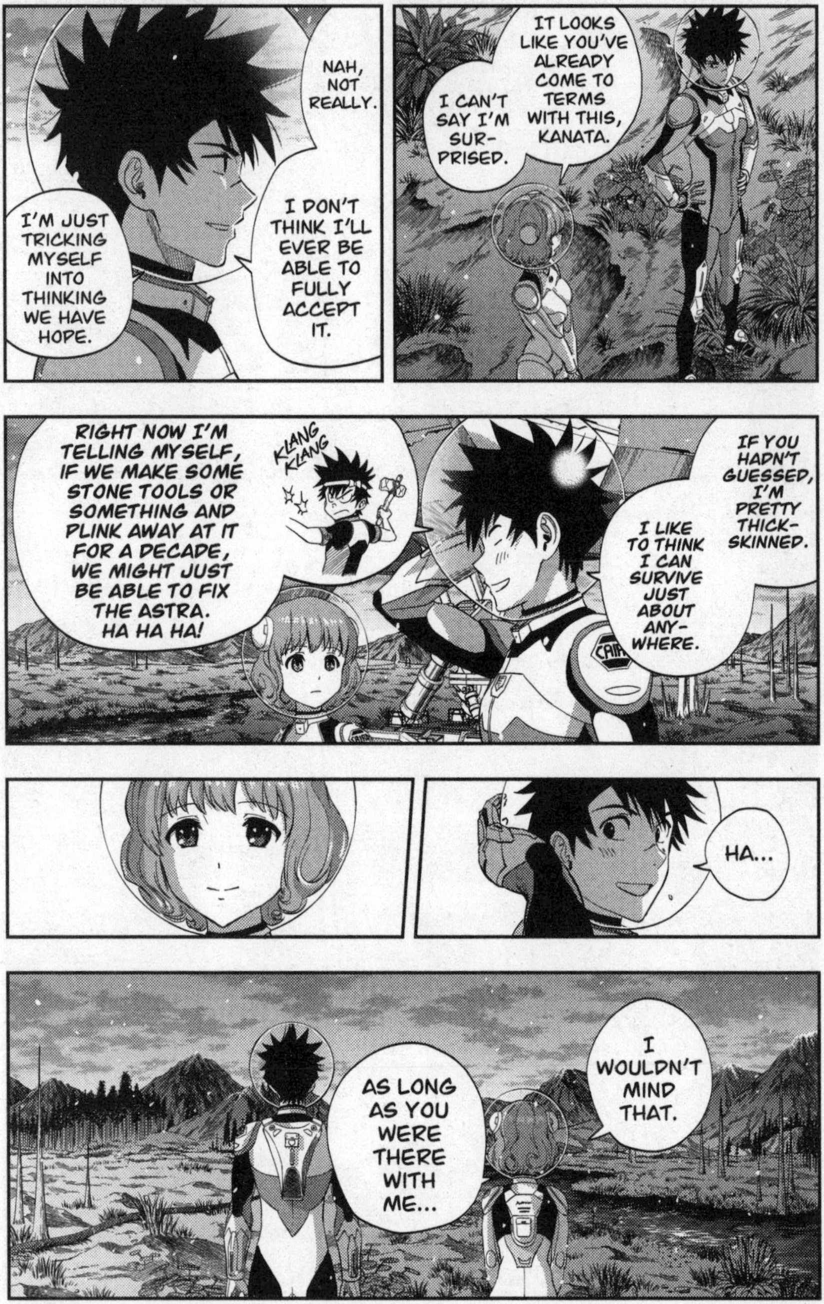
IT LOOKS LIKE YOU'VE ALREADY COME TO TERMS WITH THIS, KANATA.
I CAN'T SAY I'M SUR-PRISED.
NAH, NOT REALLY.
I DON'T THINK I'LL EVER BE ABLE TO FULLY ACCEPT IT.
I'M JUST TRICKING MYSELF INTO THINKING WE HAVE HOPE.
IF YOU HADN'T GUESSED, I'M PRETTY THICK-SKINNED.
I LIKE TO THINK I CAN SURVIVE JUST ABOUT ANY-WHERE.
KLANG KLANG
RIGHT NOW I'M TELLING MYSELF, IF WE MAKE SOME STONE TOOLS OR SOMETHING AND PLINK AWAY AT IT FOR A DECADE, WE MIGHT JUST BE ABLE TO FIX THE ASTRA. HA HA HA!
HA...
I WOULDN'T MIND THAT.
AS LONG AS YOU WERE THERE WITH ME...

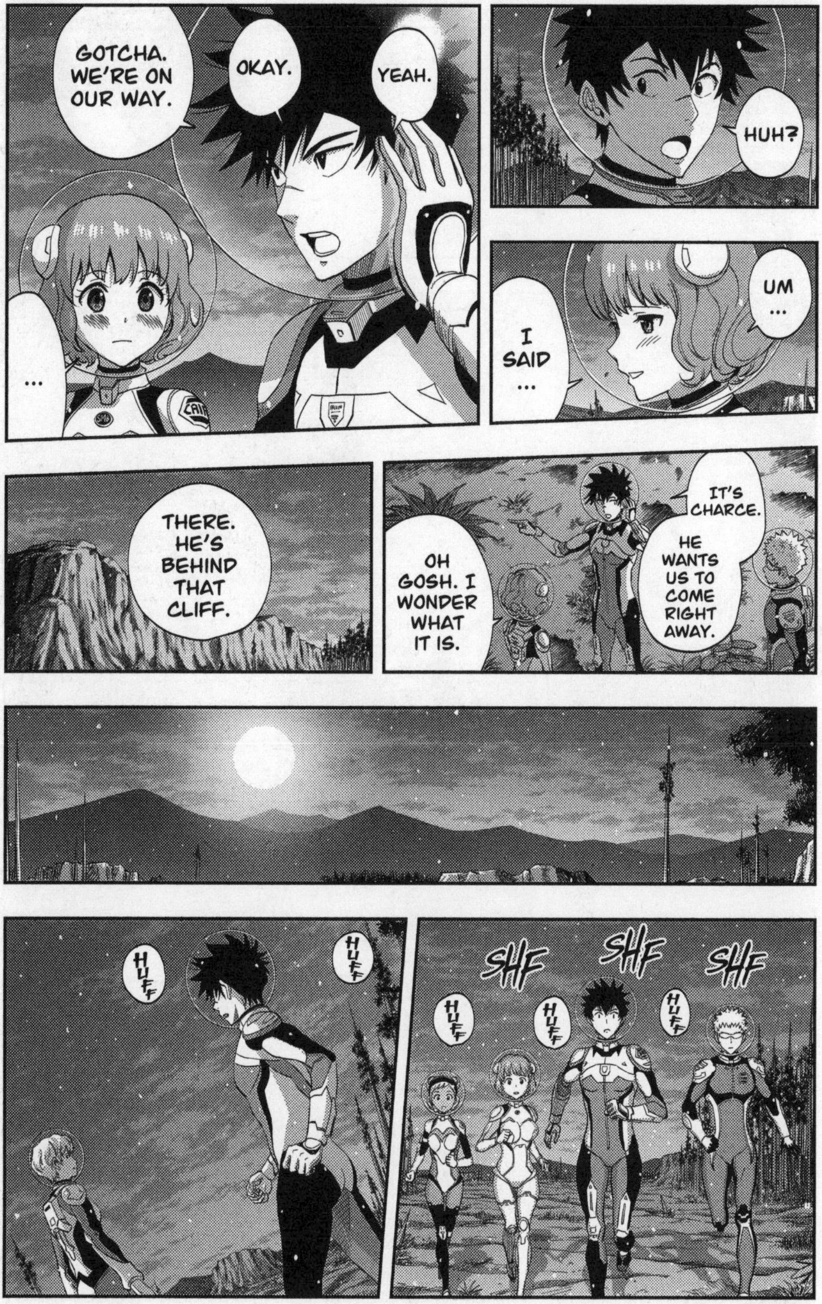
HUH?
UM ...
I SAID ...
YEAH.
OKAY.
GOTCHA. WE'RE ON OUR WAY.
...
IT'S CHARCE.
HE WANTS US TO COME RIGHT AWAY.
OH GOSH. I WONDER WHAT IT IS.
THERE. HE'S BEHIND THAT CLIFF.
SHF
SHF
SHF
HUFF
HUFF
HUFF
HUFF
HUFF

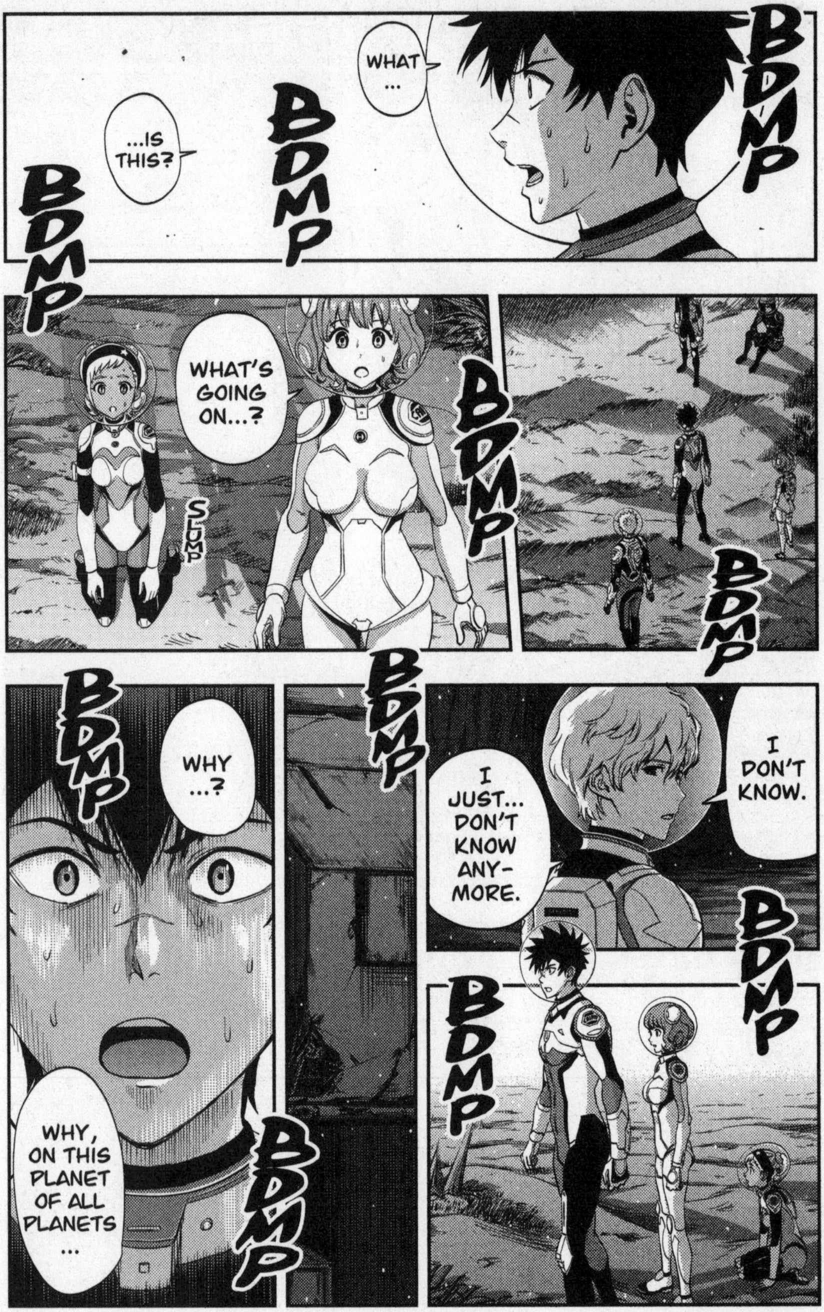
BDMP
WHAT ...
...IS THIS?
BDMP
BDMP
BDMP
BDMP
BDMP
WHAT'S GOING ON...?
SLUMP
I DON'T KNOW.
I JUST... DON'T KNOW ANYMORE.
BDMP
BDMP
BDMP
BDMP
WHY ...?
WHY, ON THIS PLANET OF ALL PLANETS ...
BDMP

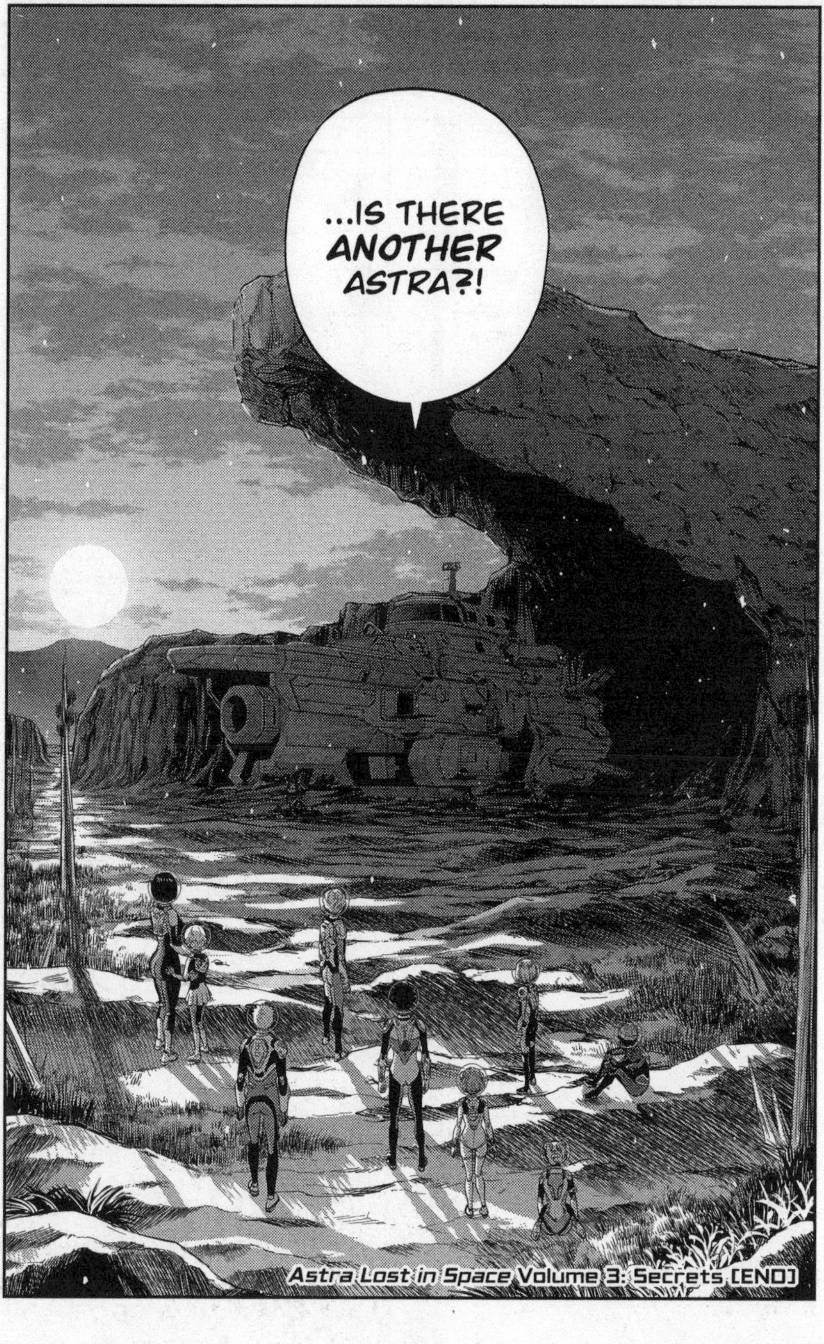
...IS THERE ANOTHER ASTRA?!
Astra Lost in Space Volume 3: Secrets [END]

A Daughter and a Fan

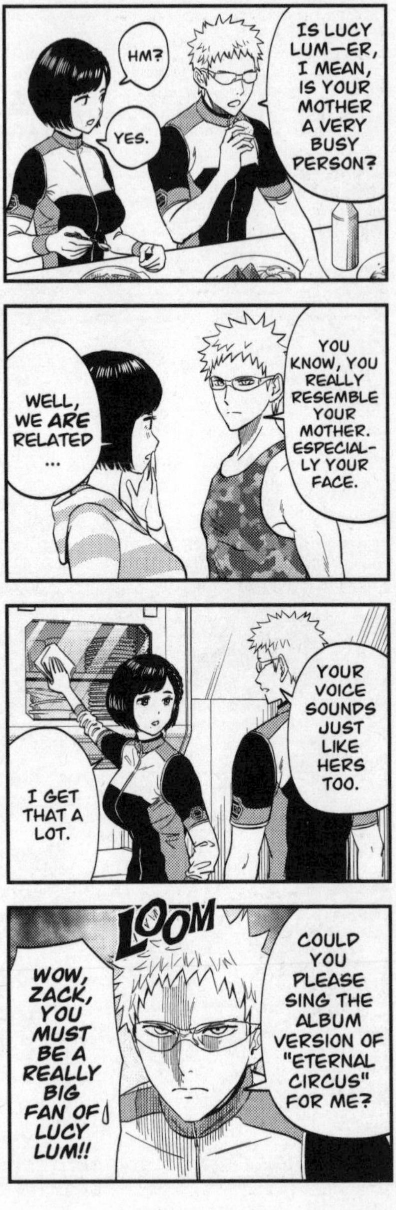
IS LUCY LUM—ER, I MEAN, IS YOUR MOTHER A VERY BUSY PERSON?
HM?
YES.
YOU KNOW, YOU REALLY RESEMBLE YOUR MOTHER. ESPECIAL-LY YOUR FACE.
WELL, WE ARE RELATED...
YOUR VOICE SOUNDS JUST LIKE HERS TOO.
I GET THAT A LOT.
COULD YOU PLEASE SING THE ALBUM VERSION OF "ETERNAL CIRCUS" FOR ME?
LOOM
WOW, ZACK, YOU MUST BE A REALLY BIG FAN OF LUCY LUM!!

Edibility Tester Additional Functionality

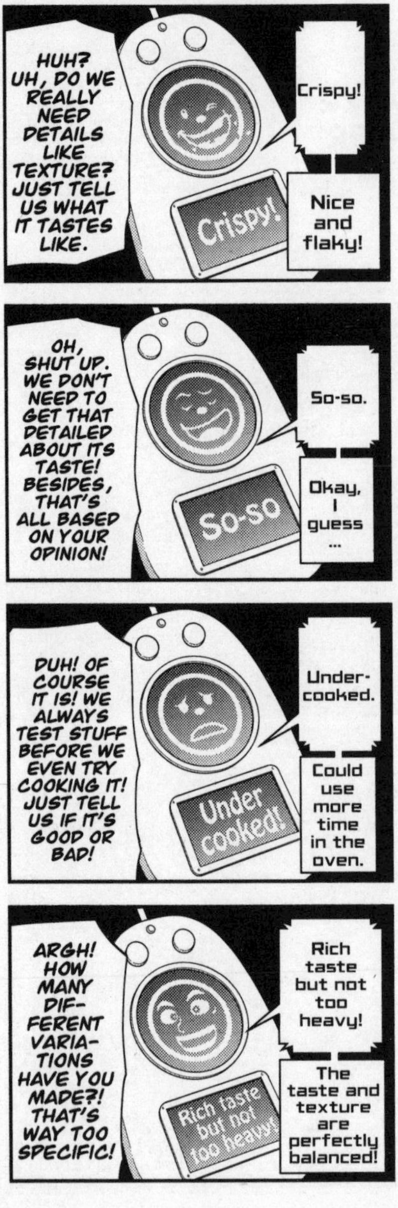
Crispy!
Nice and flaky!
Crispy!
HUH? UH, DO WE REALLY NEED DETAILS LIKE TEXTURE? JUST TELL US WHAT IT TASTES LIKE.
So-so.
Okay, I guess...
So-so
OH, SHUT UP. WE DON'T NEED TO GET THAT DETAILED ABOUT ITS TASTE! BESIDES, THAT'S ALL BASED ON YOUR OPINION!
Under-cooked.
Could use more time in the oven.
Under cooked!
DUH! OF COURSE IT IS! WE ALWAYS TEST STUFF BEFORE WE EVEN TRY COOKING IT! JUST TELL US IF IT'S GOOD OR BAD!
Rich taste but not too heavy!
The taste and texture are perfectly balanced!
Rich taste but not too heavy!
ARGH! HOW MANY DIF-FERENT VARIA-TIONS HAVE YOU MADE?! THAT'S WAY TOO SPECIFIC!

Girl Talk

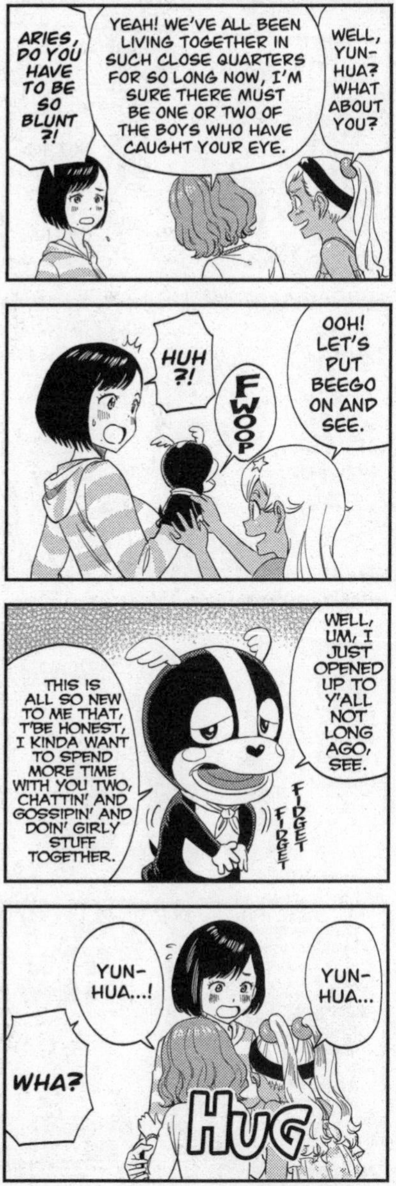
WELL, YUN-HUA? WHAT ABOUT YOU?
YEAH! WE'VE ALL BEEN LIVING TOGETHER IN SUCH CLOSE QUARTERS FOR SO LONG NOW, I'M SURE THERE MUST BE ONE OR TWO OF THE BOYS WHO HAVE CAUGHT YOUR EYE.
ARIES, DO YOU HAVE TO BE SO BLUNT?!
OOH! LET'S PUT BEEGO ON AND SEE.
FWOOP
HUH?!
WELL, UM, I JUST OPENED UP TO Y'ALL NOT LONG AGO, SEE.
FIDGET FIDGET
THIS IS ALL SO NEW TO ME THAT, T'BE HONEST, I KINDA WANT TO SPEND MORE TIME WITH YOU TWO, CHATTIN' AND GOSSIPIN' AND DOIN' GIRLY STUFF TOGETHER.
YUN-HUA...
YUN-HUA...!
WHA?
HUG

More Girl Talk

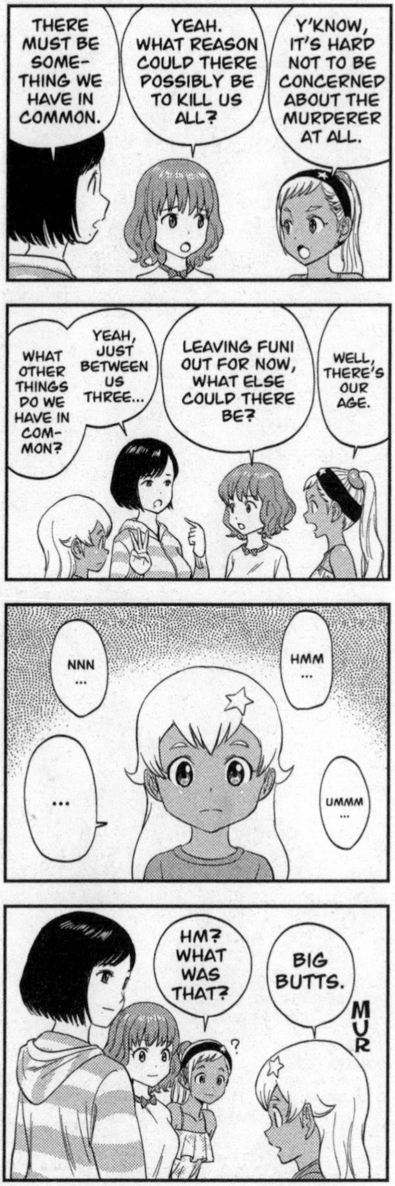
Y'KNOW, IT'S HARD NOT TO BE CONCERNED ABOUT THE MURDERER AT ALL.
YEAH. WHAT REASON COULD THERE POSSIBLY BE TO KILL US ALL?
THERE MUST BE SOME-THING WE HAVE IN COMMON.
WELL, THERE'S OUR AGE.
LEAVING FUNI OUT FOR NOW, WHAT ELSE COULD THERE BE?
YEAH, JUST BETWEEN US THREE...
WHAT OTHER THINGS DO WE HAVE IN COM-MON?
HMM...
NNN...
UMMM...
...
MUR
BIG BUTTS.
HM? WHAT WAS THAT?

The Man Named Charce #1

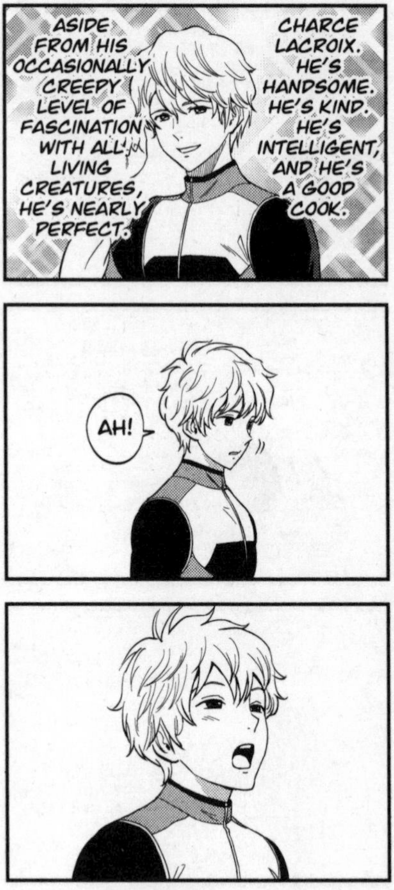
CHARCE LACROIX. HE'S HANDSOME. HE'S KIND. HE'S INTELLIGENT, AND HE'S A GOOD COOK.
ASIDE FROM HIS OCCASIONALLY CREEPY LEVEL OF FASCINATION WITH ALL LIVING CREATURES, HE'S NEARLY PERFECT.
AH!
BUT YOU DO HAVE TO TAKE INTO ACCOUNT THAT, ONE OUT OF EVERY THREE TIMES, IT KINDA SOUNDS LIKE HE SNEEZES HIS OWN NAME.
AH-SHARS!
THERE IT IS AGAIN.

The Man Named Charce #2

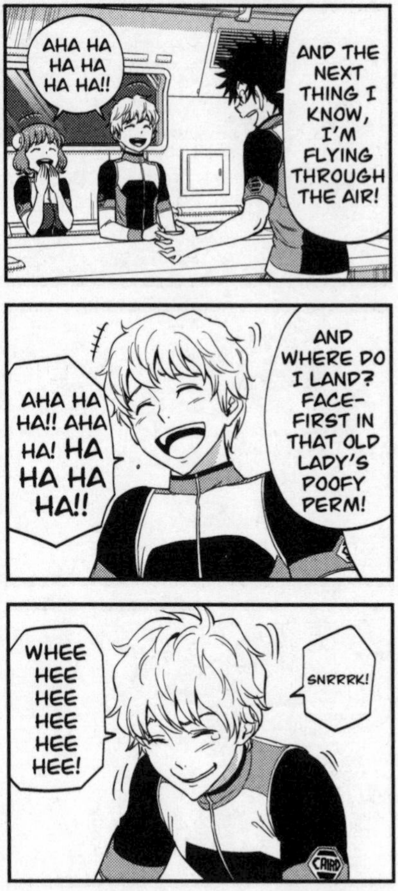
AND THE NEXT THING I KNOW, I'M FLYING THROUGH THE AIR!
AHA HA HA HA HA HA!!
AND WHERE DO I LAND? FACE-FIRST IN THAT OLD LADY'S POOFY PERM!
AHA HA HA!! AHA HA! HA HA HA HA!!
SNRRRK!
WHEE HEE HEE HEE HEE HEE!
GYAW HAW HAW!
THEN THERE'S THAT WHOLE THING WHERE, WHEN HE FINDS SOMETHING REALLY FUNNY, HIS LAUGH CAN GET REALLY CREEPY.

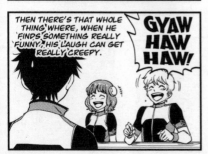

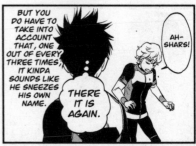

Bridge Honbasho Finals

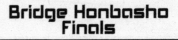

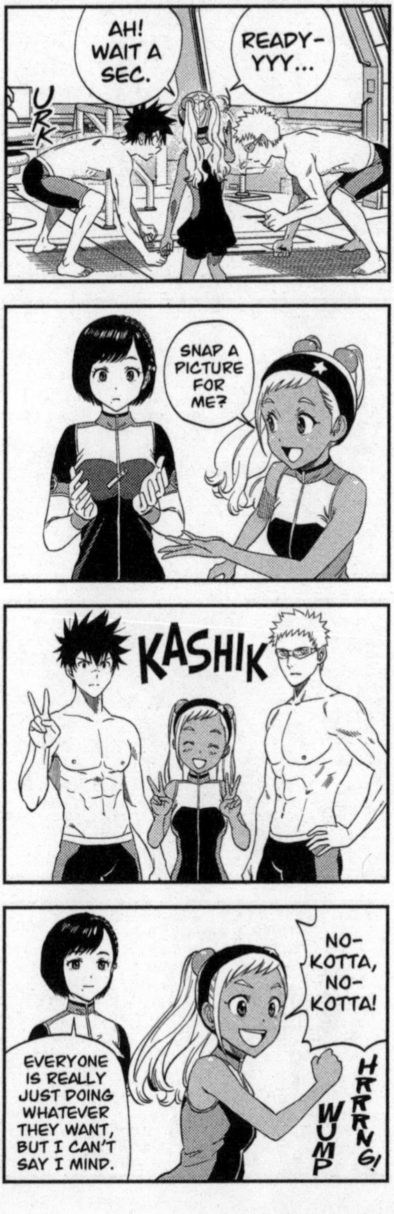
READY-YYY...
AH! WAIT A SEC.
URK
SNAP A PICTURE FOR ME?
KASHIK
NO-KOTTA, NO-KOTTA!
HRRRNG!
WUMP
EVERYONE IS REALLY JUST DOING WHATEVER THEY WANT, BUT I CAN'T SAY I MIND.

Pole-Tree Diet

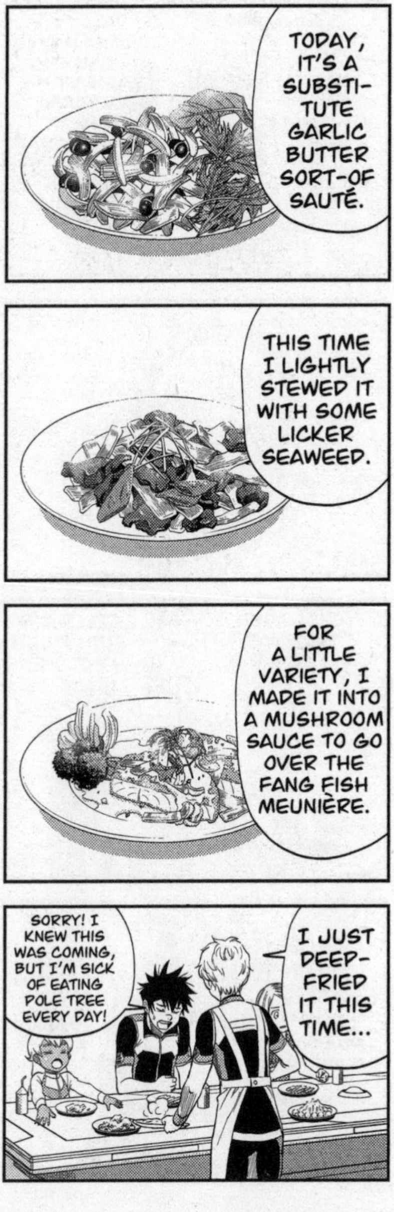
TODAY, IT'S A SUBSTITUTE GARLIC BUTTER SORT-OF SAUTÉ.
THIS TIME I LIGHTLY STEWED IT WITH SOME LICKER SEAWEED.
FOR A LITTLE VARIETY, I MADE IT INTO A MUSHROOM SAUCE TO GO OVER THE FANG FISH MEUNIÈRE.
I JUST DEEP-FRIED IT THIS TIME...
SORRY! I KNEW THIS WAS COMING, BUT I'M SICK OF EATING POLE TREE EVERY DAY!

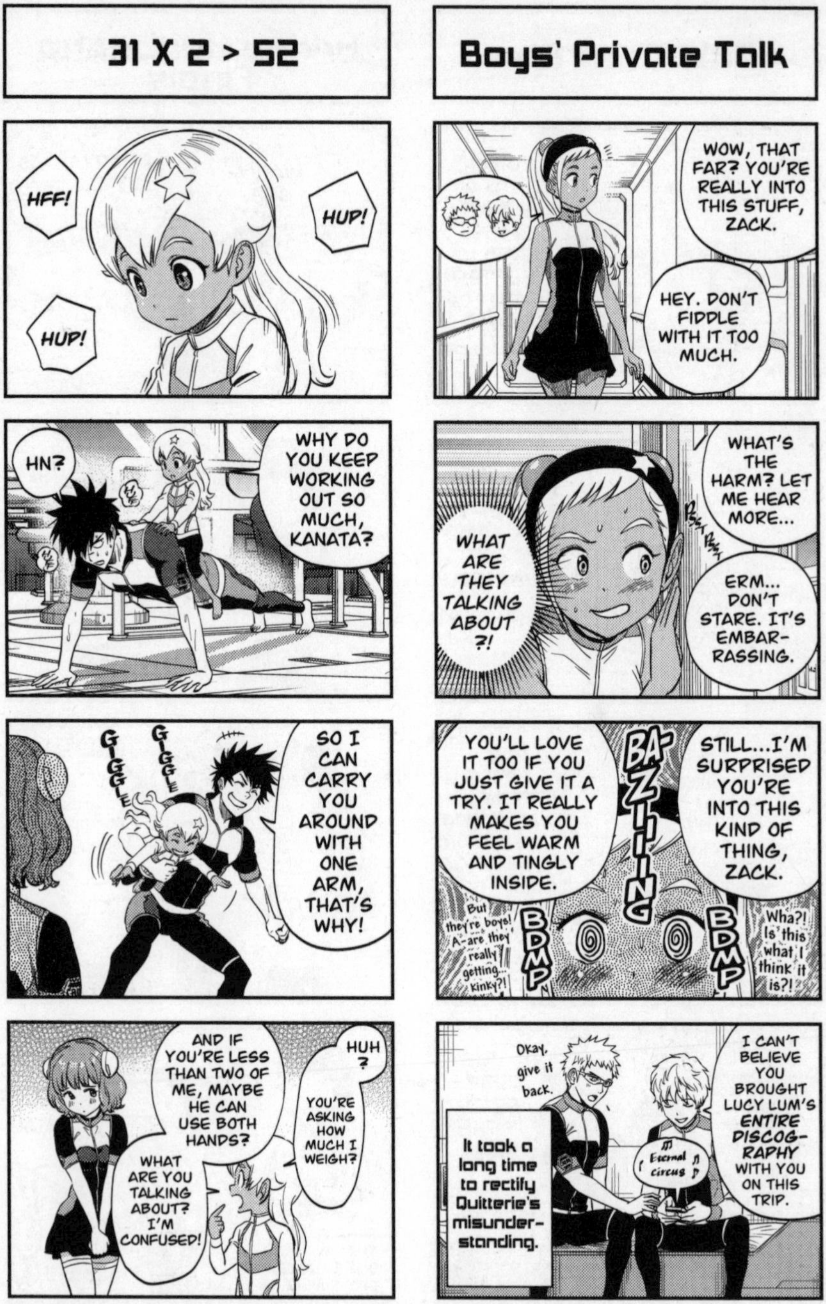
Boys' Private Talk
WOW, THAT FAR? YOU'RE REALLY INTO THIS STUFF, ZACK.
HEY. DON'T FIDDLE WITH IT TOO MUCH.
WHAT'S THE HARM? LET ME HEAR MORE...
ERM... DON'T STARE. IT'S EMBARRASSING.
WHAT ARE THEY TALKING ABOUT?!
STILL...I'M SURPRISED YOU'RE INTO THIS KIND OF THING, ZACK.
Wha?! Is this what I think it is?!
BDMP
BA-ZIIIING
YOU'LL LOVE IT TOO IF YOU JUST GIVE IT A TRY. IT REALLY MAKES YOU FEEL WARM AND TINGLY INSIDE.
BDMP
But they're boys! A-are they really getting... kinky?!
I CAN'T BELIEVE YOU BROUGHT LUCY LUM'S ENTIRE DISCOGRAPHY WITH YOU ON THIS TRIP.
Eternal circus
Okay, give it back.
It took a long time to rectify Quitterie's misunderstanding.
31 X 2 > 52
HUP!
HFF!
HUP!
WHY DO YOU KEEP WORKING OUT SO MUCH, KANATA?
HN?
SO I CAN CARRY YOU AROUND WITH ONE ARM, THAT'S WHY!
GIGGLE
GIGGLE
HUH?
YOU'RE ASKING HOW MUCH I WEIGH?
AND IF YOU'RE LESS THAN TWO OF ME, MAYBE HE CAN USE BOTH HANDS?
WHAT ARE YOU TALKING ABOUT? I'M CONFUSED!

Yun-hua's Glasses

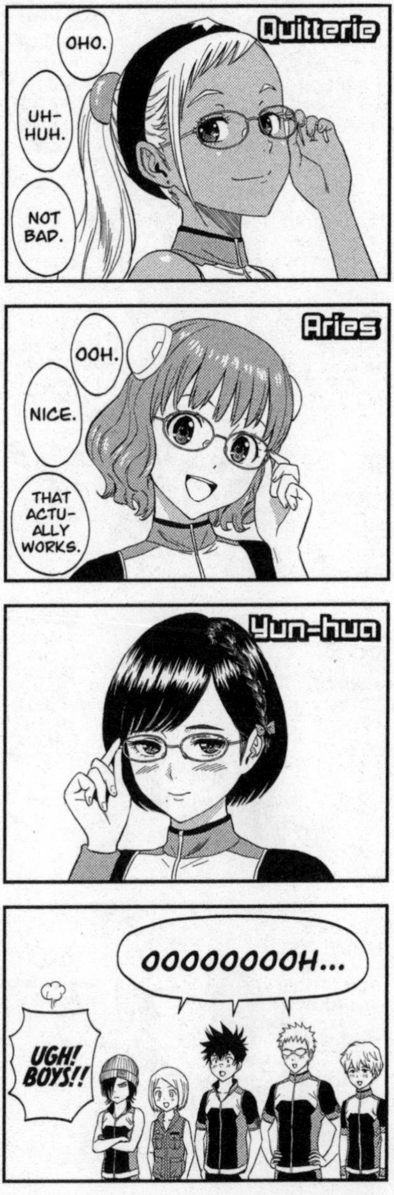
Quitterie
OHO.
UH-HUH.
NOT BAD.
Aries
OOH.
NICE.
THAT ACTUALLY WORKS.
Yun-hua
OOOOOOOOH...
UGH! BOYS!!

Sugar Shortage

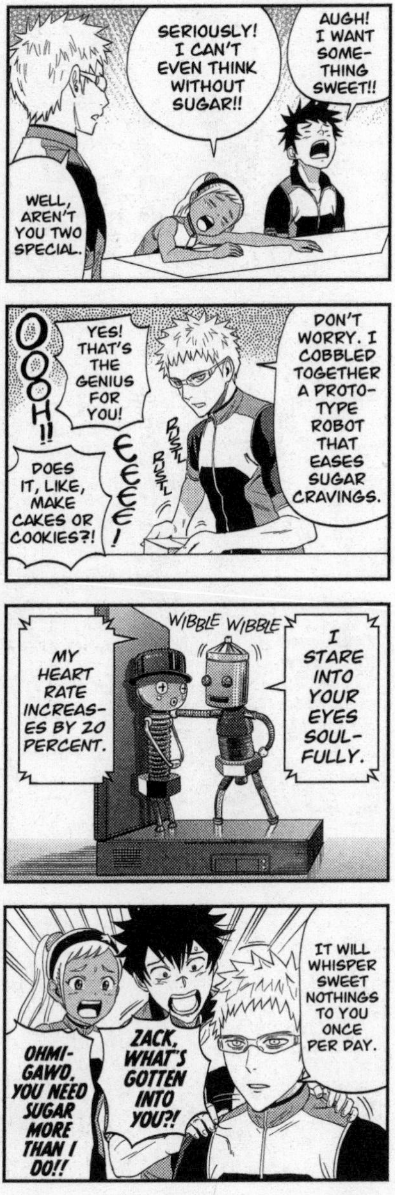
AUGH! I WANT SOMETHING SWEET!!
SERIOUSLY! I CAN'T EVEN THINK WITHOUT SUGAR!!
WELL, AREN'T YOU TWO SPECIAL.
DON'T WORRY. I COBBLED TOGETHER A PROTOTYPE ROBOT THAT EASES SUGAR CRAVINGS.
YES! THAT'S THE GENIUS FOR YOU!
OOOOH!!
RUSTL RUSTL
EEEEE!
DOES IT, LIKE, MAKE CAKES OR COOKIES?!
WIBBLE WIBBLE
I STARE INTO YOUR EYES SOULFULLY.
MY HEART RATE INCREASES BY 20 PERCENT.
IT WILL WHISPER SWEET NOTHINGS TO YOU ONCE PER DAY.
ZACK, WHAT'S GOTTEN INTO YOU?!
OHMIGAWD, YOU NEED SUGAR MORE THAN I DO!!

Messing with Ulgar

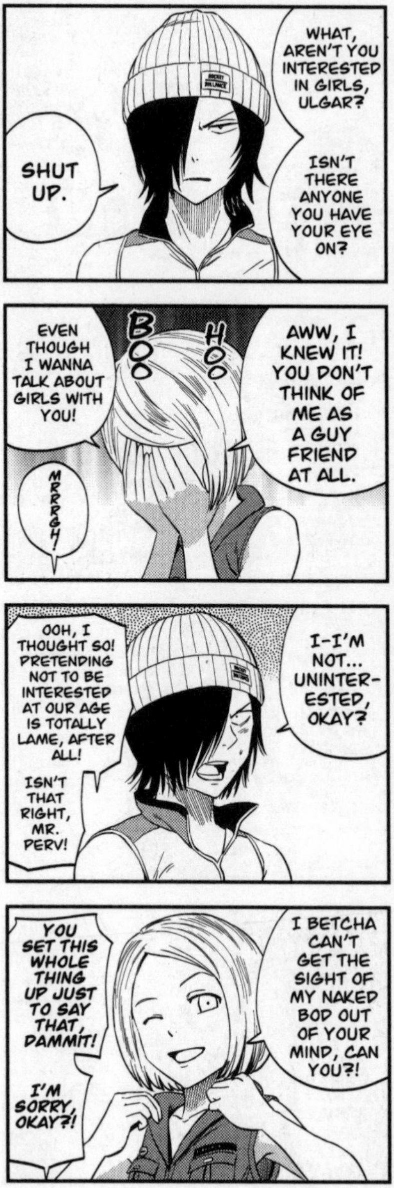
WHAT, AREN'T YOU INTERESTED IN GIRLS, ULGAR?
ISN'T THERE ANYONE YOU HAVE YOUR EYE ON?
SHUT UP.
AWW, I KNEW IT! YOU DON'T THINK OF ME AS A GUY FRIEND AT ALL.
HOO
BOO
EVEN THOUGH I WANNA TALK ABOUT GIRLS WITH YOU!
MRRRGH!
I-I'M NOT... UNINTER-ESTED, OKAY?
OOH, I THOUGHT SO! PRETENDING NOT TO BE INTERESTED AT OUR AGE IS TOTALLY LAME, AFTER ALL!
ISN'T THAT RIGHT, MR. PERV!
I BETCHA CAN'T GET THE SIGHT OF MY NAKED BOD OUT OF YOUR MIND, CAN YOU?!
YOU SET THIS WHOLE THING UP JUST TO SAY THAT, DAMMIT!
I'M SORRY, OKAY?!

More Messing with Ulgar

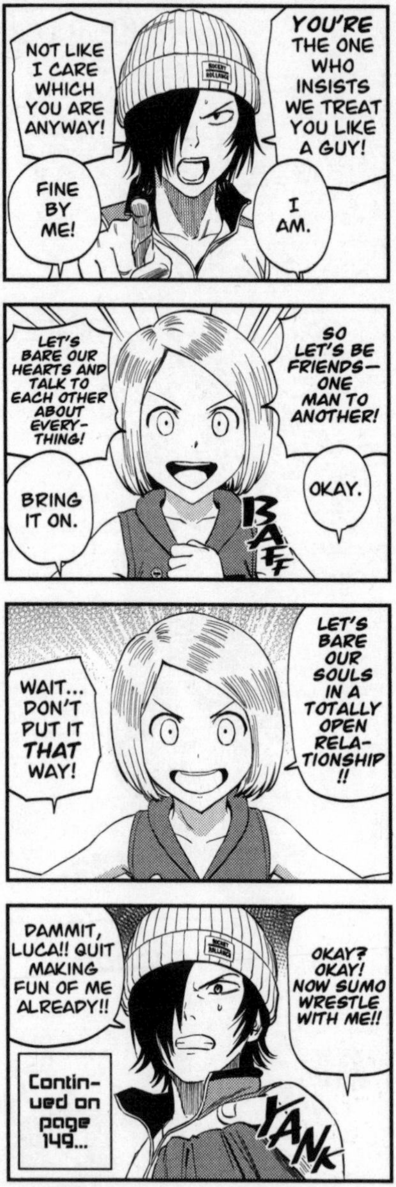
YOU'RE THE ONE WHO INSISTS WE TREAT YOU LIKE A GUY!
I AM.
NOT LIKE I CARE WHICH YOU ARE ANYWAY!
FINE BY ME!
SO LET'S BE FRIENDS—ONE MAN TO ANOTHER!
OKAY.
BAFF
LET'S BARE OUR HEARTS AND TALK TO EACH OTHER ABOUT EVERY-THING!
BRING IT ON.
LET'S BARE OUR SOULS IN A TOTALLY OPEN RELA-TIONSHIP!!
WAIT... DON'T PUT IT THAT WAY!
OKAY? OKAY! NOW SUMO WRESTLE WITH ME!!
YANK
DAMMIT, LUCA!! QUIT MAKING FUN OF ME ALREADY!!
Contin-ued on page 149...

Ulgar's Birthday

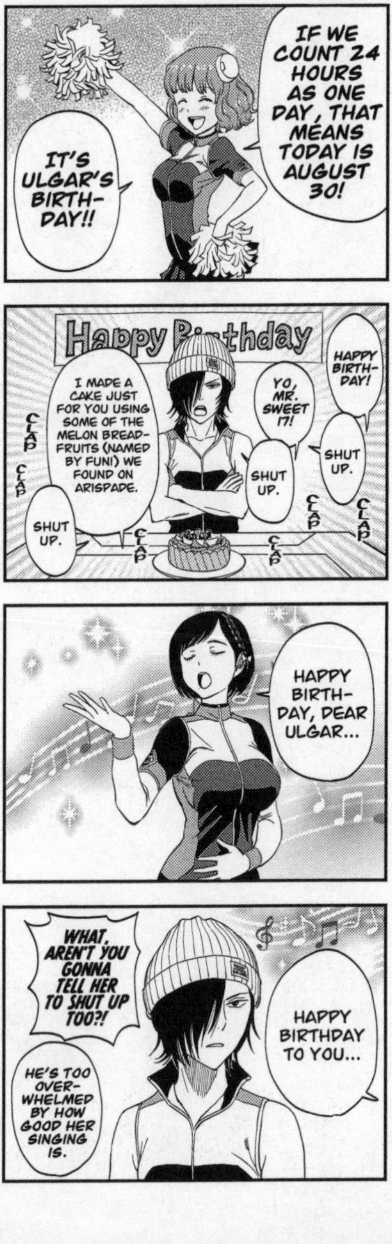
IF WE COUNT 24 HOURS AS ONE DAY, THAT MEANS TODAY IS AUGUST 30!
IT'S ULGAR'S BIRTH-DAY!!
Happy Birthday
HAPPY BIRTH-DAY!
YO, MR. SWEET 17!
SHUT UP.
CLAP CLAP
SHUT UP.
CLAP CLAP
I MADE A CAKE JUST FOR YOU USING SOME OF THE MELON BREAD-FRUITS (NAMED BY FUNI) WE FOUND ON ARISPADE.
CLAP CLAP
SHUT UP.
HAPPY BIRTH-DAY, DEAR ULGAR...
HAPPY BIRTHDAY TO YOU...
WHAT, AREN'T YOU GONNA TELL HER TO SHUT UP TOO?!
HE'S TOO OVER-WHELMED BY HOW GOOD HER SINGING IS.

Sweet Treats

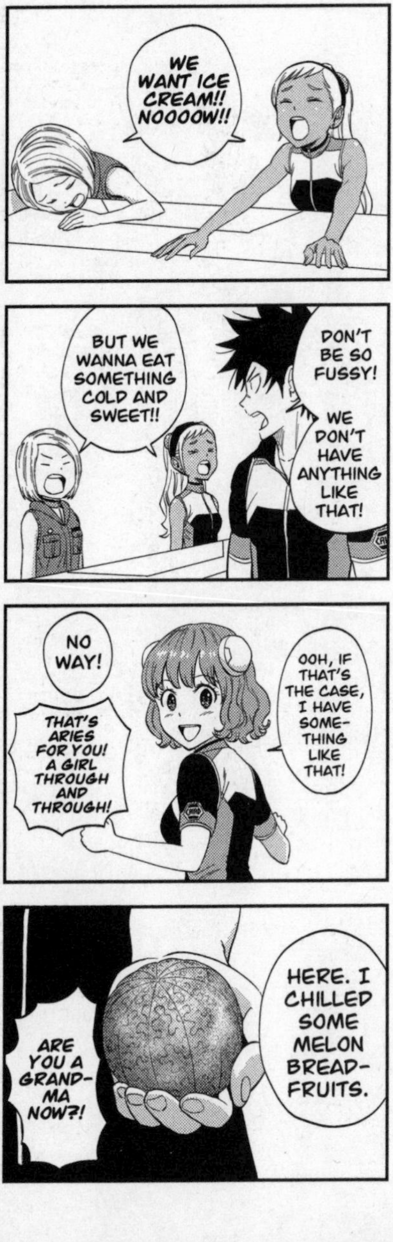
WE WANT ICE CREAM!! NOOOOW!!
DON'T BE SO FUSSY!
WE DON'T HAVE ANYTHING LIKE THAT!
BUT WE WANNA EAT SOMETHING COLD AND SWEET!!
OOH, IF THAT'S THE CASE, I HAVE SOME-THING LIKE THAT!
NO WAY!
THAT'S ARIES FOR YOU! A GIRL THROUGH AND THROUGH!
HERE. I CHILLED SOME MELON BREAD-FRUITS.
ARE YOU A GRAND-MA NOW?!

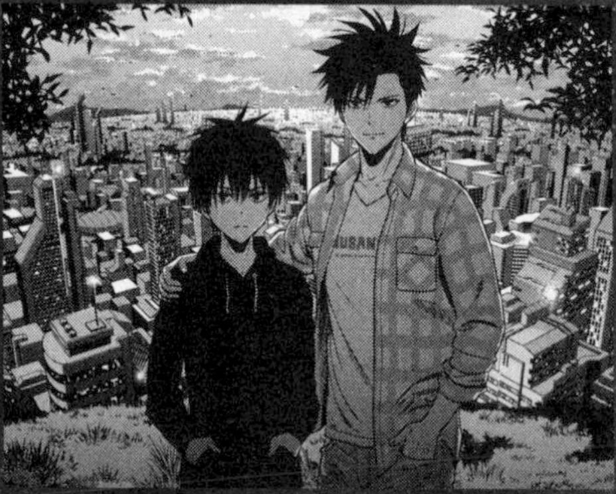
MUSAN

KENTA SHINOHARA started his manga career as an assistant to the legendary creator Hideaki Sorachi of **Gin Tama**. In 2006, he wrote and published a one-shot, **Sket Dance**, that began serialization in 2007 in **Weekly Shonen Jump** in Japan. **Sket Dance** went on to win the 55th Shogakukan Manga Award in the shonen manga category and inspired an anime in 2011. Shinohara began writing **Astra Lost in Space** in 2016 for **Jump+**.

ASTRA LOST IN SPACE 3

SHONEN JUMP MANGA EDITION

STORY AND ART BY KENTA SHINOHARA

Translation/Adrienne Beck
Touch-Up Art & Lettering/Annaliese Christman
Design/Julian [JR] Robinson
Editor/Marlene First

KANATA NO ASTRA © 2016 by Kenta Shinohara
All rights reserved. First published in Japan in 2016 by
SHUEISHA Inc., Tokyo. English translation rights arranged
by SHUEISHA Inc.

The stories, characters and incidents mentioned in this
publication are entirely fictional.

Printed in the U.S.A.

Published by VIZ Media, LLC
P.O. Box 77010
San Francisco, CA 94107

10 9 8 7 6 5 4 3 2 1
First printing, June 2018

viz.com

shonenjump.com

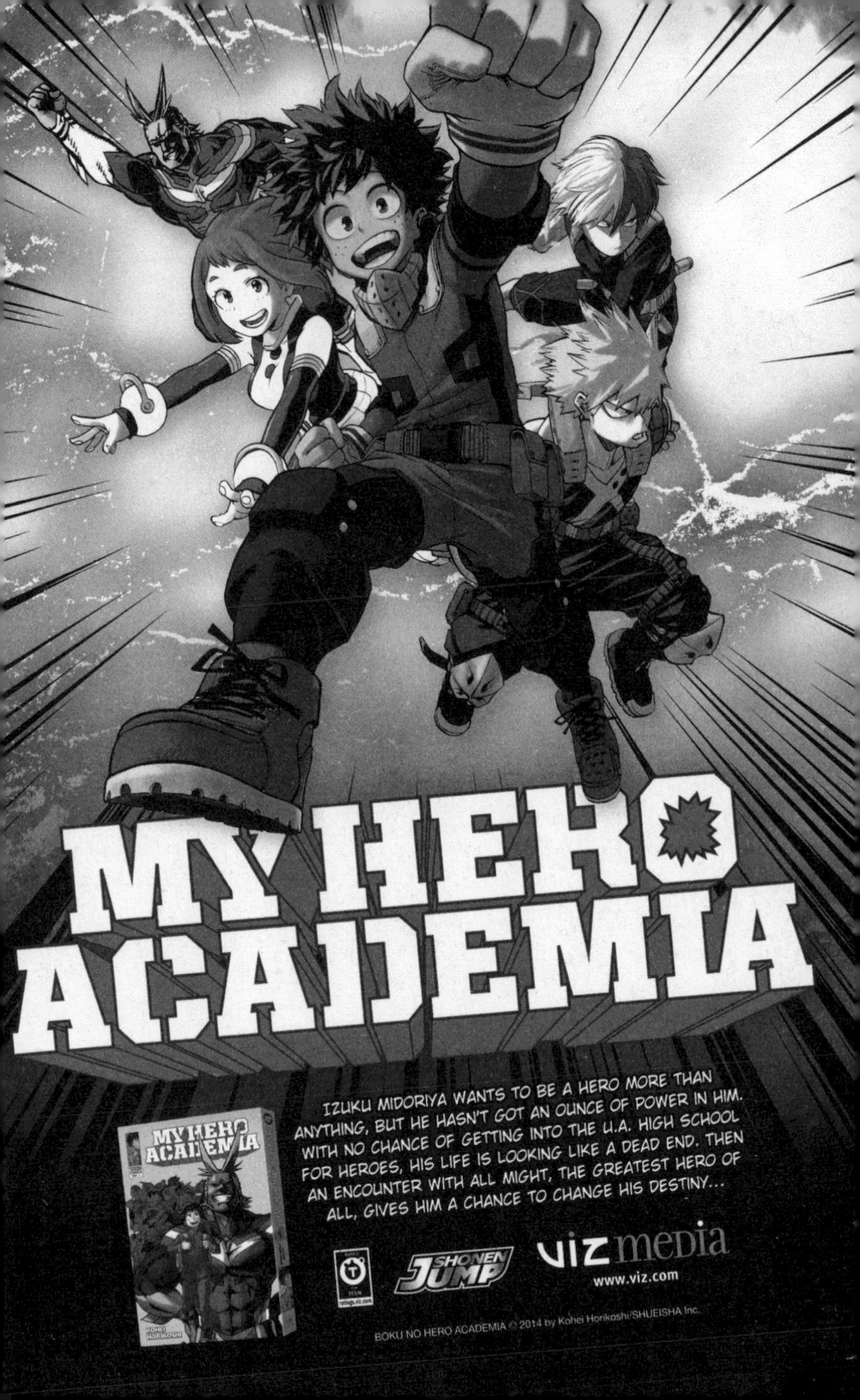
MY HERO ACADEMIA
IZUKU MIDORIYA WANTS TO BE A HERO MORE THAN ANYTHING, BUT HE HASN'T GOT AN OUNCE OF POWER IN HIM. WITH NO CHANCE OF GETTING INTO THE U.A. HIGH SCHOOL FOR HEROES, HIS LIFE IS LOOKING LIKE A DEAD END. THEN AN ENCOUNTER WITH ALL MIGHT, THE GREATEST HERO OF ALL, GIVES HIM A CHANCE TO CHANGE HIS DESTINY...
MY HERO ACADEMIA
KOHEI HORIKOSHI
TEEN
ratings.viz.com
SHONEN JUMP
viz media
www.viz.com
BOKU NO HERO ACADEMIA © 2014 by Kohei Horikoshi/SHUEISHA Inc.

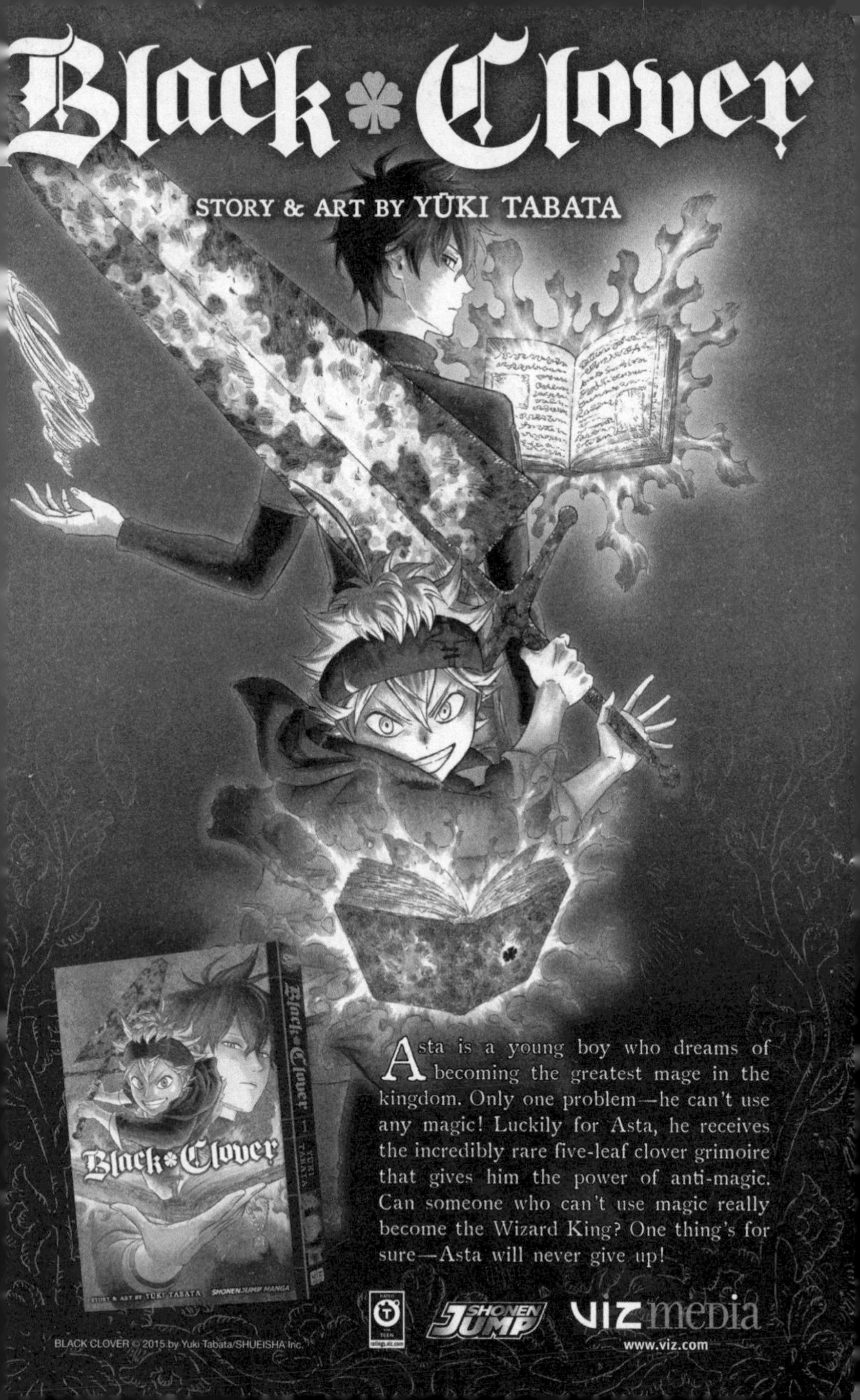
Black Clover
STORY & ART BY YŪKI TABATA
Asta is a young boy who dreams of becoming the greatest mage in the kingdom. Only one problem—he can't use any magic! Luckily for Asta, he receives the incredibly rare five-leaf clover grimoire that gives him the power of anti-magic. Can someone who can't use magic really become the Wizard King? One thing's for sure—Asta will never give up!
SHONEN JUMP
VIZ media
www.viz.com
BLACK CLOVER © 2015 by Yuki Tabata/SHUEISHA Inc.

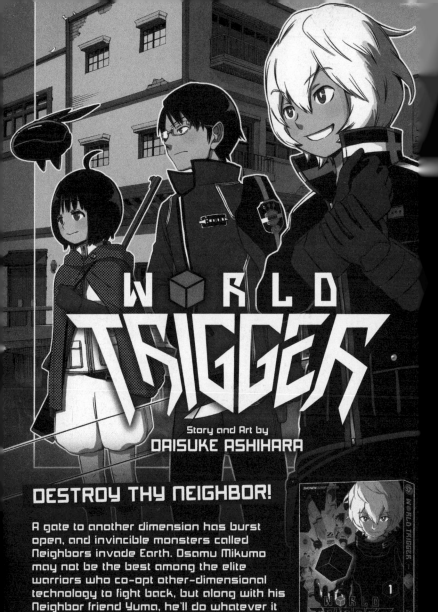

WORLD TRIGGER

Story and Art by
DAISUKE ASHIHARA

DESTROY THY NEIGHBOR!

A gate to another dimension has burst
open, and invincible monsters called
Neighbors invade Earth. Osamu Mikumo
may not be the best among the elite
warriors who co-opt other-dimensional
technology to fight back, but along with his
Neighbor friend Yuma, he'll do whatever it
takes to defend life on Earth as we know it.

YOU'RE READING THE WRONG WAY!

Astra Lost in Space reads from right to left, starting in the upper-right corner. Japanese is read from right to left, meaning that action, sound effects and word-balloon order are completely reversed from English order.

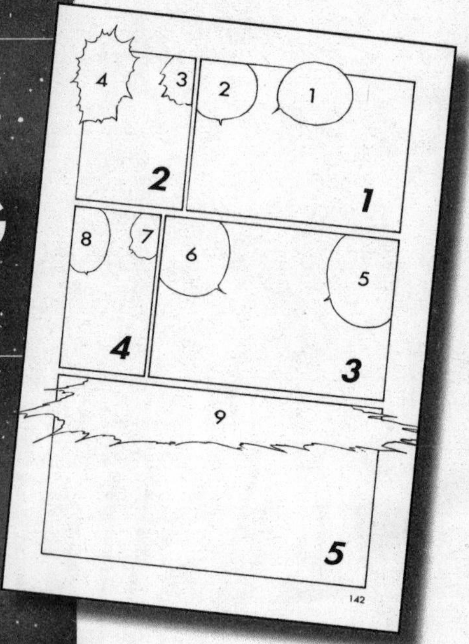

1
2
1
3
4
2
5
6
3
7
8
4
9
5
142

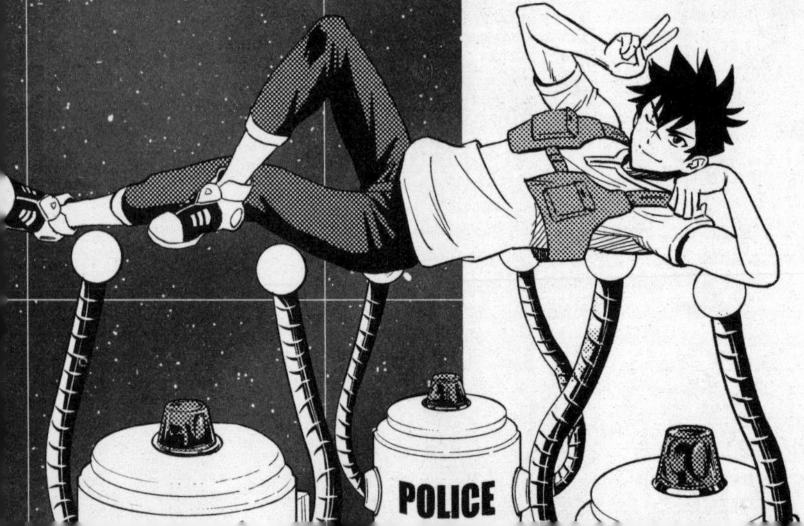

POLICE